The Wedding Feast War

Also by Keith Smith

Local General Orders of the Anglo-Zulu War 1879, 2005, 2008
Select Documents: A Zulu War Sourcebook, 2006, 2009
Studies in the Anglo-Zulu War, 2007, 2008
A Lexicon of Zulu Military Units, 2008
Harry Smith's Last Throw: The Eighth Frontier War, 1850–1853, 2011

The Wedding Feast War

THE FINAL TRAGEDY OF THE XHOSA PEOPLE

Keith Smith

FRONTLINE BOOKS, LONDON

FRONTLINE BOOKS, LONDON

The Wedding Feast War: The Final Tragedy of the Xhosa People

This edition published in 2012 by Frontline Books, an imprint of
Pen & Sword Books Limited,
47 Church Street, Barnsley, S. Yorkshire, S70 2AS
www.frontline-books.com
Email info@frontline-books.com or write to us at the above address.

Publishing history
First edition published in 2010 by Keith Smith.
Second edition published in 2012 by Frontline Books Ltd.

ISBN 978-1-84832-681-1

Typeset in Caslon Pro by JCS Publishing Services Ltd,
www.jcs-publishing.co.uk

Printed and Bound by CPI Group (UK) Ltd, Croydon, CR0 4YY

Contents

How dull it is to pause, to make an end,
To rust unburnish'd, not to shine in use!

Alfred, Lord Tennyson, 1809–1892

Illustrations

Genealogical Tables

The tables illustrate the various clans of the Xhosa people.

Maps

Map 1 was specially commissioned for this work. Map 2 is a conflation of three maps found in *Edges of War*, by John Milton, by permission. Map 3 is based on a map in BPP 1635. Map 4 is based on a map in BPP C.2000, while Maps 5 and 6 are based on maps in BPP C.1961. Map 7 is from General Cunynghame's memoirs *My Command in South Africa 1874–1878*. Map 8 is from *The Frontier War Journal of Major John Crealock 1878*, by Chris Hummel (ed.), by permission.

Plates

1 Sandile
2 Sarhili
3 Sir Bartle Frere

Pre-1877

Ninth Frontier War

Plates 1, 3, 5, 7–13, 15, private collection
Plate 14, from Streatfield's *Reminiscences of an Old 'Un*
Plate 16, Ron Sheeley collection
Plates 17–32, author's collection

1. Genealogy of the Tshawe, the Royal Xhosa Clan

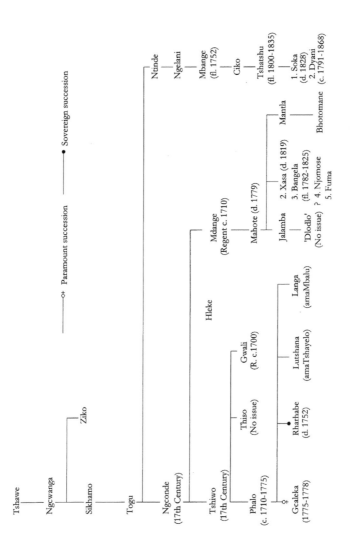

2. Genealogy of the Rharhabe

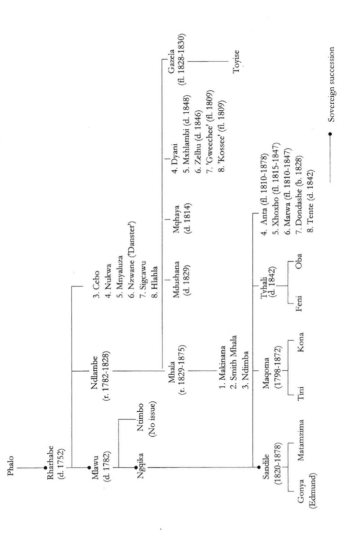

Phalo

Rharhabe (d. 1752)

Mlawu (d. 1782)

Ngqika

Ndlambe (r. 1782-1828)

Ntimbo (No issue)

Sandile (1820-1878)

Gonya (Edmund) Matamzima

Tini Kona

Maqoma (1798-1872)

Feni Oba

Tyhali (d. 1842)

4. Anta (fl. 1810-1878)
5. Xhoxho (fl. 1815-1847)
6. Matwa (fl. 1810-1847)
7. Dondashe (b. 1828)
8. Tente (d. 1842)

1. Makinana
2. Smith Mhala
3. Ndimba

Mhala (r. 1829-1875)

3. Cebo
4. Nukwa
5. Mnyaluza
6. Nzwane ('Danster')
7. Sigcawu
8. Hlahla

Mdushana (d. 1829)

Mqhaya (d. 1814)

4. Dyani
5. Mxhlambi (d. 1848)
6. Zethu (d. 1846)
7. 'Gweechee' (fl. 1809)
8. 'Kossee' (fl. 1809)

Gazela (fl. 1828-1830)

Toyise

Sovereign succession

3. Genealogy of the Gcaleka and Gwali

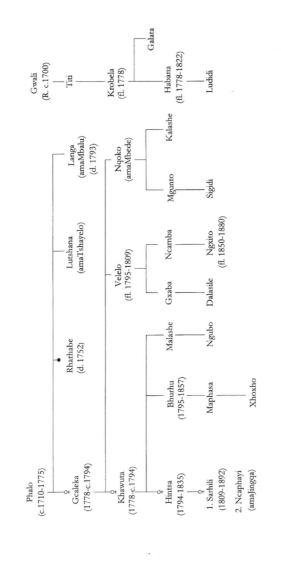

Phalo
(c.1710-1775)

Gcaleka
(1778-c.1794)

Rharhabe
(d. 1752)

Gwali
(R. c.1700)

Titi

Krobela
(fl. 1778)

Galata

Habana
(fl. 1778-1822)

Ludidi

Khawuta
(1778-c.1794)

Langa
(amaMbalu)
(d. 1793)

Lutshana
(amaTshayelo)

Nqoko
(amaMbede)

Hintsa
(1794-1835)

Bhurhu
(1795-1857)

Malashe

Velelo
(fl. 1795-1809)

Mgunto

Kalashe

1. Sarhili
(1809-1892)

Maphasa

Ngubo

Gxaba

Ncamba

Sigidi

2. Ncaphayi
(amaJingqa)

Xhoxho

Dalasile

Ngxito
(fl. 1850-1880)

—○+ Paramount succession

——— Sovereign succession

● Sovereign succession

4. Genealogy of the Tshayelo and Mbalu

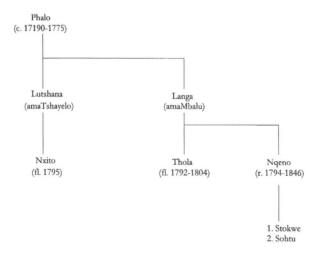

Phalo
(c. 17190-1775)

Lutshana
(amaTshayelo)

Langa
(amaMbalu)

Nxito
(fl. 1795)

Thola
(fl. 1792-1804)

Nqeno
(r. 1794-1846)

1. Stokwe
2. Sohtu

5. Genealogy of the Gqunukhwebe

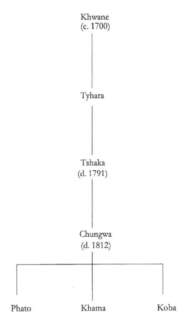

Khwane
(c. 1700)

Tyhara

Tshaka
(d. 1791)

Chungwa
(d. 1812)

Phato   Khama   Koba

Acknowledgements

This work on the Ninth Cape Frontier War of 1877–78 might be regarded as a 'prequel' to the Zulu War of 1879. The war involved some of the same British units, and many of the men, that would later fight the Zulus. In the following pages we shall witness the formation of some of the colonial units, meet the leaders of African levies, witness the first rise to prominence of familiar names and observe a political crisis of major proportions.

All wars are terrible but this one was particularly tragic: it was the last of nine to be fought by Dutch and British colonists against the indigenous people of South Africa and was to bring the Xhosa to their lowest ebb, depriving them of their land and wealth (their cattle), compelling them to work for wages and thus gradually lose touch with a vibrant culture which had nourished them for more than a thousand years.

Once more I am indebted to those curators and staff of museums and libraries who have been so helpful with my enquiries. In this respect, I must mention the staff of The National Archives, Kew, who have survived the merging of the Family Records centre with their usual aplomb, while still managing to deliver files for researchers in a remarkably short time; the National Army Museum, Chelsea; the Regimental Museum of the Royal Welsh, Brecon; the Campbell Collections in Durban; the Cory Library at Rhodes University and the Albany Museum, both in Grahamstown; the Cape Archives in Cape Town; the State Library of New South Wales, Sydney.

Part I of this work owes much to the endeavours of Noël Mostert, whose *Frontiers* is a monument to fastidious research, especially for the early years of the infant colony. It is only with the advent of British rule that one is able to make use of the British Parliamentary Papers which document the development of the Cape from 1806. Similarly, I have leaned heavily upon Michael Spicer in Part II, whose unpublished thesis 'The War of Ngcayecibi' provided much valuable information. To both of these gentlemen I owe my thanks.

During my researches I have visited the Eastern Cape three times and must thank Rob Speirs of King William's Town for his assistance during two of these visits, and for a most helpful tour of the Transkei battlefields in the area.

Some of the maps have been especially commissioned for this work, while others are contemporary documents. In the case of the map labelled 'The Advancing Frontier', I am indebted to Juta & Co., Cape Town, publishers of John Milton's work *The Edges of War*, for their kind permission to use three of the maps found in that work, which I have combined into a single map. The map depicting the area of operations in the Pirie bush is taken from *The Frontier War Journal of Major John Crealock, 1878*, edited by Dr Chris Hummel, and is reproduced here by kind permission of the publishers, the Van Riebeeck Society, Cape Town.

The task of copy-editing the typescript fell to Steve Williamson of JCS Publishing Services. In this endeavour, Steve has saved me from both error and embarrassment and I thank him most sincerely for so doing. It goes without saying that any remaining blemishes are my own.

On a more personal level, it is something of a cliché to note that we live in a small world, but it really was true for me in mid-2009. I had some dealings with a financial institution and had spoken to one of its representatives on the telephone to arrange a rendezvous. It was clear that my contact was South African so, when we met a few days later, I asked him from where he came. He replied, 'the Eastern Cape'. My interest was kindled and I pressed him further: 'Where in the Eastern Cape?' – 'You probably don't know it, but near Fort Beaufort.'

My correspondent came, in fact, from a farm between Fort Beaufort and Adelaide, at the foot of the Kroome Mountains. His name was Ryan Painter and his parents own both Blakeway's and Gilbert's farms, well known to those in the nineteenth century who endeavoured to deal with the Xhosa on the heights to the north. I made contact with his parents, Anne and Derek Painter, and they very kindly invited me to visit their farm in September 2009. They also took me to Longnor Park, which used to be Blakeway's, and there I saw the original farmhouse, now modernised and extended. From a nearby hill, one can clearly see the route up to the Kroome Heights and 'Ten Mile Pass', to which reference is made this work.

I must here acknowledge Ryan and his parents for their great kindness to a complete stranger, and the wonderful afternoon I spent at the foot of the Kroome range.

Finally, my appreciation is again due to my good friends Julie and John Parker of Durban, who have once more endured my visits, and always with a smile.

I have now visited South Africa thirteen times in twelve years and it still comes as a pleasant surprise to be greeted warmly by people whom I have met only once or twice before, or whom I have previously met only through email. I thank them all for their kindness and generosity. If I have omitted thanks to any other helpful person or institution I trust they will forgive me.

Keith Smith
Northern NSW, Australia

Abbreviations

BPP	British Parliamentary Papers
CMR	Cape Mounted Rifles (later FAMP)
CO	British Colonial Office papers in TNA
FAMP	Frontier Armed and Mounted Police
FLH	Frontier Light Horse
NAM	National Army Museum, Chelsea, UK
RMLI	Royal Marine Light Infantry
RMRW	Regimental Museum of the Royal Welsh, Brecon, UK
TNA	The National Archives, Kew, UK
WCA	Western Cape Archives
WO	War Office papers in TNA

Author's Note

It will be noted that the role of the missionaries who came to the Cape are given little mention in this work. This is largely because, while they played an important role in the colony's history, it was felt that an account of their activities would unnecessarily divert the reader from the principal military developments and make a long story longer still. Matters beyond the frontiers of the Cape Colony also receive less attention than they justly deserve but once again their story, while deeply affecting the fledgling colony, would be too distracting.

I have used modern orthography for names ascribed to the various people, groups and topographical features found in this book, if only to provide consistency of naming conventions. Where there is likely to be some misunderstanding, or potential for error, I have given the contemporary names in parentheses. Even in comparatively recent secondary works, the paramount chief of the Xhosa is referred to as 'Kreli', a British corruption of the Xhosa pronunciation of his name. I have therefore introduced him in the text as 'Sarhili (Kreli)'.

The sites of military establishments and engagements pose very special problems. Most of them were named for nearby topographical features such as a hill, river or even a trader's store. In my determination for accuracy, I have visited every site and identified their positions on modern maps. One example of the problems in determining the location of places is that of the 'Springs'. The position of this place is shown on many contemporary maps but it has since sunk into obscurity. The only way to trace it was to look on modern maps for a spot which might 'ring a bell', and about fifteen kilometres to the south-west of Butterworth there lies a site called 'Willow Springs'. Since this place is in approximately the correct place in relation to Butterworth and Toleni, I have assumed this to be the location, although nothing remains to confirm this as fact.

Preface to the Second Edition

In the first edition of this work, I determined to abandon the use of detailed notes to accompany the text, on the strength of the following statement:

> In order that this work not be encumbered with the many endnotes which are to be found in my three previous works, I have decided to omit them altogether. It is hoped that this will avoid the appearance of an academic work, a form which might frighten off otherwise interested readers, and thus appear more 'reader-friendly'.

Instead, I opted to provide what I called 'Chapter Sources', which gave details of works used in the preparation of each chapter. The major change to this edition is the reinstatement of endnotes. With the benefit of hindsight, the omission of such notes, I now believe, was a grave disservice to my readers and I have now rectified that error.

As inevitably happens, the occasional error of fact, or even a mistyped word or date, can find its way into a manuscript, and even the best of editors, lacking a detailed knowledge of the material, may not detect them in all cases. I have therefore taken this opportunity to re-examine the text and make changes to correct such errors which may have been present. As a mere mortal, I beg the reader will forgive any such material which remains.

Keith Smith
Australia, 2012

Introduction

Of the nine Kafir Wars during 1799–1877, the history of the 9th war of 1877/78 is less generally known than that of previous wars.

Dr A.W. Burton, Rhodes University, November 1967

There are few published works which deal with the last of the South African frontier wars, fought in 1877–78, and none which covers it in detail. A book which supposedly deals with all nine of these wars, but spends only a few pages on the last, is *The Kaffir Wars 1779–1877*, by A.J. Smithers. His decision to use 1877 as the cut-off date for this work is baffling, to say the least, and his discussion of the Ninth War is brief and unsatisfactory. A work with a similar objective is John Milton's *The Edges of War*. His treatment of the Ninth War is more extensive but is curiously truncated in a number of places. An epic work which narrates the history of the Cape from its first days, Noël Mostert's *Frontiers*, also describes all of the wars except the Ninth, which is inexplicably relegated to only a few pages in the epilogue. The only other secondary work of which I am aware, Philip Gon's *The Road to Isandlwana*, covers the war from the limited perspective of the 24th Regiment's campaign, and the last third of the book describes the early stages of the Zulu War.

The lack of a published comprehensive study of this important war is the more surprising because it set the final seal on the relegation of the majority Xhosa Africans, who inhabited the Eastern Cape, to the position of lowly workers for the colonists. This work, written after extensive research in British and South African archives, is an attempt to rectify the omission.

When setting out on this project, it became necessary to convey details of earlier wars so as to explain what had gone before and thus provide continuity in the work. Furthermore, it quickly became apparent that it was essential to do more than merely introduce the Xhosa leaders who took part in the Ninth War. Their forebears were almost as important as were the chiefs in 1878 in explaining the forces which were brought to bear upon them. The need to understand the evolving relationship between black and white seemed quite naturally to suggest a general explanation, albeit in brief, of the development of the colony from its birth in 1652. It has evolved, therefore, into the story of the African equivalent of the Hundred Years War, the first war between the Xhosa and the colonists taking place in 1799 and the last finishing in 1878.

The work is divided into two parts. The first, consisting of the first four chapters, briefly covers the history of the Cape from first settlement, through the first eight Frontier Wars, to the middle of the 1870s. The second part, consisting of the remaining six chapters, deals exclusively with the Ninth War.

The Ninth War itself falls naturally into two time periods: the first, between August 1877 and 4 March 1878, was waged under the command of Lieutenant-General Sir Arthur Cunynghame, and the second, from thence to its conclusion on 12 June 1878, under the command of Lieutenant-General (local rank) the Hon. Frederic Thesiger. Thesiger was elevated to the peerage as the second Baron Chelmsford on the death of his father in October 1878, but to avoid any confusion he is referred to throughout this work as General Thesiger.

The Cunynghame period was riven with disputes between the governor and high commissioner, Sir Henry Bartle Edward Frere and the prime minister of the colony of the Cape of Good Hope, John Charles Molteno, and his cabinet, so that the command of the colonial, as opposed to imperial, forces was constantly under debate. The second period began after the resolution of the Molteno issue and thus all troops – colonial, African and imperial – were firmly under the command of General Thesiger, as that officer made plain in his first despatch.[1]

We might here briefly consider what the Australian historian Geoffrey Blainey described as 'the tyranny of distance', used as the title of his work.[2] In the mid-nineteenth century, official correspondence between the Cape and London, and vice versa, could take six weeks or longer to reach its destination and this inevitably caused problems when decisions were urgently required. This situation would not improve until the advent of the telegraph in 1874, when a cable was laid between Brazil and Europe via Madeira. The improvement was not greatly significant even then, however, because communications were still required to travel from the Cape to Madeira by ship before being telegraphed to London. It was not until late in 1879 that a telegraphic link was established between Durban and London, via Zanzibar and Aden. The first direct transmission between Cape Town and London did not occur until 1883.[3]

Another difficulty faced by governors of the Cape was the changing faces of those to whom they reported: often a letter would be addressed to one minster, only to be answered three or more months later by another. This was largely due to the fact that the ruling political parties in the House of Commons came and went with elections, and with them their ministers.

Furthermore, specific ministers of state might also change during the life of a single government.

Sir George Grey (who served as governor at the Cape from 1854 to 1861) described this idiosyncratic mechanism quite concisely in a letter to Colonial Secretary Sir Edward Bulwer-Lytton in July 1859:

> I can only make the general remark that, during the five years which have elapsed since I was appointed to my present office, there have been at least seven Secretaries of State for the Colonial Department, each of whom held different views upon some important points of policy connected with this country. It was impossible that I could, in turn, have agreed in opinion with each of them; and it would have been often difficult, instantly, so to modify proceedings which I had taken in accordance with what I knew to be the wishes of one Secretary of State as to make them entirely accord with the views of each of his successors as they rapidly followed one another.[4]

Those readers who are familiar with the Zulu War fought in 1879 will already know the names of the imperial units engaged here, notably the 1st Battalion of the 24th Regiment (2nd Warwickshire) under its commanding officer Colonel Richard Thomas Glyn. In a very unusual posting, the 2nd Battalion joined its brother during the course of the war. Many of Glyn's officers' names will also be recognisable, although their ranks might differ, among them Major Henry Burmester Pulleine, Captain Russell Upcher, Lieutenant Teignmouth Melvill and Lieutenant Nevill J.A. Coghill. Officers of the 1/24th also founded a number of colonial infantry and mounted units, including Pulleine's Rangers (or 'Lambs', as they were derisively called) and Lieutenant Fred Carrington's Horse, the predecessor of the Frontier Light Horse.

The 90th Regiment also arrived in South Africa during this time, bringing with it another Zulu War luminary, Brevet Colonel Evelyn Wood, VC. Here too was Brevet Major Redvers Buller, 60th Regiment (The King's Royal Rifle Corps), soon to become the fearsome warrior leading his beloved Frontier Light Horse.

Among those who served during the war as leaders of the colonial African forces were such Zulu War figures as Rupert Lonsdale, who would later command the 3rd Regiment of the Natal Native Contingent (NNC) at Isandlwana, William Nettleton, future commandant of a battalion of the NNC and Friedrich Schermbrucker, later to serve with Evelyn Wood in Natal.

The casual reader might assume that when the Dutch first took possession of the Cape of Good Hope in 1652 it was devoid of humankind, the nearest being still in the process of extending their presence from the north, and were then still only at the Great Kei River well to the north-east. This is far from the reality: the area of the Cape teemed with indigenous people. We must therefore begin by describing the different Africans who were resident in South Africa at that time.

The San or Bushmen

Ancient stone hand axes found on the veld clearly demonstrate that men lived at the Cape more than one hundred thousand years ago. The later Stone Age people who lived around twenty thousand years ago are generally considered to be the ancestors of the San, the earliest known inhabitants of the Cape region, who came to be known to white people as 'Bushmen'. 'San' was not a name they applied to themselves – they had none – it was given to them by another indigenous people and means 'aborigine'.

They were elusive hunter-gathering nomads who shunned agriculture and the ownership of stock of any kind, preferring to hunt game where it could be found, and supplementing their meagre meat diet with fish, wild fruits and roots. They were, in short, the most primitive of the peoples of South Africa and were thus the most threatened by any encroachment on their territories by either white or black intruders.[5]

The Khoikhoi

About two thousand years ago, the Khoikhoi (a word meaning 'men of men') moved from modern Botswana into the Cape. Their lifestyle was very similar to that of the San but they also owned fat-tailed sheep and long-horned cattle. They moved with their herds into the best pastures, eventually driving the San into refuge areas such as mountain ranges or desert.

The Khoikhoi were known to the white men by the disparaging name 'Hottentot' and it was they who had coined the name 'San' for the Bushmen. These people originally descended from the San but, while continuing their nomadic way of life, this moiety chose instead to assume the role of herdsmen to cattle, goats and sheep.

Some San helped the Khoikhoi with their animals and thus became pastoralists themselves. Similarly, Khoikhoi who lost their animals during droughts or other misadventure adopted the life of the San. Both Khoikhoi and San are thought to have lived between the Great Fish and Mzimvubu rivers long before the arrival of the southern Nguni.[6]

The Xhosa

Far to the north-east was a more numerous people who, by virtue of their expanding population and the relatively inhospitable nature of the interior of central South Africa, were slowly edging down through the eastern margins of the continent in the only directions open to them: south and then west. These were a race known as the Bantu, a name with unfortunate connotations today but which was derived from their own word *abaNtu*, meaning 'people', and in the plural form *umuNtu*, meaning 'man'. The name was first applied to these people in 1862 by the German ethnologist W.H.I. Bleek. They were as advanced as any then in sub-Saharan Africa, with skills in animal husbandry, simple agriculture and elementary iron working.[7]

Bryant tells us that the Bantu were made up of three distinct 'families' called Suthu, Tonga and Nguni, labels which he himself applied in his work on the origins of the Zulu people.[8] Each of these families spoke its own variant of the Bantu language, although across the three groups the similarities of their vocabulary were striking. It is with the Nguni that we are most interested here.

The Southern Nguni was not a single entity but rather consisted of many clans who mixed, traded and fought with each other, as well as with the Khoikhoi and San. Over time, certain of these clans began to predominate and coalesce into the larger groups that we now recognise as the Mpondo, Mpondomise, Thembu, Bomvana and Xhosa.

Both Khoikhoi and Nguni placed a great deal of importance on cattle and had similar social structures. Some chiefs married San women and employed San men as rain-makers and diviners. Nguni refugees were often assimilated into Khoikhoi chiefdoms and certain Khoikhoi clans became incorporated into Nguni chiefdoms.

The most numerous of the Southern Nguni, who eventually reached the Great Kei River in the seventeenth century, were the amaXhosa.[9] By this time they had also evolved into several different clans, but all were related in the distant past. It is sufficient to note here that the Xhosa, in common with other Nguni people mentioned above, shared much of their language and could understand each other. Many of the 'clicks' in the Southern Nguni languages were the result of their contact with the San and the Khoikhoi. The word 'Xhosa' itself comes from the Khoikhoi word 'to destroy'.[10]

The Mixing of the Races

The miscegenation of the three races now living in close proximity was inevitable. Thus some Khoikhoi and San cohabited to create a mixed-race people known as Khoisan. Similarly, the Khoikhoi and the Xhosa interbred to produce new groups, most of whom chose to consider themselves as Xhosa. The Khoikhoi Gqunukhwebe chiefdom, which had settled between the Bushmans and Fish rivers by 1760, emerged in this fashion. It must also be noted that the Khoikhoi who came into confrontation with the advancing Xhosa, though generally not intermarrying, chose to live among their conquerors and eventually called themselves Xhosa. In this way the area became a great melting pot of people of different racial origins.

This, then, sets the scene and places the principal aboriginal people in their proper context.

The Structure of Nguni Society

We should next turn briefly to a subject which may be the cause of some confusion to those who know little about the nomenclature used to identify groups and subgroups of Nguni people. The names given to these groups were mostly, but not entirely, patronymics, supposedly being those of the first chief of a group. The propagation of separate Zulu chiefdoms is described comprehensively by Jeff Guy and it applied equally to other Nguni people, including the Xhosa.[11] The process is covered here in a manner sufficient merely to explain how these groups often obtained their names.

Their polygamous society was founded upon the basic building block of the *umuzi* (plural *imizi*), or 'homestead', which consisted of several beehive huts around a central cattle pen, the whole being surrounded by a crude wooden fence to keep nocturnal carnivores out and the livestock in. Guy states that:

> These *imizi* were of different sizes, according to an individual's status and wealth, but it has been estimated that 90 per cent of them were commoners' homesteads consisting of a man (the homestead-head, *umnumzana*), two or three wives, their offspring, cattle and smallstock, grazing and agricultural land. The men worked with the livestock, the women in agriculture, the two fundamental branches of production and there was a clear sexual division of labour in the many supporting tasks. The wives were ranked and housed separately within the homestead.[12]

Close to the homestead were the gardens where the women grew their produce: grains, pumpkins, melons and sweet potatoes. All around them were the extensive lands where their cattle grazed under the watchful eyes of the young men and boys of the homestead.

The local chief controlled a number of homesteads, which made up his chiefdom. Although, in principle, everything belonged to the chief, in reality the relationship between him and his subjects was finely balanced. A chief did not have absolute political or legal power: if his tenure was too authoritarian his people simply walked away and associated themselves with another chief. He was also curbed to a large extent by the advice of his councillors.

Xhosa chiefs were bound to each other by ties of marriage as well as political and military alliances. The chiefs, in their turn, answered to a principal chief of one of the two major Xhosa groups to which he belonged. The first major chief was the Paramount Chief of the Gcaleka Xhosa – that is, he was the supreme chief of all the Xhosa and the paramountcy descended through his line. The second, and subsidiary, chief was known as the Sovereign Chief of the Rharhabe Xhosa, a very large sub-family and, again, the sovereignty descended through his line. An examination of the genealogical tables will explain these matters better than words, but what they will not explain is the relationship between them. While the words 'paramount', 'sovereign' and 'supreme' have been used above, the reader will soon learn that these words were little more than niceties because the two chiefs could exercise little control over subordinates in areas other than their own, any more than could the lowest sub-chief. As Mostert explains: '[Sarhili's] was an hereditary position whose only claim upon other chiefdoms was deference and respect. His sovereignty was institutional, not absolute.'[13] The same applied to Sandile of the Rharhabe, to an even lesser extent.

The most notable feature of Xhosa culture was that cattle were central to their lives. Cattle were the external representation of wealth, because they provided the wherewithal for life: milk and meat for food, and hides for clothing, shields and other useful purposes. They also furnished the means of acquiring wives since women were given in marriage for a negotiated number of cattle, a tradition called *lobola*. This practice was not the demeaning transaction that it might be thought today. It should be seen, rather, as an insurance policy for the new wife because if the marriage was not successful and she returned to her family, she had her *lobola* on which to fall back.

The major element associated with cattle was land, because it was required to provide the animals with fodder. And a simple plot of grass was not enough.

In simple terms, grazing areas in South Africa may be classified as either sweet or sour veldt. Sweet veldt provides nutritious material even when it is mature. On the other hand, sour veldt is nutritious only during the growing season. Thus, if the local land grows only sour veldt, then the farmer is required to move his stock to alternative grazing which provides continuing nutrition.

Thus while the sweetveld allowed for a longer grazing season, people in the highlands or sourveld areas had to move their cattle to lower altitudes as the nutritive value of the grass declined in the dry season. This led to the practice of transhumance, the cyclical movement of cattle from one pasture to another as the seasons progressed. It is clear, therefore, that larger areas of pasturage were required for the good management of cattle than might at first be thought. Although land ownership was a concept foreign to the indigenous people, their right to pasturage was very much accepted, and vigorously protected. Access to adequate pasturage was, therefore, the second most precious commodity after cattle.

With the chief's acquisition of cattle, and then one or more wives, the *umuzi* grew, since each wife was given her own huts within the compound. Similarly, adult sons were also allocated their own huts, and so the *umuzi* grew still further. The sons of the chief established their own separate homestead either when they married or when the *umnumzana* died, beginning the process again, eventually leading to the formation of a clan descended from a single male progenitor. The clan was known by the name of this man so that, for example, the founder of the Xhosa people was a distant, possibly mythical, ancestor named Xhosa.

On the question of polygamy, a practice much reviled by the missionaries, it should be stated that this was not considered essential but was simply the ambition of the African male because it was an indicator of his status in society. It is certainly true that most men had but a single wife, re-marrying only after the current wife passed away. But the higher a man rose in the hierarchy, and as his wealth in cattle increased, so he might then take more wives.

Relationships in Nguni, and thus Xhosa, society were governed by two principles. The first of these was exogamy, because it ensured that the gene pools of the small clans remained open by forbidding marriage between members of the same extended family. This is really no different to the rules operating in modern society. For this same reason, Xhosa chiefs and headmen sought wives among the Thembu, also an Nguni people.

Inheritance was quite unlike the western custom of primogeniture, or inheritance by the first-born male, but was by the 'chief son'. When a chief married, his first wife was known as the first wife of the Right Hand House, because she was given a hut on the right-hand side of that of the chief. Other wives would then take other houses on the right, in diminishing order of precedence. Eventually, however, the chief would declare one of his wives to be his Chief Wife and she was given a hut on the left-hand side of the chief's, thus founding the Left Hand or Great House.[14] Even though wives of the Right Hand House may already have borne the chief sons, it was the first son of the Great Wife who inherited the chiefdom, even though he was perhaps many years younger than the first-born son.

This custom, it will be readily perceived, could lead to envy and bad feelings. Such disharmony often led to conflict between the chief's sons.[15] It is a discord which will recur as our story progresses.

Xhosa Warfare

What is most surprising about the Ninth War is the great area of country over which it was fought, stretching from the Great Fish River in the south-west to the Mbashe River in the north-east, across which lay Pondoland. This is a distance of more than 210 kilometres, or 130 miles. The fighting corridor was rarely less than 100 kilometres (62 miles) deep from the coast, giving a war zone of some 21,000 square kilometres.

The usual *modus operandi* of Xhosa warfare was based upon that practised by their forebears during the previous century of fighting with the Dutch and British colonists. Only rarely did they come together to fight a set-piece battle. It was largely a guerrilla war, in which the Africans struck at isolated farms and outposts or groups of men on the march, doing their bloody work and then fading back into the fastness of the bush. This was utterly unlike anything the British had encountered before, being used to formal European pitched battles, and it took some time for them to find a way of dealing with these will-o'-the-wisp tactics. The Xhosa were canny fighters who had great respect for British arms but little for the men who carried them.

When one flies into an airport such as East London today, it is particularly worthwhile to look at the courses of the rivers which thread the landscape below. It will be observed that they are lined on both banks with heavy bush. The bigger the river, the wider the mantle of bush on its banks, sometimes as much as a kilometre on either side; in the case of the Great Fish River, the bush may extend for several kilometres. This bush was virtually impenetrable, consisting of trees, bushes and vines which grew in wild profusion. In places, elephant, buffalo and other large animals had made permanent tracks and it was along these that both sides were able to traverse the undergrowth. For the British soldier it was a dank, dark place where at any moment he might feel the burning agony of an iron spear head as it was thrust into him as he passed by a Xhosa ambuscade. At best, he might meet one of the animals which had made the path he was following.

This was also a war in which the British took advantage of the availability of Africans keen to fight on their side against the Xhosa. These consisted principally of the Mfengu, only recently released from the economic shackles which had bound them in servitude to the Xhosa, and now anxious to demonstrate their hatred of their erstwhile masters in the most practical fashion.

Part I

The Cape Colony to 1877

Chapter 1

Dutch Settlement to 1806

If no further trade is to be looked for with [the Khoikhoi], what would it much matter if we took at once from them 6,000 or 8,000 cattle, there is opportunity enough for it, as we do not perceive that they are very strong in number, but indeed very timorous . . .

Journal of Jan van Riebeeck, 18 December 1652

The inhospitable east coast of South Africa had been, for more than a century before the first settlement at the Cape of Good Hope, the recipient of uncounted shipwrecked mariners, crews of the many ships making their way to or from the East Indies. Most lost their lives by one means or another but some managed to survive and were absorbed into the local indigenous communities.

The number of vessels sheltering, and watering, at the Cape in the seventeenth century reveals the extent to which shipping used Table Bay as a stopover, and thus the utility of the place. It was the Dutch, however, with their great trading empire in Batavia (Indonesia), who finally recognised the value of a permanent settlement at the Cape.

The First Settlement

On 6 April 1652, the first three of five ships of the Dutch East India Company (Vereenigde Oost-Indische Compagnie, or VOC) arrived in Table Bay bearing the first settlers to the Cape of Good Hope. Led by a surgeon named Jan van Riebeeck, rather more than one hundred new settlers disembarked the next day, to found what would become the city of Cape Town.[1] The object of the new settlement was simply to provide a way-station for the numerous fleets and vessels of the Company, which plied between the Netherlands and the Company's trading stations in Ceylon and Batavia. For such long voyages, ships required replenishment with the essentials of life and health: water, food, including vegetables and meat. Death from scurvy was very common aboard vessels of that day. The Company never considered that they might one day found a vast colony and considered only the establishment of a garden and the husbandry of cattle and sheep.

These ambitions were largely met by building a soil-and-sod fort near the shore in which the settlers might take shelter from attack, and the establishment of a large rectangular garden for growing food. (This garden, now largely decorative, is still extant in the centre of Cape Town, and is known as the Company Garden.) Land for the grazing of animals was appropriated nearby and hovels for the inhabitants were quickly thrown together.

The local African inhabitants, the Khokhoi, had personal habits that were to disgust the new settlers at the Cape. They went primarily naked, except in cooler weather, when they wrapped a raw sheep or cow skin (*kaross*) round their shoulders. In this respect they were little different from the yet-to-be-discovered San, although the latter did not anoint themselves with thick layers of rancid animal fat, nor wear garlands of intestines, used for both decoration and snacking. A seventeenth-century commentator wrote:

> They . . . can be smelt at twenty paces if they are up-wind. Our folk give them the pots and kettles to clean, and before all else they take off the fat by handfulls and anoint themselves from head to foot. The grease protects them from the air and the sun, and makes them healthy and fit, and they prefer these natural advantages to those of pleasing odour and attractiveness.[2]

To the Khoikhoi, however, the use of fat on their bodies made a statement as to their wealth in livestock: 'these smearings are considered by them as a sign of richness in cattle, and as an adornment.'[3]

Work began on a new stone fort in 1666, to replace the old one, which was too close to the sea and did not weather well. It was not finally completed until 1679.[4] The fortress became known as the 'Castle' and still stands today.

The first years of the colony were miserable indeed and the inhabitants were frequently on the point of starvation. They were timid and suspicious, which made them slow to establish trade with the indigenes. The Khoikhoi were, it has been noted, relatively nomadic and at first their wealth in cattle was not quickly apparent to the newcomers. As the transhumance cycle progressed, however, the Khoikhoi brought their vast herds closer to the new settlement. Since they prized their cattle as their wealth, though, they often refused to trade with the Dutch settlers and, worse, they even stole what few animals the Dutch had accumulated. They were also confused, and not a little irritated, by the presence of these white people who had appropriated the land which they were accustomed to use for grazing their own cattle.

In 1656 van Riebeeck decided that instead of binding the settlers to the Company, some should be allowed to take up their own land to develop private farms.[5] The spirit of free enterprise quickly took root, even though most of these 'freed' men found it almost impossible to survive under the stringent operating conditions laid down by the Company. The Khoikhoi were even more greatly affected by the extension of European land holding, land which they themselves had used since time immemorial.

The Dutch settlers had early discovered that the Khoikhoi were not suitable for employment as cheap labour. They were thought to be lazy and any who did undertake paid work quickly became bored and walked off. To fill this gap, the settlement became dependent on slaves bought from passing slave ships. Some of these escaped and were suspected of taking refuge with the Khoikhoi, who denied any knowledge of them. To recover them, van Riebeeck ordered that Khoikhoi hostages be taken under arms to nearby Robben Island, which even then was used as a prison settlement. By 1659 Khoikhoi resentment boiled over and for a few months armed conflict occurred.

The Khoikhoi, led by a man named Doman, attacked both the settlement and the outlying farms, carrying off livestock and destroying property, so that the farmers were compelled to withdraw to the security of the fort. Doman was severely wounded in one of the attacks and the insurrection then lost much of its impetus. In the subsequent peace negotiations the Dutch were astonished to hear the Khoikhoi accuse them of taking over the best land 'where their cattle were accustomed to graze, and trying to establish themselves everywhere'. They were asked whether, 'if they [the Khoikhoi] were to come to Holland, they would be permitted to act in a similar manner'.[6] The Dutch were unable to answer this penetrating question but van Riebeeck stated that the country had been justly won by force of arms and it was his intention to keep it. He then concluded the peace by giving the black negotiators presents and a party, at which 'all were well fuddled'.

Despite the early failure of the settlement to fulfil its original purpose, improvements gradually occurred over time. The new 'burghers' became more confident as their farms began to prosper and more and more Company men moved out to emulate the farmers. The sphere of influence of the nascent colony expanded to the north and the east and the Khoikhoi in the affected areas were increasingly deprived of land and a living. They were thus compelled either to remove themselves or find employment with the Dutch, leading to their eventual drift away from their traditional life. It was the beginning of the end for the Khoikhoi of the Cape, who were to become more and more marginalised as the colony expanded. The Dutch had inflicted debilitating problems on the indigenous people:

> The ancient balances and structure of Khoikhoi life at the Cape were deeply affected by high mortality rates from diseases brought by the Europeans, by feuds amongst themselves, and by weakening social bonds as they increasingly sought employment with the Dutch. And in April 1672, exactly twenty years after the start of the Cape settlement, the Dutch persuaded the Cape Khoikhoi to go through with a ceremony of purchase whereby the Dutch East India Company formally acquired the Cape.[7]

Expansion of the Settlement

By the year 1679 the village of Stellenbosch had been founded and the number of free farmers had reached more than six hundred: the entity was beginning the transformation from precarious settlement to unwilling colony. The village lay about forty-five kilometres almost due east of the settlement but the route had to deviate to the north to circumnavigate the intervening mountains.[8]

The original Cape Town settlement, now rather more presentable, was home to a thousand people with about 150 houses and other buildings. In the meantime, a number of white men had established relationships with some of the slaves, and even the Khoikhoi, giving rise to a mixed-white race known as Bastaards. It was a term which carried no hint of disapprobation and was borne with some pride.

The next step in the development of the settlement occurred when the expanding number of settlers began to run out of space for their farms in the small area of the Cape – limited by the crescent of mountains immediately surrounding the settlement, as well as a further range, Hottentot's Holland, about fifty-six kilometres to the south-east. It was inevitable that exploration beyond the local area should occur, especially as reports of a great people to be found in that direction became known. One early expedition simply established that the people whom they sought were just another large clan of Khoikhoi led by a very strong chief.

A second expedition set off in 1702, consisting of some forty-five young men. They returned seven months later with a huge herd of cattle and sheep. It was eventually established that they had travelled eastwards as far as the hinterland of Algoa Bay, making use of local Khoikhoi people on the way. There they had been attacked by a previously unknown people whom they called the 'Chobona'. They were very rich in cattle and the expedition members used their weapons to deadly effect to drive off the attack and then to separate the attackers from their herds, the prizes being driven back to the Cape.[9] These powerful new people used the word 'sakubona' ('I see you') as a greeting and thus the name Chobona was coined by the Khoikhoi for them. But the Khoikhoi had a second name for these people: 'Xhosa', meaning 'angry men'. The first of many battles between white men and the Xhosa had been fought.[10]

In 1713, the Khoikhoi became much less of a problem to the Dutch: a smallpox epidemic killed many of them, as well as many of the settlers.[11]

In the following ninety years the colony expanded as far as the high plateau to the north, and taking over considerable lands to the east, though always seeming to run short of that precious commodity. This was not as difficult as might be thought: each 'Boer', or farmer, demanded one or more farms of at least 3,000 morgen (6,000 acres), plus farms of the same size for their sons.[12] This usurpation was always, of course, at the expense of the aboriginal owners. Over time, the newly discovered San had attacked the Dutch, being then hunted down or driven to the mountainous or arid fringes of the expanding colony; the Khoikhoi had become totally subservient to their new masters.

The administrators of the Cape had, during this period, come to recognise that they must exercise some control over this burgeoning colony and in 1743 had set the eastern boundary at the Brak River.[13] The Boers, however, anxious both to escape the control of the Company, and to appropriate new lands, had already progressed still further east.

In 1770 the border was moved further east to the Gamtoos River and only five years later it was placed on a line from the Upper Great Fish River through the Bushmans River to the sea.[14] Even so, traders, colonists and missionaries alike continued to push far beyond these borders, the first in search of wealth, the second for land and the third for souls.

Gradually, the Boers moved still further north, then east, until by 1774 they had reached the Sneeuberg Mountains. Suddenly, trouble erupted seemingly along the whole Dutch line of advance, from the Cape to the Sneeuberg. The San had decided that they could retreat no further and began a serious resistance.

This was the first real conflict in the deeper interior of South Africa between colonists and the indigenous peoples there, the first guerrilla war sustained by an indigenous race against colonial forces; and it demonstrated all that was to become familiar in such campaigns, where the native enemy was never fully grappled with and put down, remained elusive, master of his retreat, thereby inciting the special brand of hatred, harsh and merciless pursuit and no quarter that the frustrations of such fighting invariably induced.[15]

For the first time, too, the Dutch East India Company recognised the need for a strong military presence in the colony to deal with the threat from the San and it was not long before a now-familiar unit came into being: the 'commando'. This was a well-armed mounted column made up of local burghers, a formation which was to see service through the military history of South Africa until the early part of the twentieth century. The commando had previously been used against the Khoikhoi but here was its first use in a guerrilla-style conflict.

The governor also took another innovative step: he impressed Africans as a militia force to supplement his own meagre resources. These units enrolled not just Khoikhoi but Bastaards and others 'who could be trusted and knew how to shoot'. This too was to become a familiar response.[16]

Mostert states that the Company issued a series of instructions which 'allowed ample opportunity for free interpretation', so that the Boers were given 'extraordinary licence to do more or less as they wished with nation and individuals. They could commit genocide if they wished, or take prisoners and, to all intents and purposes, indenture them as slaves.'[17]

The first commando rode out in 1774 in three columns and when it returned reported the death of five hundred Bushmen and the capture of two hundred more. The same pattern was repeated year after year and, Mostert says, there evolved a great hatred of the Bushmen, not just by the colonists but also by the Khoikhoi, Bastaards and even the Xhosa, all of whom suffered from the indiscriminate and wasteful attacks by their common foe. The conflict, to a lesser degree, was to continue for more than a decade.[18]

The Sundays River runs from its source in the Sneeuberg roughly south-east into Algoa Bay; on its left, or eastern, bank lies what became known as the 'Sour Veld' or 'Zuurveld', extending eastwards again across the Bushmans River to the Great Fish River itself. We have already seen this phrase 'Sour Veld': it denotes a country where the grass is sweet only in the summer, and sour, or of low nutritional value, in the winter and thus requires the use of transhumance for good cattle management. Boers had already been crossing the Sundays River into this country for some years and now refugees from the Sneeuberg added to their numbers.

It was perhaps inevitable, too, that the Xhosa should at this time come into closer contact with the Dutch because they too were gradually moving westwards to that same Zuurveld, having by now left the Great Fish River behind them. The original inhabitants, caught in this pincer of white and black immigrants, were the Khoikhoi and they quickly succumbed before such an avalanche of men.

Such livestock as they possessed were soon bartered away and their pastures appropriated as Boer loan-places. Economically bereft, socially disorganized, those Khoi who did not seek refuge among the Xhosa drifted into Boer employment. Within a space of two decades the traditional nomadic Khoi encampment vanished from the Zuurveld scene and the Khoi were to be found only on Boer farms, servants and dependants of the White intruders.[19]

It was only a matter of time before Boer and Xhosa collided violently. Initially the contacts had been relatively friendly, and such trading as occurred had been carried on for decades before the occupation of the Zuurveld began. Boer and Xhosa had, as a result of this trade, become mutually economically dependent. But as the bodies of men came to live physically closer, incidents of theft, particularly by the Xhosa, became progressively more frequent. Similarly, violence on the part of the Boers, attempting to recover their property, chiefly cattle, also increased. The reality of the situation was that both white and black were in direct competition for the three most important economic resources in South Africa: land, cattle and water.

With regard to the first of these, there was a vast cultural divide: while the Boer farmer received a form of lease to the land, called 'loan farms', from his government, neither the Xhosa, nor indeed any indigenes, recognised it. To them, the land belonged to the chief, being handed down from generation to generation. The people then held the land on behalf of the chief, with no thought of individual ownership.

The Xhosa

We should now pause briefly to trace events on the Xhosa side so that we become familiar with the names of the leading peoples and their chiefs.[20]

By the eighteenth century the Xhosa had roughly divided into four great families, all descended from a common ancestor, Tshawe. These families were the Tshawe themselves, the Ntinde, Mdange and Gwali. There was also an unusual clan known as the Gqunukhwebe. They were of Gonaqua (or Gona Khoi) origin but by rendering a great service to the Xhosa chief Tshiwo, their chief Khwane was adopted by Tshiwo and elevated to the rank of Xhosa chief.[21]

When Tshiwo died, he was survived by his brother Mdange and a son of the Right Hand House, Gwali. Tshiwo had taken a 'Great Wife' but she had not yet borne him a son, so Gwali became the new paramount chief of the Tshawe. But at the time of Tshiwo's death, his Great Wife had been carrying his child and Mdange hid her, and eventually her newborn son, Phalo. Years later, Mdange revealed the existence of the boy and claimed the paramountcy for him. Gwali refused to accept this claim and in the battle which followed Gwali was defeated and fled west across the Kei River, accompanied by Ntinde and his people.[22]

Meanwhile, Phalo took up his role as the new paramount chief of the Tshawe. Mdange eventually followed Gwali across the Kei, leaving Phalo to his own devices. In time, Phalo had a number of sons, the two most significant of whom were Rharhabe, son of the Right Hand House, and Gcaleka, of the Great House and thus heir to the paramountcy, each of whom founded their own families. Unusually, both men were of a similar age, Phalo having taken his Great Wife at an early age. On the death of Phalo, Gcaleka became paramount chief.

Tensions between Rharhabe and Gcaleka developed because the latter was declared to be a diviner. Rharhabe claimed that this would bring dissension to the clan because diviners were common people who dared not 'smell out' a chief. Gcaleka, on the other hand, being a chief himself, might have no such qualms. The situation eventually moved to war and in the subsequent battle Rharhabe was defeated and he too moved west into what was later called the Ciskei.[23] Here, Rharhabe tried to gather to him those people who had previously crossed over. Only the imiDange and Gqunukhwebe did not fall into line.

In 1775 Phalo, a weak ruler anyway, died and Gcaleka did not survive long either, dying in 1778. Rharhabe chose this moment to attempt to seize the paramountcy for himself but Gcaleka's heir Khawuta, despite his fear, drove Rharhabe off. In his frustration, Rharhabe hurled himself on the Dange and drove them west across the Fish River.

In 1782, Rharhabe was involved in a dispute with the Thembu and died during an invasion of their territory, together with his heir Mlawu. He was survived by his eleven-year-old son Ngqika, whose uncle, Ndlambe, took on the role of regent.

Ndlambe was the second son of Rharhabe. He was a clever and ambitious man and he immediately took up his father's mantle and proceeded against the remaining people who had obstructed Rharhabe in his quest to bring all the Ciskei Xhosa under his influence. Those remaining were the Mbalu and Gqunukhwebe. Ndlambe first brought Langa of the Mbalu into his orbit, then both of them attacked the Gqunukhwebe, who then moved still further west across the Fish River in June 1779.[24]

These explanations have now brought the Xhosa story to roughly the same point as that of the Europeans, and so we may continue.

The Dutch and the Xhosa

Hitherto, the Boers had found their early adversaries, in the shape of the Khoikhoi, relatively easy to overcome but the Xhosa were a very different proposition and they did not bend to the hard-line threats directed at them. The settlers' complaints trickling into Cape Town became a flood and finally, in a momentous departure from the norm, the governor of the Cape and director of the Company, Baron van Plettenberg, decided to make a personal inspection of the frontier.

By the time he arrived there in 1778, the Boers had already crossed the border at the Sundays River to take up residence, but van Plettenberg himself already knew that, having given the Prinsloo family permission to do so in 1774 in exchange for a modest rent, others would have certainly followed suit. When the governor appeared in person, he was besieged with complaints from the Prinsloos and others, all declaring that the Xhosa were now crossing the Great Fish River and taking land which properly belonged to them. The governor immediately approached several Xhosa chiefs and at least two of them agreed to return across the Fish, leaving the land to the Boers. In his innocence, van Plettenberg failed to realise, however, that these promises were binding only upon the minor chiefs who made them, and not upon the whole of the Xhosa people.[25] Worse, on his return to Cape Town, his council declared in November 1780 that the eastern frontier would now be moved to the Great Fish River itself. Van Plettenberg quite overlooked the fact that the Fish took a great turn to the west, then another one to the north. The original boundary following the Sundays River continued in a roughly northward direction to link up with this final turn, making a relatively straight border. By now arbitrarily setting the frontier at the Fish River, the governor was immediately seizing the remaining half of the Zuurveld for the white man.[26]

First Frontier War, 1779–1781

The Xhosa, with no constraints placed upon them, continued their surge across the Fish River and the Boer complaints continued to assail the administration at the Cape. Finally, in December 1780, instructions were issued to the field cornet at the frontier, now designated 'commandant of the eastern country', to negotiate with the Xhosa, setting the Fish River as the boundary between the two races. In the event of disagreement, the commandant was to assemble a commando and forcibly remove the Xhosa to the far side of the river boundary.[27]

The commandant was thirty-five-year-old Adriaan van Jaarsveld, a hard-bitten young man who had already experienced campaigns against the Khoikhoi, and he now took to his new task vigorously. He assembled a commando and in May 1781, without attempting to negotiate, rode to the homesteads of the local Xhosa chiefs. At each, he summarily demanded their departure to the east bank of the Fish River. Shortly afterwards he returned to find the Xhosa still in residence. He then gave them an ultimatum: leave within four days or face the consequences.[28]

On 6 June van Jaarsveld returned once more to the imiDange and sought a discussion. In *The Record*, van Jaarsveld describes what followed:

> As we approached them, they were . . . ready to push in among us with their weapons, but were forbidden by me with sharp threats, and I ordered [my men] to keep in the saddle and retire from them; but the Kafirs, following quickly, again pressed in among our men, on which we . . . drew up the commando in a line, so that we could fire to the rear as well as in front, and let the men dismount; and as I clearly saw, that if we allowed the Kafirs to make the first attack, it could not [be] otherwise than that many must fall on my side, I hastily collected all the tobacco the men had with them, and having cut it into small bits, I went about twelve paces in front, and threw it to the Kafirs, calling to them to pick it up; they ran out from amongst us, and forgot their plan. I then gave the word to fire . . .[29]

As many as two hundred Xhosa were killed in this tragic confrontation and van Jaarsveld seized a large number of cattle from them. In like fashion, he disposed of the rump of the Dange, then the Gwali, Ntinde and Mbalu, again seizing cattle and requiring the chiefs to leave.

Stunned, the Xhosa vanished, but not across the river. Van Jaarsveld had prematurely dissolved his commando before receiving reports that the Xhosa had still not yet re-crossed the Fish River. He quickly re-assembled his men – ninety-two Boers and forty Khoikhoi – and returned to the field on 9 July. On 16 July he defeated the Ntinde, taking 1,500 head of cattle. The next day he treated the Gwali in the same way; they escaped heavy loss of life by sheltering in the forest, but lost more than two thousand cattle nonetheless.

On 19 July, van Jaarsveld again disbanded his commando, having in two months slain a large number of Xhosa and seized more than five thousand cattle.[30] Thus ended the brief First Frontier War with the Xhosa people, although it better deserves the title of 'skirmish'. Van Jaarsveld could not hope to police the length of the Great Fish River and the Boers took the view that if Xhosa cattle were to cross the river into their domain, by default they would become their own property.

Within a very short time, matters between Boer and Xhosa had resumed their normal peaceful course and they were mingling and trading in the Zuurveld much as before. In 1786 the authorities appointed a *landdrost*, or local magistrate, for a newly formed frontier district, to be named Graaff-Reinet. Moritz Herman Otto Woeke built his office, or *drostdy*, on the site of what became the town of Graaff-Reinet.[31]

Tensions began to rise again, however, when the colonists' slaves and workers began defecting to the Xhosa and Gqunukhwebe. For their part, the Africans resented the arrogance and greed of the Boers. The case of Coenraad de Buys serves as a good example. De Buys was a physically huge man born about 1761. He obtained a farm on the Bushmans River but could not settle and turned his hand to hunting and trading. His behaviour became increasingly wild, assaulting and robbing Africans and abducting their women as his concubines.[32]

In 1789, the Zuurveld was suddenly invaded by a great number of Gqunukhwebe: they had taken advantage of the Boers' continuing struggle with the San and now took up occupation. When asked why they were invading Company land, their chief, Chungwa, declared that they were simply occupying their own land: they had purchased it years before from one Ruyter, a Khoikhoi chief. The astonished officials said that Ruyter had no right to do that, blithely ignoring the fact that van Plettenberg had casually resumed the land to the Company when he declared the Fish River as the Cape boundary. With a whiff of bribery in the air, Chungwa's people were provisionally permitted to remain on the land in exchange for 'rent' until the governor should decide otherwise.[33]

In 1792 Landdrost Woeke was replaced by his secretary, Honoratus C.D. Maynier, the man who had made peace with the Gqunukhwebe, a man with a philosophy more suited to a magistrate. He has been excoriated in South African history as the man who betrayed his people when he allowed the Gqunukhwebe to remain on the Zuurveld land that they maintained they had purchased, but more recent scholarship has softened his image somewhat.[34]

He began his service by undertaking to satisfy the Boers' complaints about the Xhosa by negotiation, however, in the meantime they had already come to an arrangement with Ndlambe. The hidden inducement for Ndlambe was that such an alliance would allow him to be rid of the troublesome Gqunukhwebe, but he also harboured a treacherous plan to do the same to Langa and his Mbalu.

Second Frontier War, 1793

In May 1793 Ndlambe joined Barend Lindeque, leader of the Boer mal-
contents. The sight of the massed Rharhabe army, naked, red-smeared and
noisily working itself up into a fever pitch, completely unnerved the Boers,
who suddenly lost confidence in Ndlambe and abandoned him.[35] Ndlambe
retired across the Fish River but meanwhile the commando's panic spread
to the Boer farmers in the Zuurveld and they suddenly began to pack up
and move west themselves. The Gqunukhwebe and Mbalu took immediate
advantage of the situation and fell on the Boers in their flight, burning farms,
seizing cattle and property and wreaking their vengeance on the Khoikhoi
servants. Thus began the Second Frontier War, the last war to be fought by
the Dutch against the Xhosa.[36]

Maynier immediately formed a commission and travelled about the
country trying to negotiate with the Gqunukhwebe and Mbalu, to no avail,
and by August he was forced to conclude, much against his own convictions,
that he must use force to secure the Zuurveld. Late in the month he again
took the field, and the Xhosa fell back across the Fish River as his commando
advanced against them. Tshaka and his Gqunukhwebe tried in vain to reach
the Transkei and shelter with the Gcaleka. He was intercepted by Ndlambe,
who heavily defeated him. Tshaka fell in the fighting and Langa, chief of the
Mbalu, became Ndlambe's prisoner. Further east, Maynier fell on more of the
Gqunukhwebe, killing many and taking eight thousand cattle.

As Maynier retired, he visited Ndlambe's Great Place and saw the abject
Langa, whom Ndlambe offered to him. Maynier declined the offer and
returned to the Zuurveld, where he finally met the relief commando from
the Swellendam district. From them he received news that there were still
many Xhosa in the area, some of them Gqunukhwebe who had evaded him
and slipped back into the Zuurveld. For the next few months he tried in
vain to clear them out but finally recognised that his task was impossible.
November saw Maynier finally bow to the inevitable. Agreement was reached
for a peace but the sons of Langa refused to return the stolen cattle and the
new chief of the Gqunukhwebe, Tshaka's son Chungwa, maintained his claim
to the Zuurveld and refused to give it up. On 23 November 1793 Maynier's
commando was stood down and the war was over.[37]

We left the young Ngqika, paramount chief of the Rharhabe, under the
regency of his uncle, Ndlambe. In 1793, as a fifteen year old, he had taken part
in Ndlambe's campaign against the Gqunukhwebe. Given new confidence,
and urged on by his Thembu mother Yese and his contemporaries, he decided
to throw off his uncle's shackles. As Ndlambe was making his plans, Ngqika

paid him a visit and launched his coup d'état. Taken completely by surprise, Ndlambe was just able to scramble to safety and go into hiding. Furious at his nephew's presumption, he sought help from the Xhosa paramount chief, Khawuta, only to find that he was now dead. His successor, Hintsa, was also too young to rule but Hintsa's older brother Bhurhu agreed to help Ndlambe.[38]

In the battle which followed, Ngqika defeated the Gcaleka army. Both Ndlambe and Hintsa were captured and, while he allowed Hintsa to go free, Ngqika kept Ndlambe as his prisoner. He was treated with great respect and his wives and cattle were restored to him, and Ngqika still consulted him on important matters. Mostert has this to say about Ndlambe:

> Ngqika's triumph over him was an astonishing reversal. Ndlambe was between fifty-five and sixty years of age, at the height of his strength and influence, the most powerful man among the Xhosa, and with much left still to be done, yet he had been overthrown by a mere stripling. He was by no means finished, however. He was to renew his influence upon events, and it is by him that one properly crosses over from a dimmer world into the more strongly defined landscape of modern Xhosa history. Ndlambe stands on the bridge, as it were, between the misty figures of oral history and the clearly realized ones that recorded history begins to offer from the end of the eighteenth century onward through the lives of the two young monarchs, Ngqika and Hintsa, and, eventually, their sons.[39]

Thus in 1796, at the age of only eighteen, Ngqika had established himself as the sovereign chief of the Rharhabe and humbled his ambitious uncle. He had also unwittingly rent the house of Rharhabe in two.

Arrival of the British

The next major event in the story of the Cape Colony, as it had by now become, was its accession by the British. They had long understood the vital importance of the Cape as a strategic point on the route from Britain to their possessions in the Far East, notably India, and their war with Napoleon Bonaparte had sharpened their need for this essential station.

At the Cape itself, the administration was in turmoil. The Dutch East India Company was on the verge of bankruptcy and had been compelled to withdraw what few Company troops it had there. In decay itself, the Netherlands had been drawn into the war between France and its neighbours in 1793. The Stadtholder William V, Prince of Orange, fled his country in a fishing smack on 18 January 1795 and took refuge in England. He begged the British to take the Cape and hold it on his behalf until his country was restored. Britain agreed.

The colony, receiving news several months old, lay in daily anticipation of being invaded by one of the two principal antagonists, France or Britain. On 11 June 1795, a British fleet stood into False Bay and landed troops under the joint command of Major-General Henry James Craig and Rear-Admiral George Keith Elphinstone. After extended talks, the Dutch commissioner-general, Abraham Josias Sluysken, declined to accept either William's written orders or British assurances of friendship. Following a brief flurry of military action at the battle of Muizenberg, which ended in favour of General Craig, a second, and larger, British fleet arrived in early September under Major-General Alured Clarke. When his four thousand troops came ashore and began marching on Cape Town, the Dutch garrison capitulated and on 30 September 1795, assuming the title 'Commandant of the Town and Settlement of the Cape of Good Hope', Craig took command of the British administration.[40] At the same time, the frustrated Boers at Graaff-Reinet had taken up the fever of revolution, proclaimed themselves 'the Voice of the People' and ejected the hated Maynier from the town. The British authorities at the Cape then adopted the simple expedient of cutting off their supplies of gunpowder. This action, together with the Boer propensity for dissent within their own ranks, brought the rebellion down.[41]

In 1797, a new governor was appointed, in the person of George, the first Earl Macartney. He brought with him his secretary, John Barrow, and it was Barrow who was despatched to settle matters on the frontier. On arrival in Graaff-Reinet, Barrow and the new *landdrost* of Graaff-Reinet, F.R. Bressler, determined that they should continue their investigations in the Transkei. They interviewed the chiefs of the various Xhosa clans and concluded that Ngqika was the key to unravelling the problems in the Zuurveld. The pair thus set off to see him, to persuade him to approve the departure of the Xhosa from the Zuurveld.[42]

They seemed to enjoy more success than they could have expected. The young chief, guided by his mother Yese, acceded to Barrow's request that his people not cross the Fish River while diplomatically declining to send any white men back. On the most important matter of the Zuurveld Xhosa, notably the Ndlambe and Mbalu, Ngqika was unable, or unwilling, to comply.

Despite his reluctance to give a firm promise, Ngqika did indeed try to impel the Zuurveld Xhosa to cross the Fish River, offering them land and continued independence. Nevertheless, they still refused his overtures, almost certainly because they did not want to be within his power. When Barrow sent messages to them that it was safe for them to return across the Fish, their reply was a blunt refusal.[43]

Ngqika was himself perplexed. Despite his apparent confidence, he had not understood who these new people were, other than that they were not Dutch. They were clearly unlike the Dutch, whose lifestyle closely resembled his own, so in his confusion he turned for advice to de Buys. De Buys explained to the chief that he should imagine the whole country as a single farm, with its 'Great Place' at Cape Town. The British had taken Cape Town, and thus the farm, by force, and were now trying to impose their will on all those who lived there.[44]

Such a conciliatory response did nothing to forward the hopes of the British, nor of Barrow himself. The Xhosa continued to move west, appearing for the first time in the Swellendam district, a comparatively short distance from Cape Town. The Boers were appalled and became rebellious, even freeing van Jaarsveld following his arrest for forgery. Macartney having resigned his post in November 1798 on the grounds of ill-health, the acting governor, Major-General Francis Dundas, despatched troops to quell the rebellion, which was soon to swell into Britain's first war with the Xhosa people.

A force led by Brigadier-General Thomas Vandeleur, accompanied by John Barrow, landed at Algoa Bay on 8 March 1799 and the rebels quickly surrendered. But Vandeleur had bigger fish to fry.

In the treatment of the eastern frontier of the colony, and of the aboriginal people who lived there, the Dutch and British administrations were of one mind. The Xhosa had no right of habitation on the west bank of the Fish River and, by one means or another, they were to be sent back to the eastern side. Macartney had hoped to achieve this objective through conciliation and persuasion, an attitude which did not sit well with the long-suffering Boers. The colonists had been driven to the western extremities of the Zuurveld by the encroaching Xhosa fleeing from the strife between Ngqika and Ndlambe. Now Vandeleur was to try a more vigorous approach.

He marched out of Algoa Bay in late April 1799, accompanied by Barrow, and almost immediately came upon a large group of African refugees. On enquiry, he found that they were Khoikhoi employees of the Boers, from whose cruel treatment they were now fleeing under their spokesman Klaas Stuurman. Having stolen food, weapons and clothing from their late employers in lieu of their wages, they now pleaded to be taken into the care of the British. Vandeleur urged them to stop their plundering and told them to accompany his column. One hundred of them joined his 'Hottentot Corps' and the remainder straggled behind the marching troops.

The column continued to the Sundays River, where Vandeleur met with Chungwa, who finally gave 'reluctant assent' to the Englishman's demand that the Gqunukhwebe leave their lands and return across the Fish River.[45]

Still with its rag-tag retinue of Khoikhoi, the column continued on its way around the Zuurveld, ensuring that the Boer insurrection was now quashed. Having done so, Vandeleur turned his face towards Algoa Bay, when, once again, he fell in with Chungwa. The general repeated his demand that the Gqunukhwebe return across the Fish River but this time Chungwa firmly refused to do so. The threatening nature of the chief's people became so alarming that Vandeleur's men fired a few rounds of grape shot and, when the Gqunukhwebe pressed the attack, the infantry fired volleys.[46] These were the first shots fired in the next Xhosa war.

Third Frontier War, 1799–1803

This was to be a very different affair from the two previous wars, marked as they were by the often-diffident commandos of the Dutch. The war now involved the formidable regular British army; it was the first war the British were to fight on South African soil, but it was by no means to be the last.

Vandeleur was in something of a bind: he was concerned lest the Khoikhoi refugees following him might now desert his column in favour of joining the truculent Xhosa. To prevent this eventuality, Barrow was ordered to take them on to Algoa Bay and await the general there while Vandeleur himself tried to pull together the several reconnaissance patrols that he had despatched about the country.

One of these patrols, led by Lieutenant John Chamney of the 81st Regiment, had been sent out on 5 May 1799. The patrol was ambushed and, in the hand-to-hand fighting which followed, sixteen of his men were killed. In their flight in a wagon, Chamney, on horseback, was himself killed while trying to deflect the attack on the wagon.[47]

The revolt by Klaas Stuurman's Khoikhoi workers was not an isolated incident. Throughout the Zuurveld, reports came in of Khoikhoi servants rebelling against their masters, and the British had unwittingly fostered the revolt. In order to put down the rebellious Boers, they had cut off their supply of gunpowder and ammunition. The Khoikhoi, finding that the Boers were effectively disarmed, had then taken advantage of their weakness by either leaving them or physically opposing them.

When Barrow reached Algoa Bay with his Khoikhoi charges, he was astonished to find it already occupied by a large number of refugee Boers and their families, together with their cattle. Barrow was hard-pressed to keep the two groups from tearing into each other and succeeded only by positioning a light gun mid-way between them. A more permanent solution occurred overnight when the Khoikhoi vanished. Assuming, perhaps correctly, that the British would hand them back to their Boer masters, their preferred alternative, as Maynier had feared, was to join the Xhosa and the war.[48]

In the meantime, Vandeleur packed most of his troops into their ships and sent them back to the Cape, retaining only a small rearguard at Algoa Bay. Mostert observes: 'Vandeleur had simply decided that it would be imprudent to "wage an unequal contest with savages in the midst of impenetrable thickets". Such a campaign, he felt, would add "little lustre to British arms". The loss of Chamney and the fierce attack upon his own group may have unnerved him.'[49]

It was at this time that the British soldier gained his first, if sometimes tragic, experience in South African warfare. He faced a foe who was entirely familiar with the means of passage through the dense bush, and, while remaining still, was almost invisible within its shadows. The ancient spear, or assegai as it came to be known, was at less of a disadvantage in these circumstances because a warrior was able to come within throwing, or even stabbing, range. One soldier complained: 'When you fire at them they throw themselves down on their faces to escape the ball, and the skins they wear are so tough, even if they are hit, it is doubtful if the bullets can do them much harm.'[50]

Vandeleur became isolated in his camp on Algoa Bay, able only to watch the maelstrom enveloping the colonists. Finally overcoming his suspicion of the Boers, he formed and armed a commando at the end of May but within a month it had been destroyed by a joint African force which included Klaas Stuurman. By August, the Xhosa, with their Khoikhoi allies, controlled virtually the whole of the Zuurveld and communications between the Cape, Graaff-Reinet and Algoa Bay had been severed.[51]

In that same month Acting Governor Dundas left Cape Town to take personal command on the frontier. A French warship had made an appearance in Algoa Bay and Dundas became oppressed by a fear of the French descending on an undefended colony. A prefabricated blockhouse was hurriedly shipped from the Cape and erected on a hill overlooking the beach on Algoa Bay, in what is now Port Elizabeth, and named Fort Frederick.[52]

Both Dundas and Vandeleur were at their wits' ends as to how to proceed and Dundas finally decided that the only answer, in the face of a problem that was swiftly moving towards the Cape, was to make peace. To accomplish this, he turned to his earlier saviour, Honoratus Maynier. Maynier dragged himself from his sickbed to accompany Dundas to the frontier, where, alone, he quickly concluded peace negotiations with the Khoikhoi and Gqunukhwebe in October 1799. While the Khoikhoi agreed to return to their masters, under improved conditions to be negotiated by Maynier, who now championed their cause, Chungwa and his people were clear winners because they retained their right to live on their land in the Zuurveld.[53]

Throughout all of this, Ngqika had remained neutral in his Great Place on the eastern side of the Fish River. Ndlambe was still his prisoner, although he remained respected and well treated. It was Ndlambe's Xhosa allies in the Zuurveld and beyond who had been involved in the war.

The new year brought with it a severe blow to Ngqika: Ndlambe escaped from his custody. The trigger was a plan by the young chief to kill Ndlambe's brother Siko, which Ngqika asked Ndlambe to endorse. He refused and, fearing for his own life, made plans for his flight, together with Siko and another brother. The plot against Siko, and the departure of Ndlambe and his brothers, so angered Ngqika's people that a majority of them also left him, while Ngqika himself sought the protection of a nearby Khoikhoi clan.[54]

Throughout the remainder of the year, and into 1801, conditions on the eastern frontier deteriorated. Bands of Khoikhoi continued to terrorise the settlers, and the Xhosa were little better. The peace was falling apart.

Almost lost in the confusion of events in Cape Town was the arrival in 1799 of the new governor to replace Macartney, Sir George Yonge. He barely made any impression on the colony, before being recalled in 1801 as the result of a financial indiscretion. He was temporarily replaced once again by Dundas.[55]

Treaty of Amiens

Far away in Europe, events were taking place which would have a dramatic effect in South Africa. A peace was declared between the French and British, together with their allies, and on 25 March 1802 the Treaty of Amiens was signed and the French Revolutionary War was concluded. One of its provisions was that the Cape Colony should be returned to its original founders, the Dutch, and on 8 July 1802 the new Dutch administration on behalf of the Batavian Republic of the Netherlands, led by Jacob Abraham de Mist, departed from Holland.[56]

During the fleet's procession across the ocean, affairs on the Cape frontier were once more in dire straits. In January 1802, a commando under Commandant Tjaart van der Walt rode into the Sundays River area and attacked a Khoikhoi stronghold with eighty-eight horsemen. After some slight success, they were themselves ambushed on their return and after a skirmish lasting a day and a half, van der Walt was only able to extricate his commando when he surrendered the cattle he had taken.

Dundas ordered still another commando be formed and by the end of May van der Walt was ready once more. This time he had seven hundred men under his command and for two long months he was engaged in a bitter struggle, not only to defeat the rebel Khoikhoi, but also to expel the Xhosa from the Zuurveld. On 8 August, during an attack on a band of Khoikhoi, van der Walt was shot dead and his commando fell apart. As it did so, the Khoikhoi ran riot and by September, heartened by the withdrawal of British troops to Cape Town for their evacuation, they and their Xhosa allies had again stormed as far west as Swellendam. A Boer posted to the vacated Fort Frederick lamented: 'We are stationed here, the last outpost of the Christian Empire.'[57]

The new Dutch administration, headed by de Mist, arrived in Table Bay on 23 December 1802. He was an able organiser but he had been appointed commissioner-general and was not to be the governor. That appointment fell to Lieutenant-General Jan W. Janssens, who marched his troops into Cape Town on Christmas Eve. De Mist's task after swearing in the new governor was to familiarise himself with every facet of the colony and then prepare a draft charter to be submitted to the government in the Netherlands for approval, with the intention of it later becoming the constitution of the colony.

The British administration greeted them cordially and it was agreed that the handover of the colony would officially occur on 1 January 1803. With the departure of the British the Third Frontier War would officially be over, although matters were to remain much as they had been and the Dutch would inherit a most uncomfortable situation.

Although Janssens was now formally the governor, the real administrative power remained with de Mist and the governor must have felt somewhat like a fifth wheel. He therefore embarked on a visit to the eastern frontier.

The British had taken the Cape as a strategic asset and they brought with them a strictly defensive policy. Not for them any notions of idealism; pragmatism was what really mattered. During their brief occupation, their opinion of the Boers and Africans had shifted: from a contemptuous view of the former they had become sympathetic to their position vis-à-vis the Africans. As to the latter, Mostert notes that as a result of their exasperation, 'The word "exterminate had entered their correspondence".'[58]

On the other hand, the Dutch had arrived with an entirely new policy and 'a conviction that their own high-mindedness was sufficient, their own moral superiority the means'. Their policy, however, did not include permitting the Africans to remain in the Zuurveld and the Fish River remained the frontier for both black and white. Shortly after their arrival, and following a briefing by the British, de Mist had sent an instruction to

Graaff-Reinet that a peace must be concluded and the local Boers entered into something approaching a peace agreement on 20 February 1803.[59]

Janssens' own tactics when he arrived at the frontier was thus in accord with their pacific policy and in May 1803 the governor met with the Xhosa chiefs resident in the Zuurveld. The Xhosa proved to be intractable. The split with Ngqika had caused a fracture so that the Ndlambe – which included the Mbalu, Mdange and Ntinde – were now a substantial presence west of the Fish River. Similarly, the Gqunukhwebe had remained where they were. In the meeting, at which Janssens was at a distinct disadvantage due to the odour emanating from his guests, it was made clear that that they must shift to the east bank of the Fish River and they in turn refused. The governor finally withdrew, almost overcome by the stench.[60]

Janssens set out on 1 June to meet Ngqika, sovereign chief of the Rharhabe. The meeting, on the banks of the Kat River, was described as 'by far the greatest and most splendid formal diplomatic occasion yet seen between Xhosa and Europeans'.[61] Ngqika, accompanied by his councillors and his mother, dined in the governor's tent. The moment was again spoiled for Janssens, however, by his malodorous guests.

Of equal import to the meeting was a third party, the man who since 1799 had been Ngqika's adviser on matters concerning the white man, and the chief's mother's lover, Coenraad de Buys. He was the key to the meeting because he alone was at ease in both the Dutch and Xhosa languages, and, what is more, with the conventions of each. Mostert expressed the result lucidly: 'The assurances required, the promises made, the doubts expressed, were much the same. That is, it was wholly unsatisfactory to both sides.'[62] The outcome was largely the result of a basic misunderstanding which had also dogged the British: they, and now the Dutch, believed that Ngqika had control over the actions of the Xhosa in the Zuurveld when the reality was that he did not. Ngqika himself pointed out to Janssens that his severed relations with Ndlambe placed the latter even further out of the chief's control. Their only agreement was that the Fish River was the boundary between the colony and the Xhosa.

The sole matter to be settled at the parley was that de Buys was to return to the colony and no longer live at Ngqika's Great Place. De Buys acquiesced, probably because he was aware of Xhosa ambivalence towards him and that, after living on the knife's edge for so long, it might be time to remove himself into a less perilous existence.

In Europe, the fragile peace between Britain and France was shattered when war broke out once more on 18 May 1803. When news of the outbreak reached the Cape, Janssens immediately returned to Cape Town to assure himself of its defence but the combatants were too embroiled in Europe for Britain to look yet again towards the Cape.[63]

After some time had elapsed, the Dutch grew more confident that no new invasion was likely to take place and over the next three years formulated and implemented their policy for the frontier. It was based upon two planks: that the Zuurveld must be cleared of the Xhosa, by force if necessary, and that a complete prohibition was to be placed upon all intercourse between colonists and the Xhosa people. This was not new, of course, but it was made more effective by the creation of a new military and administrative centre on the frontier. Graaff-Reinet was more than three hundred kilometres from the Zuurveld and complete control of the frontier from there was impossible. The new centre, to be known as Uitenhage, de Mist's family name, was located some thirty kilometres west of Algoa Bay and its *landdrost* was declared to be Lieutenant Ludwig Alberti. The centre of gravity now moved from Graaff-Reinet to the focus of the dispute and a policy of first, eviction of, and second, separation from, the Xhosa was embarked upon.

These were, however, only words on paper and it was quickly realised that to be able to implement them, stability in Europe was a prerequisite. It would require a Dutch military presence which could not, at that moment, be spared and so Alberti was required to walk the fine line of keeping the Xhosa and the Khoikhoi quiescent without revealing the real intentions of the government. He was remarkably successful and, as a result of his diplomacy, cattle-lifting declined markedly, and with it the principal cause of border tensions.[64]

Return of the British

In July 1805, intelligence reached London that the French again planned to seize the Cape. The Admiralty was also greatly concerned that the Americans too were casting covetous eyes in that direction. In response to these stimuli, a great fleet of no fewer than sixty-one ships was prepared in secret, and on 31 August it departed with an army of seven thousand troops under the command of General Sir David Baird. By 3 January 1806 it was standing off the South African coast.[65]

An officer of the 93rd Regiment, Captain John Graham, later to become well known in these pages, reported: 'We lay to the greater part of the night and the Fleet anchored in Table Bay for Saturday [4th January] evening. The signal was immediately made for the 38th and 39th to be in readiness to land, and about 3 o'clock on Sunday morning, these two regiments made an attempt about nineteen kilometres from Cape Town.'[66]

In the ensuing battle of Blauuwberg it quickly became clear that the Dutch troops, including the German-manned Waldeck Regiment, would not be able to stem the British tide and, despite General Janssens' personal attempts to rally his men, they were entirely overwhelmed. On 1 March 1806 a British soldier of American origin, Captain Jacob Cuyler, rode into Uitenhage and handed Alberti a letter from Janssens, informing him that he was now a prisoner of war.[67] Britain had returned to South Africa and this time it was permanent. The last of the Dutch administration left the Cape on 6 March 1807.[68] The occupation of the Cape by Britain was not, however, formalised until 1814, and only then by means of a substantial amount of treasure.

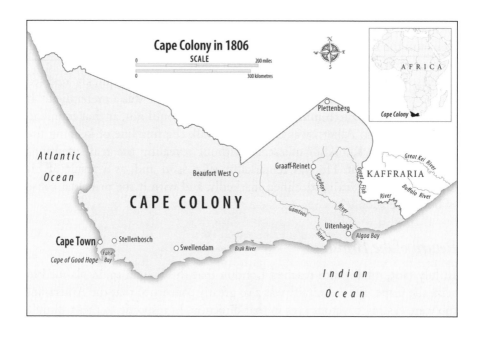

Chapter 2

The British Colony to 1834

The only way of getting rid of them is by depriving [the Xhosa] of the means of subsistence and continually harassing them . . .

John Graham

While Britain was busy taking permanent control of the Dutch colony, convulsions were also occurring among the Rharhabe Xhosa. The change in the colony's administration greatly concerned Ndlambe, who had been under heavy pressure from Ngqika, the latter having invited de Mist to join in an attack on Ndlambe, an invitation which had been declined.[1] He had now to consider that he might also be in potentially more danger by the alignment of the British with Ngqika.

Ngqika himself also faced the defection of many of his people, who disliked his abduction of Ndlambe's new wife Thuthula, supposedly a great beauty, and his subsequent seduction of her. He may have had two reasons for this action: either he might have hoped that Ndlambe would pursue her across the Fish River and thus fall into Ngqika's power, or Ngqika was simply gratifying his appetite for beautiful women. His people, on the other hand, regarded this new relationship as incestuous and they left him in great numbers.

At this point, Ngqika's chiefs rebelled against him and Ndlambe used this opportunity to join with the new paramount chief Hintsa and his Gcaleka in an attack on Ngqika. The allies defeated Ngqika, who fled into the Amathola Mountains, as his own people continued to fall away from him in favour of Ndlambe. Ngqika's confidence deserted him and he was reduced to a state of fear and indecision, hoping to win the support of the British, a support which he had previously been able to take for granted.[2]

As the months passed, the elderly Ndlambe's popularity again waned in favour of Ngqika and discussions between the two men resulted in Ndlambe finally acknowledging Ngqika's leadership of the Rharhabe.

In July 1806 the twenty-nine-year-old Du Pré Alexander, second Earl of Caledon, arrived at Cape Town to begin his term as the new governor of the Cape. From the outset he recognised, or had been warned, that there would be no additional troops available for the colony as long as Napoleon remained a threat to Britain and its interests. He therefore initiated a policy of conciliation on the frontier, noting that this policy must of necessity involve 'occasional and partial injury' to the settlers.[3]

He also found a situation very different from the one that his predecessors had left: the Great Fish River was now not just the frontier for the British, it had also become the border between the Zuurveld Xhosa, including the Gqunukhwebe, and the Ngqika. Still further to the east lay the Great Kei River, beyond which lay the land of the Gcaleka, led by Hintsa, the paramount chief of all the Xhosa. It could be argued that the choice of the Fish River as a border, adopted by both the Dutch and British, was entirely illogical. It was a river of great length, which meant that it would be almost impossible to police. Nevertheless, the British, like the Dutch before them, proceeded to demand that the Xhosa evacuate the Zuurveld.

The reality was that the reverse was happening: the Xhosa were rapidly extending their area of habitation westwards towards the Cape, often squatting on established Boer farms. In 1808 Caledon decided that yet another survey of the frontier should be undertaken, this time selecting Lieutenant-Colonel Richard Collins for the task.

Colonel Collins travelled in a great arc via the Orange River, in the course of which he met a youth who was to have a great influence on the colony in the future: his name was Andries Stockenström and he was on his way home from school in Cape Town. The sixteen year old was invited to join Collins as his interpreter.[4]

Collins continued his journey,[5] first arriving in the country of the Gcaleka, where he met Hintsa. He learned that the paramount chief would allow neither Ndlambe's nor Ngqika's people to settle in his country east of the Kei River but would permit the entry of the Gqunukhwebe. Next, the colonel travelled west to meet Ngqika in his mountain fastness. Collins found Ngqika suspicious of white men; he possessed only a few cattle and was obsessed that Collins should avoid meeting Ndlambe, against whom he railed for treachery in attacking his chief. Collins, at that point, must have realised that Ngqika could never speak for all the Xhosa, nor even the Rharhabe.

Collins' subsequent reception by Ndlambe might at best be described as courteous but cool. From the outset, the Xhosa chief tried to dominate the meeting, asking his own questions before Collins was able to do so. He acquired more information from Collins than the latter could extract from him, Collins only finding out that there was little chance that the Xhosa would willingly evacuate the Zuurveld.

Before ending his tour, Collins arranged a visit to Chungwa of the Gqunukhwebe but the chief did not make an appearance and he had to leave disappointed.[6]

The previous policy of both Dutch and British had been simply to drive the Africans across the Fish River. Collins now advocated three steps towards achieving a peaceful frontier: 'to oblige all the Caffres to withdraw to their own country; to oppose insurmountable obstacles to their return to the colony; to remove every inducement to their continuance near the boundary'.[7] He recommended a further step towards achieving these aims: that the area vacated by the Xhosa should be immediately occupied by six thousand white settlers, so preventing their return.[8] This last suggestion was eventually to lead to the greatest influx of British settlers to South Africa up to that time.

In forwarding Collins' report to London, Caledon wrote in his accompanying letter that he was averse to dispossessing the Africans of the land which they now occupied and proposed simply to allow all parties to remain where they were, deferring to a later date actions which might require the services of troops currently engaged in Europe.[9] The Boers were increasingly suffering from Xhosa depredations of their stock and property and were outraged at this delay. By mid-1810, many were abandoning their farms in the Zuurveld. It was time for a decision: Caledon had either to act or surrender much of the Zuurveld to the Xhosa.[10]

Caledon took neither course; instead he resigned his post as governor in March 1811 and his place was taken by Sir John Cradock, a professional soldier who was accustomed to defeating rebellions in both Ireland and India.[11]

Cradock arrived in Cape Town on 5 September 1811 and almost immediately issued the orders that Caledon had refused to give: the Zuurveld was to be cleared. He chose as the commander of this operation Lieutenant-Colonel John Graham, who had arrived at the Cape in 1806 as a captain. After his arrival, Graham had been placed in command of a regiment of Khoikhoi, the first African unit to be formed, and named the Cape Regiment.[12] One of the first junior officers of the regiment, and the first of South African birth, was young Andries Stockenström, who had been recommended by both Collins and Caledon.

Graham was appointed as commissioner for civil and military affairs in the frontier district on 30 September 1811 and immediately left for the frontier with orders to 'take the most effectual measures to clear His Majesty's territories from the Caffre nation . . .' Little more than a week later, the troops to accomplish his mission left by sea for Algoa Bay. The group included some

250 Khoikhoi of the Cape Regiment, accompanied by Ensign Stockenström, and more than 200 regular British soldiers, including artillerymen and cannon. They were to join up with a large commando then being formed by the *landdrosts* of Graaff-Reinet (Anders Stockenström, Andries' father) and Uitenhage (Captain Jacob Cuyler).[13]

Graham devised a plan of deceptive simplicity. He deployed his force of more than two thousand men in a line roughly parallel with the Sundays River. They would then move eastwards, driving the Xhosa before them until they crossed the Fish River. The large Boer commando led by Anders Stockenström, with his son acting as his aide-de-camp, would wait for orders to enter the Zuurveld from the north. Jacob Cuyler, meanwhile, would cross the Sundays River and march on Ndlambe's homestead. In the centre, Captain George Fraser's Cape Regiment, accompanied by Graham, was to concentrate on the Xhosa being driven towards him by the other two columns.[14]

On 28 December a remarkable incident took place. On the previous day, Cuyler had sent a message to Chungwa of the Gqunukhwebe requiring him to remove his people across the Great Fish River. Chungwa pleaded illness and undertook to give his reply on the following day. In the late afternoon of the 26th a large group of Xhosa appeared before Cuyler's camp and Cuyler rode out to meet them. It was not Chungwa who appeared, however, but Ndlambe. 'This country is mine. I won it in war, and shall maintain it,' he bellowed, stamping his foot as he spoke. He brandished his spear and immediately his Xhosa charged Cuyler and his small party. Cuyler quickly turned and galloped back to the safety of his camp.[15] War had again broken out.

Fourth Frontier War, 1811–1812

Ndlambe had, as so often, received intelligence of what was to take place and had gathered the Xhosa near Chungwa's homestead with the intention of defying Graham. Cuyler quickly saw that he could not contain Ndlambe and sent an urgent message to Graham, who decided to bring up his centre and left columns to deal with the intransigent chief. Graham later reported:

> I immediately resolved upon uniting as large a force as possible in this quarter, and accordingly on the 27th [December 1811] sent orders for two Companies of the Cape Regiment to join Mr. Stockenström from the [Bruintjes] Hoogte on the North side of Zuur Berg, and for him to cross that mountain and Riet Berg, and join me on the south side of the latter mountain without loss of time after the two Companies had joined his Commando of farmers, who were also to accompany him.[16]

The elder Stockenström decided to go down to meet Graham personally to discuss the wisdom of moving his column from its position screening the districts of Bruintjes Hoogte and, further west, Graaff-Reinet.

His route to meet Graham took him south through a mountainous area in the north of the Zuurberg which included crossing a narrow ridge between two steep valleys known as the Doorn Nek where his party met with a group of Xhosa. Against the wishes of his men, Stockenström sat down to talk to the Africans but within a short time he was stabbed in the back, dying almost instantly. Eleven of his companions were slain immediately afterwards.[17] Most of the survivors headed for Graham's camp, still many hours away, but one, a Bushman, made for the left column and the now-fatherless young man.[18]

The news arrived about two o'clock in the afternoon and Andries Stockenström immediately left for the scene of the massacre with some of his men. Arriving there, he found many Dange still in the area and immediately opened fire on them. When they tried to surround him, he led his party back to his camp and formed a laager. Soon afterwards, the Dange left.

On the same day, 28 December, Ndlambe sent a message to Graham requesting a meeting below the Zuurberg Pass, at the top of which Anders Stockenström had been killed. Graham decided to go and arrived at the rendezvous on the 29th. No one was there. 'His interpreter began addressing the thickets around them, and a voice eventually replied that Ndlambe would soon be there.'[19]

Xhosa began to appear and congregate around them until eventually Ndlambe himself appeared. He argued aggressively that the land was his, having been bought from the Dutch, and the British had no right to expel him and his people. Graham denied this and said that he had been sent to put matters right between them. During the discussion, a messenger arrived and placed a note in Graham's hand advising him of Stockenström's murder. Graham quickly glanced at it, then told Ndlambe that the message was from the governor, who acknowledged their ownership of the land and ordered him to withdraw his troops. Graham and his party hurriedly left the rendezvous and shortly afterwards stopped, at which point Graham read the full contents of the message to his party. Their dismay at the real purport of the message, which was not from the governor at all, quickly turned to grief. They knelt to say a prayer of thanksgiving for their deliverance from what they now realised had been an ambush to bring about their own deaths.[20]

On 1 January 1812, Graham set in train the plan he had formulated earlier to drive the Xhosa out of the Zuurveld. He sent his men into the bush in mixed companies of Boers and Khoikhoi. It was not entirely successful in killing Xhosa but two events saw the beginning of their evacuation. The first was the murder of Chungwa of the Gqunukhwebe[21] and the second was the discovery of the hiding place of the Xhosa cattle. Together these two events weakened the morale of the Gqunukhwebe and Ndlambe decided to move out even before Graham directly opposed him.[22]

One of the features of Graham's campaign which demoralised the Xhosa was the British killing of women and children. Throughout their history, Xhosa warfare had involved only men, and the murder of women – whom the British found difficult to distinguish from men when blindly firing into the bush – was a great atrocity to them.

About 15 January 1812 Ndlambe crossed the Fish River after having fled along the coast. 'It was an immense exodus, with the old and weak falling behind and left to die, but the quest for survival pressed them on rapidly until they had gone far beyond the eastern bank of the Fish River and settled themselves along the coast near the Buffalo River.'[23]

Over the coming weeks, Graham supervised the systematic clearing of the Zuurveld, destroying homesteads and gardens and seizing cattle. The death of Chungwa and the departure of Ndlambe left little hope for any remaining chiefs and they too departed. By early March the task was finished and no Xhosa remained in the Zuurveld. It is thought that some twenty thousand people were dispossessed and became refugees in their own land.

Graham's last order was that any Xhosa found on the west bank of the Fish River were to be shot on sight if they did not carry a pass from Ngqika. The same edict also applied to colonists who crossed the river border for any unsanctioned reason.[24] Twenty posts were erected along the river frontier, manned by companies of the Cape Regiment. Graham also sought a site for a new headquarters and, with the assistance of Ensign Stockenström, he settled on a site some thirty kilometres from the Great Fish River, in a natural bowl surrounded by hills. Work began on barracks for the troops and the place was named Grahamstown in honour of the victor of the recent war. In 1814, the eastern Zuurveld was proclaimed the district of Albany in honour of the American birthplace of Jacob Cuyler, with Grahamstown as its military and administrative centre.[25]

We have observed how brutally the new administration under Cradock dealt with the Xhosa in 1811. Two years later, in 1813, it displayed a similar harshness in its treatment of the Boers. Up until this time, land tenure had remained under the Dutch system known as 'loan farms', an unofficial leasehold system under which the farmers registered their chosen farm, or even farms, in return for which they paid a modest rent. The difficulties lay in, first, the problem of collecting these rents, and second, the many farms which remained unregistered, with the landholders paying nothing. Cradock now set about regulating the occupation of land in an attempt to bolster the government's revenue.

His chosen method was the introduction of what he called 'perpetual quit-rent', under which registered land became hereditary, thus giving the holder and his heirs perpetuity of ownership. Further, it allowed the holder to sell the property to another, thus ensuring the owner a profit on his investment. Rents would be contingent upon both the size and quality of the property, and thus would inevitably rise. The Boers were horrified by this new impost because it destroyed what they regarded as their fundamental right to acquire land on their own terms. In the frontier districts, for example, there were a large number of people who, following the struggles with the Xhosa, now squatted on abandoned farms or small unwanted blocks. The new measures were not regarded kindly by the Boers, who thought they were a prelude to dispossession.

At this point, Cradock asked to be relieved of his post and his replacement, Major-General Lord Charles Somerset, arrived in early 1814. Colonel Graham also left the country, as did Collins. On the other hand, both Captain Cuyler and Major George Fraser remained in South Africa. By this time, too, Andries Stockenström had continued his meteoric rise and become *landdrost* of Graaff-Reinet, the post held by his late father.

Emergence of Nxele

One of the oddities of Xhosa history is the occasional emergence of a sage who was able to influence his people, including the chiefs, sometimes to dramatic and tragic effect. One such mystic now made an appearance, at the same time as a persistent drought ravaged the country. His name was Makanna but he was called Nxele, meaning 'left handed'. The Boers translated this into the Dutch 'Links', which the British anglicised as 'Lynx'.[26] Nxele, coincidentally bearing some Gonaqua blood, had been exposed to sermons by missionaries in his country and had felt drawn to Christianity, although he had subsequently developed his own brand of it. His charisma among his people made him widely known and he was eventually accorded the rank of a chief. His message was that the white people were the original sinners and the Xhosa, under his leadership, would drive them into the sea.[27]

Like so many of his predecessors, the new governor, Lord Charles, determined shortly after his arrival in the colony that he would make a tour of the frontier. He had decided not to pursue the Xhosa further and, aware that Ngqika had lost favour with his people, determined to meet him to bring his popularity more into balance with that of Ndlambe. It was a policy which seemed bound to re-kindle old rivalries.

In April 1817, a magnificent panoply of British power was displayed on the banks of the Kat River, perhaps even the same spot chosen years earlier by the Dutch governor Janssens. Among the Xhosa chiefs who attended the governor sat a young man, then unknown, whose name was Maqoma.[28]

When the formalities were completed and discussion began, Somerset proposed that if stolen cattle were traced to a particular Xhosa homestead, that homestead should be held responsible for the theft, even though the cattle might not still be found there. This was later to be known as the 'spoor law', a bad pun even then. Ngqika readily assented to this proposal. He refused, however, the governor's demand that he accept responsibility for returning all stock and slaves that were found in his country. His reason for doing so was that, although he was the sovereign chief of the Rharhabe, he had no real power over the lesser chiefs, who could follow their own path.[29] Somerset was adamant, claiming that he would not deal with any chief other than Ngqika. It is said that Ndlambe, standing close by, muttered to Ngqika to acquiesce, because the white man was becoming angry.[30] Having received his agreement, Somerset brought the meeting to a close by giving the chief presents, upon receiving which Ngqika departed the scene without thanks or further ado.[31]

Battle of Amalinde

In the months following, Ngqika began to feel the results of his agreement when increasing numbers of white claimants descended upon him insisting he make good their losses. A commando arrived in early 1818 demanding his assistance in recovering some stolen cattle. When Ngqika vacillated they went off and raided Ndlambe's homesteads instead. Ndlambe, encouraged by Nxele, plotted the destruction of his nephew. Men were sent to raid Ngqika's chiefs for cattle as a reprisal and the chiefs demanded that Ngqika take his army and destroy Ndlambe once and for all.[32] Ngqika's own seer, a man named Ntsikanna, counselled against this course but Ngqika found himself with little choice. He sent a message to the British and received a supportive response, then sent his army down the Tyumie River to meet his arch-enemy in battle. Among the leaders of Ngqika's army was his son Maqoma.

In October 1818, the two armies met on a plain in the Debe Valley, some fifteen kilometres west of modern Dimbaza. From the heights, Ngqika watched with satisfaction as his warriors drove back the enemy, spread across the plain in small groups. But these were inexperienced decoys, set out as a lure to bring the Ngqika into the trap. As they advanced, veteran warriors from the Ndlambe, Gcaleka, Gqunukhwebe, Dange, Mbalu and Ntinde – led by Ndlambe's son Mdushane – rose up from the surrounding tall grass and attacked the Ngqika.

The battle raged from noon until nightfall and the shattered remnants of Ngqika's force were pursued from the field by the victorious Ndlambe in darkness. Fires were lit on the battlefield to enable the victors to find the wounded and kill them. This action, named the battle of Amalinde from the many shallow depressions (*amaLinde*, caused by giant earthworms) found across the valley, was the greatest set-piece battle ever fought between factions of the Xhosa people. Further, it was the trigger that would bring upon them the next war, in which still more of their lands would be taken from them.[33]

Fifth Frontier War, 1818–1819

Once more, the defeated Ngqika was driven back into the Amathola Mountains, from where he sent an appeal for assistance to the governor. It was not long in coming. The commander of the troops at Grahamstown was Lieutenant-Colonel Thomas Brereton, and he was now ordered by Somerset to assemble a large commando in secret with the object of driving the Ndlambe across the Keiskamma River. Andries Stockenström arrived with a number of Boers on 21 November and by 1 December the commando, consisting of British, Boer, Khoikhoi and friendly Xhosa contingents, set out from Grahamstown.

The notion that the raising of the commando could remain a secret was ludicrous. Its assembly was watched from the very first day and Ndlambe was well aware of its objective. Well before the troops arrived near his Great Place a week later, he had fled with his cattle, taking refuge in the bush on the banks of the Keiskamma River. Unable to come to grips with the Xhosa directly, Brereton unlimbered his cannon and blazed away indiscriminately into the bush. The Africans scattered and their cattle stampeded. Brereton was able to carry off more than 23,000 of them. Of these, some nine thousand were handed over to the impoverished Ngqika.[34]

It was not long before the Ndlambe began to make good their losses at the expense of the farmers. It really was Hobson's choice, in that they could either steal cattle, or starve. As a councillor of Nxele said:

> You sent a commando – you took our last cow – you left only a few calves which died for want, along with our children. You gave half the spoil to Gaika; half you kept yourselves. Without milk – our corn destroyed – we saw our wives and children perish – we saw that we must ourselves perish; we followed, therefore, the tracks of our cattle into the colony.[35]

By Christmas cattle theft was rife and by the end of January 1819 the Zuurveld, or Albany as it was now known, was almost back in the hands of the

Xhosa. As before, the farmers fled before the onslaught and the defenders of the twenty forts along the Fish River, pressed merely to survive, were entirely unable to stem the Xhosa tide moving west. In the meantime, Brereton found ample reason to request retirement to England, for which permission was quickly forthcoming.[36]

Military aid arrived by sea in Algoa Bay towards the end of February. Among its officers was Brereton's replacement, Lieutenant-Colonel Thomas Willshire, who took up his office in Grahamstown in March 1819. He once again assembled a commando, this time numbering more than 3,300 men, and planned to begin his campaign on 1 May. It was a wishful expectation.[37]

Battle of Grahamstown

On 23 April, Colonel Willshire received a strange message from Nxele that the mystic would join him for breakfast the next day.[38] After the dramatic defeat of Ngqika, Nxele had been transformed into the commander of the Xhosa army and his confidence now brought him to confront the British on their own ground – he would attack Grahamstown itself.[39]

On the following day, news reached Willshire that cattle were being driven off the town's commons. He rode out, accompanied by some Khoikhoi cavalry, and tried to rescue the cattle, only to fall into a trap set by the Xhosa. An army of three thousand warriors rose up and attempted to cut off Willshire and his cavalry and it was only with great difficulty that he was able to reach the safety of the town. Expecting an immediate attack, Willshire watched in astonishment as the Xhosa warriors lined the hills above the town, then marched nonchalantly to take up their appointed positions and stood silently watching the town below.[40]

Grahamstown consisted of a scatter of about thirty cottages along a single high street. At the western end there was a large parade ground, while to the south-east at a distance of about a kilometre lay the barracks.[41] The protection of these widely dispersed points posed a severe problem.

The total force available to defend the town was some 450 men from the 38th Regiment, the Royal African Corps, the Khoikhoi Cape Regiment and a detachment of the Royal Artillery with five cannon. The number also included civilians from the town. Opposed to them were no fewer than ten thousand Xhosa, each armed with several throwing spears.[42] Nxele had told his warriors that they should not fear the muskets of the British because their shot would turn to water.

Willshire had less than two hours to deploy his troops to best advantage. He first sent sixty men of the Royal African Corps to defend the barracks. To the east of the parade ground, the land sloped down to a small stream and it was here that Willshire set out his infantry in two lines across the slope facing the stream. The 38th took the centre, with the remaining Royal African Corps and the Cape Regiment on the flanks. The guns were in support, some distance up the hill from the infantry.

Across the valley, on the far side of the stream, the Xhosa were assembled in three large divisions. A smaller fourth division was positioned to the south to intercept any fugitives. Two of the large divisions were led by Ndlambe's son Mdushane and Kobe, son of Chungwa of the Gqunukhwebe. They were placed to attack Willshire's infantry line above the stream. Nxele himself led the third division, which was to attack the barracks.

It was not until about 1 p.m. that the Xhosa dispositions and doctoring were complete, but still they did not move. Willshire decided to advance his infantry line towards the two divisions – when they were close enough, they began firing into the Xhosa ranks. Still they did not move. In fact, they were waiting for the commencement of Nxele's attack on the barracks.

As the rattle of musket fire was heard in the distance, the two huge Xhosa divisions finally began to move down the slope towards the stream separating them from the thin British lines. Willshire ordered a retirement on the guns and when the infantry reached their original position they turned and stood fast. Seeing an attempt to turn his line, Willshire brought down the reserve of the Royal African Corps.

When the Xhosa approached to within thirty metres of the British line, the front rank of the infantry knelt in the grass and the two ranks brought their weapons up to their shoulders. On command a great volley of flame, sound and metal was thrown at the Xhosa host. At the same time, the guns above and behind the line fired canister[43] into their close-knit ranks, cutting great swathes through them. Incredibly, the Africans did not retreat but simply crouched down or knelt holding their *karosses* up in front of their faces, as if these would stave off the myriad red-hot missiles now hissing into their ranks. Their chiefs urged them on and many broke off the shafts of their spears to use as stabbing weapons when they came within arm's length. Their ranks surged to and fro under the massive volleys of musket and cannon. At this crucial moment, when the pressure was greatest, a big-game hunter named Boesak arrived in the town with 130 of his men. These were marksmen of the highest order and their shots quickly found the African leaders.

It could not last. The Xhosa mass wavered and Willshire ordered his men to advance, firing as they went. Unable to withstand the withering fire, the Xhosa fell back, then turned and ran. They were pursued up the hill, the British killing any whom they found hiding in nooks and crannies.

Whilst Willshire was thus employed engaging the two divisions to his front, Nxele's division had reached the barracks. It broke through the slight outer defences and penetrated onto the parade ground. The defenders were still fighting desperately when the Xhosa divisions facing Willshire broke and the sounds of the pursuit sowed the seeds of panic among Nxele's people, after which they too broke and fled.

By 5 p.m. the sound of firing had died away and the battle for Grahamstown was won. Estimates of Xhosa losses vary from one to two thousand dead, among whom lay three of Ndlambe's sons. The British lost three men dead, including one officer. The total wounded was a mere five men. Like Waterloo, an officer described it as 'a near-run thing'.[44]

The commando which Willshire had planned to leave Grahamstown on 1 May finally departed on 28 July 1819. As in previous campaigns, the troops were split into three columns in order to clear the country between the Fish and Keiskamma rivers.

May was the month, of course, which presaged winter's approach. The weather was cold and miserable and the Xhosa sought refuge in the dense bush which enveloped both banks of the Fish River. Mostert described it thus:

> The tangled mass of the Fish river bush, the densest jungle in that entire region, was considered by the Xhosa to be impenetrable by colonial forces, although Boers and Khoikhoi had gained experience of fighting in similar bush in the Zuurveld in 1812. But the Fish river bush was something else. Xhosa access points, as elsewhere, were through the paths trodden by elephants and along these they drove their cattle. Those inner passages were not easily found and supremely dangerous to follow in pursuit of an enemy who might be sitting mere inches away, invisible and unsuspected, and waiting to thrust his spear into a pursuer.[45]

On 15 August, Stockenström's camp was visited by two African women who gave him a message that Nxele wished to negotiate a peace. Suspicious, he accepted the message and allowed them to depart after telling them that he could only guarantee Nxele his life and imprisonment. Nonetheless, Nxele walked into the camp on the following evening, accompanied by the two women, who proved to be his wives. True to his word, Stockenström took Nxele prisoner; he was shackled and sent to Cuyler at Uitenhage.[46]

Willshire had by now completed his first task of clearing the country between the Fish and Keiskamma rivers and next decided that he would carry the campaign across the latter and up to, or even beyond, the Kei River, the home of the paramount chief of the Xhosa, Hintsa. It was a pattern to be followed by the British several times in future years. Hintsa had already been involved with Ndlambe and Nxele, lending warriors for the assault on Grahamstown and even, it is said, leading his men at the battle of Amalinde.[47]

Among those with the troops waiting for the flooded Keiskamma River to subside after heavy rain were Ngqika and his son Maqoma. They whiled away the hours consuming brandy, a habit that was to affect both of them for the rest of their lives, Maqoma in particular. The columns finally crossed the Keiskamma on 9 September 1819.[48]

Willshire carefully beat through the country up to the Great Kei River, much to Stockenström's frustration, because he had wanted to press ahead and catch Ndlambe before he escaped completely. Ndlambe had not tarried at the Kei, however, but had crossed it and scampered on almost as far as the land of the Thembu, far to the north-east.[49]

Encouraged by Ngqika into believing that Ndlambe was being protected by Hintsa, Willshire determined to cross the Kei and take on the Gcaleka. Having witnessed the defeat of Ndlambe and Nxele, Ngqika saw an opportunity to dispose of his third opponent. Stockenström was not misled by Ngqika's machinations, however, writing 'I had seen throughout that Gaika was anxious to involve us in a war with Hintsa and always doubted the accusation he brought against the latter.'[50] Stockenström was eventually able to persuade Willshire not to take this course and instead Hintsa was summoned to a meeting through his brother Bhurhu.[51]

Willshire delivered a severe lecture to Hintsa, promising to clear the Xhosa out of the country between the Kei and Mbashe (Bashee) rivers if necessary and warned him against any future hostility towards Ngqika and the British, and against his giving aid or assistance to Ndlambe.[52] The Fifth Frontier War was now almost at an end and it remained only for Willshire and his columns to retire back across the Fish River.

Nxele was eventually sent to Robben Island to serve a life sentence but on the night of 9 August 1820 he and some fellow prisoners were able to escape by stealing a boat. Approaching the mainland shore, the boat tipped its occupants into the surf and Nxele was swept to his death.[53]

Having given Ngqika military assistance to overcome his enemies, Lord Somerset now demanded that the chief pay the piper. The governor had at last noted the strategic value placed by the Xhosa on the heavy bush clothing the banks of the Great Fish River. Nxele had used it to conceal the assembly of his army before attacking Grahamstown, it offered perfect defensive opportunities and it concealed the Xhosa's own, or even stolen, cattle. This bush extended from the mouth of the river far inland and was in some places fifteen kilometres wide on either bank. Such a place of concealment on the border with the British colony ensured it could never be entirely secure along its whole length.

Somerset's conclusion was that the Keiskamma River would serve as a better boundary because the country was more open and the course of the river between its mouth and the interior was much straighter, and shorter. Having made his decision, he sailed to Algoa Bay and on 15 October 1819 he met Ngqika to impose the new boundary on him and his people. The chief was completely taken aback. He had never for one moment expected that the British would extract such a high price for their aid. The Rharhabe were given just one month to withdraw entirely from the country between the Fish and Keiskamma rivers, land which they saw as their homeland and on which they had lived for generations. The country would now be neutral territory, to remain empty except for the military posts which the British proposed to build at key points. It was to serve as a buffer between black and white.[54]

Ngqika had little choice but to agree, even though he was assenting to something that could not bind all his chiefs, especially the Gqunukhwebe. Lord Charles had his way but he too paid a price. He did not set down a written treaty, with Ngqika's mark upon it, stating the terms to which they had both agreed. To add to the confusion and misinterpretation, Somerset had spoken in English through Stockenström. He, in turn, had translated the governor's words into Dutch, which were taken up by another interpreter and translated into Xhosa. The only concession which Ngqika was able to wring from the implacable governor was that he might retain the Tyumie Valley. His plaintive remark, 'I am rather oppressed by my protector', speaks volumes.[55] Almost immediately afterwards, Ngqika denied giving his assent to any treaty. In response to a question on this matter by the Select Committee, Rev. John Philip remembered that 'I had had a letter from Brownley [sic], a missionary, in which he stated that Gaika did not understand that there was any treaty of that kind, and that he had it from Gaika himself; and Gaika declared to his dying day to the missionaries that he never entered into any treaty.'[56]

The country now appropriated by the British was to be known somewhat ironically as the 'Ceded Territory', since the Xhosa had 'ceded' it to the British. The war finally drew to its inconclusive end.[57]

Ngqika's son Maqoma was born in 1798 and was thus about twenty-two years old when the treaty was imposed on his father. He lived in the Kat River Valley, close to his brother Tyhali (or 'Charlie' as he was often known to the British) in the nearby Tyumie Valley. Both were now to lose their homes and land and both were to turn against Ngqika's former ally the British and become the vanguard of the struggle of the next generation of Xhosa.[58] Three years later, around 1822, Maqoma and Tyhali quietly slipped back to their mountain valleys, where they remained, noticed but unmolested by the administration.[59]

In June 1818, a twenty-four-year-old British officer arrived at the Cape who would come to dominate the military scene on the eastern frontier for decades. He was Captain Henry Somerset, the eldest son of Lord Charles Somerset. Henry's younger brother Charles was already at the Cape, and 'the two of them together could benefit from the patronage available to their father's office.'[60]

While writing his despatches on 15 October, the governor had called Andries Stockenström, then a half-pay lieutenant in the Cape Corps, to his tent and 'put him on full pay, raised him to a captaincy . . . and offered him a grant of land'. At that time, Stockenström was still also the *landdrost* of Graaf-Reinet. Henry Somerset was present at this meeting and had earlier been made deputy *landdrost* of Uitenhage. It was from this point that a rift developed between Stockenström and Henry Somerset, a rift that quickly developed into a deadly feud.[61]

Milton observes that Lord Charles had a motive for acquiring the Ceded Territory other than that of using it as a buffer zone. He also felt that it would provide a civilising influence on the Xhosa by exposing them to two further influences. The first was the missionaries, who were now permitted to go among them. The second was the use of British immigrants as a means of 'educating them in the modes, practices and habits of civilisation', of which the Europeans were to be the exemplars.[62]

Following the suggestion by Lord Charles that British subjects migrate to the Cape, the British government embraced the idea enthusiastically. There was a surfeit of labour in the form of the many post-Waterloo veterans who needed employment. In July 1819 Parliament appropriated funds for the migration of five thousand Britons to the Cape.[63] By April 1820, the first of four thousand of them had begun to arrive at Algoa Bay. There they were met by (now) Colonel Cuyler, who was responsible for their reception and for transport to their properties. As part of their introduction to their new country, he warned them: 'Gentlemen, whenever you go out to plough, never leave your guns at home.' It was sound advice.[64]

The men and their families were taken by a vast number of bullock-carts to the country around Grahamstown, shown their allocated block of land and left to their own devices. For many, it was a disaster from the start. Those who were able to do so sowed vegetable and grain crops almost immediately but the wheat harvest was affected by disease, although vegetables were successfully gathered. It was a hard country for agriculture and many of the immigrants became disillusioned and drifted away from their farms.[65]

The more adaptable took lessons from the hardy Boers and soon were almost indistinguishable from them. Many took to raising sheep and cattle rather than depending on the more British diet, and turned to Indian corn, or mealies, for their flour, instead of the wheat, which failed during the many droughts.[66]

Despite these travails, the British farmers who had remained on their land and, more importantly, who had begun keeping cattle and sheep, and planting crops more suited to their environment, eventually began to prosper. Those who had left the land turned to alternatives such as trading and hunting. By 1825 the venture could be called a qualified success and a year later the settlers were running good-quality merino sheep and an export market for their wool had been opened up.[67]

The Mfengu

It was about this time that Africans other than Xhosa began to appear on the fringes of their country to the north-east, arriving from the lands of the Thembu and Mpondo. These were refugees from the great upheaval now known as the *mfecane* that was taking place far to the north. The cause of the disturbance has been laid at the door of Shaka Zulu by many historians but has more recently been ascribed by Wylie to the activities of Zwide of the Ndwandwe after his defeat by Shaka.[68] The refugees were taken in by Hintsa and his Gcaleka in their hospitable manner, but they were accorded an inferior standing in their society. These were members of the amaMbo, a large clan originally resident near the Thukela River in what would become Natal. The Xhosa called them *amaMfengu*, a name derived from their words *siyam fenguza*, 'we are hungry', and corrupted by the colonists to 'Fingo'. The Mfengu were to assume a major role in the fortunes of the Xhosa people.[69]

In 1826, Lord Charles Somerset resigned his governorship – he had served longer in that office than any of his predecessors, British or Dutch. His term was marked by corruption and nepotism: indeed, the governor's advancement of his son Henry had alienated Andries Stockenström from the administration and contributed to a temporary check to his career.[70] Now Stockenström was appointed to the new office of commissioner-general for the Eastern Districts, where his antipathy towards Henry Somerset would be amply demonstrated.[71] Worse, the hatred between Somerset and Stockenström was to incubate during the coming years, and lay at the heart of much that was to follow. Lord Charles' replacement, Major-General Sir Richard Bourke, arrived at the Cape in February 1826 and Lord Charles sailed home a month later, leaving Henry Somerset at the Cape.[72] Bourke remained in office for only two years, after which another change of the guard saw Lieutenant-General Sir Lowry Cole arrive to replace him in 1828.[73]

Other changes were occurring among the Xhosa. Ndlambe finally passed away in February 1828 and was succeeded by his son, the hero of Amalinde, Mdushane, who survived him by only a year. The Ndlambe then fell to another son, Mhala, and went into decline thereafter. In the following year Ngqika himself died, on 14 November 1829. It was said that liquor had caused his death.[74] He was succeeded by his son Sandile but, because he was then only nine years old, Sandile's much older brother Maqoma was appointed regent until he came of age.[75]

Among the lesser Xhosa clans, two elder chiefs predominated: Bhotomane led the Mdange and Nqeno was chief of the Mbalu. Both men were noted for their wisdom, but in general supported the Ngqika. Finally, Phato led the Gqunukhwebe. Of all these men, however, it was really towards Maqoma that Xhosa eyes were turned.[76]

Maqoma was again expelled from the Kat River Valley in 1828, where he had lived at the whim of the administration. He had been warned a year earlier by Stockenström that he remained there at the governor's pleasure but shortly after the warning Maqoma attacked a Thembu chief and stole his cattle. Asked his advice by the governor, Stockenström responded that Maqoma had broken the terms of his agreement with the government and should be expelled from the Ceded Territory.[77]

On 2 May 1828, Henry Somerset appeared in the Kat River district, to find that Maqoma and his people had already left. Stockenström located Maqoma, who begged him to be allowed to remain on the Kat River, but the commissioner-general was obdurate. Somerset was ordered to burn every hut, making sure that all Maqoma's people had left.[78]

To add insult to injury, Maqoma then found that, far from being left vacant, as was the remainder of the Ceded Territory, the land from which he had been so recently ejected was filled up with Khoikhoi and mixed-race settlers whom the solicitous Stockenström had recommended be permitted to own land.[79] The district, which came to be known as the Kat River Settlement, went on to become a thriving, self-governing agricultural community which became the envy of both black and white.[80]

It was during this period that the enmity between Somerset and Stockenström became more acrimonious than ever. The fact that they served cheek by jowl, with one the civil commissioner-general and the other the military commander of the frontier, served only to bring them into constant friction.

Theoretically, Stockenström was required to authorise Somerset to raise a commando. In fact, the latter often evaded this authorisation and then caused havoc having done so. In June 1830 he led a commando which resulted in the wounding of Ndlambe's brother Sigcawu and the imprisonment of another chief. A year later, Maqoma told Stockenström that Sigcawu had been unarmed at the time of his shooting and Stockenström requested an inquiry. The request was denied. The shooting caused outrage among the Xhosa, and Hintsa in particular was greatly affected, his mistrust of white men increasing markedly.[81]

These events eventually led to a showdown between the two men. In 1831, Somerset requested permission from Stockenström to raise another commando. Stockenström replied that he had had 'quite enough of the one last year', a reference to the Sigcawu incident. Undeterred, Somerset applied directly to Governor Cole, who gave his consent, unaware that Stockenström had previously refused to authorise the commando. When Stockenström complained to Cole that he had earlier denied the request, the governor said that had he known the circumstances he would also have withheld his consent.

Stockenström, who by now had become entirely disenchanted with his office, stayed on for as long as he could bear it. In early 1833, however, he sought, and was granted, permission to take six months' leave. He sailed off to England, where he would present his case to the Colonial Office for review.[82] Quite coincidentally, Henry Somerset had also returned to England for leave some months earlier but, before his departure, he had allowed Maqoma to return yet again to the Ceded Territory from which he had been expelled in 1828.[83] In May 1829, Stockenström once again supervised his expulsion.[84]

In 1833, Sir Lowry Cole, disheartened by the failure of the Colonial Office to support his views, and the state of the frontier, threw up his hands and resigned. He sailed away in August of that year, leaving his military secretary, Lieutenant-Colonel Thomas Wade, as acting governor. Before he left, he gave Wade instructions to remove Maqoma's brother Tyhali from the Ceded Territory, where he had remained when Maqoma had been expelled. Wade did so and then found that Maqoma was also still resident there. In October he gave orders that Maqoma was also to be ejected.[85]

Captain R.S. Aitchison was given the task of removing the Xhosa; Aitchison was a soldier who had dealt with the Africans fairly and was entirely honest with them. Asked at the subsequent Select Committee inquiry if Maqoma and his people were distressed by their removal with crops still in the ground, Aitchison replied:

> . . . they were driven out of a country that was both better for water and grass than the one they were removed to, which was already thickly inhabited. They

took me over the country they were to inhabit, and I assure you there was not a morsel of grass upon it more than there is in this room; it was as bare as a parade.[86]

Henry Somerset returned from England in December 1833 and immediately resumed his vigorous activities against the Xhosa. Nevertheless, against explicit orders from Wade not to do so, he permitted Maqoma to return yet again.

One month later the new governor, Sir Benjamin D'Urban, arrived in the colony. Wade was infuriated to learn that not only had Somerset allowed Maqoma to return to the colony for a fourth time but had sought, and obtained, Governor D'Urban's permission to do so.[87] Once again Aitchison was called upon to remove Maqoma, both of whom were now utterly bewildered by the constant changes of mind. Aitchison subsequently responded to questions by the Select Committee:

Q. They had permission to return, then they were removed by you, and then they returned again, by the permission obtained from Colonel Somerset? – Yes.

Q. What lapse of time was there? – I drove them out in November, and Colonel Somerset returned in January. I fancy it must have been in February that the Caffres came back, but subsequently to that they were driven back again. The case is this, Colonel Somerset, who is in great favour with the Caffres, his father, Lord Charles, having been the governor, and being there ever since he was a very young man, he has got extraordinary influence among the Caffres. Whether he wrote to Sir Benjamin D'Urban, or got his sanction or not, I know not; but the Caffres were permitted to return without the civil commissioner [Stockenström] having been consulted. This gave great umbrage to the civil authorities.[88]

Among the changes initiated by D'Urban was the introduction of a Legislative Council, the first step towards responsible government, consisting of the governor, five officials and five to seven colonial residents chosen by D'Urban.

Throughout 1834 D'Urban had given numerous undertakings to visit the frontier, at the urging of both officials and Xhosa chiefs, but as a result of the pressure of work at the Cape he was unable to find the time to do so. It was an omission which was to work against him. The final step towards another war occurred when, on 2 December, a report was received at Fort Willshire that a farmer had had three horses stolen by the Mbalu. A patrol under an Ensign Sparkes was sent out to recover the animals. After ordering the seizure of forty cattle as compensation, the patrol was followed by angry Mbalu on its way back to the fort with the cattle. Chief Nqeno, learning of the warlike response of his people, sent his son Stokwe to intervene. He was only partially successful and a second group of Mbalu attacked the patrol closer to the fort, during which Sparkes was badly wounded.[89]

Henry Somerset saw this as an act which required immediate and heavy retaliation. Riding out with a strong force behind him, he demanded 150 cattle from Nqeno and further demanded that the chief remove himself and his people to the far side of the Keiskamma River.

Somerset next moved against Tyhali. A patrol led by Lieutenant William Sutton went into the area of the lower Kat River and there he burnt huts and took cattle. In the process, Tyhali's brother Xhoxho received a slight wound to the head, a mere graze but sufficient to knock him down. To the Xhosa, Xhoxho was now 'dead'.[90]

Sixth Frontier War, 1834–1836

The Xhosa chiefs met in council but were largely driven by the fury of their people. Only the Gqunukhwebe stood aside, they having a good understanding with the British. Hintsa too counselled peace but his opinion was also discarded: 'Hintza is king; but if any insult is offered to Hintza's people, and they are going to make war on any one, and Hintza tries to restrain them, they would not listen to him. He is something in council, but not out of it.'[91]

On 22 December 1834, as many as fifteen thousand Rharhabe and lesser Xhosa clans invaded the colony along almost the whole of its 150-kilometre border. Mostert describes the appearance of these warriors as they approached farms and villages:

> Naked, masked from head to foot in red clay, around his shaven head a beaded band adorned with blue crane feathers, a plumage that nodded in elegant rhythm with the wail and whistle of the war cry, the Xhosa warrior was unrecognizable from the passive, amiable and pliable 'kaffir' whom the missionaries sought to convert, with whom colonists and military traded ivory or shouted at or threatened from the saddle.[92]

The Dutch burghers, experienced in skirmishes with the Xhosa, did as they had done in earlier incursions: after an initial defence they packed up and left their farms for the safety of the nearest location where a laager had been established. The British settlers panicked and fled to the nearest village or town.

The military too was overwhelmed by the Xhosa numbers and the extent of the incursions. Somerset, having vainly tried to come to grips with the many bands of marauding Xhosa, ordered his troops to abandon Fort Willshire and the smaller frontier forts and fall back on Grahamstown while he locked himself in Fort Beaufort. By Christmas Day the Xhosa had burnt out the frontier farms, taken their cattle and were well on their way through the Zuurveld towards the Sundays River. As the days passed, exaggerated stories emerged of the murder of every trader on the frontier.[93]

One of the victims was the British settler leader Thomas Mahoney, who owned the Clay Pits. On Christmas Eve, his family and those of two other neighbours, were suddenly surrounded by warriors as they made their way from their farm towards the nearest military post. Every man was killed but, as was the usual Xhosa courtesy, the women and children were allowed to go unharmed. The warrior who had just cut Thomas Mahoney's throat brought her wrap to Mahoney's wife, gently put it around her shoulders and told her to run.[94]

On the 28th, nine hundred refugees, being the whole of the populace of Bathurst, arrived to take shelter in Grahamstown. Somerset had himself finally abandoned Fort Beaufort, arriving in Grahamstown on 29 December.[95]

The Xhosa now took the political initiative, with both Maqoma and Tyhali instructing their respective missionaries to write to the governor on their behalf. That of Maqoma, dated 1 January 1835, is contained in a Parliamentary Paper of the day and reads in part:

> I take the liberty of writing to your Excellency to inform you of the causes of the present quarrel between the colonists and Caffres. No one has told your Excellency how the colonists have been accustomed to deal with the Caffre people. It is true Colonel Somerset communicates with you about the transactions of the frontier, but he tells you only one side of the story. Colonel Somerset for a long time has killed the Caffres; he has disturbed the peace of the land, and torn it in pieces, and matters are now come to such a crisis that you alone are able to rectify them. Colonel Somerset has also ruined me. This he did in 1829, when I aided Bowana in punishing some Tambookies who had stolen from the colony . . .[96]

Tyhali's letter was less passionate than Maqoma's but just as telling, setting out his arguments in fourteen points, each detailing a particular incident in which the Xhosa were badly treated. The thirteenth item came to the heart of the rebellion and reads as follows:

> 13. That there were three things which were great in Caffreland; 1st: It is a great thing to kill a chief, or to wound him; 2d: It is a great thing to take land from the Caffres; 3d: It is a great thing to seize the real cattle of a chief.
>
> That the Caffres cannot say that their chief's cattle were beyond the boundary line, as they consider that the lawful boundary line is the Great Fish River.[97]

Somerset made no answer to the letters but did send them on to the Cape, where they arrived weeks afterwards, too late to do any good.

Neither Henry Somerset, nor Sir Benjamin D'Urban for that matter, should have had cause for concern, because, at that very moment, there was a white knight riding to the rescue of the colony and Britain's honour. He was an unlikely hero, having languished in obscurity at the Cape for the last seven years, but a hero he was, having already established his credentials in South America and the Peninsular War.

Chapter 3

The British Colony, 1835 to 1847

I cannot admit that the British sovereignty over the country between the Fish River and the Keiskamma rests on any solid foundation of international law or justice.

Lord Glenelg, Colonial Secretary

On 6 January 1835, there strode on to the stage of the Cape frontier arguably the most controversial Englishman ever to serve in South Africa. His name was Lieutenant-Colonel Henry George Wakelyn Smith, who preferred to be known as 'Harry'. Mostert describes him as 'one of the most extraordinary personalities of all, dashing, vain, self-glorifying, reckless, somewhat mad, and often ludicrous, as well as silly.'[1] Born in Whittlesey, England on 28 June 1787, Smith was about forty-eight years old in 1835 and had already served with great distinction in South America and in the Peninsular War.[2]

Seventh Frontier War, 1835

Smith was no stranger to South Africa, having served at the Cape since 1829 as deputy quartermaster-general.[3] It was a post in which he chafed for action and, as the year 1834 came to a close, his opportunity arose. In Cape Town, Governor D'Urban had received many pessimistic messages from Henry Somerset on the eastern frontier but only with the arrival of a despatch on 28 December had he finally become aware that a Xhosa irruption into the colony was actually under way. As the second most senior military officer at the Cape after D'Urban, Smith was ordered to take ship with reinforcements and leave for Algoa Bay immediately. Instead, he chose to ride the one thousand kilometres to what had become known as Port Elizabeth, on Algoa Bay, leaving in the early hours of 1 January 1835 and arriving just six days later. It was a remarkable, if unnecessary, achievement.[4]

I have been puzzled as to why Smith made the choice he did, hazarding his personal safety for an unnecessary ride, instead of taking the comfortable option by sea, while gaining little, if any, time. I now think I may have the answer. In June 1828, Henry Somerset had gone to Cape Town in order to resign his military command so that he could accept a civil post. On arrival, he was told that he had been appointed to the command of the Cape Mounted Rifles instead, a post he much preferred. So delighted was he with the appointment, and here I quote: '[Somerset] returned post haste to Graham's Town, covering the 600 miles on horseback in six days. Jubilation reigned in the Somerset household, where none had wished to leave the Frontier or their comfortable home at Oatlands Park.'[5] So the marathon ride had already been accomplished seven years earlier, and by a man with whom Smith was now to serve. It might be speculated that, given Smith's vanity and propensity for theatricality, he would want to prove that he could do just as well as Somerset.

On arrival in Grahamstown on 6 January, armed with plenipotentiary military and civil powers, Smith took immediate action to quell the panic that had taken hold of the town. He declared martial law, compelling males between sixteen and sixty to register for military service, ordered the demolition of the 'ridiculous' barricades which had been hurriedly thrown up across streets.[6] He then sent a strong message to the Xhosa chiefs, ordering them back beyond the colony's boundary, at the same time surrendering the result of their pillage. Smith believed that attack was the best form of defence and immediately adopted his own doctrine. His troops were ordered out of their barracks into the field, so that they might recover the forts hastily abandoned. Major William Cox, like Smith an officer of the Rifle Brigade, was given the command of a column and ordered to re-occupy Fort Willshire.[7]

Cox left on 10 January and the next morning at dawn, after a lightning march, descended on Nqeno's homestead. The deserted homestead was burnt and Cox then made his way to Fort Willshire. It had been sacked by the Xhosa and he rested there for a day before marching on Tyhali. His homestead was also deserted and it too was razed to the ground.[8]

Smith's next step was to secure his border with the Xhosa. Patrols were despatched to secure the abandoned forts and to establish new ones. Colonel Somerset was ordered to secure the road to Port Elizabeth to ensure that the supply line remained open. Governor D'Urban arrived in Grahamstown on 20 January, by which time border security had been re-established: the rebellious Xhosa had, for the most part, been pushed back across the colonial border on the Great Fish River.[9]

D'Urban next ordered that the fight be pursued into the Xhosa homeland and prepared four columns of troops to undertake the reprisal invasion.[10]

Harry Smith Takes Command

Throughout the remainder of January and the whole of February, Smith, now Chief of Staff to D'Urban, laboured to prepare the invasion force. On 29 March 1835, a general order was issued identifying the troops assigned to each of the four columns, numbering some two thousand men in total, of whom eight hundred were mounted. The invasion was to be directed towards the Amathola Mountains, where the Rharhabe chiefs were said to have concentrated.

On 31 March the 1st Division, under Lieutenant-Colonel John Peddie, marched out from Fort Willshire and found only empty Xhosa homesteads, all of which were burnt, and their gardens destroyed. The division arrived in the Amathola Mountains two days later and sat down to await the remaining columns. Lieutenant-Colonel Henry Somerset's 2nd and Major William Cox's 3rd divisions arrived on 4 April, and on the 5th D'Urban started his troops up the lower slopes of the mountains. Another force was placed to the north where it was expected to intercept any fleeing Xhosa.[11]

It was not long before D'Urban became disenchanted with the task of driving his men into the Xhosa mountain refuge and, leaving Cox to continue the toil, took both Peddie's and Somerset's divisions across country to the Great Kei River. His plan was to cross into Gcaleka country and harry the man whom he thought responsible for permitting the Rharhabe rebellion: Hintsa.[12]

On 15 April, the 1st Division reached the Kei and descended into its deep valley to reach the drift far below. Their progress was observed by hundreds of Gcaleka lining the heights on the far bank. A shouted conversation across the river then followed, in which Smith was given permission for his force to cross the river in order to have a meeting with Hintsa. They crossed and proceeded some thirty kilometres to the area now occupied by the town of Butterworth, near the site of the abandoned Wesleyan mission station, where they set up their camp.[13]

Almost immediately a host of warriors appeared. Despite being armed with assegais and shields, they waved strips of white cloth as if in surrender and asked to speak to D'Urban. In the subsequent meeting with their leaders, it transpired that they were Mfengu refugees who had left their Gcaleka hosts as a result of their ill treatment and now sought his protection. D'Urban had some sympathy for their plight and allowed them to stay near the British camp. In the following weeks, the host swelled until it reached about sixteen thousand people. On 24 April, British cannon shots announced the admission of the Mfengu into the British fold and, at the same time, the declaration of war against Hintsa.[14]

Hintsa's silence was in fact the result of his deep suspicion of white people, whom he believed were responsible for the deaths of Ngqika and Ndlambe. The subsequent seizure of thousands of Gcaleka cattle, however, forced him into attending a meeting. On 19 April, about forty horsemen thundered towards the camp and were met by two British officers. A tall African came forward, shook hands and gave his name: Hintsa.[15]

The Gcaleka chief sat down to talk with D'Urban and Smith. The governor immediately launched into a condemnatory speech in which he held Hintsa responsible, as paramount chief, for failing to prevent the war with Maqoma and Tyhali. Hintsa, he said, had encouraged the attacks and now harboured stolen cattle in his country. D'Urban demanded reparations of fifty thousand cattle and a thousand horses as a condition of peace. Hintsa was also required to order the recalcitrant Rharhabe chiefs to cease their rebellion. He was given just forty-eight hours to consider his response; if he agreed to the terms he was to leave two hostages in the camp until the conditions were met.

These were savage terms, a reminder of similar conditions imposed by Lord Charles Somerset on Ngqika in 1817. Hintsa was plainly shocked at their severity, and was puzzled at the reference to the power he supposedly held over the Rharhabe chiefs. He tried to explain that his paramountcy was largely symbolic and the reality that he had little control over the Rharhabe, but his argument fell on deaf ears.

Harry Smith had Hintsa dine with him that night and was impressed at how well the chief was able to argue his position. Nevertheless, by the end of the evening, the chief had agreed to the terms imposed upon him. The following morning, amidst a resplendent British host, and to the accompaniment of more cannon-fire, peace was declared. For the governor and Smith, it was an exercise in self-delusion: it was most unlikely that the paramount chief would turn against his clan chiefs so precipitately. Hintsa had, in fact, secretly sent messages to Maqoma and Tyhali telling them that he was a prisoner of the British and that they should send all their cattle eastwards beyond the reach of the white men.[16]

Hintsa and his son Sarhili (known to the British as 'Kreli' due to their inability to pronounce the Xhosa name properly) declared themselves to be the British hostages that the governor had earlier demanded, only to be told by D'Urban that they were free to leave whenever they wished.

On 2 May, D'Urban began the march back to the Kei. On the way, they came across Hintsa's brother Bhurhu driving about two dozen cattle: all he could find of the stolen beasts, he claimed. D'Urban was furious that he was to be offered so few cattle instead of the fifty thousand he had demanded and declared that the army would camp on the spot until his demand was met in full.

On that same day, news was received that the Gcaleka had begun killing Mfengu in retaliation for their disloyalty. In fact, the Mfengu had begun to seize Gcaleka cattle as soon as they were given British protection and already many of them had been formed into a levy to serve with the British column. Now the Gcaleka were attacking those Mfengu who had not yet joined the British, killing them and carrying off their stock.

D'Urban exploded at the news and ordered Hintsa to stop the killing within three hours, or else he would hang the chief, Sarhili and Bhurhu from the tree under which they were sitting. Hintsa gave the order but his anger was apparent in his questions: 'Why is there so much made of the Fingoes; are they not my dogs? Cannot I do with them as I like?'[17]

The honeymoon was over and D'Urban and Smith's semblance of warmth towards Hintsa evaporated. The chief was told that he, Sarhili and Bhurhu were prisoners and might be sent to the Cape.

By this time the column had reached the Kei, where they were to await fulfilment of Hintsa's reparation obligations. There too D'Urban reached another decision: he would extend the colony's border beyond even the Buffalo River up to the Kei. Furthermore, he would remove the Transkei Mfengu to the land between the Keiskamma and the Kei, thus providing a human buffer between the Gcaleka and the colony, also making them the first indigenous people to become British subjects in South Africa.

On 9 May, amidst much singing and shouts of joy, in a column two and a half kilometres wide and more than twelve kilometres long, the Mfengu horde began crossing the Kei into the colony; their destination was the Fort Peddie area, where they were to be re-settled, despite the fact that this was part of Gqunukhwebe territory.[18] The man in charge of this host was a young Theophilus Shepstone, who was D'Urban's interpreter. On 27 April, Shepstone recorded in his diary: 'Today I received my appointment as Commander in Chief of the Fingoes – about 6,000 in number.'[19]

Smith, meanwhile, was working on Hintsa, dining with him and Sarhili every night. It was a period of what might now be called 'brainwashing', in which Smith alternated his mood constantly, from threatening through menacing to frivolous. If Hintsa became morose, Smith made him laugh, then immediately changed his own mood. After a week of this, Hintsa finally suggested of his own volition that he accompany Smith on a patrol to bring in cattle.[20]

On 10 May, the governor ordered his troops to form a large square facing inwards. Hintsa, Sarhili and Bhurhu were brought into the centre of the square and there listened to D'Urban proclaim the new border of the colony, naming the country between the Keiskamma and the Kei as the new province of Queen Adelaide. All the rebellious Rharhabe were to be transported across the Kei to the Gcaleka country, leaving behind only the Gqunukhwebe and the newly transplanted Mfengu. A new military headquarters town was to be established on the upper Buffalo River and given the name King William's Town.[21]

Death of Hintsa

Almost immediately after the governor's proclamation on 10 May 1835, Harry Smith left with a large force for a destination known only to Hintsa, who accompanied him, where the promised cattle were to be delivered.[22] Hintsa had twice asked Smith for clarification of his situation, only to be told that should he attempt to escape he would be shot. Otherwise, the peace would be established when the requisite number of cattle were delivered.

In his report on the events following, Smith stated that he was at the head of the column leading their horses, with Hintsa and his two followers several horses' lengths behind him. Nearing the crest of a hill, the chief dashed past him through the bushes and then back on to the track they were following. Smith called out the chief's name and drew his pistol and, pointing it at the chief, called his name again and ordered him to stop. 'He stopped and smiled,' Smith recalled. Smith berated the small group of guides, who had quickly come up, for failing to watch Hintsa properly. Smith then described what followed:

> Upon nearing the top of this steep ascent, the country was perfectly open and a considerable tongue of land running parallel with the rugged bed of the Kebaka, upon a gradual descent of about two miles to a turn of the river, where were several Caffre huts. I was looking back to observe the march of the troops when I heard a cry of 'Look, Colonel!' I saw Hintzta [*sic*] had set off at full speed, and was 30 yards ahead of everyone.[23]

There now followed a race between Smith and the Xhosa paramount chief through more than a mile of scrub. Hintsa had the better horse but Smith was the better horseman. Smith drew his pistol and pulled the trigger but it misfired and he threw it down. He drew a second weapon and it too misfired. Spurring his horse, he drew level with the chief and struck him on the head with the butt of the useless pistol. As Hintsa surged ahead, Smith threw the pistol at him, striking him on the head for a second time. Smith was now effectively disarmed while Hintsa still had his bundle of assegais. Angrily spurring his horse, Smith drew level with Hintsa again and seized him by the throat with one hand, twisting the other into the chief's *kaross*. Summoning all his strength, he threw Hintsa from his horse but the chief immediately bounced to his feet and, after throwing an assegai at Smith, ran down towards the nearby river. Smith's horse now became unruly and it was some moments before he regained control. In that time, George Southey, leader of the Corps of Guides, had ridden up and, while still some two hundred metres from the chief, called to him twice in Xhosa to stop or he would fire. Smith's report described the tragic end of the episode:

> He ran on; Mr. Southey fired, and only slightly struck him in the leg, again calling to him to stop, without effect; he fired, and shot him through the back; he fell headlong forwards, but springing up and running forwards, closely pursued by my aide-de-camp, Lieutenant Balfour, he precipitated himself down a kloof into the Kebaka [River], and posting himself in a narrow niche of the rock, defied any attempt to secure him; when, still refusing to surrender, and raising an assegai, Mr. George Southey fired, and shot him through the head.[24]

A group of men closed in on the body and removed all his ornaments as souvenirs; one of the men, reputed to be Southey's brother William, cut off one of Hintsa's ears whilst another man cut off the second. Smith, learning of the death, sent for the body, but while it was being brought up to him draped over a horse, he sent word that he no longer wanted to see it and it was dropped unceremoniously in the bush and left there.[25]

Undeterred by the murder of a great chief in his own country, Smith continued to gather up Gcaleka cattle and had taken more than three thousand before he at last turned back to the Kei River and the governor's camp. D'Urban was greatly shocked by the news of Hintsa's death and anxiously considered the reaction which might be drawn from the Colonial Secretary in London.[26]

On 19 May, the governor sent for the twenty-seven-year-old Sarhili, now the new paramount chief of the Xhosa, and induced him to accept the Great Kei River as the new border with the colony and that the Rharhabe Xhosa would be removed into the Transkei. He then arranged an escort to accompany him back to his own country. His uncle, Bhurhu, remained behind as a British hostage.[27] Like his father, Sarhili would not trust a white man for the rest of his life.

On 24 May, D'Urban officially proclaimed the establishment of Queen Adelaide Province, extending from the Keiskamma River to the Kei. Harry Smith was given command of the province, with his headquarters in the newly founded King William's Town, where building was already in progress.[28]

Meanwhile, the troops left in the Amatholas had continued to thrash through the mountain bush to little avail. The elusive Xhosa had been able to avoid capture although their huts were burnt, their stock taken and crops destroyed. They were virtually without the basic means of subsistence but continued to fight on, even extending their raids into Albany from the Fish River bush. On the other hand, the British forces were little better off. The burghers had been given permission to return to their farms to sow a new crop and the Khoikhoi auxiliaries were bitter that they had not been allowed to do the same. The regular troops were tired of beating through endless bush, their uniforms were in tatters and some did not even have boots. Under these circumstances, D'Urban was anxious to conclude a peace that would allow him to concentrate on other matters.

On 15 August, Major Cox met with a submissive Maqoma and Tyhali to discuss a peace.[29] He gave them assurances that they would be granted secure land on the west bank of the Kei River, the governor having by now abandoned his former policy of moving them into Sarhili's country. Cox was unable to respond to their enquiries as to the land that was to be given to them but a truce was agreed. D'Urban next sent a strong message to the two chiefs in which he demanded that Sandile and his mother should live in the colony while all Xhosa living in the Amatholas should go to King William's Town to surrender their firearms and be 'reallocated'. The message was conveyed to the chiefs and another meeting was arranged, this time at the Burnshill site of the ruined mission station and within sight of Ngqika's grave.

When the British negotiators arrived at the rendezvous, they were astonished to be surrounded by about six thousand mounted and foot Xhosa warriors who moved into seemingly predetermined positions in a highly disciplined fashion. It immediately gave the impression of a force that was not defeated and certainly not in disarray. A sardonic message was received from Maqoma: 'The chiefs hope you will not be alarmed at seeing so many warriors assembled; they have brought them together merely to show you how many Xhosa are dying of hunger!'

Maqoma and Tyhali then arrived, Maqoma riding and Tyhali walking by his side. Both wore magnificent clothing and assumed a confident bearing. The meeting which followed was very different from that which had taken place earlier; gone was the submission and deference and in its place was a confidence bordering on arrogance.

The chiefs were equally surprised at the belligerent tone of D'Urban's message, with Maqoma responding, 'That is not peace; is that the way of making peace?' After a five-hour discussion, the chiefs were no closer to accepting the terms and insisted that they would not leave the Amatholas. It was up to the governor to make the next move.[30]

D'Urban was by now anxious to achieve a peace under almost any conditions and was furious that his officers had failed to press one on the Rharhabe. He was even more angry at the display of force demonstrated by the Xhosa and their change of 'tone and temper'. He decided that the only person able to satisfactorily conclude the next round of talks was Harry Smith, who made his way to Fort Cox. On arrival, he sent a blustering message to Maqoma giving him two hours to appear before him, otherwise Smith would 'sweep him and all his host off the face of the earth'. The two hours came and went and Maqoma did not appear. Eventually Smith received a message saying that Maqoma would meet him on the following day, 6 September 1835.

Smith must have calmed down a little by the time the chiefs appeared because he was able to conclude a preliminary agreement with them. On 17 September, the governor himself arrived at Fort Willshire for the final agreement. It was not just the Ngqika chiefs who were present on this occasion: Mhala of the Ndlambe, Nqeno of the Mbalu and Bhotomane of the Mdange were also present. All signed or made their marks, the Xhosa agreeing to become subjects of the king. As with Queen Adelaide Province, doubt was also cast on this decision since it was argued that only the Crown could naturalise aliens.

The Xhosa on the west bank of the Kei River were now subject to the laws of the Cape Colony but were permitted to retain their own native law. As to land assignment, Maqoma and Tyhali were permitted to remain lawfully in their chosen country of the Amatholas and Sandile was allowed to stay near his father's grave near Burnshill. The remainder were placed in separate locations throughout the new province, except the large area where the Mfengu had been settled between the Keiskamma and Fish rivers. Each chiefdom was to be assigned a commissioner who would administer his area, reporting to Smith at King William's Town.

Although the war had lasted some nine months, the casualties, in European terms, were relatively light: one hundred colonists and Khoikhoi, while the Xhosa had lost a thousand (as many as two thousand according to Cox). The loss of cattle and crops was very high for all parties, even the Gcaleka being unable to pay their reparations because of a drought, despite retaining the Rharhabe cattle that were being harboured by them.[31]

In terms of winners and losers, it can be argued that the governor and Smith came off worst because they had allowed the Xhosa to retain their land on the west bank of the Kei and, most notably, the Amathola Mountains. This area had been, and would remain in the future, the key to Ngqika resistance. At the same time, the Xhosa did not regard themselves as having been defeated, despite their material losses – in view of D'Urban's avowed intention to remove them to the Transkei and his subsequent change of mind, they had indeed won.

Governor D'Urban wrote a belated report of the war and its progress, dated 19 June 1835, to the Earl of Aberdeen, Secretary of State for War and the Colonies.[32] It was also accompanied by many enclosures, some of which have been noted here. Aberdeen had, however, already lost his post following the election of a new Whig government under Viscount Melbourne in April 1835 and Charles Grant, Lord Glenelg, had taken his place.[33]

Glenelg's reaction to the report was beyond anything that D'Urban could have expected; 'he read and re-read it in horror, disbelief and bewilderment,' writes Mostert.[34] The reply is dated 26 December 1835 and in its 150 pages Glenelg excoriated D'Urban for his failure to explain the reasons which caused the irruption of the Xhosa into the colony and demanded that the omission be rectified.[35] His informants in London (among whom was William Ellis, secretary of the London Missionary Society and, indirectly through his testimony to the Aborigines Committee, Andries Stockenström) had given him contrary and additional facts and he now demanded answers.[36]

Harry Smith Under a Cloud

Glenelg also demanded an explanation of D'Urban's reason for holding Hintsa responsible for the rebellion as early as February 1835 when he had no evidence to justify it, nor for invading his country while the fighting with Maqoma and Tyhali remained unfinished. Glenelg was also highly critical of the circumstances of Hintsa's imprisonment and subsequent death, and the matter of important details which Smith had omitted from his report:

> It is stated to me, however, on evidence which it is impossible to receive without serious attention, that Hintza repeatedly cried for mercy; that the Hottentots present granted the boon, and abstained from killing him; that this office was then undertaken by Mr. Southey, and that then the dead body of the fallen chief was basely and inhumanly mutilated. I express no opinion on this subject, but advert to it because the honour of the British name demands that the case should undergo a full investigation, which it is my purpose to institute.[37]

The Colonial Secretary's decision with regard to the proposed Queen Adelaide Province was a bombshell, although it should not have been unexpected. Glenelg could not agree that British sovereignty over Queen Adelaide Province 'rested on any foundation of international law'. The claim to sovereignty of the new territory was to be renounced, since it rested 'upon a conquest resulting from a war in which . . . the original justice is on the side of the conquered, not of the victorious party'. Occupation of the territory was to be resigned effective from the end of 1836, 'by announcing that the British occupation of it is temporary and provisional only'.

The decision affected more than the Cape administration; it raised a cry of horror from the settlers themselves. For the Boers, it simply reinforced what they had always held: that they must shift for themselves since no overseas government could determine their future for them. The announcement was thus the immediate cause of the 'Great Trek' out of the colony in search of independence. For the British colonists, more recently arrived but now closely aligned to their new country, it caused a rift between them and their origins and they could never see Britain in the same light again. Like the Dutch, they had, almost without noticing, become South Africans. For Boer and Briton alike it was to entrench in them the most bitter racist feelings towards the Xhosa.

For the Xhosa, the war had forced them to give up some of their ambitions but they had not sacrificed what they cherished most – their land. Under Harry Smith's aegis, the chiefs, particularly Maqoma, were able to convey an appearance of submission to his alternating displays of pique and foolish pomp (which included a throne in his residence at King William's Town) which in reality masked a secret contempt for him that would have shocked him. So well was his egocentric character understood by them that they were able to obtain, through their apparent deference and supplications, concessions which would not otherwise have been granted.

There was also a sting in the tail of Glenelg's very long letter which affected Harry Smith:

> For the due regulation of the future relations between the Caffre tribes and the colonists, as well as for other purposes of local convenience, His Majesty proposes immediately to appoint a lieutenant-governor of the eastern districts of the colony. On the lieutenant-governor will be devolved the administration of the executive government within the boundaries to be assigned to his command.[38]

Worse was to follow. The appointee was none other than Andries Stockenström who, after three years in England, arrived back at the Cape on

25 July 1836, where he was immediately sworn in as lieutenant-governor of the eastern frontier districts. It is notable that even at this late date, with the new official actually about to take up his appointment, the tardy D'Urban had still not yet addressed the matter of writing his defence of the annexation of Queen Adelaide Province for Lord Glenelg.

Stockenström left for his new office on 17 August but, on his arrival at King William's Town, he was astonished to find that martial law had been revoked in the province. D'Urban had made no mention of this at the Cape, even though the decision had been made on the day of his departure. He regarded the rescission with considerable concern, since it would not now underpin any decision he might make.[39]

Harry Smith had agreed that he would leave his command when Stockenström arrived and the revocation of martial law was an additional incentive for him to depart.[40] Still more imperative was his need to address his defence in the forthcoming inquiry into his actions in the death of Hintsa, which was then being convened in Cape Town. Commencing on 29 August and lasting just one week, the inquiry proved to be a whitewash for Smith and failed to identify the mutilators of Hintsa's body, even though everyone knew that it had been the Southey brothers.[41]

On 14 September, Harry Smith left King William's Town with his wife after hosting a meeting between the Xhosa chiefs and the new lieutenant-governor. There was no love lost between Stockenström and Maqoma, the latter never having forgotten that the former had been responsible for his first eviction from the Kat River Valley in 1828.

Left to manage the fading Queen Adelaide Province, Andries Stockenström decided to move the line of colonial defence back to the Great Fish River, even though the official frontier would remain on the Keiskamma. He had determined that the Xhosa should be permitted to occupy the Ceded Territory even though it was to remain under British control. The land was to be given to the Xhosa as a loan in perpetuity, conditional only on their keeping to the terms of the individual treaties which Stockenström intended each of the chiefs to sign. The many military posts and forts, including Fort Cox and even the King William's Town headquarters, were to be abandoned.[42] When the treaties were discussed with the Xhosa two objections were raised. First, the chiefs were still furious with the Gqunukhwebe for refusing to join the war with them. Stockenström told them to reach an amicable accommodation between themselves. The other problem lay with the Mfengu, whom the Xhosa saw as interlopers. Here Stockenström made it clear that they were now under British protection and the treaties included provision for them to remain in their location without let or hindrance.

D'Urban was incensed when he was notified of Stockenström's decision regarding the movement of the effective border back to the Fish River. This was more even than Glenelg had required and in a fit of pique he declared that the whole of the Ceded Territory from the Keiskamma to the Kei was to be completely evacuated. The relationship between the governor and his lieutenant-governor was ruptured beyond repair.[43] He now also sent off his defence of the annexation, even though the value of the document was by this time entirely academic. It was couched in such insulting language towards Glenelg that even King William IV was shocked. Whatever else D'Urban might have expected as a result of his letter, its only consequence was his immediate recall.[44]

Stockenström did not survive in his position for long either. Such was the antipathy throughout the colony towards him that a matter from long ago was dredged up by D'Urban. Stockenström was alleged to have murdered a Xhosa youth in 1813 in revenge for the death of his father and much dubious evidence was collected to demonstrate the fact.[45]

Stockenström was exonerated by an official inquiry into the allegations but he felt it was necessary to go to England to clear his name there. Glenelg was sympathetic but he was then replaced by Lord Normanby, who offered Stockenström a consolatory knighthood and a governorship in the West Indies. Stockenström declined the governorship but accepted the baronetcy and a pension, resigned his post as lieutenant-governor, and returned to the Cape as a private citizen.[46]

On 20 June 1837, William IV passed away at the age of seventy-one. He was succeeded by his eighteen-year-old niece Victoria, a granddaughter of George III, thus ushering in the great Victorian era.[47]

D'Urban was replaced in January 1838 by Sir George Napier, though the former remained at the Cape in a private capacity until 1846, the city of Durban being named after him. Harry Smith, meanwhile, who had thought that his military career might be finished, received news in 1840 that he had been appointed adjutant-general of the British forces in India and sailed away immediately.[48]

The departure of Stockenström introduced Colonel John Hare to the post of lieutenant-governor of the frontier. He was an older man and, lacking the experience of his predecessor, depended heavily on intelligence from his diplomatic agents resident with the Xhosa. John Bowker was assigned to the Xhosa near the coast, including the Ndlambe and Gqunukhwebe, until his dismissal and replacement by Theophilus Shepstone.[49] Charles Lennox Stretch, based at Alice, was attached to the Ngqika at Tyumie in the Amatholas.[50]

In 1840, Hare was visited by a number of Rharhabe chiefs, who introduced him to a young man with a withered leg. This was the new sovereign chief of the Rharhabe, Sandile (known to the British as Sandilli) who had undergone his coming of age ceremony only recently. He had done so with some bitterness on the part of his older brother Maqoma, who had served his people as regent since the death of Ngqika in 1829. Maqoma's dependence on the bottle had increased in recent years, especially after Sandile assumed his leadership of the Ngqika, and it was not unusual for him to be seen in Fort Beaufort canteens. He and Tyhali had gone their separate ways, Tyhali being disgusted with his brother's alcohol dependence.[51]

Mostert describes Sandile, who by now was emulating his older brother's intemperance, as having 'a more difficult personality to penetrate than most'.[52] Other historians were less generous, Meintjes recounting: 'Character assessments of Sandile are not flattering.' Cory described him as weak-minded. Theal says that he was 'a wretched stupid sot'. Brownlee also calls him weak, as well as irresolute and foolish. Soga says he was a weakling, pliable, 'and without a settled or reliable mind'.[53]

These conclusions may be accurate, but they may also reflect the conditions under which Sandile lived during his minority, being in the shadow of his more dynamic and influential brother Maqoma. Certainly the events about to be described indicate that he was making an effort to cast off Maqoma's dominance and assert his own personality. One might also suggest that his withered leg, the result of infantile paralysis, or poliomyelitis, might have induced a reserve in him as a youth which bred a lack of confidence as he grew older.

Stockenström's 'treaty system' lived on after his departure until the encouragement it gave to the Xhosa proved to be too much. Hare was constantly bombarded by complaints of cattle-lifting by the Xhosa, an old story by now, but just as infuriating as ever.[54] Governor Napier refused all Hare's requests for armed intervention with the Xhosa.[55] What the farmers and traders really wanted was the abandonment of the hated treaty system altogether, but Napier obdurately refused, and continued to do so until his replacement in March 1844. Mostert observed that he had 'presided over an entirely new and different atmosphere of hate and mistrust on the eastern frontier . . .'[56]

The new governor was Lieutenant-General Sir Peregrine Maitland, yet another veteran of the Peninsular War and Waterloo. Mostert describes him as having '. . . drawn sarcasm and anger in Canada for indolence and incompetence'.[57] When he visited the frontier for the first time in September 1844, Maitland surprised everyone by announcing the abandonment of

Stockenström's treaty system, which he now deemed unworkable. He did this without recourse to either Sandile or Maqoma, both of whom were angered by their treatment, learning of a new general treaty only by messenger.[58]

The treaty, which was finally read to Sandile and Maqoma on 2 October, re-instituted the 'patrol system' which had so angered the Xhosa before Stockenström had swept it away. The Ngqika were convinced that these changes were aimed at taking away their land again, especially when Maitland announced that the military occupation of the Ceded Territory, set in train by Hare earlier, would now be made permanent. Far from putting a stop to the cattle-lifting, the sudden change of system imposed on the Xhosa increased its frequency, encouraged by another drought. And thus the pot simmered throughout 1845.

Seventh Frontier War, 1846–1847

In the middle of March 1846 a Dange sub-chief named Tsili entered a trading post in Fort Beaufort. It was not a fort in the true sense of the word, its only fortification being a Martello tower, but the village contained a barracks and a hospital, and a few houses straggled along its two streets.

Tsili took a liking to an axe he saw in the store and walked out with it without payment. It was not unlike an incident in which Sandile had been involved two months earlier[59] and this may have been the model which Tsili was following. He was quickly arrested, manacled and put in gaol. His chief Thole was advised of the arrest and sought to have Tsili released, a request which was denied, perhaps due to Thole's own unsavoury reputation as a horse thief.

On 16 March, Tsili, shackled to a Khoikhoi fellow detainee, and with two white prisoners, was sent under escort to Grahamstown for trial. On the way the little convoy was intercepted by a large number of Thole's warriors and the escort fled in the brief mêlée that followed. As he rode off, one of the escort fired at the Xhosa, killing one of them, ironically a brother of the Xhosa thief. The Khoikhoi prisoner was then stabbed to death and his hand hacked off in order to release Tsili from the shackles.

Lieutenant-Governor Hare demanded that Tsili and the murderers of the Khoikhoi be surrendered at once, only to be advised by Bhotomane, Thole's brother, that Tsili's brother's death compensated for the death of the Khoikhoi, while Thole himself suggested that the best course was to do nothing. Sandile was of the opinion that the magistrate who had consigned Tsili for trial in Grahamstown had erred because he had over-reacted to the theft of a utensil worth a mere four pence.[60]

Hare continued the over-reaction by immediately concluding that a war was unavoidable and informed Maitland on 24 March that he was calling up burgher forces to be thrown against 'the hostile chiefs'. On 11 April, a large force, including regular, burgher, Khoikhoi and Mfengu troops, assembled at Grahamstown under Colonel Henry Somerset. They were, again, divided into three columns, and their orders were to converge on Sandile's Great Place near Burnshill. When they arrived there it had been abandoned and word came that the Xhosa had assembled in the recesses of the Amathola Mountains.[61]

This war, which came to be known as the War of the Axe, was to be fought very differently from its predecessors. The most dramatic change was that many of the Xhosa were now mounted, equipped with firearms or both, the firearms being sold to them by rogue Grahamstown traders and the horses being stolen from their white owners.

The spread of forts across the frontier also meant that supplies and forage had to be transported to them from supply centres such as Grahamstown and Port Elizabeth. Recognising this important fact, Maqoma devised the means of disabling wagon convoys, either by cutting the traces or killing the oxen, leaving the convoy at the mercy of the attackers. Together these innovations were a winning combination.

Hare found to his dismay that his opponents were not just the Ngqika: Phato of the Gqunukhwebe had stood aside from the war in 1835 and had been castigated for it. Now he was quickly persuaded to join Sandile and chose to attack the Mfengu who had recently been given his land near Fort Peddie. There Colonel Richardson, commanding the fort, gathered two hundred troops and attacked Phato. The Gqunukhwebe chief immediately turned his attention away from the Mfengu and onto Richardson, who promptly retreated to the safety of his fort.[62]

Phato was not the only chief to join the war, his example being followed by Mhala of the Ndlambe, who attacked the supply line between Grahamstown and the Fish River. Indeed, the only chief who chose not to do so was Nqeno of the Mbalu. He died on the first day of the war, but not before he had made his heir Stokwe promise not to become involved.[63]

These early successes were the signal for a general invasion of the colony and the Xhosa quickly began to take cattle and burn farms, an ironic reversal of fortunes for the settlers. Even Stokwe was sufficiently encouraged to break his promise to his dying father. The colonists, having been forewarned, went into laagers or moved into Grahamstown. With little else he could do, Maitland took command of the frontier, concentrated his troops at Forts Beaufort and Peddie, as well as Grahamstown, and declared martial law.[64]

With so many mouths to feed at Fort Peddie, on 18 May a convoy was arranged to take supplies and fodder from Grahamstown to Peddie. The wagons were attacked after crossing the Fish River, while they were making the long ascent out of the valley. With his convoy at a standstill because of the new Xhosa tactics, the officer in command gave the order to withdraw and the escort fell back onto Trompetter's Drift.[65]

The supply problem for the fort was finally solved by the assembly of more than eighty wagons with an escort of no fewer than twelve hundred troops.[66] The convoy only reached Fort Peddie on 31 May after yet another ambuscade and a desperate fight while climbing out of the Fish River valley.

On 8 June, Colonel Somerset, anxious to return his wagons to Grahamstown safely, set out on a diversionary foray. For once his luck held. Setting out to attack Stokwe's Mbalu homesteads, he stumbled on the tracks of a large Ndlambe force under Mhala. Following the spoor, he came upon the camp site of a large number of Ndlambe on their way to attack another convoy. In the fighting that followed, the Ndlambe scattered and took refuge in thick bush. Undeterred, Somerset sent his men in after them and after several hours, with only partial success, he called them back.[67]

He next sent an officer forward to find a suitable site for the troops to take a meal. This individual was the ubiquitous Jack Bisset, now a staff officer. Only recently, Bisset had had a close shave:

> On one occasion, after the enemy had been driven into the bush beyond our reach, and were firing long shots at us (in two senses of the word), I was watching the result, when all at once I heard a wobbling, whizzing-sound approaching me; and looking to my front, I saw a blue line in the air falling at an angle of about sixty degrees direct for my head. I had only just time (and I am not ashamed to say so) to bob on one side. A long piece of lead grazed my cheek and struck Major Walpole, of the Royal Engineers, who was standing immediately behind my horse. It sounded like a thud as it struck him on the thigh, tore out a piece of cloth about two inches long by one broad, and fell to the ground, but did not enter the leg. The pain for the moment must have been excruciating, for it made the major jump about on one leg and grind his teeth.[68]

Bisset's horse, 'a vicious chestnut brute', took flight and his rider found himself carried into the Gwangqa River valley in which was another large column of Ndlambe, this time led by Siyolo, a son of Mdushane. Coincidentally, they were also on their way to ambush the same convoy as the earlier force.

Bisset gave his mount its head and made his way back to Somerset, who then formed up his cavalry and Cape Mounted Rifles to make an attack in what was perfect cavalry country. Siyolo drew his men into a tight mass to meet the horsemen and, as they drew within a few yards of them, ordered a volley, just as he had seen the white troops do. Their shots went high and seconds later the cavalry were on them. They passed through, sabres flashing, and then wheeled and rode back hard into them again. The second blow broke the Ndlambe and they scattered across the field. They were followed for some eight kilometres before the pursuit was abandoned. But the slaughter continued on the field as the Mfengu footmen searched out hidden groups and the wounded, finally leaving three hundred dead and dying on the banks of the Gwangqa. Bisset took three prisoners during the five-hour battle, one of whom turned out to be a councillor of Sarhili, evidence that the Gcaleka were taking part in the war in which they professed neutrality.[69] According to Meintjes, it also emerged that the Gcaleka had taken part in an earlier attack on Fort Peddie.[70]

This action seemed to be a watershed in the war. Following their heavy defeat at the Gwangqa, the Xhosa withdrew from the colony and by mid-June the governor was able to report that the colony was once again secure.

Maitland immediately set about raising a new force to cross the Keiskamma and by the end of the month had gathered together fourteen thousand troops, auxiliaries and transport men, of whom three thousand were regular British soldiers. The drought, however, interposed and this, together with the Xhosa tactics of attacking extended convoys, made commissariat operations almost impossible. Wagons were now ordered to carry powder and a lit match so that supplies could be blown up in preference to being captured. By the middle of July, however, Maitland had regained sufficient confidence to arrange his troops into two divisions. The first, under Somerset, was to operate in the south while the second, under Hare, was to be centred on Fort Beaufort in the north.

Somerset, with some fifteen hundred men under his command, set out to deal with Phato of the Gqunukhwebe. The chief withdrew with his stolen cattle all the way to the Kei River and then crossed into Gcalekaland. Somerset followed him across and managed to seize a few cattle before retiring again to the west bank of the river. Exhausted by their march, the column set out for home, harassed all the way by the Xhosa, who fired into their camps at night. It was a weary division that finally reached Fort Peddie with very little to show for their efforts but their lives.

At the end of July, Hare began an offensive against the Ngqika in the Amatholas. After ten days he too withdrew with virtually nothing accomplished. He retired in August, dying on board the ship taking him to England.[71] The fort at Block Drift was renamed Fort Hare by Maitland in his honour.

August saw Maitland and his army at their lowest ebb. They had withdrawn to the mouth of the Fish River, it being the only place where supplies could be safely landed by sea. However, Maitland was not the only one in low spirits.

In mid-September the drought which had ravaged both colonist and Xhosa finally broke. This immediately turned African minds to their fields because they returned to agriculture and refused to fight. It was, notes Mostert, 'a strategy that much later would be invented by Mahatma Ghandi'.[72]

In the same month, Maqoma approached the British under a flag of truce. He said that the Xhosa wanted peace, and a meeting with the chiefs was arranged. At this conference, with Sandile, Maqoma, Bhotomane and Thole present, Maitland presented the three conditions for peace: the Xhosa were to surrender their firearms, return all stolen cattle and forfeit all land west of the Kei River.[73] The chiefs, although wishing for peace, could not accept the conditions. Sandile left the conference, saying that he was going home to sow his fields. The governor's terms having been rejected, Maitland terminated the discussion.[74]

Shortly afterwards a sick Maqoma surrendered himself and his goods and Maitland allowed him to live in a small building near the governor's camp. Sandile made another overture for peace by surrendering Tsili, the man who had started the war, together with the man who had killed the Khoikhoi prisoner manacled to Tsili.[75] On 26 November, Maitland, at Fort Hare, wrote in his despatch to the Colonial Secretary in London: 'With the Gaika tribes we are at this moment neither at war nor at peace, nor is there even a defined truce between us; but no hostilities take place, and while they continue to bring in arms and cattle, and to maintain a peaceable demeanour, they shall not be attacked.'[76]

The governor again crossed the Kei to gather up more cattle and during this expedition, on 6 January 1847, he received a message that he had been recalled.[77] This decision had been precipitated by another change of government at Whitehall, when a Whig government under Lord John Russell assumed power. The new Secretary of State for War and the Colonies was the third Earl Grey. As Maitland passed through Grahamstown on his way to the Cape, he rescinded martial law on the frontier.

The new incumbent in Cape Town was Sir Henry Pottinger, who arrived at his post on 27 January 1847 confident, from Maitland's despatches, that the war was over. Late governor of Hong Kong, Pottinger was a martinet with a very short fuse who had spent the majority of his career in India. He regarded his appointment at the Cape as a temporary expedient, with the expectation that he would soon be appointed to another governorship in the sub-continent.

Suffering from a kidney ailment, by the time he had reviewed the frontier position his temperament, described by Mostert, was not encouraging:

> Pottinger's physical discomfiture obviously added many degrees to his permanent condition of hot displeasure with the world about him. The shoddy disorder and makeshift way things were managed on the Cape Colony's frontier, the venality, crookedness and subterfuge that lurked behind the shabby facade, permanently inflamed his mood. His rage was cumulative, overheated by impatience, by contempt for the way things had been left and by the shortcomings of those with whom he had to deal.[78]

In his consultations with the various informants on the frontier, he found opinions were divided, as he reported to Earl Grey on 20 February from Port Elizabeth:

> In making this attempt, I must premise that the reports I have had ever since I landed here are as contradictory as they are various. Some of them aver that the Kafirs are really subdued, and ready (with a few straggling exceptions) to come into any terms and arrangements that we may prescribe for them; others, on the contrary, would lead to the supposition that little or nothing had yet been done towards breaking the power of, and combination amongst, the chiefs, and that they are only awaiting a convenient time to reassemble and carry fire and sword into this colony.[79]

Pottinger thought that the truth lay somewhere between these extremes, although he believed that 'the announcement by my predecessor, that the war was at an end, and the consequent abolition of martial law . . . have already been demonstrated to have been altogether premature . . .'

Like Maitland, Pottinger also found that the Ngqika would not go to war: the onset of rain meant they were far too busy with their gardens and cattle. The governor then turned his attention to Phato of the Gqunukhwebe and Sarhili. Unlike his predecessors, however, the governor could not prosecute the war himself. He was still an employee of the British East India Company and was therefore barred from commanding Her Majesty's troops. Instead, he employed the services of Lieutenant-General Sir George Berkeley, who had accompanied him from England.[80]

Berkeley went off to deal with Phato but the chief was always two steps ahead of him and the general quickly found, like his predecessors, that this was a war unlike anything he had experienced in his career before.[81] The constant thrashing through heavy bush tore his soldiers' clothes from their backs, destroyed their boots and wore them physically almost to a standstill, to little or no avail.

Pottinger, meanwhile, when not railing against the indolence and venality of all those about him, had tried to return the burghers and Khoikhoi to their military duty. Even a sickly Stockenström, though, was unable to gather together more than twenty men, largely due to their fury with the way Stockenström himself had been treated, and the fact that they had served without pay.[82]

With Berkeley unable to bring the Gqunukhwebe to heel and Sarhili at too great a distance, Pottinger next turned to Sandile. The chief of the Rharhabe inadvertently gave the governor a pretext when fourteen goats were stolen from the Mfengu in June 1847. As Mostert notes, while Hare and Maitland had used a stolen axe as an excuse for war, Pottinger now used 'a small herd of goats as a pretext for resuming hostilities with Sandile and the Ngqika'.[83] He sent a force of 170 men to Sandile's Great Place at Burnshill to arrest the chief but Sandile had gone into hiding. They took cattle from both Sandile and his brother Anta and returned to the colony under heavy attack from the Ngqika.

General Berkeley now began a campaign against the Ngqika in the Amatholas. It was conducted in a most ruthless fashion and even British commentators were highly critical of the treatment meted out to the Xhosa and the way so many cattle were taken. It was not long before Sandile was compelled to negotiate but the British were in no mood for compromise. On 18 October, he sent a message that he wished to come in. The next day Captain Jack Bisset met Sandile, who was accompanied by a brother and a large number of councillors. After stating that he was too junior an officer to negotiate with Sandile, and guaranteeing the chief his personal safety, Bisset declined to say anything more. He escorted Sandile first to King William's Town, where the chief met Berkeley and enjoyed an expansive lunch at the expense of the government. Berkeley also told Sandile that he wished the chief to go on to Grahamstown to meet the governor.[84] On his arrival there, Sandile only realised his predicament when he found himself in a locked room, accompanied by only two councillors.[85] It was an act of gross British duplicity, and was regarded as such by Sandile.

It is uncertain what was meant to happen to Sandile after his capture – perhaps consignment to Robben Island. In the event, the military found themselves in possession of a hot potato and began to entertain grave doubts about the validity of his detention, Pottinger no less than any of his officers. Sandile remained a prisoner and, like his father and his brother Maqoma before him, took to drink, demanding a daily allowance of wine.[86]

Pottinger abandoned his plan to attack Sarhili across the Kei but continued his campaign against Phato and his Gqunukhwebe. For three months, until December 1847, Somerset chased him from one end of his country to the other but Phato always seemed to elude him. In mid-December, Phato sent messages to Somerset that he had had enough and wished only for peace. He surrendered his arms and was escorted to King William's Town.[87]

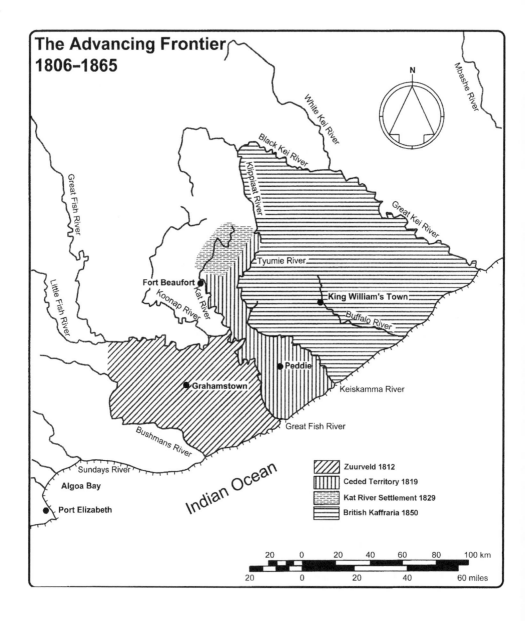

Chapter 4

The British Colony, 1847 to 1877

[British soldiers] are so accustomed to closing up in rank that they get bewildered when they are scattered singly in the bush . . .

T.J. Lucas, *Camp Life and Sports*

At the beginning of December 1847, there was a reception in Cape Town for Governor Pottinger's replacement. His name was Sir Harry Smith and that vain, quixotic figure strode onto centre stage for a second time. After leaving South Africa under a cloud, and as a mere colonel, he now returned in triumph as a major-general, the hero of Aliwal, and the new governor and high commissioner, after gathering a baronetcy and an honorary Doctor of Laws for his services in India.

Ten days after his arrival at the Cape, Smith began his journey to the frontier. On his way, he chanced to see Maqoma in the jubilant crowd; according to his autobiography:

At Port Elizabeth he saw the chief Macomo, and, having upbraided him for his treachery, ordered him to kneel, when he set his foot on the chief's neck, saying, 'This is to teach you that I am come hither to teach Kafirland that I am chief and master here, and this is the way I shall treat the enemies of the Queen of England.'[1]

This episode was never to be forgotten by Maqoma, who would soon repay the humiliation.

Smith continued on his way to Grahamstown, where he was again received by rapturous crowds. There he received the prisoner Sandile, whom he allowed to kiss his foot in submission, after which he was lectured and allowed to go free.

His next action was to abandon Maitland's general treaty system: it was annulled on 17 December 1847. The Mfengu, who had so often demonstrated their loyalty to the Crown, were settled at a number of locations in the Ceded Territory.[2]

Smith's triumphal procession moved on to the abandoned King William's Town which he had begun to develop nearly a decade before. There on 23 December he met all the great Xhosa chiefs whom he had summoned to meet him: Sandile of the Ngqika, his brother Anta, Thole of the Mbalu with his nephew Stokwe, Siyolo, Mhala and Siwani of the Ndlambe, Tshatshu of the Ntinde. Present too was Phato of the Gqunukhwebe, one of the prisoners brought in that day by Henry Somerset.

Here once again Smith was to indulge in theatrics. While remaining mounted, he had two poles brought forward, a tent pole with a brass knob on the top and a pike. He declared one to be the Staff of Peace and the other the Staff of War. He now required the chiefs to come forward to touch a staff indicating their choice of war or peace. Led by Sandile's mother Suthu, they all approached and touched the Staff of Peace.

The new governor next read a proclamation which announced the resumption to the Crown of all the lands between the Keiskamma and Kei rivers, which was henceforth to be known as 'British Kaffraria'. The Xhosa would be allowed to continue to live there and Smith would be their supreme chief. He then symbolically threw down the Staff of War and declared that the war was over. Once again, the chiefs were summoned forward to kiss his stirruped foot.[3]

On 7 January, Smith convened yet another meeting of the chiefs, the major feature of which was the destruction of a wagon using explosives to the accompaniment of Sir Harry's threat to treat them in like manner if they dared make war again. The date was no coincidence – it was eleven years to the day after the original proclamation of Queen Adelaide Province.[4] It was also Smith's way of thumbing his nose at Glenelg and his decision to abandon the province.

The war was over but nothing of consequence had been achieved. The Xhosa were cowed but not defeated and their apparent surrender was simply their pragmatic way of preserving their existence. The colonists had lost greatly by the war; some of them had lost everything. For the British government, the war had cost it an enormous amount of treasure.

Smith now put in place the infrastructure through which he proposed to govern the Xhosa. He appointed Colonel George Mackinnon, a new arrival in the colony, as chief commissioner. Under him were appointed Captain John Maclean as commissioner to the Gqunukhwebe and Ndlambe, while

Charles Brownlee was appointed commissioner to the Ngqika.[5] Brownlee, then twenty-five years old, was a particularly happy choice because he was fluent in the Xhosa language, having previously served as interpreter to both Stockenström and Stretch. He had also virtually grown up with Sandile.

In his annual report to Smith on the year of 1848, Chief Commissioner Mackinnon set out the great strides forward made by the administration of British Kaffraria. One year later, his second report was equally fulsome. But while matters in the colony were seemingly going well, Smith's own star had waned in spectacular fashion. The British government had sent out convicts to the colony, a development to which the locals objected strongly, and for which they held Smith responsible.[6] He also had problems with emigrant Boers leaving the colony. He had sent home three regiments of infantry and the Dragoon Guards, leaving the colony only thinly protected. Finally, at the age of sixty-three, his own health was failing.[7]

Eighth Frontier War, 1850–1853

The reader will recall the emergence in 1819 of Makanna-Nxele as a mystic who subsequently rose to the military leadership of the attack on Grahamstown by calling on the shades of the Xhosa people. Now another such individual appeared whose name was Mlanjeni. The new seer was reported to have spent a long period of time immersed up to his neck in an enchanted pool, and to have emerged speaking the words of spirits. It is perhaps no accident that his appearance coincided with yet another of the many droughts with which the country was afflicted.[8]

On 26 August 1850, John Maclean, commissioner to the Ndlambe, wrote from Fort Murray:

> I have the honour to report that Umlanjeni, a Kafir of Umkye's tribe and location, has lately revived the witch-doctoring craft, and great numbers have attended his meetings from all parts of Kafirland; in consequence of which I ordered him to appear before me, also his father Kala (at whose kraal Umlanjeni had erected several witchcraft poles). Both parties failed to appear; I therefore ordered the second division Kafir police to apprehend them, and to seize two head of cattle for their disobedience.
>
> The police apprehended Kala and seized one head of cattle, but they found Umlanjeni so weak and emaciated that he could not leave his kraal without assistance; they, however, pulled down all his witchcraft poles; and I have had him removed to the immediate vicinity of Umkye's [Mqhayi's] kraal, near Mount Coke, in order that I may keep him under observation.[9]

This and other reports eventually found their way to Sir Harry Smith and his response was to instruct Mackinnon to arrest Mlanjeni as soon as practicable. It did not happen and Smith was compelled to go to the frontier himself in October 1850.

Smith seemed to be completely unaware that he had unwittingly encouraged Mlanjeni as a result of his own policies. He had resumed the Ceded Territory and given it to the Mfengu and new British settlers; he had compelled the Xhosa to move their homes into British Kaffraria; he had undermined the power of the chiefs by appointing white commissioners with greater powers; perhaps worst of all, he had coerced the Xhosa to adopt European ways at the expense of the own traditions. It is hardly surprising, then, that the Xhosa would be so easily swayed by Mlanjeni, who offered a solution to their problems.

Smith convoked another conference with the Rharhabe chiefs on 26 October but Sandile chose not to appear.[10] Brownlee, Sandile's friend, was ordered to compel Sandile's appearance but the chief argued that he had accepted a similar British invitation once before, only to find himself their prisoner at Grahamstown: he was not going to repeat the error.[11] Smith was infuriated by Sandile's contumelious behaviour and on 30 October a proclamation was issued deposing Sandile as chief of the Ngqika and appointing Brownlee in his stead. Smith then returned to Cape Town on 24 November.

Mackinnon reported in a despatch to Smith dated 2 December 1850 that Maqoma had quit his home near Fort Hare to join Sandile in the bush.[12] Although Mackinnon did not expect any overt hostile action from the Xhosa, he did feel that they 'might drive us to some act which will give them a pretext for rising'.[13] Such a pretext would be forced upon them very soon, and Mackinnon himself was the willing tool.

On 5 December, Smith again felt it necessary to return to the eastern frontier and took ship to the newly established port of East London and brought with him reinforcements from the 73rd Regiment. When he arrived at King William's Town he found the frontier farmers in a state of panic, many of them having already abandoned their farms for safety in laager. To stabilise the frontier and reassure the colonists, on 14 December he issued orders for the formation of the inevitable three columns. The left, under the command of Lieutenant-Colonel Eyre, 73rd Regiment, was to move to the Kabousie Nek; the centre, under Colonel Mackinnon, was to be based, with headquarters, at Fort Cox 'for the purpose of penetrating the Amathola Mountains'; the right, under Henry Somerset, was to concentrate at Fort Hare.[14]

On 19 December, Smith called another conference of Xhosa chiefs at Fort Cox, which he opened by dramatically brandishing his Staff of Peace, complete with brass knob, after which the chiefs pledged their loyalty to the Crown. The single exception was Maqoma, who characteristically exchanged sharp words with the governor.[15]

Battle of Boma Pass

Perhaps driven by his angry exchange with Maqoma, Sir Harry now decided to send troops to patrol the Amathola Mountains and on 24 December 1850 his centre column under Colonel Mackinnon left Fort Cox to patrol as far as the Uniondale mission station at modern-day Keiskammahoek.[16] Their route followed the course of the Keiskamma River, close by Ngqika's grave. Beyond Burnshill, river and track turned north until, some three kilometres from Keiskammahoek, the hills closed in on the river and the track again to form the Boma Pass. Thomas Lucas was present with the column and could not help criticising the poor defensive posture of the venture, even to the extent of the men marching with unloaded weapons.[17]

The pass consisted of a narrow track, so hampered by huge boulders and tangled undergrowth that the troops were forced to march in single file. On their left reared a massive, crescent-shaped cliff while on their right, close to the track, ran the Keiskamma River, with lightly bushed meadowland beyond. There was a large conical hill at some distance to the right.[18] It was here that Maqoma exacted his revenge.

The attack on the column began with a single shot fired from a Xhosa musket, and was then followed by further sporadic Xhosa fire. The troops were marching with unloaded weapons and it took them time to load their firearms. Even then, though, they were unable to open fire because their commanding officer was more than a kilometre ahead of them and could not issue the necessary order.

The troops fled into the cover of nearby rocks and undergrowth but they were in a most perilous situation. Thousands of Ngqika warriors were bounding down from the conical hill to attack the stalled column across the river. The troops belatedly opened fire on the command of their immediate officers, who then urged them forward out of this defile of death.

For more than a kilometre the men struggled on, leaving twelve dead in their wake, until the whole column emerged into more open country, then sprinted for the safety of Keiskammahoek two kilometres away. They formed a square near the Uniondale mission station and spent a sleepless night awaiting the next attack – an attack that never came.

Colonel Mackinnon recognised the impossibility of returning by the way they had come and decided instead to take his column by an alternative route.

Most likely he took the Red Hill Pass, which would bring the column down to the area of Bailie's Grave.

The next morning, Christmas Day, the column left their overnight bivouac as the dawn mist began to burn off, promising a hot summer's day, and the men gasped their way over the pass, carrying their personal equipment, unloaded firearms and fourteen wounded men. Lucas commented: 'Will it be believed that on the morrow when we continued our route to Fort Cox . . . the same orders to forbear from hostilities were repeated, on the supposition that the disaffection was limited to the particular tribe that had attacked us?'[19]

At the top of the pass, they thankfully set down their burdens and dropped to the grass to eat and rest. Almost immediately they were subject to yet another hail of missiles and musket fire from the nearby forest. The troops were again only able to return fire after loading their muskets, but were in so exposed a position that their officers urged them forward yet again. After a bitter fight, the panicked column emerged onto more open ground and their enemy withdrew. They made their way down to lower ground where they finally managed to swallow something to eat and drink.

They approached Fort White at four o'clock that afternoon, where yet another horror awaited them. While passing over the Debe Flats near the fort they came upon the remains of a sergeant and fourteen soldiers of the 45th Regiment, decapitated and their bodies mutilated: they had been ambushed that same morning.[20] Mackinnon continued to Fort White, where he found a friendly Ngqika who was prepared to take a message to the governor at Fort Cox.

Meanwhile, at Fort Cox Smith was fuming, having received word of gunfire in the Boma Pass – news which he had initially dismissed but shortly afterwards Mackinnon's messenger arrived to confirm the rumours. He spent an anxious night and much of Christmas Day awaiting further information, which only came in the evening when Mackinnon himself arrived.[21]

Smith, rather than being the aggressor, now found himself besieged. He had few troops in the vicinity, the majority of those being the exhausted and dispirited column at Fort White. Worse was to follow. Some of the military villages established by Smith were also attacked the same day. In Woburn and Auckland their male occupants were killed and the houses burnt to the ground. In Juanasburg (named after Smith's wife), the occupants were able to escape with their lives to the safety of Fort Hare but still lost their homes.[22]

On 28 December, Colonel Somerset tried to break the siege of Fort Cox but was forced back by the weight of Ngqika numbers. Heeding a message sent to him by Somerset, Smith finally escaped from Fort Cox on 31 December: dressed as a trooper of the Cape Mounted Rifles (CMR), he led his cavalry in an attempt to reach Fort Hare. He was intercepted by a Ngqika force and changed direction and arrived at King William's Town instead, just after noon.[23]

While Phato and his Gqunukhwebe remained loyal to the Crown, promising to keep open the road between King William's Town and East London, Smith soon found himself still further isolated. The disaffected Khoikhoi population of the Kat River Settlement decided that their own loyalty to the Crown was worthless, threw in their lot with the Xhosa and began sacking the area around the Kat River under their leader Hermanus Matroos. Many of the rebels were trained soldiers, having served with the CMR.[24] An appeal for the support of the Boers fell on deaf ears: they too had had enough. It is notable that both had proved to be formidable adversaries of the Xhosa, yet both had served without remuneration.

On 6 January 1851, Matroos appeared before Fort Beaufort and attempted to overrun the village. His force occupied a part of the place but, as Matroos was leading a flank attack on the upper part, he was shot dead and the rebels left hurriedly, leaving their slain leader behind.[25] His place was taken by Willem Uithaalder, a full-blood Khoikhoi and a pensioner of the CMR.

Yet another British setback occurred on 22 January when Uithaalder led his Kat River rebels in an assault on Fort Armstrong. The fort was built on a peninsula of land thirty kilometres north of Fort Beaufort, almost entirely surrounded by the Kat River except for a narrow access point to the north-west only three hundred metres wide. It was strategically well placed, sporting a single stone tower and walled enclosure, but was poorly armed and without troops. Uithaalder permitted the safe departure of the British occupants the next day after extensive negotiations with the commandant and a cleric.[26]

In the far north-east corner of the frontier, the Thembu had resented a British decision to extend the colonial border to the White Kei River, thus taking Thembu land which had then been settled by white farmers. In early January 1851, their chief Maphasa openly revolted against the British.

It was fortunate for the British that Captain Richard Tylden, Royal Engineers, who was undertaking a survey in the area, assumed command. He gathered around him men of the loyal Gqunukhwebe under Phato's Christian brother Khama, a body of eight hundred Mfengu and seventy mounted Boers under Thomas Bowker. Between them, they were able to drive off the marauding Thembu. They re-grouped, to be joined by a party of Kat River men. The new alliance of Khoikhoi and Thembu engaged Tylden and his men for a number of days, each time being driven off. A shortage of ammunition caused Tylden to send an urgent message to Cradock over three hundred kilometres away. Two days later, and just in time, Boers with pack horses came to their aid and the following day a wagon train arrived. The fighting continued almost daily with no decisive result, until the Thembu drifted off to engage another party of Boers further north. The Khoikhoi left to return to the Kat River and by mid-February the Thembu emergency was over, Maphasa having been killed in the fighting.[27]

Things began to look a little brighter for Sir Harry Smith by the end of January 1851. A levy of fifteen hundred Khoikhoi had arrived by sea from Cape Town and with their help Smith trounced an over-confident Siyolo of the Ndlambe outside King William's Town. He then sent a column numbering about 2,750 men under the command of Colonel Mackinnon to relieve and supply Forts Cox and White on 13 February. Mackinnon left four hundred levies with Henry Somerset (who had been promoted by Smith to major-general at the beginning of January) and on 15 February both columns moved into the Tyumie Valley. There was no resistance and they moved through the valley laying waste every human habitation.

The next success was gained by Henry Somerset, who took back Fort Armstrong on 22 February.[28] Somerset followed up the victory with a sweep through the Kat River Settlement, where every man was disarmed and many of them arrested.

Smith now had some reason for optimism. The Khoikhoi rebellion was seemingly over, the Thembu problem was largely resolved and his agreement with the Gqunukhwebe to secure his lines of communication had held firm. His buoyant mood was shattered, however, when on 13 March Lieutenant-Colonel Edward Napier, commanding the CMR, was awakened to the news that his men were deserting. Smith received reports at midnight and a hasty court of inquiry was convened the next morning, which heard that nearly fifty men had left to join Uithaalder and his Kat River rebels. Smith paraded the rump of the King William's Town corps and, on the evidence of the inquiry, disarmed and disbanded them all.[29]

Autumn drifted into winter and still Smith struggled in the Amatholas against both the Ngqika and Uithaalder. The Khoikhoi question dogged him and in May, with his 'army' supplemented by deserters from the CMR, Uithaalder began attacking settlements in Albany. From there, he took up a position in the infamous Fish River bush. July saw the contracts of 1,800 African levies raised in January expire and, despite Smith's pleas, they left to return to their homes. This loss was in part offset by the landing of small drafts of troops from Britain in May through September.

Smith's immediate plans were: first, to deal with the Khoikhoi in the Fish River bush; second, to eject Maqoma from the colony and, when both of these objectives had been achieved, to make still another sweep of the Amatholas. The first task met with near-disaster although Smith's account dressed it up as a success.

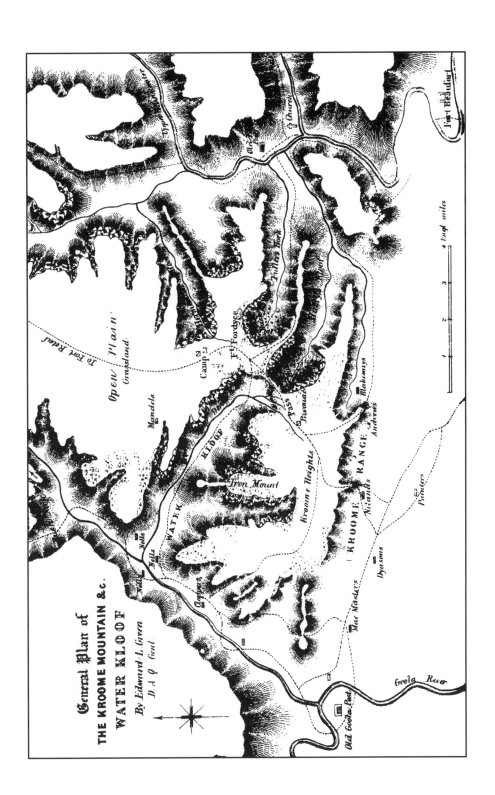

General Plan of
THE KROOME MOUNTAIN &c.
WATER KLOOF

By Edward L. Green
D A Q. Genl.

Open Plain

To Fort Relief

Ormsland

Mandels

Iron Mount

WATER KLOOF

Pells

Bella

Caspers

Kroome Heights

Pass

Trumans

Blakeways

Andrews

Nickolds

Printers

Mac Masters

Dyasons

Old Goola Post

Goola River

KROOME RANGE

Fuller Post

Church

Camp

F.t Fordyce

Fort Beaufort

1 2 3 4 Engl miles

Colonel Mackinnon led a strong force to the Fish River, arriving on 9 September. He continued his demonstrations until 16 September, when he marched back to King William's Town. Although his expedition was hailed as a victory, with many enemy killed, he had paid a heavy price, losing twenty-nine killed, forty-one wounded and eight missing, presumed dead. The 2nd (Queen's Royal) Regiment, which had arrived in South Africa only three weeks earlier, suffered particularly heavily.[30]

Kroome Heights

The governor's second objective was the ejection of Maqoma from the colony. For many years Sandile's older brother had wanted to return to the Kat River area from which he had been expelled so many times. With the rebellion of the Kat River Settlement, he had seen his opportunity and had stolen back, taking up residence in the deep, wooded valley known as Fuller's Hoek.[31]

The Kroome Heights were also contemporaneously known, as if to confuse us, as the Waterkloof. It described a mountainous region to the north of the Fort Beaufort–Adelaide road, the southern escarpment of which formed a plateau extending many kilometres north in the direction of Post Retief. This plateau was split by a number of steep-sided, heavily wooded valleys. To the west, running roughly north-west to south-east, was the Waterkloof itself. There was a narrow neck between this and two other valleys running approximately west to east; these were Aries Kloof to the south and Fuller's Hoek a little to the north. Still further north lay the valley known as Schelm (or Hermanus) Kloof, while running north to south still further east was the Blinkwater Valley.

The campaign for the Kroome Heights was to last from July 1851 to mid-March 1852, and consisted of no fewer than nine separate operations. Space precludes a detailed description of each of these sorties into the mountains in that period, other than a brief account of that in which Lieutenant-Colonel Thomas Fordyce, one of Henry Somerset's senior officers, was killed in November 1851.

On 6 November, two columns concentrated on a small knoll north of the end of a neck between the Waterkloof and Fuller's Hoek, a mere bump that was to become known as Mount Misery. From there, a column under Lieutenant-Colonel John Michel fought its way into the Waterkloof while Fordyce's column took guard around the knoll. All parties came under a galling attack from both Khoikhoi and Xhosa and the conditions for the British troops were wretched.

It was at Mount Misery that Fordyce was killed that morning, shot through the chest as he deployed his troops, waving his cap and shouting commands that were carried off by the wind. When night fell, there was a terrible thunderstorm and the men, including the wounded, were left exposed to the elements and sickness stalked through the camps. Two days later, Somerset withdrew his force, claiming a victory that was never his. The Xhosa remained masters of the Kroome and its deep valleys whilst the British were able merely to scratch the surface.[32]

Invasion of the Transkei

It was in these circumstances that Sir Harry Smith made an astonishing decision. He perhaps recalled the ease with which he and D'Urban, and others before him, had been able to penetrate Sarhili's country across the Kei, and the supine nature of the Gcaleka. He now decided that he would punish Sarhili again, for the same reasons as those adopted by D'Urban: Sarhili had harboured Rharhabe cattle and had encouraged Sandile in his resistance against the British. The probability is that he was trying to gather accolades for achieving something, rather than the constant criticism that was being levelled at him for his inability to deal with the Ngqika and Khoikhoi rebels.

The troops from the Kroome had recovered from their ordeal sufficiently to enable them to march by late November and Smith sent a force of five thousand men across the Kei on 1 December. His instructions to Somerset were quite explicit: he was marching 'for the purpose of seizing the Gaika rebels' cattle . . . and also for the purpose of chastising the Chief Kreli for his treachery'. The objective was not to defeat the Gcaleka in the field and was further expounded in the instruction:

> 2. The attempts on the cattle of the rebel Kafirs must be made with the greatest possible vigour. Not a day must pass upon which the troops do not move upon them, by which the double purpose will be served of at the same time assaulting Kreli, whose warriors and cattle are intermixed with those of the rebels.[33]

Somerset returned triumphantly to King William's Town on 11 January 1852 escorting more than thirty thousand cattle, as well as many horses and a great number of goats.

The exercise had only been a diversion and soon Smith was again confronted by the intractable problem of Sandile, Maqoma and the Ngqika. He now planned to overrun the Amatholas with his troops and apply a scorched-earth policy; it began in early February 1852 when seven columns moved through the mountains, burning everything in sight and destroying gardens. It was not long before overtures were received from the Rharhabe chiefs but Brownlee was instructed that the governor would accept nothing short of unconditional surrender, after which the Rharhabe would be removed across the Kei River.

Brownlee met Sandile and his chiefs in an open meadow and gave them the governor's terms, which they found entirely unacceptable. The destruction by the troops continued unabated until virtually nothing was left standing, but still the Xhosa would not submit. Once again, Smith decided that he must revert to his strategy of killing Sandile's warriors and began to put his plans in place.[34]

His efforts, however, were in vain. He received a despatch from Earl Grey on 1 March telling him he was dismissed from his post and that his replacement was already on his way. Grey included a catalogue of Smith's 'errors' which had led to his replacement.[35]

Smith recognised that he had but a brief window of time during which he might pursue Maqoma. He took personal command of the troops and led them into the Kroome Mountains. On 10 March three columns began their work scouring the three major valleys, including Fuller's Hoek, the seat of Maqoma's personal domain. On the 11th Maqoma's homestead was shelled and overrun, and his Great Wife taken prisoner.

The operations demonstrated with great clarity Smith's own genius for bush fighting: in five days he had achieved more than the three previous operations in the Kroome combined. The kloofs were not entirely cleared but they were very nearly so. From 21 to 25 March he turned his attention on the Amatholas and achieved a similar result.[36] Despite these successes, Smith could not bring the chiefs to surrender. The Ngqika were no fools: Milton quotes a letter of Charles Brownlee which noted that the Ngqika proposed to continue their resistance 'until the arrival of His Excellency's successor . . . when the Xhosa hope to obtain peace on their own terms'.[37]

The new governor was Sir George Cathcart, who had enjoyed a long career as a soldier serving, as had so many of his predecessors at the Cape, under Wellington. Immediately after his arrival Cathcart went to the frontier, arriving on 10 April. Smith left the Cape on 18 April, a man broken in both health and spirit. He lived for another eight years, dying from heart failure on 12 October 1860.[38]

Another, less heralded, departure was that of Henry Somerset, who had served at the frontier for no fewer than thirty-four years. He sailed from the frontier on 7 September 1852, bound for India, leaving behind a legacy of corruption and incompetence which would not prevent his receiving a knighthood in his new command. He died at Gibraltar in 1862.

George Cathcart carefully assessed the situation on the frontier. Sandile and his people were still in the Amatholas and, despite the ravages to their agriculture, had managed to sow a second crop. Maqoma still controlled the Kroome and its valleys, the fugitive Ndlambe chief Siyolo was hiding somewhere in the Fish River bush and the rebel Khoikhoi had broken up and scattered in small groups, now reduced to random acts of banditry.

While the new governor ordered some rest and recreation for his exhausted troops, he devoted his energies to the formulation of a strategy for dealing with his many difficulties. Mostert asserts that the result was hardly different from that of Sir Harry Smith, except in minor details.[39]

Cathcart's first task was to secure the road from King William's Town to Grahamstown, which passed over the Fish River. It was here that Siyolo was active and to restrict his marauding Cathcart ordered the setting up of small manned posts, which he called 'castles', along the road, at the centre of which lay Fort Peddie. He also enlisted a corps of armed mounted police for each of the five frontier districts, to be used to patrol their own area in search of rebels.[40]

In late June 1852, Cathcart assembled a force which spent nearly a week scouring the Amatholas, building several of his 'castles' there. Nothing of any substance was achieved. In July, he did much the same thing around the Kroome Heights. His troops again went into the Waterkloof and Fuller's Hoek, both of which he then assumed he had cleared.

Like D'Urban and Smith before him, Cathcart chose Sarhili as his next target and the Transkei was invaded on 28 July 1852. Sarhili's Great Place was once again reduced to ashes and a great many cattle were taken before the country was evacuated yet again.[41]

In September, the Waterkloof again became a target and this time no mercy was shown, prisoners being either shot or hanged from the nearest tree. Maqoma now fled and two more castles appeared, one in the Waterkloof and another overlooking Fuller's Hoek.[42]

Cathcart's policy of circumscribing Siyolo's actions eventually led the latter to surrender in October 1852, when he was seized and tried by court martial. He was found guilty and sentenced to death, but this was commuted to life imprisonment and he was despatched, as so many before him, to Robben Island.[43]

In the same month Cathcart declared the war to be at an end, a unilateral declaration with which the Xhosa disagreed. Their struggle continued with no sign of surrender. Other signs, though, were more propitious. In November, the Kat River rebels had had enough, being hunted by the military and settlers alike. Uithaalder and a few of the chiefs went into exile across the Mbashe far to the north while the remainder surrendered. The price they paid was heavy: they were banished from their old homes and the Kat River district was settled by white farmers.[44]

Sandile and Maqoma remained at large, pursued relentlessly by Colonel Eyre, whose cold-blooded purpose and spectacles so impressed his quarry that they named him Ameshlomani or 'Four Eyes'.[45]

In January 1853, Cathcart reached a settlement with Sarhili and issued a proclamation on 14 February giving effect to the peace.[46] Cathcart met Sandile for the first, and last, time on 9 March. Maqoma and the other chiefs were also present. They were told that they were never again to live in the Amatholas. As for the man who began it all, Mlanjeni fled across the Kei at the conclusion of the war and later died, an object of contempt.[47]

Although D'Urban, Smith and then Cathcart had determined that the Ngqika were to be forced across the Kei into Sarhili's country, simple pragmatism compelled this governor also to change his mind. Sandile and his people were settled on land to the immediate east of their beloved mountain home, stretching as far as the upper Kei River. The Amathola Mountains were proclaimed a 'Royal Reserve', to be occupied only by the military.[48] The rebel Thembu were also dealt with severely. Their lands on the west bank of the Black Kei River were confiscated and made the new district of Queenstown, being then thrown open to white settlement. The Thembu were forced to the east bank, an area then labelled 'Emigrant Tembu' on contemporary maps.

Those Africans who had remained loyal to the Crown were rewarded: the Gqunukhwebe under Phato and most of the Ndlambe were confirmed in their locations along the coast; the Tyumie Valley and land on the middle reaches of the Keiskamma River were allocated to the Mfengu and Khama's Christian Gqunukhwebe.[49]

In December 1854, Sir George Cathcart was replaced by a much younger man, forty-two-year-old Sir George Grey.[50] He was destined to leave a more indelible mark on the colony than any of his predecessors, particularly in the area of indigenous education. He also had, according to Peires, a darker side, which was alleged to emerge when the Xhosa were faced with a spiritual disaster.[51]

Representative Government

The Legislative Council in Cape Town had been arguing for several years over the form which a constitution for a Cape parliament might take. No fewer than seven drafts were considered but a draft was finally agreed in 1852 and sent off to London for endorsement by the 'Mother of Parliaments'. There it again underwent revision but on 23 May 1853 Queen Victoria signed letters patent constituting a parliament in Cape Town. The new parliament was to consist of the governor of the colony, an upper Legislative Council and a lower House of Assembly. The Legislative Council was to consist of the chief justice of the colony, who was the president of the council, with fifteen elective members.[52]

The House of Assembly was to consist of forty-six elective male members, to represent the twenty-three divisions of the colony. Remarkably, any person qualified to vote in an election was also qualified to stand as a candidate for the House of Assembly. The speaker was to be elected by the members. It should be noted here that there was no restriction on the colour or race of members, so that any indigenous African might, and eventually did, become a member.

Together with the governor, the parliament was empowered to 'make laws for the peace, welfare, and good government of the said colony'. The governor was required to assent to any bill before it could be enacted, and he retained the power either to veto the bill, or to reserve it 'at Her Majesty's pleasure'. The colony of the Cape of Good Hope had now taken its second step towards 'responsible government'.

The Cattle Killing, 1856–1857

In September 1853, a ship arrived in Mossel Bay bearing perhaps the greatest scourge ever to visit the shores of South Africa. It was a disease that affected only cattle and had already devastated the herds of Europe. It began with a dry cough and developed into a fatal infection of the lungs which was given the name 'lungsickness'.[53] Government regulations failed to stop its spread across the colony. By March 1854, it had reached Uitenhage, a year later it was to be found in King William's Town and in the Transkei by January 1856. Cattle losses were enormous, especially among the Xhosa, and in these times of severe stress, they again turned to a mystical solution.[54]

The first news of the emergence of yet another sage was brought to Charles Brownlee in June 1856.[55] He heard the story of a teenage girl named Nongqawuse, the niece of a baptised member of the Methodist church named Mhlakaza of the Gcaleka. Accompanied by another girl, a distant relative named Nombanda, she had gone down to a pool in the Gxara River, just north of Kei Mouth, where she alleged they had been visited by two men. They told her that she was to spread the word that they were spirits of men long dead and asked that all the Xhosa people kill their cattle, plant no more gardens and renounce witchcraft. This would prepare the way for the rising of the dead, who would help drive out the white men and usher in the new world which would emerge. Cattle would also emerge to replace those killed, or which had died as a result of lungsickness.[56]

At first, their words were ignored but were then gradually taken up until Sarhili himself believed what was prophesied. Over the coming weeks and months, the prophecies spread rapidly through the Xhosa people and thousands of cattle were killed, in part because it was thought that this new millennium would solve the problem of the lungsickness disease which was killing more and more of their cattle. Mhlakaza announced that the resurrection of the 'new people' would take place on 16 August. That date came and went, the non-appearance of the 'new people' being blamed upon those Xhosa who had failed to kill all their cattle, or who had planted crops. The date of the new millennium was changed to 11 December, to be heralded by a full moon. The night proved to be wet and misty, so no one could see if the moon was full or not.

Soon the belief had spread across the Kei to the Rharhabe and the Gqunukhwebe. Brownlee constantly criss-crossed Ngqika country trying to dissuade them from what he knew would be a disaster. Grey, on the other hand, saw such a catastrophe as an opportunity to undermine the authority of the chiefs further, an ambition he cherished.

By the end of 1856, some forty thousand cattle had been destroyed and their rotting carcases were scattered across the countryside. No crops were planted and the people were beginning to starve.

Thousands of Gcaleka gathered at Butterworth and in early January 1857 Sarhili and a large group of his councillors went down to the Gxara to meet Mhlakaza and Nongqawuse. They were not to be found. They had left a message saying that the dead chiefs had departed as a result of the disbelief of the Gcaleka chiefs and Sarhili should return to the Gxara if the next full moon, due on 10 January, were to rise blood-red. If not, then they should look to the February full moon. There was no change to the colour of the January full moon.

There was yet another great meeting of the Gcaleka at Butterworth, after which Sarhili announced that he would go down to the Gxara once more. On 8 February Mhlakaza announced that all remaining cattle were to be killed within eight days, after which the sun would rise blood-red, then set, and after the ensuing darkness a great storm would erupt, following which the supernatural events would take place. By this time Sarhili entertained grave doubts about the event but gave instructions for the killing of all remaining cattle except for one cow and one goat.

The Xhosa carried out his instructions, killing all their remaining animals and digging grain pits for the new era which they thought was approaching. The eight days also came and went and still no supernatural events occurred, no dead heroes or cattle arose. Hope springs eternal, and it took some time for the people to accept that their expectations would not be realised.

In the meantime, many lost their lives, the aged and infirm being carried off first. Among them was Mhlakaza, but Nongqawuse survived. She fled to Pondoland and was arrested there in 1858. She too was tried and sent to Robben Island though she was eventually permitted to return to live near Grahamstown and died in 1898.[57]

Peires asserts that in the two years of the Cattle Killing, the black population of British Kaffraria fell from 105,000 to 38,500. In that same period, the white population increased from a mere 949 to 5,388. 'While this did not exactly equalise the racial mixture . . . to the extent that Grey had hoped, it did increase the white population from less than 1% to a more healthy 12.5%.'[58]

The number of dead must have been at least as high among the Gcaleka. There is evidence of some cannibalism during this period. Survivors strong enough to do so flocked into the colony in search of work, leading to the fragmentation of a hitherto stable society, while the remainder endured appalling conditions. It was, perhaps, the worst catastrophe ever to befall the normally happy-go-lucky Xhosa.

Maqoma was another victim of the Cattle Killing, although not directly. Its impact had had the effect of increasing his appetite for alcohol and in a fit of anger, probably while under the influence, he had assaulted a magistrate in the street. He also applied for a pass to pursue a woman whom he had seized as a concubine who has fled into the Amatholas. The pass was denied but in August 1857 Maqoma pursued her anyway, was arrested and taken to Grahamstown, where he was allowed a pint of wine a day in his cell.[59]

Reduction of the Chiefs

Governor Grey, in an attempt to subvert the power of the chiefs further, chose to blacken Maqoma's name. His lieutenant-governor, John Maclean, was not convinced that the pass offence was enough to silence Maqoma and dredged up the alleged murder of an informer named Vusani by a number of Maqoma's adherents in July 1857.[60]

Maqoma, with nine other men, was charged on 17 November with Vusani's murder and also with receiving stolen goods. The defendants were left to defend themselves in court and Maqoma averred that he had ordered Vusani's cattle to be stolen as a fine, and denied the remaining charges. The next day, in what must have been a speedy trial, three of Maqoma's followers were found guilty of the murder and the remaining six guilty of robbery. Maqoma was found guilty of inciting the robbery and receiving stolen goods, and all the defendants were sentenced to transportation to a penal colony outside South Africa for life. When the sentences were brought to

Grey for confirmation, the governor commuted the transportation sentences to twenty years' hard labour. Maqoma, on account of his advanced years, was excused the hard labour. In December, he was moved to Cape Town gaol and then Robben Island.[61]

Grey's second victim was Mhala of the Ndlambe. He was charged with conspiring to levy war on the basis that he had 'created' Nombanda, the second prophetess of the Cattle Killing. He was given a light sentence of five years on Robben Island. Phato of the Gqunukhwebe was next, charged with horse-stealing. He was acquitted but a retrial was ordered at which he was found guilty, despite objections from the attorney-general. He too was sentenced to five years' transportation, to be followed by Xhoxho, Thole, Stokwe and numerous minor chiefs. By the beginning of 1858, nearly a thousand Xhosa were brought to Cape Town to be imprisoned and more served their sentences locally.[62]

The only major chiefs remaining at large were Sandile, Bhotomane and Sarhili. Bhotomane was both aged and infirm and was thus not regarded as a threat. Sandile piteously begged forgiveness for his belief in the Nongqawuse prophecies and was ordered to make a public declaration of obedience to the government in front of his council, being then reduced to the position of a paid hireling. Grey blamed Sarhili entirely for the Cattle Killing and wanted him prosecuted too. The paramount chief was reduced, like Sandile, to begging for forgiveness but Grey was in no mood to be placated. A column of troops was despatched in February 1858 to arrest him and bring him in but Sarhili managed to escape its clutches and crossed the Mbashe River northwards into exile with some of his supporters.[63]

Grey also began to set in place plans he had harboured for some time. He encouraged the immigration of German settlers and allotted them land in British Kaffraria, despite several attempts by his London master to stop him doing so.

Even the Gqunukhwebe and Mfengu lands were not immune and were broken up into small farms for settlement by Europeans. To his credit, however, Grey ensured that chiefs and their families were granted plots of freehold land in perpetuity and more was thrown open to purchase by the Xhosa.[64]

On 15 August 1861, Governor Grey finally left South Africa to take up the post of governor of New Zealand for the second time.[65] Robert Henry Wynyard replaced him temporarily until the arrival of the next permanent appointee, Sir Philip Edmond Wodehouse, who arrived at the Cape in 1862.[66]

Throughout the 1860s, the Xhosa chiefs were brought back one by one from Robben Island but Wodehouse did not allow Maqoma, Siyolo and Xhoxho to return until 1869. Maqoma again established his household surreptitiously in the Waterkloof but one night in November 1871 his home was surrounded and he was arrested. He was taken to Fort Beaufort where, without trial, he was again bundled off to Robben Island, to spend the rest of his days in idle contemplation. Possessing perhaps the greatest military mind of the Xhosa leaders, Maqoma died alone on 9 September 1873. He was, notes Mostert, about as old as the century.[67]

A postscript to this tragic tale is that in May 1978 what were alleged to be Maqoma's bones were exhumed and brought to the apartheid National Party government's black homeland of Ciskei, where they were interred on 13 August with great ceremony in what was then called the Hero's Acre atop the Ntaba kaNdoda.[68] The place is now neglected and dilapidated, surrounded by the concrete skeletons of buildings that were once erected to honour great Xhosa men. No other heroes were brought to be interred there and his untended grave remains alone.

Another man reduced to a life of indigence was Sarhili, paramount chief of all the Xhosa, who eked out an existence which bordered on starvation. Both Grey and Wodehouse had planned to annex Gcalekaland but they were forestalled by the announcement of a Sarhili plot to re-cross the Mbashe and invade his old country. There was, of course, no truth to the story, the chief being quite unable to undertake such a venture. Wodehouse ordered one of his officials to interview Sarhili. The official's conclusion was that 'it was impossible for him and his people to subsist much longer in the miserable hole to which they had been banished.' He recommended that Sarhili be given back a part of his land and Wodehouse concurred. In September 1864, Sarhili was told that he could return to re-occupy the southern portion of his original country. A month later they began their return to a land that, being uninhabited for so long, was now a paradise.

Wodehouse had intended that the northern portion of Gcalekaland be opened up to European settlement but this proposal was vetoed by the Colonial Secretary. Instead, the governor was allowed to settle indigenous people there. Offered a portion of this land in the Transkei, Sandile refused it but the Mfengu accepted with alacrity. 'There was', says Milton, 'a delightful piquancy about the offer since it gave them land where they had once lived as "dogs" of the haughty Gcaleka.'[69] Forty thousand Mfengu settled there, cheek by jowl with the Gcaleka, where the close proximity of these two old enemies would bring about the last frontier war and the final humiliation of the Xhosa.

In 1865, after extensive correspondence with Wodehouse on the subject, the British government annexed British Kaffraria to the Cape Colony.[70]

Conditions in the late 1860s and early 1870s were substantially different from those in 1852 for a number of reasons, principal among which was the presence of political entities other than the Cape Colony. Natal had finally been annexed to the Crown in 1843 (whose lieutenant-governor was responsible to the governor of the Cape) but there were also the children of the Great Trek. The Boers had established the Orange River Territory, later called the Orange Free State, and the South African Republic, later to be the Transvaal, both of which were self-governing. In addition there were far-flung areas which included such other entities as Griqualand East and West, and Basutoland, which over time were annexed to the Cape Colony.

The discovery of a small gold deposit in the Transvaal in 1867 and diamonds a year later at Kimberley in Griqualand West gave the British government pause, and resulted, in time, in the annexation of the Transvaal and the diamond fields. Such discoveries brought about a great mining boom which recruited unskilled labour throughout South Africa, leading many indigenous people, including Zulu and Xhosa, to seek work in the mines. Their reward was often in the form of firearms and these were soon seen by the Africans as a mandatory acquisition. Such employment also brought wealth to the Xhosa communities from cash remitted to dependants at home, and it was by the use of this wealth, added to their income from agriculture and cattle, that they began the purchase of land. It was a sweet twist of irony that in 1876 a son of the Mbalu chief Stokwe would purchase the land on which stood the abandoned Fort Willshire.[71]

There had also been a long-running debate about the number of troops based at the Cape, centring on the British requirement that most of the troops be withdrawn while the Cape government paid the cost of the remainder. On 29 January 1867, the Earl of Carnarvon wrote to Governor Wodehouse setting out the pertinent details, and making the following exactions: (a) the five infantry battalions were to be reduced to four immediately, one of which was to be shared between Natal and St Helena, leaving three effective battalions at the Cape at no cost to the colony; (b) in 1868, two battalions would be provided at no cost whilst the third battalion would be charged at the rate of £40 per man, this being the approximate cost of infantrymen in Australia; (c) in 1869, battalions in excess of one would be charged at £40 per man; (d) for three years after 1869, payment was required for every infantryman at £40 and £70 for every artilleryman. In default of any of these contributions by the Cape, the British government reserved the right to withdraw the troops from the colony.[72]

Wodehouse wrote in reply on 16 July giving the response of the Cape parliament.[73] As might be expected, some of its arguments in favour of retaining the troops at no cost were quite specious; one of them, for example, being that 'Great Britain must continue to provide military protection because in 1819 certain settlers were brought out and located on the frontier, under an implied pledge of protection' – despite the fact that the frontier had moved forward substantially in the years between 1819 and 1867, leaving the British settlers far to the rear.

Wodehouse's own views were rather more carefully considered. He asked, first, 'by whom, and how, is the Colony to be governed; by its own people or by Great Britain, and under what form of constitution?' He came to the nub of his argument:

> I do not see how any Governor appointed by the Crown, not having a Responsible Ministry, and not supported by the presence of Her Majesty's troops, could attempt to regulate the affairs of the Colony. It may be said with truth, that the troops never interfere in civil matters; but the consciousness of their presence at command has its effect. It is not exaggeration to say that without them the Government might be quite unable to control the enmity of the two races, and hold a just balance between them. Recent events have tended in the clearest manner to establish the truth of what I now submit to you. My opinion is, that if Her Majesty's Government contemplate retaining any serious amount of responsibility for the character of this Government, and its conduct towards the Natives, they must carefully avoid any diminution of the power of the Governor, must keep troops here, and if they keep any, must keep a sufficient number. If, on the other hand, they contemplate divesting themselves of all such responsibility, and by some means forcing the people of the Colony to set up Responsible Government (which, I believe, would be very prejudicial to them), then the troops ought all to be withdrawn, and the Colony and its rulers should clearly understand that the consequences of any wrongs done to the Natives must fall entirely on themselves.[74]

As had so often occurred, there was a new incumbent as Secretary of State for the Colonies and the reply on 9 December came from the Duke of Buckingham and Chandos. The plea that the colony was simply unable to pay for the troops was treated with sympathy so that, while the principles previously enunciated were not retracted, an undertaking was given that there would be no withdrawals due to non-payment in 1868. For later years, the British Government 'must rely on the Colonial Legislature's continuing their efforts to retrieve the finances'.[75]

On the matter of 'responsible government', the Colonial Secretary took the following view:

The policy therefore which I shall enjoin on your successor will be that of pointing out to the colonists that, in one way or another, a change in their constitution is inevitable, and of explaining to them that Her Majesty's Government look upon the present constitution as an inadequate and transitional one, which, as they are unable to administer it effectually, they are only content to administer at the desire of the colonists, and until a decision is arrived at as to what change should take place.[76]

Wodehouse continued to argue for the retention of troops in the colony, and against responsible government, until his departure from the colony in 1870, when he was replaced by Sir Henry Barkly.

Responsible Government

On 17 June 1872, a bill for the introduction of responsible government was passed by both houses of the Cape parliament, sponsored by Governor Barkly, largely at the behest of the British government. There were objections from some local members, who argued that every clause reviewed at the committee stage was passed only on the casting vote of the chairman of the committee but this objection was brushed aside. On 9 August, an Order in Council was signed by Queen Victoria giving her assent to 'An Act to amend the Ordinance enacted on the 3rd of April, 1852, by the Governor of the Colony of the Cape of Good Hope, with the advice and consent of the Legislative Council thereof intituled "An Ordinance for Constituting a Parliament for the said Colony"'.

In January 1873, Barkly began the process of forming a government but it was not an easy problem to resolve. After several potential candidates had declined the privilege of being the first prime minister of the colony, the post was taken up by John Charles Molteno. Three weeks later, as prime minister elect, Molteno put forward the names of his proposed ministerial colleagues – it is notable that Charles Brownlee accepted the position of secretary for native affairs, resigning his post as civil commissioner to do so.

Charles Molteno was born in London in June 1814, emigrated to the Cape Colony in 1831 and settled in Cape Town, where he became an assistant to the public librarian. He had served as a burgher in the War of the Axe, remembering that he had slept in a 'dung cart' and was fed on 'bony, dry poor and black raw beef'. His experience at this time informed his view that the British military was incompetent, a recollection which was to have a grave effect on his ministry in the future.[77]

From 1872 to 1877 several other significant changes occurred. The first of these introduces Mr John X. Merriman. Born in 1841, Merriman became a member of the Legislative Assembly in 1869 and was subsequently appointed Commissioner of Crown Lands in Molteno's ministry in 1874.[78]

Enter Sir Bartle Frere

Another change involved the rotating position of governor and high commissioner of the Cape of Good Hope. Sir Henry Barkly served until April 1877, when he was replaced by Sir Henry Edward Bartle Frere. Born on 29 March 1815,[79] Frere had enjoyed a long and distinguished administrative career in India, where he served from 1834 to 1866, the latter years as governor of Bombay.[80] An intellectual who quickly learned to speak Hindustani, Marathi and Gujarati, Frere has nevertheless been described as having 'a certain recklessness, strange perhaps in so experienced an administrator, and yet the natural defect of his strongest qualities'.[81]

The Frere family, comprising the governor, Lady Frere and their four daughters, arrived at Cape Town on 31 March 1877.[82] His son, Lieutenant Bartle Compton Arthur Frere, was serving at that time in Gibraltar. Although Sir Bartle appreciated Table Mountain and the beauty of the local flora, and found the climate agreeable, he was less than impressed with the town itself: writing to Lord Carnarvon, he said, 'it would be difficult to imagine anything more sleepy and slipshod than everything about the place, or more dirty and unwholesome than the town.'[83] In the event, he was to spend little time there.

We should note that Frere was also high commissioner for South Africa. What did this second title mean? In fact, it enhanced his power considerably, giving him authority in the lands and territories external to the colony, including those still held by African chiefs. The letters patent appointing Sir Harry Smith to the post described its responsibility as 'the settling and the adjustment of affairs of the territories adjacent or contiguous to the eastern and north-eastern districts of our settlement and its dependencies'.[84]

Frere and Confederation

The subject of the federation of the various South African colonies and territories was not a new matter in 1877. Based on the model which had served Canada so well since July 1867, it was widely believed that the principle should also be applied in South Africa. Indeed, it had been discussed at length both in Britain and at the Cape for several years and an informal conference had been held in 1876 to discuss the matter, attended by representatives of the various South African colonies and republics.

While the subject is too complex to be discussed at length here, the matter of the several states and territories which had emerged in South Africa, particularly those which came into being as the result of the Great Trek, is vitally important. Suffice to say that there was a history of British annexation of these small states.

In August 1876, President Burgers of the Transvaal had led a force against the rebellious baPedi chief Sekhukhune and had been soundly defeated. It was suggested at that time that the king of the Zulu, Cetshwayo, was giving encouragement to Sekhukhune to retain his independence and was also in correspondence with the Xhosa and other southern people. The leaders of the Cape Colony saw at once that what had happened to Burgers might also happen to them, should the Xhosa choose to fight. To meet this potential threat, Lord Carnarvon, the Colonial Secretary, determined upon two steps. The first was to send back the newly knighted Sir Theophilus Shepstone on a secret mission to annex the Transvaal to the Crown.[85] The second was to appoint Sir Bartle Frere as the next governor of the Cape.

Frere stepped ashore at Cape Town in March 1877, completely unaware that the annexation was to take place. Shepstone had arrived in Pretoria in January, and the annexation of the Transvaal was summarily announced in April 1877. Such was Frere's surprise on hearing of the annexation that he exclaimed: 'Good Heavens, what will they say in England!'[86] As the new administrator, Shepstone would report to Frere.

The last changes define the nature of the imperial military presence at the Cape. First, in November 1873, Lieutenant-General Sir Arthur Cunynghame arrived at Cape Town to assume his new post commanding Her Majesty's troops in South Africa.[87]

Finally, the reader will recall the formation of the Khoikhoi Cape Regiment during the early development of the colony. In 1827, what remained of this corps was renamed the Cape Mounted Rifles, still largely consisting of Khoikhoi troopers serving under white officers. After the Khoikhoi rebellion in 1850, the proportion of white troopers was greatly increased and in 1855 it was designated the Frontier Armed and Mounted Police (FAMP), taking an increasingly military role in addition to policing. The Artillery Troop of the Frontier Armed and Mounted Police was raised in 1874, although its equipment was of very poor quality, a defect which was to become apparent at an early stage.[88] According to Cunynghame himself, the total number of FAMP, on paper, was about one thousand men.[89]

The actors in our drama have now taken their places in the wings and are waiting for the curtain to rise.

Part II

The Ninth Frontier War

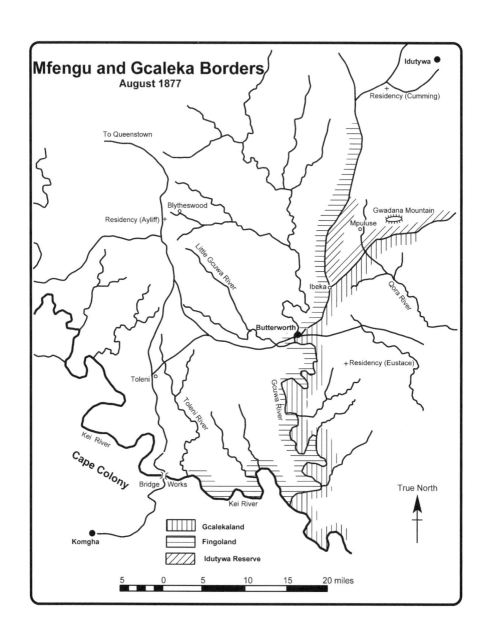

Mfengu and Gcaleka Borders
August 1877

Idutywa

+ Residency (Cumming)

To Queenstown

Blytheswood

Residency (Ayliff) +

Little Gcuwa River

Gwadana Mountain

Mpuluse

Ibeka

Qora River

Butterworth

+ Residency (Eustace)

Toleni

Toleni River

Gcuwa River

Kei River

Cape Colony

Bridge   Works

Kei River

Komgha

True North

	Gcalekaland
	Fingoland
	Idutywa Reserve

5   0   5   10   15   20 miles

Chapter 5

A Spark in the Tinderbox

I am perfectly convinced in my own mind that the old fox [Sarhili] has been acting a very treacherous part, and I am sorry to find that the officials were hoodwinked.

Inspector F.B. Chalmers, FAMP, 2 September 1877

The first inkling to the British government that something might be amiss was a report from Charles Brownlee, secretary of native affairs:

On the 10th of the current month (August 1877) a party of Kreli's tribe under two petty chiefs named Umxoli and Fihla crossed the border between Fingoland and Kreli's country for the purpose of taking part in a marriage festivity in Fingoland.

At night, an altercation arose, ending in blows, and the Galekas were eventually driven across the border, the two chiefs being severely bruised, and one of their party mortally wounded, dying shortly after the affray.

The report of the Resident with Kreli throws the blame for the fray entirely upon the Fingos; while the Government agent with the Fingos considers that the Galekas were the aggressors and that the Fingos acted simply on the defensive.[1]

A more accurate account, giving the correct date of the incident, was given by one of these men, the resident with Sarhili, Colonel John Eustace, on 18 August 1877 and published many pages later in the same Parliamentary Paper:

On the evening of the 3rd instant, about four miles from Butterworth, two Galekas, chiefs Mxoli and Fekla, crossed the Fingo boundary with some 10 followers to join in a beer drinking party at the hut of a Fingo; towards morning they all became more or less drunk, and calling at an adjoining hut belonging to a Fingo named Malceli, a fight ensued, brought about by a Fingo seizing the chief Mxoli by the leg and endeavouring to drag him out by his heels; this indignity was resented by his followers, who, however, being the minority, were badly treated, and obliged to return to their own kraal, taking with them, however, one of their number, Ngge, who was mortally wounded and died two hours afterwards. The chief's brother, Fekla, was very severely injured, and all the party were more or less hurt.[2]

It is clear that even at this early stage the two government agents were each taking the side of the people to whom they were allocated.

At the time the incident occurred, Sarhili, the paramount chief of the Gcaleka, was at Colonel Eustace's home at Ntlambe near Butterworth. Eustace's clerk, Mr West White Fynn, wrote on 11 May 1911 in the *East London Daily Dispatch*:

On August 3rd, 1877, at a kraal owned by Quenquas, a Fingo, another Fingo named Nchayechibi held a marriage feast. It was on the border between Fingoland and Gcaleka land. Some Gcalekas were there by special invitation and they went home peacefully at the close of day crossing the Gcuwa river.

Another party of Gcalekas under two chiefs, Mxoli and Fehla, of Mapassa's location, arrived from a distance. The two chiefs were the sons of Bune and they had not been invited to the wedding. They joined in and late in the day were asked to leave. More beer was demanded and a collision ensued in which the Gcalekas were the aggressors. The Fingoes overpowered them and drove them over the Gcuwa river. The two chiefs were wounded and a Gcaleka of their party, who was severely wounded, died during the night. I went to the spot on the next day, took evidence and examined the body of the Gcaleka whose head had been smashed. The body was found in a crevice of the rocks on the Gcuwa river.[3]

The Gcuwa River formed the border between the lands allocated by the British to the Mfengu from the northern portion of what had been Gcalekaland, and the southern portion of that country to which the Gcaleka had been confined after their return from across the Mbashe. A final version gives a slightly different perspective, perhaps explaining why any of the Mfengu's bitter enemies were at the feast at all:

The immediate cause was a quarrel at a beer drink concerning which the Fingoes had a different tale to tell from that of the Gcalekas. The Gcalekas said, 'Some of Nquenqwa's people who, it is said, were in habits more like Kafirs than Fingoes through residing on the border between the tribes, came over to the Gcalekas to borrow large clay pots specially used for brewing beer.' If the Fingoes did so they were to blame for having regarded those who loaned the pots as uninvited guests at the wedding feast. In accordance with custom those who loaned the pots were privileged to attend and did so. The Fingoes denied having borrowed pots for the occasion and reported the brawl very soon.[4]

Early Skirmishes

The Mfengu reported the affair to their magistrate, James Ayliff, and soon further raids took place along the length of the boundary. West Fynn wrote:

> Three days after the brawl, Mapassa's son Xoxo assembled a force of Gcalekas and invaded Fingoland at four different points, and from five or six Fingo villages swept off 150 cattle and 500 goats. Mapassa and Xoxo did not restrain the Tsonyana people. I warned them of the risks that they had taken by taking the law into their own hands. They yielded and assisted in collecting the stolen stock. Great difficulty was experienced in tracing 30 other cattle stolen from the Fingoes by other Gcalekas . . . A few days later I was aroused at midnight by two of Kreli's [Sarhili's] councillors who were sent by Kreli to report that the Fingoes and Gcalekas were fighting on the Qcuwa river. Kreli said that he was afraid to go there as his moving would arouse the whole of his tribe. In accordance with Kreli's wishes I went over to stop the fighting if possible. It was a moonlight night and when I arrived the fighting was still in progress. Nine dead bodies were seen. Xoxo was there and when I informed him that Kreli had sent me to stop the fighting, he withdrew the Gcalekas and ordered them to return to their kraals.
>
> I then crossed the Qcuwa river where the Fingoes were assembled. I was told by the Fingo headman that the Gcalekas had crossed the boundary, set fire to several huts and burned several children. The Fingoes denied the accusation made by Xoxo that they had crossed the river during the night and stolen some goats from a Gcaleka.
>
> When the Fingoes understood that Kreli had sent me to order Mapassa's people back home, they were satisfied and dispersed.[5]

On his return home, Fynn found Sarhili and two of his sons sitting comfortably in his dining room drinking coffee. Sarhili explained that after Fynn had left for the scene of the fighting, he became concerned for the safety of Fynn's wife and family and had come over to protect them.[6]

This latest skirmish had taken place on the night of 9 August when, at the Gcuwa River about six kilometres from the Butterworth mission station, between twelve and fifteen hundred Gcaleka had fought under Maphasa's son Xhoxho (not to be confused with Sarhili's brother of the same name). Ayliff had warned his Mfengu charges that they were neither to attack nor defend themselves without his instructions. However, they could not be restrained and joined in the fight against orders. Afterwards, they crossed the boundary river themselves, firing on the Gcaleka. Burton also noted: 'For a long time the lawlessness of the Fingoes as British subjects was the talk of Kafirland and they took no heed of Government officials who were endeavouring to avert war.'[7]

The increasing seriousness of these clashes along the border between Mfengu and Gcaleka presented the Cape government with a dilemma. Its local agents had tried to calm down both groups but matters were now developing beyond their control. As Frere had observed earlier, 'We are under the strongest obligations . . . to protect the Fingoes who have been placed in this country under our Government.'[8] It was clear that the weight of Gcaleka numbers compared with the Mfengu might result in the latter being swept away and the government felt it should throw its weight behind the Mfengu. On the other hand, however, such support could be interpreted by the Gcaleka as favouritism and what had begun as an inter-tribal dispute might well turn into a white-versus-black confrontation.

Charles Brownlee, also determined that he must support the Mfengu, decided to send a troop of the Frontier Armed and Mounted Police (FAMP) to Butterworth. To sugar the pill, he told the Gcaleka, through Colonel Eustace, that they were being sent to restrain the aggression of the Mfengu.

> On Tuesday evening, the 21st instant, I got your telegram of the 20th instant, informing me that Mr. Chalmers and detachment of police were coming to Butterworth. In order that there should be no misunderstanding as regards the object of their coming, I requested Mr. West Fynn to ride over the following morning, and inform Kreli of the same. I think he thoroughly understood it, and as he has not, I believe, left his present kraal, I hope will soon be reconciled to their presence on his border; he feared, however, that their coming would not tend to allay the somewhat dangerous excitement of his people, and though I do not, under the circumstances, see what else the Government could have done, still I think the excitement which has been on the increase during the last two or three days is partly owing to that circumstance.[9]

On the night of 24 August, a serious clash took place at Endochanga, near Butterworth, when the Mfengu resisted another Gcaleka raid in which seventeen of the attackers were killed.

On the night of the 24th there was a sharpish fight below Butterworth, in which many Galekas were killed and some few Fingos. Kreli informs me he has gone fully into the case, and from what both he and Mr. West Fynn, who went to the spot the next morning, says, I am inclined to think the Galekas were caught in a trap when pursuing some Fingos who were trying to drive away some of their goats. With considerable difficulty Mapessa [Maphasa] and his son Zo Zo [Xhoxho] kept their people quiet.[10]

At about that time, Inspector E.B. Chalmers arrived at Butterworth with a detachment of the FAMP. Their arrival had the inflammatory effect forecast by Sarhili.

We have already noted the prominence given in this narrative to West Fynn, Colonel Eustace's clerk, and it is pertinent here to relate other matters to which Eustace was not made privy. Some days before the clash on 24 August, Fynn had met with Maphasa, who had a most unusual request:

Mapassa, a cousin of Kreli's, a few nights previously [to the 24th] had roused me out of bed urgently requesting a Pass for the purpose of crossing the Kei river into colonial territory and placing himself under the protection of the Colonial Government, because Kreli, under the influence of his chief advisers and generals, had decided to attack Fingoland. Mapassa admitted that he had invariably lost land, people, and stock in fighting against the Government and that now he wished to separate himself entirely from Kreli. I asked Mapassa why he had not informed Kreli of his intentions instead of deceiving him while professing loyalty. I also asked him to remember that his people (Tsonyana) were the instigators of the trouble now on Kreli's shoulders. In his reply Mapassa said that if he told Kreli he intended to remain neutral, Kreli would most certainly 'eat him up' (confiscate all his property and possibly destroy him).

I gave Mapassa the Pass for the whole section of the tribe under him numbering about a thousand men, women and children.[11]

Fynn then goes on to relate his involvement in the dispute of the 24th:

On August 22nd 1877, a large number of armed men (about 9,000) had assembled along the border from below Butterworth almost as far as the

Gwadana Mountain (Mount Wodehouse). They had massed at the nearest kraals on the boundary line until Sunday August 25th.

I noticed as I was leaving Graham Villa for church at Tutura that a body of men which had hitherto assembled at Botman's place, had moved and taken up the highest positions they could find on all the Kopje's just opposite the Residency (Ntlambe). I was of opinion that this meant mischief. During the Service I noticed through one of the church windows another large body of men (about 800) armed to the teeth and making for the Residency at the Ntlambe. I left the church at once, mounted my trap and went home. On overtaking the army I found that the warriors were under the chief Sibozo from the Qolora sea coast. I at once reported these proceedings to Colonel Eustace, telling him that I was now sure that war was certain since the coast Kaffirs had come up.

Colonel Eustace replied, 'No, I cannot agree with you, these people, hearing rumours of war and the continued war cries, have come to see for themselves what is going on.'

I then said: 'You do not understand the Natives, they have been ordered up; Natives at their kraals are as well posted in the news of the day as those on the immediate border.'

Fynn next went to see Sarhili at his Great Place, Holela, where he found the Gcaleka being doctored for war.

Observing all these serious indications of war, and knowing that if war came the Gcalekas would simply sweep across Fingoland, as the only support the Fingoes had was forty-five Police under Inspector Chalmers, I thought I could stave off the war for a moment by giving away Mapassa's movements and intentions and that it would be good policy to do so under the then precarious circumstances.

Fynn took Sarhili to one side, out of the hearing of his councillors:

Addressing the chief, I asked, 'Is it definitely your intention to attack the Fingoes?' Kreli replied, 'Wesi, you know as much of what has been going on as I do; since the fight at the Gquwa, in which nine of my people were killed, my people are like madmen, I cannot control them any longer.' I then asked 'Are you sure of the support of all your chiefs without exception?' Kreli anxiously replied, 'Be candid with me Wesi, why do you ask me?'

'Are you depending upon Mapassa with others?' I asked. In a querulous tone Kreli asked, 'Is not Mapassa now with his sons at the Gquwa?' I then decided, considering it the only course under the circumstances, to give Mapassa away and said, 'Yes, certainly Mapassa is at the Gquwa, but supposing I assure you that, at this present moment, he holds a Pass from me which will protect his people and cattle across the Kei (into the Colony) immediately you order a rush into Fingoland – that Mapassa may leave with all his people and property tonight – what then?'

Kreli turned the colour of ashes and said, 'Wesi, Wesi, don't, don't, you are trying to deceive me'.

Fynn now explained why Sarhili should not go to war, the reason being the same as that which had impelled Maphasa's defection.

In response to Kreli's appeal, I said, 'I have been with you over twelve years and do you not know me better than that? It was my sympathy for you that led me to tell you Mapassa's secret; could I stand by and see you led into a trap by a man whose subjects have brought this trouble on your shoulders and whose intention was, having saved their own skins, to leave you in the lurch? I wanted you to realise your true position before you had gone too far. The Fingoes will be supported by the Government and the result will probably be that you will be captured, your country taken away from you, and possibly Mapassa may become chief in your stead. Anyhow, after this you cannot charge me with having kept anything from you, I have spoken to you frankly and openly.'[12]

There is no doubt that the assembled Gcaleka then returned to their homes and a war which had seemed inevitable was, at least temporarily, averted.

Another clash took place on 29 August, when fighting broke out at the trader John Barnett's shop, the site of the future Fort Ibeka, where Chalmers' FAMP detachment and a group of Mfengu warriors were drawn up. Sarhili blamed Gcaleka resentment against the apparent collusion between the Mfengu and FAMP for the fight. Chalmers, with the aid of some of Sarhili's councillors, was able to persuade the Gcaleka to withdraw.[13]

On 2 September, Lieutenant Teignmouth Melvill, of the 1/24th Regiment, wrote a report of a three-day tour of the Transkei which his commanding officer, Colonel Richard Glyn, in his capacity as the commandant of the frontier districts, had ordered him to make 'to obtain and transmit . . . information concerning rumoured disturbances'. Melvill reported:

On the 30th I left [Kei Drift] and arrived at the Zolein [Toleni?] trading station, 7.30 a.m., thence I sent you a telegram informing you that there had been fighting between the Galekas and Fingos the day previous, and that I had seen armed parties of the latter on their way to the Bawd drift, over the Butterworth River. At this drift on the 23rd ultimo, I am reliably informed that there was a fight at which 24 Galekas and several Fingos were killed; the Galekas crossed [the river] and attacked, but were repulsed.[14]

He arrived at Butterworth in the late morning, where he found Inspector Chalmers and his FAMP detachment nearby. He left with Chalmers and some of the FAMP to visit Ibeka on the Idutywa Reserve. At Ibeka, he found 'Kreli's army occupying positions in the immediate vicinity. On the slope of a hill about two miles off we could see natives to the number of several thousands, and a very large number of horses off-saddled.' He went on to describe the engagement of the 29th narrated earlier, during which the Gcaleka had advanced 'on Government ground' to within a few hundred yards of the FAMP detachment. Melvill stated that 'only a small portion of Kreli's army was engaged, but they were advancing to the number of 6,000 or 7,000 . . . This appears to have been a deliberate attack on the Fingos in their own territory'.

Melvill arranged an interview with Colonel Eustace but by the morning of the 31st the Gcaleka army had dispersed. Colonel Eustace arrived at Ibeka shortly thereafter and declined an offer from Melvill for a detachment of the 24th to go to Komgha.

Lieutenant Melvill left Ibeka about noon on the 31st and rode back to Butterworth, noting on the way that a party of about forty Gcaleka was following a wagon escorted by two men of the FAMP.

The road here forms the boundary between the two tribes, and six armed Fingos were walking on the further side of the waggon. The Galekas appeared excited and I halted the waggon and questioned the police. I ascertained that the Galekas alleged that the Fingos had made a raid into their country, and had shot a man, and that then they had retreated for shelter behind the escorted waggon. I immediately ordered the Fingos away to their own side of the valley, and with the assistance of the police, prevented the Galekas from attacking them; at the same time I explained to them, through a native policeman who was with me, that the police were on neither side, but only to keep the peace, and that they must go and complain to their magistrate. Several of the Galekas in this party had the war paint on their foreheads.

From Butterworth, Melvill travelled back to Toleni and then to Komgha via Pullen's farm. He several times observed armed groups of Mfengu around

Butterworth, even a 'small regiment marching into town'. Nothing, he noted, suggested that they were paying the slightest attention to the orders given to them that morning that they were to return to their homes. In his summary, he noted that the Mfengu were in 'a high state of irritation' and they considered that they were 'being made targets by the Government'. He repeated a rumour that the Ngqika were sure to join the Gcaleka if Sarhili asked them.

With regard to the Gcaleka, Melvill was convinced that 'Kreli wants war with the Fingos, and he attacked them in an open and unprovoked manner.' On the other hand, he had seen no instance of a premeditated advance of any substantial number of Mfengu to attack the Gcaleka. He reported that the general feeling on the frontier was that if Sarhili were not severely punished, there would be fresh disturbances within a short time.

Melvill was particularly scathing in his report that there was 'not the slightest attempt at organisation for the purpose of defence on the Frontier'. There were no defensible posts where farmers might take shelter or where volunteers in the neighbourhood might rally. The farms in the Komgha district, for example, had been deserted by their owners and their families, and by their African workers. He concluded that the dispersal of Sarhili's army was either a ruse, or because he was thoroughly frightened, especially by a rumour that 'troops were to be landed at Mazeppa Bay in his rear'.

Quite coincidentally, senior elements of the government arrived at the frontier towards the end of August. Governor Frere wanted to have first-hand knowledge of conditions on the frontier and travelled there with J.X. Merriman, minister for Crown lands and public works, arriving at Port Elizabeth on 21 August.

On his arrival at the frontier, the governor was besieged by deputations of citizens 'in a state of most genuine apprehension and alarm'. Frere tried to calm their fears but could not help feeling that 'our assurances that the war seemed to be only an inter-tribal quarrel . . . were listened to with incredulous impatience.'[15] In Cape Town, meanwhile, Prime Minister Molteno was concerned at the lack of news from his representatives resident with the Mfengu and Gcaleka and wanted to send up a wing of the 88th Regiment, but Frere vetoed the move for the time being.[16]

For his part, Inspector Chalmers remained convinced that Sarhili was deeply involved in trying to foment war. Writing to his commanding officer from Ibeka on 2 September, he stated, 'I have it on the most reliable sources that the Galekas intended war with the Fingos, and Kreli himself was as much for it as anyone else.'[17]

Frere and Merriman arrived at King William's Town on 4 September and Brownlee arrived there a day later. Frere at once introduced an informal daily meeting between himself, Merriman and Brownlee, with General Cunynghame also attending when he was able. Frere wrote in a private letter to Carnarvon on 8 October of the two minsters' initial discomfiture with these arrangements:

> Merriman and Brownlee were at first aghast at such an innovation as a daily council, at which the General would sit as Commandant of the Forces, where we could interchange intelligence and suggestions and settle the orders to be given, which could be issued at once and communicated to Cape Town without further correspondence. They had evident misgivings as to the view that their colleagues would take of such an intimate relation with the military authorities, but they concurred when I pointed out its necessity . . . I am certain that without it some great disaster must have occurred.[18]

It was agreed that Ayliff and Eustace should complete their interrupted inquiry into the causes of the clashes between Mfengu and Gcaleka and report. In the meantime, the governor and his ministers continued their tour through the frontier districts.

On 16 September, they arrived at Butterworth, where the governor received reports from his officials and from the Mfengu. Frere had requested that Sarhili also meet him there but the chief sent a number of excuses for not attending. Anxious to meet the paramount chief, he expressed his willingness to go to Sarhili. All parties must surely have been aware of the chief's suspicion towards white people after the way his father had died at their hands. Frere's advisers pressed him not to go to Sarhili, disregarding the precedent set when Barkly had done so three years earlier.[19]

Unable to see him face to face, a disappointed Frere sent a letter to Sarhili on 20 September, explaining that he had 'heard that there has been trouble here between Galekas and Fingos, and I am come to see and judge for myself who is at fault'. The letter was couched in moderate terms, without resort to threats or browbeating. Frere was anxious to establish the truth, he said, and wanted to believe what he had heard: that Sarhili 'was wise and would do nothing to stir up strife, which must entail ruin on his people and family'.

The governor ended his letter thus:

> These words I intended to have spoken to you if I had seen you. You have not come to see me, and therefore I have spoken them to those of your family and people who I have seen, and now I send them in writing, in order that you may have them read over to you and reflect on them at leisure, and that you

may be able from them to warn your people that if they do not in future obey your orders and abstain from making wars or raids and from all wrong-doing towards the Fingos and all others, the Government will take matters into their own hands and very severely punish all the guilty.[20]

In less than a week Frere would receive his answer.

Before leaving Butterworth on 20 September, Frere put in place what he hoped would be two obstacles to further conflict: he moved Inspector Chalmers with his FAMP to the Idutywa Reserve and ordered that one half of the remaining FAMP be stationed in the Transkei, undertaking both police and military responsibilities. He also announced, through Merriman, that Charles Duncan Griffith was appointed as commandant of the FAMP to replace the ailing James Bowker, yet another of the numerous Bowker family members.[21]

Griffith was to assume a considerable role in the war to come. He was born in Grahamstown in 1830. Being frontier born and bred, he was a fine horseman and a good marksman, qualities which had served him well in the Seventh and Eighth frontier wars. At the conclusion of the Eighth War in 1873 he was given the command of a division of the frontier police at Queenstown and was then commissioned in the newly formed Frontier Armed and Mounted Police.

In 1858, Griffith was appointed as magistrate for the district of Albert and from 1859 to 1868 was the magistrate at Queenstown, greatly assisting with the consolidation of the new settlement. He was subsequently appointed as magistrate in Grahamstown and then King William's Town. In June 1871, he was made high commissioner's agent in Basotholand, becoming the governor's agent when the territory was attached to the Cape. He was particularly successful in his endeavours and the rebellious Langalibalele was arrested in 1873 as a result of his initiative.[22] He returned from Basotholand to take command of the FAMP.[23]

These actions, following several more, were to make clear that Merriman was quickly becoming the de facto minister for war for the Molteno government. These additional responsibilities were assumed with the entire approval of the governor: in early October he wrote a note to General Cunynghame which included the following:

Your Excellency is aware that since the present disturbances came to a head the Honourable the Commissioner of Crown Lands has, with my full concurrence, and with, I have every reason to believe, the full consent of the whole Cabinet, taken the principal share of all the duties which would devolve on a Minister of War and Internal Police . . .[24]

From Spark to Flame

It was at this point that the Gcaleka made a commitment to war. Their reasons were entirely logical, if not fully considered: it had become clear that the government was intent upon supporting the Mfengu at their expense, and that there were insufficient troops available to act as a deterrent to immediate action. At the root of everything, though, was their burning fury that the Mfengu, their erstwhile 'dogs', now occupied land that had previously been theirs while they themselves were crammed into a corner of their previous territory.

Two events led them into war. The first, which occurred shortly after Frere's departure from Butterworth, was the return of an emissary from a visit to Sandile, asking him to join with Sarhili in defeating the Mfengu. On 29 September, Fynn visited the governor at King William's Town, where he reported that a Gcaleka envoy had gone to Sandile and asked him to join them in an attack on the Mfengu. Sandile had replied that 'he had had enough of wars, and his leg troubled him; he was getting old, and would have nothing to do with war.'[25] Fynn made a second visit to Frere on 3 October, when he reported on the emissary's return:

> I first noticed the change after Runeyi came, which was after your Excellency left Butterworth. Up to Runeyi's arrival Kreli said, 'I will abide by the decision of Government,' and did not want war; but when Runeyi, who is a cousin, came, many people said, 'Now there will be war.' He is a chief of the Guawaka tribe, who are great warriors, and he is the bravest of them. It was he who visited the Gaikas, and was, I rather think, still among them when the Governor was over the Kei. His tribe lives on the Bashee. He is not particularly hostile to the British Government, but, like all Galekas, thought that the police would stand by and look on, as before, and that they would be allowed to settle things with the Fingos . . .[26]

The second incident was a raid on 21 September by three hundred Gcaleka into Fingoland and the Idutywa Reserve 'about four miles beyond Ibeka', where they seized cattle, sheep and goats. Intercepted by the FAMP, they handed over the sheep and goats but refused to return the stolen cattle.

Fynn visited Sarhili's Great Place just after the raid to deliver the previously mentioned governor's letter and he asked the chief what he proposed to do about the stolen cattle. If they were not restored, then Colonel Eustace would leave his country, but remain on the border if further communication were needed. To this Sarhili replied:

[He] was sorry Colonel Eustace should think of leaving the country, but it was now in such a muddle that there was no settling anything, not only in his (Kreli's) country, but also in the Idutywa Reserve, where the magistrate [Cumming] could not manage his people. How could Colonel Eustace expect him to manage his people when they had gone so far? It was useless his collecting cattle; as fast as he collected them more were taken.

Colonel Eustace, thinking this not at all satisfactory, left on the following morning (Monday, 24th) for Ibika [*sic*] with his family.[27]

Fynn continued that, shortly before, he and his family also left Gcalekaland (escorted by six of Sarhili's sons, including Sigcawu, and an honour guard of three hundred warriors).

During Fynn's visit of 29 September to Frere, Fynn had told the governor that Maphasa and his son Xhoxho had come to him on 26 September and asked what they were to do if 'farmers or police came across to his place and asked me for a white flag. I gave him a dozen and told him to give them to his people, and no one would harm them.'[28]

While Frere was now more convinced than ever that war was inevitable, he asked Eustace to make one more effort to convince Sarhili to hold his people in check.[29] He also heard that Chalmers had sent for reinforcements, believing that he would not be able to hold his position without them.[30]

On 23 September, confirmation of an imminent confrontation came from a trader who had just left Gcalekaland and from a missionary, both of whom reported that men were flocking to Sarhili's Great Place from all over the country and that the war cry was being sounded.[31] On the 24th, Merriman sent a telegram to J. Rose-Innes, the civil commissioner at King William's Town, asking him to publish a government warning of impending war.

Affairs in the Transkeian territory having assumed a threatening aspect, and a collision between the police and Galekas being imminent, in which contingency it is possible that the tribe might seek to revenge themselves by raids on the farmers in yours and the neighbouring division, his Excellency the Governor thinks it advisable, as a precautionary measure, to detail, for the information of the public and those concerned, the actual position of our defensive organisation.[32]

The notice gave a list of those places where posts had been set up by the FAMP, advised that colonists should arrange laagers for their safety and appointed John Cowie and Captain E.Y. Brabant as burgher commandants. Particular attention was given to the railway then being constructed between East London and Queenstown. The line had only reached Kei Road and recommended the use of stations (sixteen kilometres apart) and platelayers' cottages (at six-kilometre intervals) as defensive posts, firearms being placed in each one as points at which colonists might rally.

The spark was about to become a conflagration.

Battle of Gwadana

When West Fynn and his family had quitted Gcalekaland for safer quarters, Sarhili's son Mcotoma had confided to him that he would be safe if he crossed the Kei before 26 September.[33] Fynn might have wondered at the significance of that date but he was left in no doubt when it arrived.

Gwadana (or Guadana) is an eminence now known as Mount Wodehouse. It lies fourteen kilometres south of Idutywa and consists of a broad plateau extending about fifteen hundred metres by a thousand metres, at a height of two hundred metres above the surrounding country. It is extremely difficult to approach from either north or south owing to the steepness of the drop from the plateau but is readily accessible from the west and only a little less so from the east.

Commandant Griffith reported that on 26 September he had arrived at Ibeka, where he found Inspector Chalmers with a hundred of his FAMP. Chalmers had just arrived back from a patrol into the Idutywa Reserve, where he had seen Gcaleka as far as eight kilometres into the reserve. He had also observed an engagement between Mfengu and Gcaleka, 'the latter drawing off on the appearance of the police'.

Chalmers' report, dated 25 October, gives us a detailed account of the following action.[34] On his way to the Idutywa Reserve, he had been told of a Gcaleka attack on the Mfengu near Gwadana. At that time he must have been marching north on the Ibeka–Idutywa road because he goes on to say '. . . when about two miles from the Mpeluse [Mpuluse River], opposite the Guadana, I observed the Galekas had crossed [the river] in numbers and attacked the Fingos, and that an engagement was taking place between the two tribes.' The Mpuluse is a small tributary of the larger Qora River that, during its short length, flows due east towards Mount Wodehouse. Near its upper reaches stands a small village, also bearing the name Mpuluse.

Before proceeding, Chalmers sent a message to James Ayliff, who was then at Mpuluse with about a thousand Mfengu, telling him that the Gcaleka had crossed into British territory. Ayliff brought his Mfengu up and they continued together. On arrival, Chalmers found the Gcaleka had taken up a position at the foot of the mountain in three divisions. Chalmers halted his

FAMP near the road on the west side while Ayliff took his Mfengu further east onto the plateau on top of the mountain.

When the FAMP and Mfengu made their appearance the Gcaleka 'made a move toward us'. Chalmers' men were 'extended in skirmishing order on the brow of the hill, the horses having been left out of sight in hand, and in charge of the usual number of men'. He placed Ayliff and his Mfengu on the left of his single seven-pounder gun with his own FAMP on its right.

As the Gcaleka approached, Chalmers ordered Sub-Inspector Cochrane to open fire with his gun. As the Gcaleka continued to advance, they were also fired upon by the FAMP and the Mfengu when they came within range. Chalmers reports that the engagement lasted 'nearly two hours, which checked the enemy . . .' After firing ten rounds the trail of the gun carriage broke, upon which Chalmers gave the order for the gun, its crew and an escort of twenty-five FAMP to retire. (This seems a remarkably slow firing rate for an engagement that lasted the best part of two hours, but we do not know how much ammunition was carried for the weapon.)

When the Mfengu saw the gun retiring they flew into a panic and began to run.

> Finding that we were deserted by the Fingos, and that by remaining on the ground any longer the lives of the whole of the European police would be sacrificed, I ordered the men to retire.
>
> The confusion caused by the Fingos rushing about in all directions caused several of our horses to break loose and through this unfortunate circumstance one officer and six men fell victims of the enemy.

Chalmers successfully broke off the engagement and fell back on Idutywa. Leaving his men and the gun there, he rode over to Ibeka to report to Griffith.

It is noteworthy that Chalmers' report is accompanied by a separate note by General Cunynghame. It would seem that the FAMP officer's report was sent to him by Merriman for his comments, and these make fascinating reading.[35]

His opening remarks take an acid tone, noting that he had not been placed in command of the colonial forces. He continues that he had examined the battlefield on 28 October, accompanied by a member of the FAMP who was present at the battle.

Cunynghame notes that the gun 'was advanced to an excellent position and must have done excellent service until the trail broke'. He blames this defect on the colonial manufacture of the carriage, 'in consequence . . . of the proper Woolwich carriages being lost in the [sinking of the] *Windsor Castle*.[36]

He found that the Mfengu were being outflanked by the Gcaleka when they broke and the subsequent confusion kept the gun and its escort too long on the field. This led to the deaths which followed. Cunynghame commended the courage of Sub-Inspector von Hohenau, telling us: '. . . in fact he lost his own life in his endeavours to carry off the field one of the men who had been wounded, and that while he was endeavouring to place this man on his own horse, he himself was shot through the body, and that he died like an English soldier.' The general mentions that he assisted with the raising of a cairn on the mountain in honour of von Hohenau: 'its position commands Galekaland.'

He concludes that the troops had done well until the gun was disabled, 'and [admired] the way in which they retained their position until they were compelled . . . to retire'.

Due to his shortage of troops, Griffith was unable to continue to defend both Idutywa and Ibeka, and decided to concentrate his forces at Ibeka. A village had not yet developed on the site and it was occupied only by Barnett's house, shop and stables. Ibeka lies some eleven kilometres north-east of Butterworth on the Idutywa road. Sarhili's Great Place, Holela, was about the same distance away to the south-east. Griffith left a description of the shop and its surrounds: 'It is sufficient to say that the Ibeka post consists of a trader's house, shop, and out-offices, built of brick, and roofed with corrugated iron, and with a piece of ground, about 80 yards square, enclosed by a sod bank about 3 feet 6 inches high and a ditch 3 feet deep.'[37]

The morning of the 27th saw a large assembly of Gcaleka warriors in front of the post. In anticipation of an attack, Griffith sent all the women and children away to the safety of nearby Blytheswood but no attack materialised, either then or on the 28th.

For the next two days the defences of the shop and its surrounds were improved in the expectation of a Gcaleka attack. The author of a contemporary work on the Cape Mounted Rifles also described his service there:

> Mr. Barnett was a Kaffir trader on a large scale, and had resided several years at Ibeka. After the battle of Guadana he sent all his family away, and his house and premises were taken possession of by the police, the house being converted into quarters for the Commandant and Staff, the store into a hospital, and the shop into a magazine. We were now daily employed digging rifle trenches and making sand-bag bastions for our three guns at three different corners. Out-lying and inlying pickets were posted every night, and every precaution taken to prevent a surprise.[38]

Meanwhile, a meeting of the Gcaleka chiefs had taken place at Holela at which Sarhili attempted to persuade them that they could not win against the colony in the long run, but the victory at Gwadana so elated them that Khiva, a particularly aggressive chief who had taken part in that battle, was able to bully the paramount into submitting to the will of the majority.

Battle for Ibeka

Michael Spicer identifies several factors which influenced Gcaleka strategy. They had not, unlike the Ngqika, fought the colonists in any previous war. Instead, they had chosen to withdraw before them on the several occasions when the colonists had crossed the Kei. They therefore had no experience in attacking fortified posts, and did not consider the more usual Ngqika guerrilla tactics. Yet again, they turned to vaticination, influenced by a young prophetess named Nita. In addition to the war mark applied to each warrior's forehead to protect him from bullets, she gave each of them a charm to be worn around the neck for the same purpose.[39] A report quoted by General Cunynghame in his autobiography says:

> It was said this prophetess or sorceress had told the Galekas that one of the messages from the spirits of their ancestors was a mandate to give up their old tactics of loose skirmishing, and to attack the enemy in heavy close columns, after the manner of the English soldiers; and that this was the cause of the departure of the Galekas from their usual system of fighting, and of their attacking our posts at Ibeka and elsewhere in masses.[40]

On the afternoon of 29 September, a huge Gcaleka army appeared before the Ibeka post. The fort was manned by a mere 180 FAMP but was supported by two thousand Mfengu. Three guns and a rocket tube were under the command of Sub-Inspector Cochrane. A recent recruit to the FAMP, who would now help to defend the post, was Thomas Shervinton, aged about nineteen. Recently arrived from England, Thomas was the younger of two sons of Colonel Charles Shervinton of the 46th Regiment. The elder brother, Charles Robert St Leger Shervinton, was born on 4 June 1852 and was thus twenty-five years old. Both men had arrived at King William's Town in August 1877 to join the colonial forces: Charlie joined a new unit formed by Colonel Pulleine called 'Pulleine's Rangers' as a lieutenant; Tom chose to join the FAMP as a humble trooper, and both men were immediately sent to the frontier. We shall return to the Shervintons periodically to see how they fared.[41]

The Mfengu were led by Sub-Inspector Allan Maclean of the FAMP. Under him were several Mfengu chiefs, including one whose name will become familiar to the reader, the senior Mfengu chief Veldtman (also spelt Veldtmann or Feldman) Bikitsha. The small size of the enclosure round the buildings suggests that the FAMP manned the sod wall while the Mfengu took station outside.

The men prepared themselves as the Gcaleka stood poised before the small post:

> About eight o'clock we saw them on a hill, immediately south of us, in their usual formation, as intimated. Their numbers were estimated to be between 7000 and 8000. They halted about a mile and a half from us. Of this we took advantage to have breakfast, and to make a few more preparations for defence. The horses, which had been kept grazing close to what I shall now call the fort, were at once brought in, saddled, bridled, and tied up to a picket rope stretched between the trees in the garden. Shells and case-shot were brought out and placed in proximity to the guns; ammunition boxes were opened and placed all round the walls, and men told off to keep up the supplies. Barrels of water had been filled, and these were now set in convenient positions all round the enclosure.[42]

After some initial skirmishing, in which Veldtman was prominently successful, the Gcaleka attacked the post directly and en masse at about 3 p.m. 'in a perfect cloud of skirmishers'. The guns and rocket tube opened up and when the enemy came within rifle range, the FAMP inflicted a withering fire. The Gcaleka were checked, at which point the Mfengu again drove them back.[43]

While the defenders were taking a brief rest, a second huge force appeared out of the nearby Qora River gorge to the east and marched directly at the post. The artillery opened fire but appear not to have been effective and the Gcaleka continued advancing until they disappeared behind a ridge some eight hundred metres away. Griffith ordered the guns to be laid for the top of the ridge, which had been evacuated by a vedette only a short time earlier. As soon as the Gcaleka appeared on the top of the ridge the guns opened fire but 'owing to their great numbers and to the configuration of the ground they succeeded in turning our flank before the guns could be turned on the main body.' A gun was rapidly moved into a better position from where it could rake the advancing column. When the gun opened up the Gcaleka were 'thrown into disorder', at which point Maclean led his Mfengu in another attack, driving the column back down the ridge.

While this action was taking place, the earlier column re-grouped and attempted to threaten the right flank of the post. It was repulsed by Chief Veldtman, who drove them back with about four hundred Mfengu, launching his attack from a stone enclosure near the Butterworth road. The prophetess Nita was killed here while leading her division; her body was decapitated by the Mfengu. Cunynghame was shown the head, kept in a sack of lime, when he later visited Ibeka, reporting: 'The features and woolly hair were quite perfect. It was not a pleasing object, and one look was enough. Such was the end of this would-be enchantress, revered with trembling fear in life, in death a curiosity to a white stranger.'[44]

A gun and the rocket trough were redeployed to the right face of the post, supported by another three hundred Mfengu, and directed their fire on to a body of Gcaleka threatening that side. 'This gun alone', reported Griffith, 'fired 18 rounds before the enemy began to retreat.'

A last futile attempt was made by a small reserve of the Gcaleka to attack the front of the post again but it was quickly repulsed by artillery and rifle fire by the FAMP, after which the whole Gcaleka force withdrew.

The action, which had begun about 3 p.m., ended about 6.30 p.m., during which time the guns fired forty-three shrapnel and nine plain shells, as well as thirty-seven nine-pounder rockets. Laconically, Griffith reported that one gun had to be taken out of action because 'the trail (of colonial manufacture) and which had given way on a previous occasion, broke down altogether after the fifth round.'[45] It was almost certainly the same gun which had failed at Gwadana three days earlier, and which had been hastily repaired.

The British defenders had only one European casualty, who was 'slightly contused in the neck by a musket bullet'. The Mfengu lost six men killed and six wounded.

That night a mist fell on the post, during which the Gcaleka could be heard moving about. The mist turned into a heavy fog the following morning, and the sound of mounted men approaching was heard. The post came to the alert and waited for an attack which did not eventuate. About 5.45 a.m. the fog started to lift, revealing a Gcaleka force on a hill to their left. The guns and rocket tube were brought into action, one shell apparently killing seven men. Allan Maclean, assisted by magistrate F. Pattle, again led his Mfengu in an attack in which they were supported by sixty FAMP under Inspector Chalmers. They dispersed the Gcaleka force, driving it three kilometres down the ridge, killing about thirty and 'burning the Galeka huts right and left'.[46]

There has been some suggestion that, had it not been for the presence of the Mfengu, the post at Ibeka would have been quickly overrun, and this is probably true. Spicer argues that the colony stepped in to prevent the Gcaleka from overwhelming the Mfengu in a war which the latter had themselves helped to precipitate. The Mfengu had also unintentionally contributed to the Gcaleka victory at Gwadana. At Ibeka, the skirmishing ability and large numbers of the Mfengu had complemented the firepower of the numerically weak colonial troops. 'The truth is, whites and Mfengu played a true complementary role throughout the war.'[47] The battle of Ibeka was to prove a watershed in the early war with the Gcaleka.

Status of Imperial Troops

The reader might with reason ponder the status of the British troops. Where were they and why had they not played any part in the war to this point? The more observant might also have noted the opening comment in General Cunynghame's opinion on the battle of Gwadana, in which he stated that he had not been placed in command of the colonial forces. These matters now need some explanation.

Cunynghame had at his immediate disposal a mere two battalions at the Cape: the 88th and the 1/24th. (The 1/13th was in the Transvaal and the 80th and five companies of the 3rd were in Natal.) Most of the 88th was based in Cape Town while the 24th was spread in penny packets about the Ciskei. On 10 October the general reported that his troops were allocated to the following posts:

King William's Town	HQ and 3 companies, 1/24th
East London	50 men, 1/24th
Komgha	200 men, 1/24th
Draaibosch	50 men, 1/24th
Pullen's farm	50 men, 1/24th
Fort Cunynghame	100 men, 88th and one seven-pounder gun
Cathcart	100 men, 88th

Cunynghame had briefly considered whether he might withdraw some of the troops in Natal or the Transvaal to the Cape, then decided against doing so.

When war seemed inevitable, General Cunynghame had recommended to Sir Bartle Frere that he (Cunynghame) was 'the proper person to take the superior command of all troops in the field' and the governor had 'entirely concurred' and 'was so gazetted'. He also offered to supply the colonial FAMP and burgher forces with transport and supplies but his offer 'has not yet been replied to'. In that same letter, Cunynghame told the Under-

Secretary of State for War that he had asked Frere to consider 'whether a Brigadier-General should not be appointed to the Eastern Frontier. In the event of anything happening to myself, it is difficult to forsee [*sic*] on whom the command would devolve.'[48]

Like Melvill, Frere was highly critical of the 'absence of unity or concentration of authority' on the frontier. In a report to London on 28 September, he had written:

> 4. Foremost among this want of co-operation and concentration was the total severance of the Frontier Armed and Mounted Police from other Departments of the Administration, and the yet more distinct separation and want of communication between the civil and military authorities.
>
> 5. On inquiring the cause I found a general belief in the existence of district orders forbidding any intercommunication between the civil and military authorities otherwise than through the Government at Cape Town.'[49]

This may have had its origins with Governor Barkly. In a memorandum to Frere on 24 September, Cunynghame had mentioned that in November 1876 he had given instructions that his military commandant should maintain communications with the resident commissioner and the commandant of the frontier field force. Barkly had then vetoed this suggestion, requiring instead that the civil authorities should communicate only with the government secretary and the military commandant should report to Cunynghame without reference to the civil authorities. It seemed that this protocol was still in force and Cunynghame had cancelled it.[50]

A second memorandum, sent by Cunynghame to Frere on 26 September, noted that Colonel Glyn, commanding the 1st Battalion, 24th Regiment, was required to give assistance in the organisation of burgher forces. He said that he would be happy to give those directions to Glyn, but wished to know 'with whom he is to be placed in relation to in carrying this into effect'. He went on to quote an order which stated: 'No communications shall take place between Her Majesty's Commandant of the frontier [Glyn] either with the Civil Commissioner or with the Commandant of Police [Griffith], but that all communications between the civil and Her Majesty's military authorities on the frontier should pass through your Excellency or myself and the Honourable the Secretary of the Government.'[51]

Frere had not found any further documentary evidence of these 'district orders' and the presence on the frontier of the governor, together with ministers Merriman and Brownlee, 'representing the authority of the Cabinet',[52] had temporarily circumvented the prohibition of communications, but the matter was sufficiently serious to cause Frere to take some formal action. In his response to Cunynghame on 28 September he was unequivocal:

> I am not very perfectly informed as to the reasons which induced my predecessor to give your Excellency, last year, the instructions you refer to, but I entirely agree with you that those instructions are quite inapplicable to the present juncture, and should be cancelled.
>
> I have requested all civil commissioners, officers of the police, and magistrates to have the freest [sic] possible communication with the military authorities nearest to them, and I have no doubt of their cordial co-operation to the best of their power.
>
> I have requested that in every case where it is possible any application for assistance or advice to Colonel Glyn should be sent through the Civil Commissioner of the district or the senior police officer.[53]

This whole matter was to take a far more dramatic turn in the weeks ahead.

Aftermath of Ibeka

The decisive defeat of the Gcaleka at Ibeka had several immediate consequences. On 5 October, the governor published a proclamation which deposed Sarhili as chief of the Gcaleka:

> His country is taken from him, and will be disposed of as Government shall direct; and, pending instructions from Her Majesty's Government, will be ruled directly by officers appointed by the Governor of the Cape of Good Hope.
>
> Commandant Griffith has been instructed to occupy the country heretofore governed by Kreli, and to arrange for its future administration as part of Her Majesty's possessions in South Africa.[54]

Sarhili sent a message to Brownlee asking what terms he would be granted if he surrendered. Brownlee responded that it was too late for terms, and that the governor intended to punish the Gcaleka. Frere asked the attorney-general, then the younger Andries Stockenström, son of Sir Andries, for his opinion on the legal status of Sarhili as a combatant. Stockenström responded: 'The position of the chief Kreli is somewhat anomalous, and I fear that grave technical difficulties would stand in the way of any legal proceedings against him, or any of his people, in the courts of this colony for his or their acts beyond the Kei.'[55]

As might be expected, however, there was a way by which the same end could be achieved using different means:

Having regard to the conditions upon which Kreli was allowed to reoccupy the land to the west of the Bashee, and the wanton manner in which those conditions have been broken, as also to the position in which Kreli placed himself by accepting, as a matter of grace, a habitation at the hands of our Government, I consider that the Government is clearly entitled to repossess itself of the land so allotted, and to incarcerate the chief and those of his followers who have taken part in the recent outrages.

The final step would be to undertake the occupation of Gcalekaland promised in the proclamation. Frere suggested that such an invasion might be delayed in order to rectify some of the deficiencies in Griffith's force, in particular the state of the FAMP, which was at half its nominal strength of 1,100.[56]

Although it was now generally agreed that occupation was the best course to be adopted, there was at least one objection to the means by which this should be accomplished. Prime Minister Molteno sent a telegram to the governor in which he stressed that there should be no delay in advancing into Gcalekaland, and he requested that Griffith be given sole military responsibility. Frere complained, in a note to Merriman, dated 5 October: 'This is not encouraging, but we must do our duty, and not care what men . . . may say of us – or to us!' He went on to enumerate a number of his complaints that Merriman might informally mention to Molteno, the first of which was the injunction on communications between the civil and military authorities to which reference was made earlier.[57] In a footnote to the governor's first point, Phyllis Lewson, the editor of the publication in which the quotation appears, writes that it was 'an example of Molteno's intense suspicion of the "military". His aim was to prevent any interference with Colonial self-government, which included responsibility for defence.'[58]

The breach between the military and civil authorities, despite the best efforts of the governor, was already widening and was soon to lead to serious difficulties. In the meantime, General Cunynghame, having been officially recognised as commanding all troops in South Africa,[59] undertook not to interfere in any Transkei operations under Griffith's command.[60]

Chapter 6

The Transkei Campaign

A snake if trodden upon will bite.

Sandile

There was some debate as to the next military step to be taken, Frere arguing that Griffith's forces were in no fit state to invade Gcalekaland. It was eventually determined that the commandant should make a demonstration in force and, at daybreak on 9 October 1877, he set out with his troops in four columns.[1]

In the first, a large number of Mfengu under James Ayliff and Allan Maclean set out from Butterworth and the Veldtman and Smith Poswa locations. (Smith Poswa, another senior Mfengu chief, was named after Sir Harry Smith.) A second, the Gonubie and Maclean Town Volunteers, under their respective leaders, Captains Gray and Sprigg, left from the 'Springs', while a third, part of No. 6 troop, FAMP, the Queenstown Burgher Force and a body of Thembu levies, all under the command of Major H.G. Elliott, the chief magistrate of Thembuland, advanced from Idutywa towards the Toleni River. The fourth was led by Griffith himself, who left Ibeka with two troops of FAMP, two guns of the FAMP Artillery and the King William's Town Burgher Force. Each of the four columns was directed towards Holela, Sarhili's Great Place near the river of the same name.

The first to arrive, soon after sunrise, were Griffith and a division of Maclean's Mfengu, the former having had only about ten kilometres to travel. The Gcaleka were taken entirely by surprise:

The Frontier Police and the artillery drew up on the slope of a hill commanding the enemy's position, and the guns immediately opened fire, dislodging the enemy with a few rounds, when the Fingos of the first division, led by Messrs. Allan and W.A. Maclean, charged down and drove the Galekas before them through the Cora [Qora] river and a long way beyond it. Another body of the enemy tried to make a stand on a high ridge along which the King William's Town Burghers were advancing, but they were attacked with great spirit by Commandant Bowker and the Butterworth and other Fingos, and were driven with loss through the Cora, and pursued for some distance beyond the river.[2]

Holela was burnt to the ground, as were Sigcawu's homestead and many others in the vicinity, and a vast amount of 'booty' fell to the Mfengu.

It is thought that Sarhili had left Holela about a week before the attack, but that it was re-occupied by Bhotomane a few days later. He was still there when the attack began but escaped to join Sigcawu and his brothers nearby, where they re-grouped but were again driven off.[3]

Meanwhile, the Idutywa column under Major Elliott had met with a body of some three hundred Gcaleka, heavily defeated them and then burnt all the homesteads found nearby.

Battle of the Springs

Leaving sixteen men to guard the camp at the 'Springs', Captain George Gray and his volunteers had crossed the Gcuwa River south of Butterworth and almost immediately became 'hotly engaged with the enemy, who fought with great determination and courage'.[4] The force consisted of 134 men from several bodies of the Kaffrarian Volunteers, including Gray's own Gonubie Troop, Captain James Sansom's Komgha Troop and Captain Howard Sprigg's Maclean Town Troop.

The force moved south-west to the Gcuwa River valley, then in a southerly direction towards the Tutura mission station. After marching only a few kilometres, and approaching the confluence of the Gcuwa and Kei rivers, they were attacked by a second large body of Gcaleka, said to number as many as two thousand, under Khiva and Bhotomane. There followed a noisy engagement, much of the clamour coming from the Gcaleka. Each side manoeuvred to maintain their ground, and, if possible, to gain some. The superior firepower and accuracy of the volunteers turned the tide of the attack. Gradually the Gcaleka began to melt away in the direction of the Qora River and the volunteers, their ammunition almost exhausted, were compelled to return to their base at the Springs.[5] Gray had suffered two men and several horses wounded while the Gcaleka were thought to have lost as many as fifty men.

Griffith declined to pursue the Gcaleka, refusing to expose his column any further due to a shortage of ammunition, and instead took his force back to Ibeka. He was heavily criticised for not taking up the pursuit.[6]

On 15 October, Griffith sent a telegram to Merriman in which he said that he had received two messengers from Sarhili, who had asked Griffith to delay sending more troops into Sarhili's country until the paramount had had an opportunity to treat for terms. Merriman immediately responded, instructing Griffith: 'you may give Kreli, or any of his chiefs, any assurance you think proper of their life and treatment . . . but you will inform him that, pending his surrender, the movement of troops will not be suspended nor delayed.'[7]

First Clearance of the Transkei

Nor were they. Within days, Griffith was ready to make a full invasion of Gcalekaland with three columns. He led his headquarters column out of Ibeka on 18 October, camping overnight just north of Kentani (Centane or Quintana) Hill. He left very early on the 19th, and about 8 a.m. set up a more permanent camp on the southern slope of Kentani Hill itself, where the column took breakfast.[8] Leaving a strong force to guard the camp, Griffith then took the main body of his column on a patrol in the direction from which the contingent from the Springs, now under Inspector Chalmers, was to join him. After meeting with Chalmers, who reported that he had swept the country through which he had moved clear of Gcaleka, they both returned to the Kentani camp.[9]

The following morning, the 20th, the combined Mfengu forces from Chalmers' and Griffith's columns were led out under the command of James Ayliff with instructions 'to secure the country from the Kobonqaba River [just south of Kentani] to the sea'. The Kei River mouth lies almost due south of Kentani while the Qolora River meets the sea some five kilometres further north-east of Kei Mouth. The line which Ayliff was to clear was some twenty-five kilometres long.[10]

At the same time, the remaining white troops, including the artillery, moved with Griffith to the mouth of the Qolora River, to be joined there later by Ayliff's Mfengu. On the morning of the 21st, the whole force crossed the Qolora at its mouth and moved north-east along the coast, crossing the Kobonqaba mouth at what was called the 'Ebb and Flow Drift'. (In fact, it will be seen that the same name is used for drifts near the mouth of several rivers but the principal one is that near the mouth of the Kei.) At the same time, the Mfengu scoured the country along the Nxara River for several kilometres inland from the coast.

Early on the 22nd, Griffith continued his march north-east along the coast, reaching the top of the ridge overlooking the Qora River. It was here that he had planned to effect a junction with Inspector Hook's No. 2 Column, which Griffith found at the source of the Lusize River north of the Manubi Forest.

Hook, with a combined mounted force of 225 FAMP and burghers, some two thousand Mfengu under Allan Maclean and a single gun, had left Ibeka on 18 October and, passing by Holela, continued on the track towards Mazeppa Bay. After twenty-five kilometres he camped overnight and continued on the 19th, keeping the Qora River on his left. He arrived at the Lusize River later in the day and set up his camp within 'two or three miles of the Manubi Forest'. Throughout his march he had encountered little opposition and had burnt a number of Gcaleka homesteads.

On the 20th, he sent out four hundred mounted Mfengu towards the Manubi 'to spy'. They returned later in the day with a large number of sheep, together with a number of Gcaleka women and children. They also reported a large number of Gcaleka along the Qora and many cattle and horses in the Manubi Forest.

Hook himself took Maclean and a party of FAMP on a reconnaissance towards the Kei River, where, from a great distance, he saw Griffith's column 'burning and moving towards the sea'. He sent off a messenger telling Griffith where his camp lay.

On Sunday 21 October, Hook was advised that a Gcaleka force was in sight 'advancing towards the camp in numbers'. He posted the Mfengu on the ridge in front of them, with a piquet of FAMP. There followed several skirmishes, which ended when the Gcaleka withdrew, leaving sixty-seven dead on the field. Hook's own losses amounted to two Europeans killed and one slightly wounded. Of the Mfengu, two of their officers, brothers named William and Michael Goss, were killed, with nine Africans, and twenty-one wounded. On 22 October, Griffith joined Hook in the latter's camp on the Lusize.

Major Elliott's contingent arrived at a ridge about six kilometres south of Toleni on 17 October, where he made camp. During the evening there was a skirmish between a small party of Elliott's force and some Gcaleka but they were defeated with minimal loss. Elliott thought that the various groups were concentrating in a kloof east of his camp, with a view to making a later attack. To prevent such a sortie, on the 18th, while Elliott remained in his camp, Inspector Bailie, FAMP, took out half of the mounted Europeans and a third of the Thembu, meeting a number of groups of Gcaleka, each between fifty and three hundred strong, which he scattered.[11]

Griffith's next report was dated Fort Bowker, 5 November.[12] The fort had been built in 1860 near the west bank of the Mbashe River and was now to prove a useful asset.

Bad weather prevented Griffith moving out until the 30th, when he crossed the Qora River at its mouth and moved north along the coast to make camp on the Jujura River about two kilometres from the coast. There he was finally

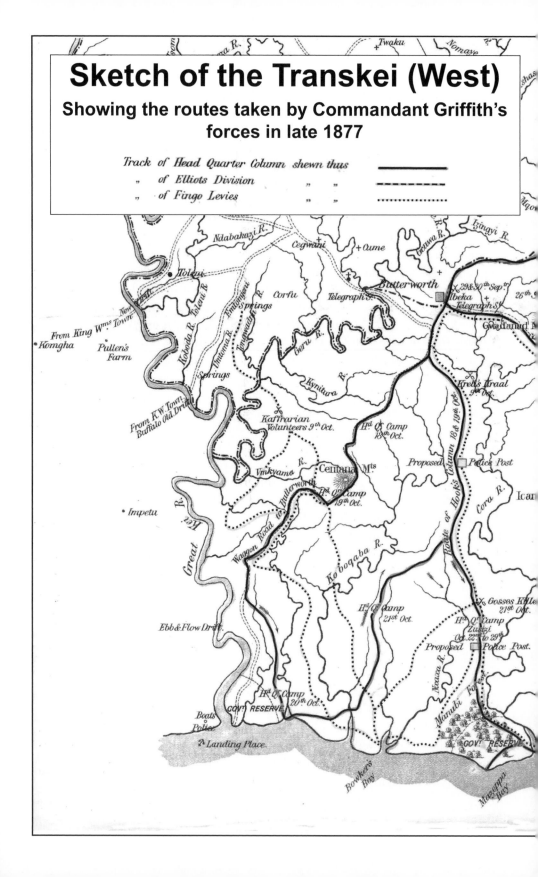

Sketch of the Transkei (West)

Showing the routes taken by Commandant Griffith's forces in late 1877

Track of Head Quarter Column shewn thus
" of Elliots Division " "
" of Fingo Levies " "

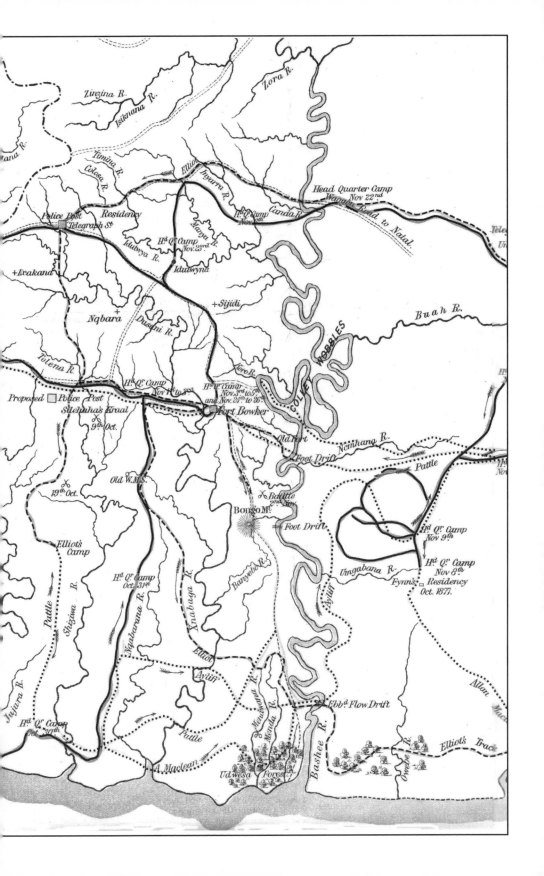

able to make contact with Major Elliott's contingent, which he found some twenty-five kilometres north-west of his bivouac, on a tributary of the Shixini River. The next day, 31 October, he crossed the Shixini, again at its mouth, where he broke up his column. No. 7 Troop of the FAMP, supporting a division of Mfengu levies under Commandant Maclean, was detached and sent across the Nqabara River towards the Dwesa (Udwessa) Forest. Part of a second division of the Mfengu under Commandant Pattle was sent slightly inland to cross the Nqabara at (yet another) Ebb and Flow Drift, there to support Maclean's contingent towards the Dwesa. The last portion of the Mfengu, under Commandant Ayliff, and with the support of the Kaffrarian Volunteers, crossed the Nqabara still higher up to sweep north-east across the ridges in concert with the other two groups.

Griffith himself, with the headquarters column, pressed on north-west up the ridge separating the Shixini and Nqabara rivers. Little Gcaleka contact was found and Griffith bivouacked at the source of the Nqabarana, a tributary of the Nqabara, no more than five kilometres from the sea. The next day, 1 November, in a heavy spring rainstorm, his column continued north-west until it struck the wagon road from Butterworth to Fort Bowker, where he found Major Elliott's division on its way to the fort. After seeing Elliott on his way, Griffith made camp for the night near the road as the rain continued to beat down.

On 2 November, with the downpour continuing to make movement difficult, and being short of provisions, he remained in camp awaiting the arrival of his convoy from the Lusize camp, which he had ordered to meet him there. The wagons and their welcome supplies arrived about 5 p.m.

On the 3rd, with the bad weather abating, he struck camp and made a short day's march to Fort Bowker, joining Major Elliott there. Elliott himself was out on patrol when Griffith arrived and did not return until late on the 4th. Griffith ordered him out again on the 5th, with his contingent and a gun, first to assist with the scouring of the Dwesa Forest, and then to cross the Mbashe and occupy the heights on the left bank from the Ebb and Flow Drift down to the river mouth. He sent a message to Ayliff to complete his work in the Dwesa, then to cross the Mbashe and cover the left bank from the Ebb and Flow Drift inland. He ordered Inspector Chalmers with his FAMP troop back down the ridge they had followed earlier towards the coast, to get as close as he could to Ayliff's position, there to offer support as needed and also to sweep up any Gcaleka who might slip past Ayliff.[13]

On 20 November, Griffith reported that he and his various columns had moved from the left bank of the Mbashe in Bomvanaland towards the Mtata River, the commandant reaching the mouth of that river on the 13th.[14] Near here he met with Nqwiliso, the Pondo chief. Griffith held the chief responsible for allowing the Gcaleka to enter his territory but Nqwiliso repudiated the accusation, stating that he himself had cause for complaint because the colony's troops had driven the Gcaleka into his country 'without warning or requests to close his drifts'. He went on to say that that there was a major concentration of Gcaleka nearby and, with the assistance of some of his troops, Nqwiliso could defeat them. Griffith was reluctant to press on beyond the Mtata: 'Most of the horses were knocked up; the Native Levies were footsore and disinclined to advance beyond the Umtata; the weather was extremely wet and inclement; we were almost entirely out of provisions, and a very long distance from our depot of supplies . . .' He therefore pressed Nqwiliso to continue harassing the Gcaleka with the promise that he should keep all the cattle he could capture. Walter Stanford was interpreting for Griffith at the time and recorded a conversation between a Captain Scott and the commandant in which the former told Griffith that his decision not to co-operate with Nqwiliso had been an error and that 'the Gcaleka still unbeaten would re-cross the Mtata River and resume operations in Gcalekaland before long.' Griffith, however, was convinced that the Gcaleka were beaten and withdrew his force back across the Mtata.[15]

On 19 November, Griffith had released the mounted volunteers to return to their homes and on 21 November began his own return, reaching Fort Bowker on the 24th. He waited two days before the Mfengu arrived there and, leaving two troops of the FAMP, with a gun detachment, at Fort Bowker to patrol the banks of the Mbashe, he marched for Ibeka on the 26th, arriving there the same day.

After summarising his campaign, his report of 29 November naïvely maintained that 'the war with the Gcaleka tribe may now, I trust, be considered at an end.'[16] He had taken large numbers of cattle but had fought few engagements. The Gcaleka had, in fact, withdrawn in front of his sweeps, eventually retreating halfway to the St Johns River, leaving small pockets behind them. As quickly as Griffith had returned to Ibeka, the Gcaleka returned – eluding the few men left behind to guard the Mbashe – leaving families and cattle behind.

On 21 November, the governor issued a proclamation deposing Sarhili and depriving him of his lands.[17] Also at this time, government notices called for prospective white farmers to apply for grants of three hundred acres between the Kei and Qora rivers.[18]

Makinana Crisis

We left Maphasa having withdrawn his support for Sarhili. Just before the battle of Ibeka on 29 September, he had crossed with his people into the

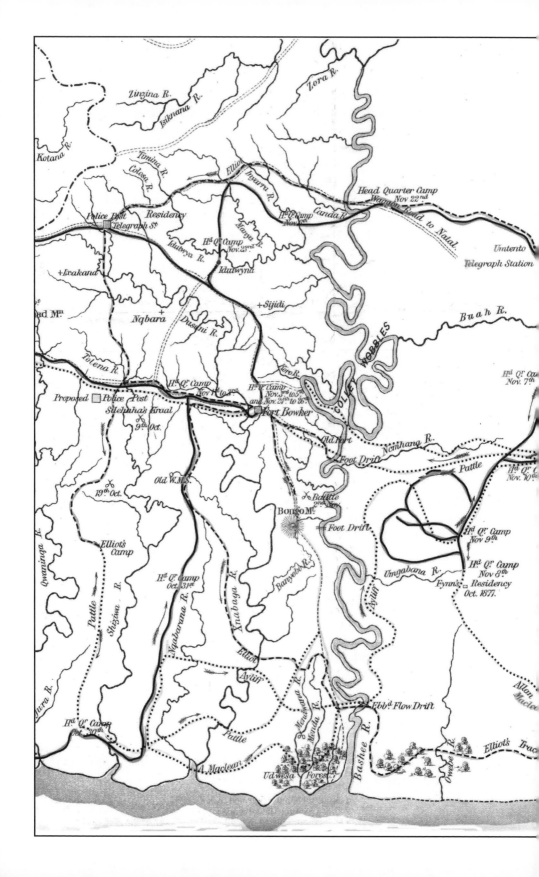

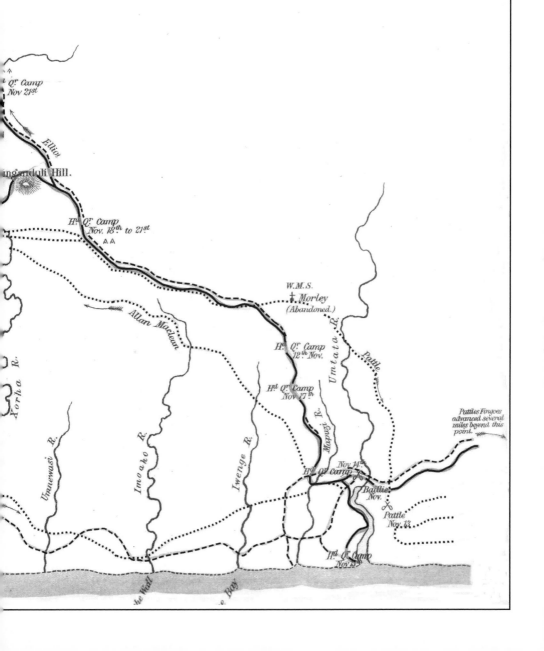

Sketch of the Transkei (East)

Showing the routes taken by Commandant Griffith's forces in late 1877

Track of Head Quarter Column shewn thus ———————
„   *of Elliots Division*   „   „ – – – – – –
„   *of Fingo Levies*   „   „ ················

Q.ʳ Camp
Nov 21ˢᵗ

Elliot

ing—nduli Hill.

Hᵈ Q.ʳ Camp
Nov. 18ᵗʰ to 21ˢᵗ
A A

W.M.S.
† Morley
(Abandoned.)

Hᵈ Q.ʳ Camp
12ᵗʰ Nov.

Hᵈ Q.ʳ Camp
Nov 17ᵗʰ

Allan Maclean

Umtata R.

Pattle

Pattles Fingoes
advanced several
miles beyond this
point.

Xorha R.

Imoako R.

Iwenge R.

Ununewasi R.

Mapesi R.

Nov 14ᵗʰ
Hᵈ Q.ʳ Camp

Baillie
Nov.

Pattle
Nov. 13.

Hᵈ Q.ʳ Camp
Nov 15ᵗʰ

he Wal

Bay

colony to Impetu on the west bank of the Kei River. The numbers involved were of the order of 4,300 people.

Opinions in the colony were divided on Maphasa's defection: Brownlee felt that it was a positive step because it indicated a split in the Gcaleka leadership and might discourage other chiefs from joining Sarhili. Others were not so sure, fearing that Maphasa's treachery might cause trouble in the colony. Cunynghame was among the latter and strongly advocated Maphasa's disarmament, a step which Brownlee was able to delay for a short time.[19]

Maphasa was soon joined by Makinana (known to the British as Mackinnon), a son of the Ndlambe chief Mhala and the brother of Ndimba and Smith Mhala (yet another African named after Sir Harry), bringing with him a mere fifty or sixty warriors.

By mid-November, Gcalekaland had been supposedly cleared by Griffith and steps were being taken to relocate Maphasa and his people there. This came as a welcome relief to their white neighbours, who had found their livestock numbers being rapidly depleted. The Tsonyana were allocated an area between the Qora and Shixini rivers.[20]

Sir Bartle Frere, who had agreed with Cunynghame, ordered that the Tsonyana be disarmed before being moved to their new location and Brownlee was despatched to Impetu to make the arrangements. Inspector Hutchison, second-in-command of the FAMP, was deputed to give effect to the disarmament order with his troop of police.

When Brownlee arrived at Impetu on 15 November the Tsonyana had had time to consider their position. It was not a comfortable one. Maphasa argued with Brownlee that he had left Sarhili so that, with the paramount's defeat, he and his people might return to their own country in safety. Now he was to be re-settled in the midst of hostile Gcaleka and, worse, was to be deprived of the means to defend himself. Brownlee was implacable and Maphasa, with great reluctance and misgiving, eventually had to acquiesce.[21]

Before the war began, Makinana had several times requested permission to relocate from Gcalekaland to be near his brother Ndimba, situated in the south of the Ngqika location in the colony. Despite Sarhili's support for the move, Brownlee had turned his requests down. Now, not only was he to be sent back to Gcalekaland, but he was to be disarmed and, because he had chosen to accept 250 of Maphasa's men, he was to pay a part of the cattle fine imposed on Maphasa. The situation, he felt, was intolerable, and he again appealed to Brownlee to be allowed to settle with his own people. Brownlee curtly told him to do as he had been told.[22]

As part of the disarmament process, a German volunteer, Baron Wilhelm von Linsingen (of whom we shall hear more) had over-zealously searched the huts of the Ndlambe, finding three firearms which he had confiscated.[23] Makinana and his people became extremely alarmed, fearing that their disarmament would be the prelude to the seizure of their cattle and perhaps their own massacre. On the pretext of looking for lost cattle, Makinana then sought, and was given, a pass permitting him to go to Ndimba's location. In dead of night, he and his people fled from Impetu to his brother's location near Draaibosch.[24]

Before he left, Makinana had told Maphasa of his intention; the latter had lost no time informing Brownlee, who immediately sent Hutchison and his FAMP in pursuit. One troop of police managed to intercept a large group of men and cattle entering the Draaibosch location but were deterred from intervening because of their inferior numbers. The next morning, they entered the location and attempted to seize some cattle they found there without enquiring to whom they belonged. Both Ndimba and Makinana resisted the police attempt to seize the cattle. Inspector Hutchison arrived in time to prevent any escalation and castigated the sub-inspector responsible for not having sought the permission of the magistrate or Sandile to enter the location, and instructed him to return the cattle pending Brownlee's arrival. Brownlee was able only to plead lamely that the incident was the result of a mistake over the location's exact boundary.[25]

It was too late. The first clash between the authorities and the Ngqika had taken place, the very confrontation that Brownlee and the governor had sought to avoid. Ndimba refused to meet Brownlee because, he said, he was too frightened. When he went to see the chief, Brownlee found a strong armed contingent posted, overlooking the homestead.

Ndimba asked why Makinana had been denied permission to join his own people and refused Brownlee's demand to surrender him to the authorities until the troops were withdrawn. Sandile reacted even more strongly, angrily asking why permission had not been sought to enter the location, and saying: 'A snake if trodden upon will bite.'[26]

Brownlee took these events to presage the extension of the war to the Ngqika and, as if in confirmation, there was a massive increase in stock losses in the following days. There is some evidence to suggest that a tentative Sandile had originally sought to keep aloof from the war but with the increases in cattle theft in October, Sandile refused to punish the offenders and began to disregard the advice of his resident, William Wright, and his councillors. Spicer argues that despite these signs, the majority of the Ngqika wanted peace, and that the increase in theft was the reaction of a more hot-blooded 'war party' among the young warriors.[27]

The story of Makinana eventually reached the press and a huge panic ensued when rumours flew, examples of which Frere reported to Carnarvon:

'The Gaika war-cry has been sounded on all sides during the night. Machinnon [*sic*] was making for the Amatolas. The Kaffirs were assembling on all sides, and flocking to march on Komgha.'[28]

It was nonsense, of course. Makinana, as Frere rightly pointed out, had fled in fear, not with hostile intent. Frere enjoined Merriman to expand the FAMP with all speed and appointed W.B. Chalmers, previously a commissioner with the Ngqika, as a special commissioner to resolve the Makinana matter. According to Spicer, 'Chalmers was instructed to tell Makinana that he only need pay the fine and hand in the arms of his people and then he would be allowed to settle where he wished.'[29]

On 24 November, Chalmers arrived at Ndimba's location and began a series of meeting with Ndimba, Makinana and Sandile. It quickly became clear that misunderstandings had occurred and Chalmers was able to stabilise the situation. Makinana agreed to pay the fine and hand in his arms, while Sandile apologised for unwittingly creating a panic among the white colonists. It took some time for a reluctant Makinana to collect a small number of cattle and firearms. Chalmers reported:

> On the 3rd [December] I proceeded to Dimba's where I found Mackinnon. He handed over to me 22 head of cattle, 16 bundles of assegais, and three guns, stating that he was doing his best to comply with the Government demands, and requesting me not to send off to Sandilli.
>
> The number of cattle now handed over to me was 55 head. In compliance with the Government instructions, I informed Mackinnon that with these 55 head of cattle, and the cattle, sheep, and goats, captured from him, the Government would now consider the fine imposed on him fully satisfied. He expressed himself as being very thankful. He also handed over to me four guns and about 60 or 70 assegais, stating that four guns and four bundles of assegais had already been seized from him. He requested me to ask the Government not to send him across the Kei, but to allow him to remain in the Gaika Location, and be under Government. I informed him that I would communicate his wishes to the Government.[30]

While Chalmers regarded the fine as paid, he told Makinana that he was not satisfied that sufficient firearms had been handed in. Accordingly,

> on the 6th [I] returned to Dimba's, where I found Mackinnon. He handed over to me his own gun, which he stated he had had in his possession for the last 20 years, and that he handed it over to show his full submission to the Government. He also handed over to me three more guns, and some more assegais, stating

that he really could find no more; and that his people had become scattered over the country through fright. Seeing that everything had been done which could be accomplished without using force, I informed Mackinnon that he may now consider the matter at an end . . .[31]

With the resolution of the Makinana affair, and with the Gcaleka apparently cleared from their country, the government believed, like Griffith, that the war was over.[32] On 21 November a proclamation was published in the government *Gazette* to the effect that, despite the bellicose actions of the Gcaleka, '[Government], considering the chiefs more at fault than the people, is willing to forgive all, who have not been leaders in acts of rebellion, who may now lay down their arms and submit.'[33] At the same time, advertisements appeared in the local press offering prospective white settlers grants of land of three hundred acres between the Kei and Qora rivers.[34]

Battle of Holland's Shop

We have already noted that as soon as Griffith withdrew from the Mbashe, except for a token force of two hundred men which he left at Fort Bowker, the Gcaleka had begun to return to their homeland. Those who had never left, but simply gone into hiding and remained undetected by Griffith's massive sweep of the country, also now began to return to their homesteads. This movement not only demonstrated the futility of Griffith's campaign, but brought home the fact that the war with the Gcaleka was not at an end. Frere himself did not hesitate to point out, in a report to Colonial Secretary the Earl of Carnarvon on 5 December, the discrepancy between Griffith's claim to have cleared Gcalekaland, and the reality of their re-appearance:

> Since my despatch of the 28th ultimo, no further progress has been made in the settlement of Galeka land, owing to the re-appearance of armed bodies of Galekas in considerable numbers throughout that part of the Transkei, hitherto supposed to have been effectually cleared by the columns under Commandant Griffith, which lately swept through the whole country.
>
> There appears little doubt that some of these armed bands must have eluded observation during the advance of Commandant Griffith's columns; others appear to have returned in small parties across the Bashee River.[35]

Confirmation of the assembly of Gcaleka in their homeland came in a telegram from Captain Wardell, of the 24th Regiment, to General Cunynghame dated 2 December:

Information just received from some of Mapassa's people that large parties of Galekas are congregating between the Qora and Koligaloo rivers with intention of attacking Mapassa; I have wired this through Captain Upcher to Griffith, Ibeka. Xoxo tells Raymond tribe will be obliged to recross [Kei] river if not protected, having no guns and but few assegais.[36]

On 3 December 1877, Inspector J.H.W. Bourne reported to Griffith that two days earlier he had begun a routine six-day patrol from Ibeka with a troop of twenty-five FAMP and one gun with men of the Capetown Artillery and a detachment of Capetown Volunteers. His total force consisted of 152 men.[37]

He bivouacked that night near Sigcawu's homestead, close by Holela, fifteen kilometres to the south-east. On the 2nd, he started out with his mounted men at 4.30 a.m., intending to sweep the area to the east of the road towards the Qora River. He ordered his infantry to march as early as possible with the wagons, along the 'main road' towards Mazeppa Bay. He continued down the road to an abandoned shop owned by a trader named Holland, some six or seven kilometres further to the south-east. The shop was located near the present African location of Msintsana, close by the river of the same name. When Bourne reached the store, he 'observed Galekas moving along the heights and making for the Cogha [Qora] . . .' The two parties exchanged shots from a distance and Bourne followed them, leaving a small party of men on the road to cover his rear. He succeeded in driving the Gcaleka across the Qora, from where they 'collected in large parties and observed his movements'.

It was now about 11 a.m. and Bourne next saw the Gcaleka moving up the hills towards Holland's shop. He retired towards his support party on the road, to be met by a messenger informing him that the horse of one of the men left behind had been shot and the rider 'narrowly escaped with his life', as did two others of the party. 'It appears that these [three] men, not expecting any Galekas were in their vicinity, had ridden on to the ridge to the right of the support for the purpose of reconnoitring, when they suddenly came face to face with several mounted Galekas.'

There was an exchange of shots in which one of the horses was wounded, and the FAMP quickly retreated, followed by the Gcaleka, who gave up the pursuit only when Bourne and his men appeared. Shortly afterwards, they were joined by the wagon party. Again at full strength, Bourne arranged for his force to take the offensive.

Captain Bayley and volunteers and Capetown Artillery [were ordered] to overlook the densely wooded kloof, and cover our rear; myself and police with

1. Sandile, sovereign chief of the Ngqika Xhosa. (*Private Collection*)

2. Sarhili, paramount chief of the Xhosa people

3. Sir Bartle Frere, governor and high commissioner at the Cape. (*Private Collection*)

4. Charles Molteno, prime minister of the Cape colony

5. General Sir Arthur Cunynghame, commander-in-chief to March 1878. (*Private Collection*)

6. Lieutenant-General Hon. Frederic Thesiger, commander-in-chief from March 1878

7. Fighting between Mfengu and Gcaleka on the Butterworth River. (*Private Collection*)

8. An Mfengu camp at Fort Fordyce. (*Private Collection*)

9. Xhosa prisoners escorted by Mfengu. (*Private Collection*)

10. A British patrol on the heights above McNaghten's Krantz. (*Private Collection*)

11. Ngqika skirmishers recovering their wounded. (*Private Collection*)

12. The battle at Holland's Shop. (*Private Collection*)

13. The battle of Kentani. (*Private Collection*)

14. General Thesiger and his staff: left to right: Crealock, Molyneux, Wood, Thesiger, Buller, Gossett. (From Streatfield's *Reminiscences Of An Old 'Un*)

15. Troops sweep the broken country around Ntaba kaNdoda. (*Private Collection*)

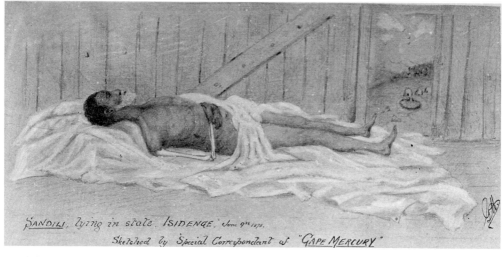

Sandili, lying in state ISIDENGE. June 9th 1878.
Sketched by Special Correspondant of "CAPE MERCURY"

16. The end: Sandile's body on display at isiDenge, 9 June 1878. (*Ron Sheeley Collection*)

17. The Boma Pass today

18. Kroome escarpment from the south

19. Fort Fordyce remains

20. Waterkloof

21. Debe Nek

22. Maqoma's grave

23. Fuller's Hoek

24. Fort Armstrong

25. Gwadana Hill (Mount Wodehouse)

26. Barnett's Shop, Ibeka

27. Site of the battle of Draaibosch

28. KwaKentani

29. McNaghten's Krantz

30. Ntaba kaNdoda

31. Tyityaba Valley

32. Sandile's grave

Grahamstown Artillery to move round the head of the kloof and take up a position on high ground on the other side of the kloof. The Galekas had retired and did not make their appearance until we were over them, when they rose up in far larger numbers than any of us had anticipated; we estimated their numbers at about 200. The gun delivered one shot which told with good effect, the police stuck well to their work considering their numbers, but were (after one of the warmest fires ever delivered by the natives for about half-an-hour) forced to retire. Private Wesley was near me holding my horse, at his request I took it from him, he was leading his horse in front of me, and I told him to mount and retire. It appears he did mount, but again dismounted to deliver a shot, his horse left him and he fell into the hands of the Galekas who stabbed him to death at once. Several Galekas were shot over his body and many others put 'hors de combat'. My time was too busily occupied in rallying my men and dragging another out whose horse had left him. We all made a stand until the gun was limbered up and retired on to the volunteers without any other casualty. During the time we were retiring Lieutenant Stigant delivered some beautiful shots which completely routed the enemy.

Faced with a more serious situation than he had expected, Bourne wisely decided to retire into more open country and make camp. Having prepared his position, he awaited further developments. He did not have long to wait. About 4 p.m. he noticed mounted reconnaissance parties of Gcaleka on distant ridges and at 6.30 p.m. the enemy advanced on his position 'from the direction of Holland's [shop] in one dense mass'.

The cavalry rode round to our left flank, infantry to our right, and a column of at least 500 or 600 Galekas steadily advanced to our front. Then commenced one of the most deadly and raking fires that has, I think, ever been delivered this war. The artillery to our front and right flank dealing death by wholesale, if I might use the term. The infantry to front left, and rear, as we were then completely surrounded by, at the lowest average, 800 or 1,000 well armed Galekas who kept up on all sides a brisk fire until 8 p.m. The casualties on our side are; killed – Henry Philip Baron, P.A.V.G., shot through the head, and will be interred this morning. Six volunteers wounded . . . The enemy kept up the firing until 9 p.m., but the actual engagement only lasted until 8 p.m. I am thankful to say they were driven back at all points.

Around 10.30 p.m., Sub-Inspector Hatton arrived with some relief troops and Bourne was clearly very pleased to see him. The slightly enlarged force spent the whole night under arms in hollow square formation.

Bourne's ammunition was by now all but spent and he had lost many of his horses and cattle to the Gcaleka during the engagement. He sent a message to Ibeka requesting a supply of ammunition as soon as possible and noted that the Gcaleka were still in force in the vicinity and might resume the attack later in the day (the 3rd) if reinforcements were not sent. There were two postscripts to Bourne's report. The first requested medical assistance for the wounded, as 'we have no medical comforts, bandages, or anything of the kind.' The second was in a happier vein: 'Dr Hartley and everyone just arrived. Thanks. We can hold our own against these rascals, who are moving off now they see the reinforcements.'

A telegram from Griffith to Merriman dated 3 December advised that he had sent fifty FAMP to reinforce Bourne, together with Mfengu levies under Allan Maclean; Veldtman was also collecting his men to move there. It was in this telegram that Griffith first mooted the suggestion that 'it would be a good move to send "Active" to Mazeppa Bay with marines, also blue jackets.'[38]

It was now very clear that those Gcaleka who had surrendered to the authorities were in the minority and the rest were determined not to be driven from their homeland. The inevitable result of this fact, when it reached the ears of the colonists, was immediate panic. A report in Kei Road, not far from King William's Town, stated that inhabitants there threatened 'to take the law into their own hands and shoot every nigger found on their farms'.[39] Frere believed that Sarhili was with the rebellious Gcaleka and intended to bring his warriors across the Kei to join up with the Ngqika.

On 5 December, Griffith wrote to Cunynghame requesting an 'increase of 500 men – 300 infantry and 200 cavalry – to enable me to form a good camp in the heart of Gcalekaland . . .' He also repeated his request for a landing at Mazeppa Bay.[40]

After bringing up most of the 88th Regiment from Cape Town, in bits and pieces over several weeks, General Cunynghame found that they and the 24th were insufficient to provide the necessary protection for the colony. Once again, they were spread across the frontier in penny packets, interspersed with some volunteers.[41]

Arrival of the Naval Brigade

The shortage of troops was so serious that Cunynghame had to request the landing of a Naval Contingent from HMS *Active*. On 10 December, the ship left Cape Town in company with the hired steamship *Florence*, with the last two companies of the 88th on board.[42] The ships arrived at East London on the 13th and Commodore Sullivan went ashore to meet the governor and

General Cunynghame. There it was agreed that a Naval Contingent of about two hundred men would be put ashore at Mazeppa Bay with fifty men of the 88th.[43] The weather, however, intervened – the Mazeppa Bay expedition was cancelled and the whole force was landed at East London on 15 December. The Naval Brigade consisted of Commander H. T. Wright, commanding, with seven other officers, two clerks, 121 seamen, forty-two marines and twenty-three Kroomen, a total of 196 men.[44] Six twelve-pounder guns, two rocket tubes and a Gatling gun were also put ashore.[45] At the temporary camp at the railway terminus in the suburb of Panmure, Naval Surgeon Henry Norbury was given some sage advice by a veteran of an earlier war:

> The Kaffirs were all bad shots, and in consequence invariably fired high, and that the tall men were the only ones who ever got hit; indeed, all the men, without exception, that he had ever seen killed were tall men, and that I was certain to fall; he would give nothing for my chance of coming back.[46]

On the 16th, the Brigade, in company with about 150 men of the 88th Regiment, took the train to Kei Road and from there marched towards Draaibosch. After crossing the Gonubie River, about halfway to their destination, an order arrived to despatch two of the guns and a hundred men to Fort Cunynghame. The remainder marched on to Draaibosch, where stood 'a very fair hotel and in a valley close by, a detachment of the 88th Regiment . . .'[47] After lunch, they continued their march, arriving at Komgha late in the afternoon. Norbury described the town:

> Komgha is a place of some size, possessing two very good hotels, and three or four large general stores, in which almost anything may be bought; and there is a never-failing supply of good water. Most of the houses were surrounded by a double wall of planking about six feet in height, filled in between with earth, and loop-holed; this had been done by direction of the authorities, in view of the threatened Gaika rising. Numerous Europeans, with their families and goods, had fled thither, and were living in sheds or tents, and the surrounding country was covered with their cattle, which were regularly driven in at sunset. Near our camp was a barrack of the F.A.M.P.: we found that the low walls which surrounded it had been heightened by means of bags of earth, and loop-holed for musketry.[48]

Leaving behind two more guns and the Gatling gun for the town's defence, with ten seamen to man them, the Brigade left Komgha for the Kei River. They passed by Pullen's farm, located just before the long descent to the Kei

River. It had recently been placed in a state of defence by Lieutenant Edgar Anstey of the 24th and nearby rested fifty men of the 88th under Lieutenant Maurice Moore. The march continued down into the Kei River valley, then up and on to Toleni, arriving at Butterworth on Christmas Eve. The first building to be erected at Butterworth had been the mission station years before but now the town was more substantial:

> Butterworth is situated close to a small river [the Gcuwa]. There are a few European houses, the best of which is occupied by the Rev. Mr. Warner, a Wesleyan clergyman, whose church was close to his residence; there is a large store, a wine merchant's establishment, and great numbers of Fingo huts, which not only fringe the summits of the hills surrounding the place, but also occupy the major portions of the sides . . .[49]

On Christmas Day they set out on the last stage of their journey, an eleven-kilometre march to Ibeka, which was accomplished by mid-morning.

A Rift Develops

The shortage of troops had by now become acute, mounted men in particular. Mfengu levies had been drafted to the maximum and there was considerable reluctance to bring in Thembu levies. There was also a divergence of opinion between the governor's council and the Molteno government. Spicer says that 'Molteno and Merriman considered that Imperial troops were slow, cumbrous, expensive and unsuited to local conditions, and therefore rejected . . . Imperial reinforcements and an Imperial campaign.'[50] On the other hand, Frere, Cunynghame and Brownlee took the opposite view. Merriman was finally compelled, through the scarcity of local troops and in spite of his growing animosity towards Cunynghame, to agree to an imperial-led campaign. Merriman admitted, in a letter to Molteno, dated 15 December, which was designed to blunt the prime minister's criticism of him: 'You seem to think that I rush into the arms of the military but you little know what personal pain it causes me to have to confess that Griffith had blundered and that there seemed no course open but appointing some man [Cunynghame] and giving him the assistance he required . . .'[51]

In a letter to Carnarvon dated 12 December, Frere announced that he had appointed Colonel Glyn, 24th Regiment, to the command of all imperial troops in the Transkei,[52] effective from 9 December, although the only imperial soldiers there at that time were three detachments of the 24th, at Ibeka, Toleni and another further south at the Springs. Similarly, the FAMP were spread across the whole of the Transkei, one detachment even being on the east bank of the Mbashe near Mtentu.

At the same time, Colonel William Bellairs assumed command of all troops on the west bank of the Kei from Glyn.[53] To assist with the shortage of troops, two officers of the 24th lent their services in creating two new units. The two officers, however, were like chalk and cheese.

Brevet Lieutenant-Colonel Henry Burmester Pulleine had served with the regiment since 1855, mainly in an administrative capacity. He was a popular officer as a result of his gregarious nature, but he was an infantryman and a stolid infantryman at that. Pulleine recruited a group of unemployed East London louts to form an infantry unit called Pulleine's Rangers (or Lambs as they became derisively known).[54] (The commanding officer of No. 2 Company was Captain Charles R. St Leger Shervinton,[55] yet another officer who would take part in the Zulu War.)

Born in 1844, Lieutenant Frederick Carrington was a very different man from Pulleine. He was described as 'physically restless' and joined the 24th in May 1864, just before his twentieth birthday. The long periods of peace had encouraged him to take an interest in sports and he became an accomplished horseman. In 1875, rebellion in Griqualand West and the unwillingness of Prime Minister Molteno to send a party of FAMP there as a relief force, required that General Cunynghame make do with the resources at his disposal. In a rare stroke of brilliance, he created a troop of mounted infantry drawn from the 1/24th Regiment. Carrington's horsemanship and his association with Cape Town's Green Point Racecourse led to his appointment to the command of the innovative unit.

After three months in Griqualand West, the troop returned to the Cape, where they were disbanded. In late 1876, Carrington received a letter from General Cunynghame asking him to go to King William's Town to purchase horses for a new mounted unit. Within two weeks he and forty-two volunteers from the 24th were based at Komgha and patrolling the Kei River border near a bridge then under construction.

By early 1877, this unit was also threatened with disbandment but, with trouble threatening in the Transvaal, the troop was sent to Newcastle in Natal where Carrington established a training camp for mounted infantry units. While there, his troop was expanded to squadron size by taking more volunteers from the 3rd (the 'Buffs') and 13th regiments then in Pietermaritzburg. In spite of the fact that the squadron was drawn from several regiments, it was given cohesion by naming it 'Carrington's Horse'. The outbreak of the Ninth Frontier War brought Carrington's recall to the Cape Colony, where he was given the local rank of major and ordered to form a new mounted unit of volunteers, to be called the 'Frontier Light Horse'. It was a name that was to become the stuff of legend in South African military history.[56]

Sarhili and Sandile

It seems plain that Sarhili was responsible for the return of the Gcaleka to their homeland, whether he himself was present or not. It is also clear that he either ordered or condoned the attack on the FAMP at Holland's shop, but it is mere speculation to define what his intentions were in so doing. He must have known that the Transkei was to be settled by Europeans, and probably that Maphasa was also to be settled there, hence the threats. His intention was most likely to improve his negotiating position in any discussions which might follow if he were to surrender.

The paramount chief had, of course, maintained constant communication with Sandile but the latter, while himself being willing to fight, was unable to carry his councillors with him, most of whom preferred to remain aloof from the war despite the Makinana incident.[57]

The colonists' fear had not, however, abated and the Mfengu living within the colony became intensely arrogant as a result of their brothers' success across the Kei. This led the Ngqika to manifest their hostility towards them by stealing their cattle, acts which increased in number as the weeks passed.

On 19 December, Bhotomane and several other Gcaleka chiefs surrendered at Holland's shop, also indicating that a fearful Sarhili was seeking terms for his own submission. While the chiefs were anxious that Sarhili remain with his people, the government was determined that he should not. Thus the best terms that Glyn could offer was a guarantee of his personal safety, at the same time granting a six-day armistice while Bhotomane conveyed the government's terms to Sarhili.

A meeting was arranged between Sarhili and Colonel Eustace for 24 December near the burnt ruins of Holela, and the paramount chief arrived there on Christmas Day with a large armed bodyguard. Sarhili professed his wish for peace but said that the government's terms were very harsh and he saw no reason why he should not live in his own country. Eustace was unable to convince Sarhili otherwise and the meeting concluded without achieving anything. Also on Christmas Day, Cunynghame advised Bhotomane that there would be no further armistice and, with a price of five hundred cattle or £1,000 on Sarhili's head, preparations for Colonel Glyn's own Transkei campaign continued.[58]

Spicer rightly places considerable emphasis on the activities of Khiva, the aggressive Gcaleka chief who had played a prominent role in the earlier fighting. As Glyn's column moved forward through Gcalekaland, Khiva was forced southwards and became active near the Kei River.[59] Merriman was anxious that Khiva not be permitted to cross into the colony to make contact with the Ngqika but he managed to slip through the colonial net. Indeed, General Cunynghame himself was one of those who observed his progress, writing in his memoirs:

> On the following morning [22 December] at six, when starting for the river, I was informed that Kiva, a noted warrior of the Galekas, had crossed the Kei with a large force, and that he was but a few miles in my front.
>
> All the cavalry and mounted men that I had were but a few orderlies, and not more than eight mounted police could be assembled.
>
> With this force my aide-de-camp and Major Moore advanced to the frontier between the Komgha and the river . . .
>
> The few police under Major Moore came up with the rear of Kiva's force just as they were entering Murderer's Kop, but could do little more than watch their movements. Thus this dangerous character had crossed into the colony, as he could not have done had a sufficient force of mounted burghers been stationed in the positions I had indicated long before.[60]

When they heard of Cunynghame's own failure, Molteno and Merriman added this incident to their arsenal of criticism.

Charles Brownlee issued a telegraphic alert on 23 December to William Wright and other civil commissioners regarding Khiva's movements:

> Kiva, an influential Galeka chief, is reported to be near junction of Kei and Kabousie, with a small party. He may attempt to move into some place in the Gaika location. A sharp look out should be kept to stop and arrest him, if necessary by force of arms; and he or any of his party who resist may be shot. Be careful and make no mistake as to persons.[61]

Spicer analyses Khiva's movements relative to those of other chiefs, including Sarhili. He argues that the surrender of Bhotomane, and the subsequent failure of Sarhili to convince Eustace to allow him to stay with his people, may well have caused him to send Khiva on a mission to recruit the Ngqika to his cause. He therefore concludes that Khiva's was not an independent mission: the paramount sent him to make contact with Sandile.[62]

Lieutenant Craigie, RN, commanding the naval contingent based at Fort Cunynghame, accompanied Wright to a meeting with Sandile at the chief's Great Place on the Kabousie River on 24 December and his report is sufficiently detailed to record the conversation between the two men. Sandile admitted that Khiva had been to see him but said that whatever message he had passed had been referred to four other chiefs for their opinion. This would be given in the next few days. Wright stressed the danger in delay and stated that 'Armed parties might be in search and might come into collision, in so doing, with the Gaikas.' The meeting ended after further fruitless discussion, and without Wright learning the content of Khiva's message.[63]

According to another report, Siwani, a son of Mdushane, had gone to see Brownlee and there stated that three messengers had come to his homestead from Sandile on 26 December. Their message was:

> that Kreli had sent to Sandilli to say that he been abandoned by his friends and chiefs across the Kei, and had now resolved to die, that it was his intention to cross the Kei and fight, and that he intended first to attack the Komgha, that he had appointed Kiva to be his representative, that he did not seek for peace but intended to fight, that Sandilli and Kreli's subjects, i.e., the Kafirs on this side of the Kei, were to be ready to join and assist him. The messenger further informed me that Kiva was on the Galeka side of the Kei, and was in communication with Sandilli, and that Sandilli sent to report this to me, desiring me to report the matter to Jali [Tyali], Sujolo [Siyolo], and W. Kama. The messengers did not inform me what answer Sandilli had returned to Kreli, but said that Sandilli was at his kraal near the Kei and Ruhusi [Kabusi] junction and had a number of armed men with him. The messengers informed me that they were directed to lose no time in returning, and they imagined that there would be an outbreak before they got back.[64]

Also on Christmas Eve, Commandant Edward Yewd Brabant was tracking some stolen cattle on the banks of the Gonubie River and was hindered by some men of the Gqunukhwebe. He withdrew because he was substantially outnumbered. The special magistrate for Tamacha, Richard Tainton, persuaded Brabant not to return to seize the cattle and offered to mediate.[65] Accordingly, he, his brother John Tainton and Field Cornet W. Brown of the divisional police, with some fifty of his Mfengu policemen, went to the location. They found the offending homestead and were promised that the cattle would be returned. Tainton and his men returned to their camp on the Kwelerha River where, shortly afterwards, they were confronted by a number of armed men from the homestead they had just visited. The Mfengu police bolted, leaving the three white men to be murdered.[66] The offending Gqunukhwebe sent their cattle across the Kei and joined the Ngqika war party.

It would be pertinent here to enlarge briefly upon the relationship at this point in time between the governor and John Merriman – in particular the latter's assumption of the unofficial role of minister for war. In a despatch dated 4 December, Frere noted:

> I should not omit to record my sense of the degree in which the services of the forces in the field were aided and supported by the unflagging energy and quick intelligence of the Honourable Mr. Merriman, the Commissioner of Crown Lands, who was charged by Mr. Molteno and his colleagues in the Ministry with the civil duties which usually devolve on a Minister for the War Department.[67]

On 26 December, Frere included mention of the minister in another despatch to the Colonial Secretary: 'I cannot speak too highly of the ability and energy shown by the Honourable Mr Merriman for months past, whilst he has been discharging the usual functions of a Minister for War and Police on this frontier.'[68]

A further indication of pending escalation of the war was reported on 28 December:

> On Christmas Day, Sandilli, with great consideration and perhaps some kindly feeling towards the man at whose house he had enjoyed so many pleasant drinking bouts, sent warning to the owner of the hotel and store at Draibosch [sic] (a station about thirty-five miles on the main road between King William's Town and the Transkei), telling him to 'trek', as he proposed to burn his place the next night.
>   The Draibosch hotel and store was accordingly sacked and burnt, and news was spread through the colony that the Gaikas had at last broken out, and that our communications with the Transkei were cut off.[69]

Two farmhouses in the area were also burnt down, and a white trader was killed.[70]

Whether or not Sandile was directly responsible for this act, he must have realised that action against the colonial Mfengu would bring the British authorities to support them, just as they had supported the Transkei Mfengu against the depredations of the Gcaleka just a couple of months earlier.

White attitudes towards the colonial Mfengu were ambivalent. On one hand they urged that, like the Mfengu in the Transkei, they should be armed. On the other hand, when they found that the stock and divisional police introduced by Merriman were Mfengu, they were highly indignant. Spicer sums up the position of the Ngqika thus:

Open rebellion for the Ciskeian blacks was, in their fragmented, depressed and weak state, an act of desperation. While it was clear from the Makinana affair that resistance would be offered to any threat to the people and their property by the colonists, it required some striking act or success by the Gcaleka to kindle the flame of open rebellion.[71]

The Draaibosch developments were confirmed in two short telegrams from Komgha, both dated 29 December. The first reported incidents involving the Ngqika:

The Draaibosch Hotel was burnt down last night.

A Mr. Smith, trading for Mr. Hedding at Shiniki was killed by Gaikas yesterday. The late Josias de Kok's house, three miles from this village, is on fire.

The police mail was stopped this morning between this and Draaibosch, and had to return.

The Gaikas are taking cattle off the out-span.[72]

The second report was more menacing, noting a clash between Ngqika and police in which one of the latter was killed:

An engagement with police has taken place at Mr. Nicholas de Kok's, near Draaibosch. Major Moore was wounded through the arm, one policeman killed. The patrol is supposed to have killed 20 Gaikas. Commandant Cowie was present, and all behaved splendidly.

A Fingo wagon has been found at Draaibosch, with driver killed, and the oxen taken.[73]

Battles of Draaibosch

The first telegram above notes that the mail between Komgha and Draaibosch had been interrupted by groups of Ngqika. This was the more serious because vital government mail between King William's Town and the Transkei was also affected.

On 29 December, about 1 p.m., a patrol consisting of thirty-two men of the FAMP under Sub-Inspector Mitchell, and all under the command of Brevet Major Hans Garrett Moore, 88th Regiment, left Komgha for Draaibosch with the intention of securing the passage of the mails. Just over ten kilometres (Moore says four miles but this must be incorrect) west of Komgha, he turned right off the road, passing by de Kok's house, which had been burnt down a few hours earlier. Moore took a patrol, which paused on a nearby hill, to secure their route and Moore noted a number of armed Ngqika (for so they proved to be) on the further slope. He called on the nearest of them to lay down their arms and was answered by a shot from a man some thirty or forty metres away from him. The rest of the FAMP came forward, upon which the Africans retired down the hill towards the Kabusi River, followed by the dismounted police in skirmishing order.

The men remounted and Moore led them about fifteen hundred metres closer to Draaibosch, where he again took up a position on another eminence. From there he saw another body of Ngqika approaching from the Kabusi River, trying to get to Moore's left. Once again, his dismounted police formed a skirmishing line and drove the Ngqika off, towards the river.

He then remounted his men once more and, turning sharply to the left, proceeded towards Draaibosch to meet an ammunition convoy bound for Komgha, accompanied by Lieutenant Wood and forty men of the 88th Regiment. After a further three kilometres his right troop came upon a body of three hundred Ngqika who were advancing in their direction. The troop dismounted to receive them but after firing a few shots they were forced to retire. The Ngqika quickly followed them up and were able to seize one man, who was dismounted, and killed him. Moore tried, but was unable, to retrieve the body of this man, Private Giese.

Moore continued his movement and the Ngqika disengaged, for shortly afterwards the party met with Deputy Commissary Strickland, Lieutenant Wood and the convoy, who had hastened towards him on hearing the firing.[74] Moore's self-effacing report makes light of this last incident but he was subsequently awarded the Victoria Cross for attempting to rescue Private Giese. The citation reads:

> Major, now Brevet Lieutenant Colonel Hans Garrett Moore, late of the 88th Regiment, when 2nd in Command of a Detachment of Frontier Armed Mounted Police on the occasion of the action with the Gaikas near Komgha fought on the 29th December 1877, observed, when a small body of Mounted Police were forced to retire before overwhelming numbers of the enemy, that Private Giese was unable to mount his horse and was left at their mercy.
>
> Seeing his danger Major Moore rode back alone into the midst of the enemy in order to rescue him and did not desist in his endeavour until Private Giese was killed, he himself having shot two Kaffirs and received an assegai wound in the arm in his attempt to save the man.[75]

It was not the only act of courage on the field that day. Moore's report goes on to commend the bravery of Colour-Sergeant Harber and Corporal

Court, both of whom attempted to rescue Giese while he was surrounded by warriors. 'Harber further distinguished himself by halting, when the enemy were within a few yards, and taking up behind him Private Martindale, whose horse had broken loose, thus saving him from sharing the same fate as Private Giese.'

Such a feat might prove sufficient for some men but Moore was in action again on the following day. Once again he set off from Komgha towards Draaibosch, in command of forty men of the 88th under Captain Acklom, and twenty-one FAMP troopers under Sub-Inspector White.[76] As the party proceeded, Moore noted the presence of many Ngqika scouts on ridge tops on both sides of the road. Ten kilometres from Komgha, as they approached Savage's shop, where Moore had met with Strickland the previous day, he found large bodies of Ngqika collected about fifteen hundred metres away on the right (north) side of the road. Expecting an imminent attack, he took up a position 'on the crown of a hill about half a mile beyond Savage's shop and close to the road'.

He extended his infantry behind some rough ground and prolonged the line by using half of the police dismounted. The remainder of the police, also dismounted, guarded the wagons in the rear. 'We were not kept long in suspense as to the enemy's intentions, for about the time our arrangements were completed about 600 footmen and 50 mounted men . . . were seen advancing rapidly and in perfect order.'

The tiny force opened fire at five hundred yards and the bullocks ran off with the ammunition cart. As they continued their advance, the Ngqika threw off large bodies to left and right to attack the flanks. Some also continued towards the rear, where they took the ammunition cart.

The engagement lasted from 2.15 p.m. to 3.45 p.m. with the Ngqika sometimes coming within assegai range. Moore ominously noted that not many were thrown, most of the warriors being armed 'with guns and rifles'. The loss of the reserve ammunition caused a severe problem because each man had only forty rounds on their person. To conserve his dwindling supply, Moore resorted to repeated bayonet charges, 'before which the enemy always gave way'. Eventually, the Ngqika tired and withdrew the way they had come. Moore then continued on his way, halting when he reached Savage's shop. About 4.15 p.m., he met with a relief force of the 88th under Lieutenant-Colonel Lambert.

Moore's losses were again quite heavy, losing two men killed and two men wounded, with another two missing. These latter were the men with the ammunition cart.[77] One aspect of the last action which is seldom mentioned is the inexperience of the soldiers of the 88th Regiment. It had only recently arrived in South Africa and consisted of mainly very young men. A week later, Colonel Bellairs, commanding troops in the Ciskei, wrote an illuminating comment on this fight:

> The fact that over 600 of the enemy were, in the latter action [of the 30th] driven off by a mere handful of very young soldiers, imperfectly trained in the use of their weapons, cannot be without good effect on the troops generally, and tend to give them confidence in themselves and in their arms. Its disheartening influence on the enemy must be great.[78]

In July 1878, Charles Brownlee wrote a concise biography of Sandile, probably as the result of the Ngqika chief's death a month earlier. With reference to the identity of those who had participated in the attack on Moore and his party on 29 January, and the extent of Sandile's involvement, he wrote:

> He also appears up to December [1877] to have been opposed to the rising of the Galekas, but in December there appears to have been a yielding to the war party by accepting a share of the cattle captured by the rebels from Colonial farmers and loyal natives, and when Kiva crossed the Kei on the 26th December, as Kreli's representative, Sandilli at once gave in [sic] his adhesion to Creli [sic] by sending Gamna, his right hand son, to join Kiva, whom he immediately afterwards joined in one of his raids into Fingoland; furthermore a number of Sandilli's people had joined Makinnon and Kiva in an attack on a small detachment of the 88th Regiment under Major Moore at Sangi's [Savage's] shop on the 28th [sic] December.[79]

On 31 December, at the suggestion of Brownlee,[80] who hoped to exploit any rift in the Ngqika leadership, Wright invited all the Ngqika chiefs who wished to distance themselves from the conflict to meet him at the Emgwali mission station and there register their alignment with the government. A number of them appeared – including Tyali and a son and nephew of Maqoma, Kona and Feni, together with their followers – and were duly registered as non-combatants.[81]

Chapter 7

A Crisis of Government

The resignation of the ministry was announced this morning.

Cape Times, 4 February 1878

We have already noted that on 17 June 1872 the constitution of the colony of the Cape of Good Hope was changed to embrace what is known as 'responsible government'. That is a phrase that assumes vital importance in what is to follow and for that reason alone it deserves a definition. Quite simply, it means that the prime minister and his ministers are collectively responsible for their actions to the parliament, and through it, to the people.

This most important change in the constitutional government of the colony greatly altered the relationship between the head of the Cape government, the prime minister, and the head of state representing the sovereign, the governor. In the light of the political crisis soon to develop, it is important to note the key phrase pertaining to this form of government, and the relationship between these two men: 'the head of state rules only with the advice of the government.'

The first prime minister of the Cape of Good Hope, John Charles Molteno, arrived in King William's Town on 9 January 1878,[1] where he had a series of long discussions with the governor. The prime minister expressed a wish that Frere return quickly to Cape Town but the governor thought 'while his presence was considered desirable by the military authorities, he did not think it could be consistent with his duty to leave the frontier.'

It is not a coincidence that, after Molteno's arrival, the daily informal meetings between the governor and his two ministers, at which executive and military decisions had previously been made, were discontinued.

Until this time, the Ministers present on the frontier had met the Governor in council, and no formal minutes had passed between them. Now, however,

Mr Molteno said that it was no longer possible to act in this manner. The proceedings must be conducted in the proper constitutional method and minutes between the Governor and the Prime Minister must embody the final decisions, whatever informal conversations might take place in the first instance.[2]

Molteno argued that this was constitutional practice but ever since he had adopted this method of proceeding, the governor had resented it, calling it 'being placed in quarantine'. The prime minister's argument for the changed method of proceeding was simply this:

> The Sovereign, or Governor in the Sovereign's place, communicates with the Cabinet through its Prime Minister, and not with individual members of the Cabinet; much less is the Sovereign present at the discussions of the Cabinet. If Ministers were to act constitutionally at all, and to be responsible for their advice, this was the only possible procedure. The informal method on the other hand suited the Governor admirably, as he was thus able to impress his views on weaker members of the Cabinet and obtain their support as against their colleagues, and so divide the Cabinet and enable his own views to prevail.[3]

It was a telling argument in favour of the governor's actions being dependent solely upon the advice of his prime minister.

Very soon thereafter, the prime minister advised Frere that he (Molteno) had authorised the formation of two columns, for an attack on the Ngqika in the southern part of their location.

> Commandant Frost was . . . to take a position . . . between the sources of the Bolo and Umquali rivers, and to operate thence in a southerly direction assisted by Captain Rorke, who was to cross from Fingoland, the object being to sweep that part of the location where Sandilli and those Gaikas and Islambies [Ndlambe] who had joined in rebellion were said to be with Kiva and the Galekas who had invaded the Colony.[4]

This was similar to an operation planned some time earlier by Colonel Bellairs, which had to be postponed because of the delay caused by Wright being unable to complete his registration of loyal Ngqika in time. The delay was also attributed to the unavailability of burgher and Mfengu forces, for which several requests had been made to the colonial government by Bellairs, but which had not been satisfied.[5]

Bellairs himself commented on the planned operation, in which he noted: 'To attack the enemy with an imperfectly organised column in the manner proposed by the Colonial Government would, in my opinion, be unwise, and even should the operation not lead to failure, would certainly be calculated to cause unnecessary bloodshed.'[6] Bellairs added that an imperial operation would be opened in the Tyityaba (Chichaba) Valley in a few days' time and all available troops in the Komgha area would be involved. He concluded that there would be serious disadvantages to the colony from 'a dual system of commands and operations in the field'.

The governor pointed out to Molteno the risks involved in embarking on such 'isolated operations entrusted to several independent leaders, under no one general head, and with very feeble and imperfect attempts at com-bination and co-operation'. He also reminded the prime minister that by withholding the requested Mfengu levies, he essentially rejected the benefit the operation might derive from the use of regular infantry and artillery, thereby reducing imperial troops to 'compulsory inaction'. Molteno would not be persuaded, averring that the burgher forces would not serve under the command of any but their own officers, nor co-operate with imperial troops. The governor noted that, while he had not been officially informed of the fact, Commandant John Frost was to operate entirely under the orders of the colonial government and was not subject to the imperial mili-tary authorities.[7]

Inconvenient Superfluities

Sir Bartle Frere issued a minute to his ministers on 11 January concerning the intention of the colonial government to embark on these operations. In the last paragraph of the minute the governor made mention of the fact that he had been advised that morning by Molteno that 'the Cabinet desired an operation on this side of the Kei, to be entrusted exclusively to Colonial officers and Colonial forces, unfettered by any co-operation or control from Her Majesty's officers and forces.'[8]

Captain Henry Hallam Parr was at that time serving as military secretary to Frere and allegedly told the governor that he no longer wished to collaborate with Merriman, who was now completely absorbed in his role of unofficial minster for war. In a letter to Merriman, dated 14 January, Frere stated: 'He [Parr] quite agrees with me that, considering the new position taken up by you with regard to all military matters, his continuing to attempt to assist you would place you both in a very undesirable position.'[9] In his own published story of the war, and the later Zulu War, Parr makes no mention of this incident, so one might infer either discretion on Parr's part or that it was at Frere's suggestion that his military secretary took this action.

Merriman sent back a note questioning Frere's meaning of the term 'new position' in his note about Parr. This gave the governor the opportunity to make known his views on the developing situation, a position which would certainly be conveyed to Molteno.

> Since Friday [11 January, three days after Molteno's arrival] my position has in no wise, as far as any action of mine is concerned, been altered; but you and Brownlee have kept aloof, have withdrawn such information and assistance as you used to afford me, and treat the Governor, Commander-in-Chief and High Commissioner, and all Forces and Departments which take their orders through him, if not as rivals, as inconvenient superfluities, whose absence would improve your prospects in suppressing this rebellion. This is the 'new position' you have taken up, and to which I referred.[10]

There is an interesting anecdote regarding the cooling between the governor and Merriman, recording the chill the latter had sensed in his relations with Frere. It is also a valuable look past the formality of the correspondence, showing the actors in our drama as human beings. A letter from Merriman's wife Agnes to her mother-in-law, dated 19 February, relates the following:

> Up to December [Frere] was on terms of the warmest friendship with us, when Jack began to notice a slight coolness towards him, which ripened and at last the cool manner became an insulting one, which reached its height one day when Jack went up to His Excellency's quarters to introduce Sir Henry Tyler . . . He left Sir H.T. in a room downstairs and went up to His Excellency's apartments – was met by H.E. in the passage who said in a very offensive way without waiting to hear what Jack had come for, 'Come in here', and was led into a sitting-room where Colonel Bellairs and Mr. Littelton [Hon. W. Littleton, Frere's secretary] were sitting. Without another word the Governor immediately began abusing Jack before these two for not having given him, or rather the General, some Fingo levy which he said had been promised. His tone and manner was so insulting that Jack very calmly said, 'I think, Sir, what you have to say had better be put on paper and I think it is time I left the room', or words to that effect. The Governor in a towering passion bade him 'sit down' – and upon his continuing his tirade Jack withdrew and bowed himself out of the room. This was his last private interview with His Excellency.[11]

On 12 January, Frere issued a further minute to his ministers, in which he declined 'all responsibility for enterprises undertaken with what seems to me great want of precaution'.[12] He continued:

> It is unnecessary for me to add that Her Majesty's forces will everywhere do their best to assist when they know what is to be done, but to enable them to do this, it is quite necessary to know who is in command? Who directs the general operations? What power have Commandants Frost, Schermbrucker, Rorke, Surmon, Brabant, and the Commandant of the Tarkastad volunteers, to direct co-operation other than in the way that any officer commanding a detachment may ask another to exercise his discretion and give him aid?

From Rift to Chasm

The breach between Molteno and the governor deepened from 12 January. On the previous day, Frere had held another long meeting with the prime minister and subsequently wrote a letter enclosing a copy of the notes he had made about the matters under discussion. He now asked that Molteno 'run his eye over the note I made, and let me know whether it accurately represents the conclusions you expressed to me'.[13] It is worthwhile to reproduce here at least a part of those notes, for a fuller understanding of current Cape government thinking.

1. There is a strong impression in the Colony that the conduct of military operations has been entrusted too exclusively to military men, and that the management of affairs has passed too much from the hands of the colonial ministry, into those of officers of Her Majesty's service, in whose ability to manage them economically, and efficiently, the Colony has less confidence than it has in its ministers.
2. That the result of this feeling has been to impede a ready response to the call for reinforcements.
3. That ministers are quite competent themselves, to do with Colonial forces, all that is now required to restore peace and order to the Colony.
4. That to enable them to do this it is desirable that the operations of Her Majesty's forces should be confined to the Transkei, leaving operations in the Colony entirely to Colonial forces under the direct control of the ministry.
5. That the reinforcement of Her Majesty's troops asked for by the Governor in his communication with the Secretary of State for the Colonies, are not needed for any Colonial purpose in this Colony.

6. That Commandant Griffith should be brought back as soon as possible to this side the Kei, for duty under the direct control of the Colonial Government.

Frere remarked that he was ready to accept the fourth point but pointed out that it was necessary to 'retain their present positions at King William's Town and on the Kei Road in order to secure communications with the Transkei'. He also accepted the fifth proposition, with the proviso that the government was able to raise sufficient forces to put down the Ngqika rebellion and to prevent its spread, which the governor rather doubted.[14]

On 12 January, Molteno returned the governor's notes unread, stating in his reply:

I cannot help thinking that it will be exceedingly inconvenient to introduce so entirely new and novel a mode of procedure as that of reducing to writing and formally placing on record, conversations necessarily of so confidential and delicate a character as those in many cases which must take place between the Governor and Prime Minister of the Colony.[15]

There now ensued a series of exchanges in which Molteno, after a 'cursory glance' at the governor's notes, continued to object to the recording of conversations between them, while Frere insisted that it was perfectly normal 'between men of business, or official persons, when the interlocutors are, as in my case, anxious to be accurate in their conception and recollection of the conclusions stated by either party'.[16]

In his second response, of 14 January, Frere said that he had no wish to discuss the practice of cabinet councils any further but had chosen the one means by which 'two men can talk for four hours on very important subjects and make sure they have accurately understood each other's conclusions'. He then set out what he believed to be the salient points of their original conversation – it was a formidable list:

That the slackness of Colonists to answer the call for reinforcements was due to an impression that the management of affairs had been left too much to the military, that as a remedy you proposed to exclude the military from all active share in the operations in the Colony; that you did not wish Her Majesty's troops to be at once withdrawn from the Colony, but simply to remain inactive where they are, till relieved by Colonial forces; that, ultimately, they were to be all withdrawn, and the Colony to be defended exclusively by Colonial forces; that you were well assured the Colonial forces actually coming up were ample for these purposes; that you wished me to countermand any demand I had made to Her Majesty's Government to send out two regiments in anticipation of the usual reliefs, and to prepare the Secretary of State for the entire evacuation of the country by her Majesty's troops; that for the more vigorous prosecution of measures to suppress rebellion, you would abandon the plan of united action under one head, which we have hitherto followed here since the first outbreak; that the Colonial Cabinet would undertake the management of all Colonial forces entirely uncontrolled by any reference to military authority; these were some of the important conclusions at which, in our conversations on Friday and Saturday I understood you to say the Cabinet had arrived, and regarding which I was naturally anxious I should be under no mistake, more especially as I must address the Secretary of State on the subject by next mail.

The sting lay in the final paragraph:

I am sorry to trouble you at such length, but the subjects are far too important to be dealt with cursorily, and I trust you will give what I have written more than a cursory glance. I am bound not to misunderstand you. I am bound to tell the Secretary of State of any change in contemplation so important as the evacuation of the Colony by Her Majesty's troops, or any change which has taken place so momentous as the exclusion of the Colonial forces from military command, and the substitution of many leaders and generals and plans of operation for one; and I am bound, when I see danger from such changes to warn you of it, though I do not wish to dictate in any way as to the course your duty to the country requires.[17]

On that same day, 14 January, Commandant Griffith had been recalled from the Transkei. On 18 January, Frere received a minute from his ministers in Cape Town recommending that Charles D. Griffith, commanding the FAMP, be appointed commandant-general of colonial forces, effective from the 15th.[18] According to Percy Molteno, this appointment was in response to a suggestion by Frere, in a telegram dated 18 December 1877, for the appointment of 'an officer with very large powers' if he were to accede to the advice of his ministers to return to Cape Town. On 16 December, he had suggested Griffith as the officer to be appointed to the post and the prime minister had agreed, it being in accord with his own view.[19]

On the 21st, Frere approved the appointment 'in anticipation' of a reply to his reference to the prime minister 'to ascertain what duties it was proposed to entrust' to the new appointee. There were now two commanders of forces in the colony: Commandant-General Griffith commanding colonial troops and Colonel Bellairs, acting for General Cunynghame then in the Transkei, commanding the imperial troops.[20]

Frere's note of 14 January gave the prime minister pause. It was not until 19 January that he responded by personally handing a letter to Frere on that day, the tone of his letter being in marked contrast to those preceding it. He made it clear that the proposals in the letter were simply that, and were of a 'tentative character, subject in all respects to such modification and alterations as may be considered necessary by your Excellency'. It went on, however, 'the principal not being lost sight of . . . of separating the command and direction of Colonial forces from that of Her Majesty's troops, the former being under the direction of the Colonial Commandant-General'.[21]

The letter principally referred to comments made earlier by General Cunynghame on various military matters, with almost all of which Molteno now agreed. He noted that Commandant-General Griffith concurred with 'the number of infantry and cavalry necessary' to occupy Gcalekaland – to the extent that he proposed that, rather than withdrawing all FAMP forces to the colony, he would leave three hundred of them there under military control. The remaining colonial forces, mainly burgher volunteers, would be withdrawn.

He also agreed with the general that 'troops cannot garrison posts [in the] Transkei till the line of railway from East London to the Kei Road, and along that road to Toleni is held by forces at least equal in number and composition to the troops which at present hold it.' Griffith was to liaise with Cunynghame on the implementation of this process.

The prime minister was 'very sensible of the kind and cordial manner in which Sir A. Cunynghame has responded to the enquiries and suggestions' which he had made to the general and expressed the wish to work 'cordially and harmoniously with the military authorities'. He added that there was no wish 'at the present moment' to discuss the evacuation of imperial troops from the colony to the Transkei, other than those movements thought necessary by the general. Nevertheless, and in spite of the genial tone of the letter, Molteno could not resist adding that it would become necessary, within the colonial boundary, to withdraw military control, placing all colonial forces under Griffith.[22]

Frere submitted the letter to Bellairs, in his capacity as deputy adjutant-general, for his comments. For himself, he wrote a provocative minute on 22 January which said that he had not entirely understood Molteno's intention, asking whether 'Mr Griffith, as Commandant-General, shall now take command of all Colonial forces . . . under the General Commanding the Forces, and the Governor, as Commander-in-Chief in the Colony'.[23] Thus did he set another hare running regarding his own position as commander-in-chief.

Molteno's terse response to this minute, on the same day, was unequivocal, and was, perhaps, more distasteful because the prime minister referred to himself in the third person. The key paragraphs read:

> Mr. Molteno's proposals to be acted upon at once, and with regard to the future, to continue until alterations may be found necessary.
>
> For the present, subject, of course, to any alterations Parliament may determine upon, it is proposed that Mr. Griffith, as Commandant-General, shall take command of all Colonial forces, police, burghers, and volunteers, and be under the sole control and direction of the Colonial Government.
>
> Governor has no special powers over Colonial forces as Commander-in-Chief, but as Governor of the Colony acts in exactly the same manner with regard to Colonial forces as he does with regard to any other Colonial matter.[24]

The governor wrote an extensive reply to the two Molteno memoranda on 26 January, in which he stated that he was unable 'to concur in their proposals as far as I understand them'. He went on to remark that, for present purposes the proposals were 'far too violent, impracticable, and unconstitutional' while, for future purposes, they were 'quite inadequate'.[25] He made the first mention of the threat of possible illegality in their actions, observing:

> I would further ask Mr Molteno to consider that what he proposes to do appears to me to be entirely unconstitutional and illegal, and that it must inevitably expose all who act in accordance with his suggestions to legal penalties, of which it would be difficult to predict the extent, and from which it will not be easy for Parliament to protect the parties concerned by any general act of indemnity.

Frere went on to describe the constitutional instruments of the colony as being: the governor, 'who is also Commanding-in-Chief and High Commissioner'; a lieutenant-governor (General Cunynghame) and the Executive Council. This latter consisted of the premier and the colonial secretary (both positions held by Molteno); the treasurer-general (Dr H.D. White); the attorney-general (thirty-three-year-old Andries Stockenström, the youngest son of Sir Andries Stockenström); the commissioner of Crown lands and public works (Merriman) and the secretary for native affairs (Brownlee).

The governor noted that while there was no formally appointed minister for war or police, both positions were held de facto by Merriman, 'but in no case . . . have the large ministerial duties combined in that important office been considered to include either the personal command of troops in the field or the independent power to direct military operations in the field, without reference to or control by either the Commander-in-Chief or the General Officer commanding in the field.' This was a remarkable volte-face when one considers the previous statements made by the governor regarding Merriman's portfolio.

Citing quotations from his own commission as governor, Frere wrote that the 'clear intention of the constitution' was that there should be only one person, the governor and commander-in-chief, in command of military forces of every kind, colonial as well as imperial, performing all executive duties through a commander of the forces.

The governor covered this ground in tedious detail but then went on to excoriate Molteno for proposing 'to invest an office, to be created by himself, unknown as yet to Parliament and the constitution, and unsanctioned by law, with powers of supreme command over all Colonial forces, entirely independent . . . of all control and subordination to the Governor or any other executive military of civil officer, recognised by Parliament or the constitution.'

He next asked to whom the new officer so created was responsible. It was clearly not to the governor, nor to the general commanding the forces, for Mr Molteno had said so, nor to the parliament 'for Parliament has never heard of him'. The fact was, for the previous ten days, executive control of all military operations had rested entirely with the commissioner for Crown lands and public works, and, as far as he had heard, was to remain so.

Frere then requested that should Molteno remained unconvinced by the governor's words, he should seek formal legal advice on the matter from the attorney-general. He went on to issue a warning as to the possible legal consequences which could follow from pursuing this course.

The governor concluded his remarks by noting that before Molteno's arrival in King William's Town, affairs had proceeded in a 'legal and constitutional manner' and asked that the old method continue to be used, rather than the system proposed by the prime minister.[26] It was at this point that the rift between governor and prime minister became a chasm, and it was immediately recognised by Merriman:

When we received the Minute we felt at once that for the first time a serious difference had arisen; I thought everything was going as merry as a marriage bell till the 26th of January. Then we saw that a difference of opinion had arisen. On the Monday morning my honourable friend the member for Beaufort [Molteno] came to me and said, 'I see no answer to this: there is a difference of opinion between the Governor and my Ministry. I see no answer but resignation.' . . . He then went up to the Governor on the Monday to resign. When he came back I said, 'Well, what has taken place? Have we to pack our portmanteaus?' He said, 'No, not at all; the Governor would not hear of resignation. This memorandum, His Excellency said, is merely the basis for discussion; it is a subject upon which he wishes to get the Attorney-General's opinion, and he desires me to send it to the Attorney-General.' This was done . . . the resignation was withdrawn, and for the next few days things went on somewhat as usual.[27]

A serious deficiency in Molteno's policy of an independent military command was reflected in a criticism by Deputy Commissary-General Edward Strickland, amply demonstrating the practical difficulties of the policy, and the lack of infrastructure that should have accompanied it. On 21 January, he wrote a memorandum to the surveyor-general of ordnance in London, in which he observed:

> To my great surprise I have just learnt that the Colonial Government are suddenly raising volunteer corps on their own account, which they are sending into the field on their own responsibility and under their own orders. They are to act entirely independent of the General, and are not in fact to be under his orders. They are supposed to be rationed by a Colonial commissariat. I say supposed, as from the enclosed correspondence . . . a sudden demand is made upon one of my depots by one of these corps, of the existence of which I am not officially aware, for a large supply of rations and forage as their own commissariat could not supply them.[28]

He enclosed a copy of a note from Deputy Commissary Warneford at Komgha: 'A large body of mounted volunteers from Queenstown have applied for rations, and being without any provision for themselves I have under Departmental Order of 8th December issued one day's rations pending your sanction. These men are not under orders of the Imperial authorities.'[29] Strickland continued his memorandum:

> The Colonial commissariat has already twice broken down – (1st), in their campaign across the Kei; and (2nd), in rationing the Fingo levies. Both times I have had to take over the supply of these troops. Now, while everything is going on right, the Colonial Government hampers my arrangements by bidding against me in the South African markets, and raising the price of everything; by borrowing my transport when their own breaks down, and, as I have shown above, by suddenly demanding the supplies which I have collected for the Imperial troops.

Strickland also wrote in similar vein to Sir Bartle Frere personally, under the same date of 16 January, in which he stated that he had been advised that 'Captain Mills in Cape Town has directions to purchase biscuit and forage (for Colonial Government) which was playing mischief with the market . . .' He argued that the competition from such colonial purchases was driving up the price of everything in the market, citing the example of mealies, which had risen from fifteen shillings to thirty or thirty-two shillings per hundred pounds weight, over a period of only three weeks. 'It is right that I brought it to the notice of your Excellency that in protection of Imperial interests it is needful that strong measures should be adopted to arrest a system as vicious as it is extravagant and mischievous.'[30]

On 29 January, Frere sent a telegram to London, advising that the Ngqika location had been 'repeatedly traversed by burgher and Fingo forces' and the rebels had been defeated with a heavy loss of stock. Sandile had escaped, presumably southwards. More disturbing, however, was the news that Frost's operations had spread into the Thembu location where Civil Commissioner Hemming had defeated Gungubele.[31]

Frere wrote a report to Lord Carnarvon on 30 January 1878, in which he epitomised for the Colonial Secretary the protocol which Molteno advocated for his government's dealings with the governor:

His view of the proper action of responsible Government, as far as I can understand it, is that all matters of policy and all measures of importance are to be settled by the Cabinet, in separate consultation, without the Governor being present; that the Premier is to be the sole medium of communication between the Cabinet and the Governor on such matters, direct communication between the Governor and any other Cabinet Minister being only permissible on matters of departmental detail not involving any question of policy or principle; that the meetings of the Executive Council are simply for the formal registration of measures decided only by the Cabinet and sanctioned by the Governor, at which the attendance of the Commander of the Forces is generally unnecessary and inconvenient, and that anything like discussion of measures at the meetings of the Executive Council is, if not absolutely prohibited, so likely to be embarrassing that it is to be avoided as far as possible.[32]

Frere convened a meeting of the Executive Council on 1 February in order to discuss a minute which he had distributed to ministers the previous day, 31 January,[33] and to hear a statement by General Cunynghame. This minute was still another of Frere's verbose documents which repeated much of what had gone before: he criticised the attacks in the Thembu location, regarding even their successes as 'mischievous in their results, tending to spread the rebellion rather than suppress it'; he viewed Merriman's proceedings with disfavour, asking what were the limits of the authority of ministers; he again expressed his opinion that it was 'absolutely necessary that one authority should command all military forces in these Eastern districts and in the Transkei'; he asked that ministers define the duties and responsibilities of the proposed commandant-general, having as yet received none. Finally, stressing what he regarded as the illegality of what was being undertaken, he requested 'an early and decided answer on this subject'.

The premier then handed a minute of his own to the governor, asking that it be placed in the record of the meeting. This minute was a protest by Molteno that he had received no earlier notice of the meeting, nor the business to be discussed and had had no time to consult his colleagues. He added that this was the first meeting of the Executive Council to be convened without prior notice to the prime minister since the introduction of responsible government in the colony.

Frere read the Molteno minute to the council, then reminded the prime minister that it rested with the governor to summon the Executive Council whenever he saw the necessity for doing so, and asked the prime minister when ministers would be ready to discuss the governor's own minute. Molteno prevaricated, stating that he 'felt himself unable to specify any date'. At this, Frere said that 'he must summon the Council in that case every day until the ministers were in a position to discuss the question', an action that Molteno's biographer (and son) regarded as treating his ministers 'like schoolboys'. After a short discussion, Molteno agreed that the next meeting should be on the following day, 2 February.

The final business of the meeting was a statement made by General Cunynghame, who deprecated 'the operations which were being carried on in the Tambookie [Thembu] Location as an infringement of his position and command'. Frere asked the general to commit his protest to paper for the record of the council minutes, and adjourned the meeting.[34]

Dismissal

The drama came to its climax when the Executive Council met the following day, Saturday 2 February 1878. The tension began early when the minutes of the previous day's meeting were read, the prime minister objecting to his own spoken words being recorded as 'having declined' and the words 'feeling himself unable' being substituted.[35]

Once again, Molteno pre-empted the governor, handing him another minute, asking that it be recorded in the minutes of the present meeting. This was a response to Frere's minute of 31 January. The response, also dated 2 February, is among the many documents which the governor placed before the newly convened Cape parliament on 10 May.[36] Unlike Frere's prolix style, it consisted of shorter, pithy paragraphs, but merely repeated much of what had been said before. Early in the minute, we read:

> Ministers are prepared to undertake the responsibility of putting down rebellion in the speediest and most effectual manner, and they have expressed to his Excellency their opinion that this may best be carried out by Colonial forces, led by Colonists, and not encumbered by military impediments.
>
> They consider that to place such a force under the control of the military authorities would seriously impair its usefulness, and would tend to prolong the operations for an indefinite period.

With regard to the activities of Merriman, the response was also much the same:

> By the Constitution the responsibility of ministers was established, and their duties are to carry out the laws of the Colony and to administer the business of the country according to the wishes of the Parliament. The Governor acts solely by and with their advice. Should an emergency fraught with danger to the country arise, for which the law makes no provision, ministers act on their own responsibility, and will be prepared to answer for their acts to that body whose representatives they are.

As for the dual military administration which had been created by his government, Molteno argued:

> [Ministers] would observe that the Government of the country being by the constitution vested in a Governor and a responsible ministry, to hand over the control of the Colonial forces and the conduct of military operations within or adjacent to the Colony to an officer not accountable to the Government of the country, and not in any way controlled by them, would be giving practical effect to dual government of the worst kind.

The conclusion was inevitable, and it was stated with elegant finality:

> Either the Government of the Colony is responsible for the military operations conducted in the name and at the expense of the Colony, or it is not; if it is,

then the officer conducting these operations, be his name what it may, must be under the control of that Government. If the Government of the Colony is not to be held responsible, and if the conduct of these operations is to be made over to the officers of the Imperial Government, it is manifest that there must be an entire reversal of the policy of the last few years for which neither the ministers nor the Colony are prepared.

The minute having been read out by the clerk, the governor asked whether the matter had been referred to the attorney-general as had been requested. Molteno answered that it had been so referred but no answer had as yet been received.

Frere then addressed the council, regretting that, despite no reply having been received from the attorney-general, his minsters should have arrived at the conclusions set out in Molteno's minute and placed on the formal record. After briefly referring to the prime minister's first reaction to the governor's minute of 26 January, which had been to resign, Frere pointed out that it was Molteno who had wished to refer the matter to the attorney-general, but they were now taking a position without waiting for that officer's advice. 'This left the Governor no course but to intimate to Mr Molteno and those of his colleagues who agreed with him, that their resignations would be accepted.'[37]

Molteno responded that when he had first tendered his resignation, he had then withdrawn it, and he 'considered it in the same light as if it had not been made'. Frere replied that Molteno had withdrawn his resignation in order that the matter be referred to the attorney-general but had now acted without waiting for that advice and, since he was 'carrying on a system of conducting the war, which the Governor believed to be illegal', if he persisted in that view, then the governor could not support him and was ready to accept his resignation.

The government crisis now came to a head: 'Mr. Molteno repeated that he had withdrawn his resignation. His Excellency could not accept a resignation which had been withdrawn. He could of course dismiss his ministers. His Excellency replied that in that case it would of course be necessary to dismiss them.'[38] With that, the Molteno ministry was dismissed, to remain in office only until such time as an alternative government could be formed. Perhaps Sir Bartle Frere did not consider, when he accused Molteno and his ministers of taking decisions before the opinion of the attorney-general had been received, that he had just dismissed his prime minister without waiting himself for that same opinion.

Martineau wrote of the dismissal:

It was a bold step for him to take; for a Governor to dismiss on his sole responsibility a ministry which had hitherto possessed, and was supposed to possess still, the confidence of the Legislative Assembly, was an act without precedent in Colonial Constitutional government, and was likely to meet with severe criticism in a newly enfranchised Colony morbidly sensitive to dictation from the representative of the Queen.[39]

While in many respects Martineau's work, by its very nature, is less than objective, he does cite in a footnote that Todd's *Constitutional Government*, a reputable publication, referred to Frere's action as entirely constitutional and as establishing a valuable precedent.[40]

Reactions to the Dismissal

With regard to the dismissal itself, the question remains: who was actually dismissed? Certainly Molteno was dismissed, but what of his ministers? Merriman was also certainly dismissed: on 6 February, the governor wrote to him in the following terms: 'I have the honour to inform you that, by the authority vested in me as Governor of this Colony, I remove you from your office as Commissioner of Crown Lands and Public Works, and that from the receipt of this letter you cease to hold the said office.'[41]

On that same date, Charles Brownlee addressed a brief note to the governor, responding to Frere's words at the council meeting that the governor would accept the resignation of his ministers, in which he tendered his own resignation, despite the governor's request that he remain in office.[42] Frere accepted it with reluctance.

There was, however, some confusion in the cases of the attorney-general and the treasurer, both of whom were in Cape Town and thus far removed from the centre of activity. In the case of Andries Stockenström junior, Frere had stated in the telegram to the attorney-general: 'I gather from the messages you sent me, through Captain Mills . . . that you had no wish to retain office after Mr Molteno leaves it. If I rightly understand your intention, I ought now to inform you that your resignation of office will be accepted whenever it is tendered.'[43]

Stockenström was not a little puzzled by this and responded on the same day that he was not aware of having sent any message to the governor through Captain Mills, the Colonial Under-Secretary, nor was he aware of the details of Molteno's dismissal. 'Wherever the mistake,' he concluded, 'your Excellency's dismissal of Mr Molteno involves my dismissal, and I bow to your Excellency's decision.'[44]

On 7 February, Frere sent off another telegram to Stockenström in which he gave the details of the message from Mills but concluded, 'Mr Molteno's dismissal does not necessarily involve yours, and I shall, unless you otherwise instruct me, consider what you tell me as a virtual resignation, and shall accept it with great personal regret . . .'[45]

Stockenström replied on the 8th, stating that he had been unaware of the precise terms and grounds of the dismissal.

> Being in such position I was bound, out of courtesy to Mr. Molteno, not to communicate except through him. Had your Excellency been here, I might have known what the points at issue were, and decided whether I should support Mr. Molteno or not. From what I can learn it appears that the difference between your Excellency and Mr. Molteno took place on points upon which I had no opportunity of expressing an opinion. As Mr. Molteno's dismissal involved that of all ministers, a formal resignation on my part is unnecessary.[46]

Frere responded on the same day, his brief telegram indicating that he had not authorised the extension of the terms of his letters of dismissal to Molteno and Merriman 'so as to include anyone else, and much regret the mistake which led you to a different conclusion'. Frere was clearly anxious to retain his attorney-general but was just as clearly not prepared to make it plain. He ended his telegram with the starchy words: 'As I intended no dismissal in your case, you will, I trust, allow me to regard the expression of your wishes as virtual resignation, and unless I hear to the contrary, I purpose so to record it.'[47]

This telegram crossed with another that Stockenström sent explaining that he had compared the governor's earlier telegram with information given to him by Mills, and found that the ministry was not dismissed 'in the ordinary sense' but that the services of Molteno and Merriman 'were dispensed with on personal grounds'. That being so, the remaining minsters should have been given the opportunity of making known their own views, and of assisting in the formation of a new ministry. The attorney-general was unwilling to lose his position, but was every bit as proud as the governor in not wishing to make this fact apparent. He therefore begged 'to be understood as declining to tender my resignation, and as your Excellency will now probably dismiss me, I beg that your reasons for doing so may be recorded in the Executive Council minutes'.[48]

On the 9th, Stockenström sent off another telegram stating that he had no wish to resign, 'as by so doing I should virtually approve of the acts of Messrs Molteno and Merriman' and as yet had insufficient data on which to base

such a decision. He went on to say that while he did not wish to be understood as wishing to retain his position, 'although willing to serve my Queen
and country', a dismissal would leave him unfettered, unlike a resignation.[49]

Frere now wanted to make the position clear to Stockenström and
abandoned telegraphic correspondence in favour of a more considered letter.
On 9 February, he wrote to Stockenström, giving him a full summary of the
events as he had observed them, noting that Mills had informed him that
the attorney-general wished to communicate with the governor only through
the prime minister, and that, following the dismissal, it had been reported to
him that Stockenström had declined to carry on the duties of his office. He
mentioned the telegrams which passed between them, observing that they 'led
me to doubt whether you had not been misinformed as to the occasion and
character of the crisis'. He said that he wished to regard Stockenström's act as
a virtual resignation, and to treat it as such. The only other course of action was
to regard him, having neither resigned nor been dismissed, as having thrown
up his office, as an act 'attended with grave constitutional consequences'.

He concluded that he had no wish to aggravate current dissensions and
would regard the attorney-general's act as a virtual resignation from office. If
Stockenström wished to view the communications which had passed between
the governor and his two senior ministers, he was free to do so, after which he
might re-open the question with Frere. In the meantime, he could not now
dismiss him, having been informed that he had already vacated his office.[50]

On 14 February, Stockenström replied, also by letter. He explained the
misunderstanding that had emanated from Captain Mills and the series of
errors into which he had been guided by that misunderstanding. He said, too,
that he had received a note from the former prime minister which, in stating
the circumstances of the dismissal, inferred that all ministers had also been
dismissed.[51]

On Wednesday 6 February, Molteno had copied to him the text of Frere's
letter of dismissal. From the moment that Molteno had received the letter,
Stockenström 'considered the ministry as dead in law'. He did not, however,
leave his office, nor had he done so up to now. Nor had he refused to perform
the duties of his office, except that in one case he had declined to sign a
letter in his official capacity 'when he had been under the impression that he
also had been dismissed'. He concluded by saying that he wished, until fully
informed of the facts, 'to be understood as neither endorsing Mr Molteno's
acts, nor repudiating them; and as a resignation on my part might be regarded
as pledging me to the former course, I most respectfully decline to tender it.'

The letter was given short shrift by Frere; he replied on 26 February in the
briefest terms:

I have given the matter every consideration. I cannot record your dismissal as you suggest, as it would not agree with the facts as they appear to me.

I therefore propose recording that, consequent upon the dismissal of the Premier, and the dissolution of the ministry which followed, you vacated your office.[52]

The case of Dr White, treasurer-general, was very much simpler. He had already received the same copies of notices which Molteno had sent to Stockenström. In reply to a telegram from the governor, White had tendered his resignation.[53] On 7 February, he had sent another telegram to Frere in which he confirmed his resignation, at the same time suggesting that he did not consider his resignation necessary since, like the attorney-general, he had believed that the retirement of the prime minister 'necessarily involved the retirement of the other members of the ministry', which required him to then vacate his office and decline to perform any further duties of his office. He also, like Stockenström, averred that he had received the same mistaken information from Captain Mills.[54]

The reply was even briefer than that to the attorney-general: 'I have accepted your resignation of your office of Treasurer-General tendered in your telegram of the 6th instant.'[55]

Frere did, however, respond in a more courteous manner by a letter dated 15 February, which offered the same arguments as those offered to Stockenström, but adding that White had held his office from the Crown, not from Molteno, and that he could not see 'how the removal of the Prime Minister could affect the tenure of office by another minister, or the validity of this act'.[56]

Mention has already been made several times of the request from the prime minister to the attorney-general for his opinion on the question of the validity of the Cape government wishing to provide for its own defence, and appointing a commandant-general to command all colonial troops. The opinion is published in the appropriate Parliamentary Paper, but it remains undated. It is cited here in full.

In my opinion Governor's Commission as Commander-in-Chief places under his control all Her Majesty's troops stationed in this Colony, but does not give him any power as Commander-in-Chief over the Frontier Armed and Mounted Police, the Volunteers, or Burghers. Over these Colonial forces he has no greater authority than is vested in him by the various Acts of Parliament under which they are embodied; and the powers so vested in him by these Acts he cannot now constitutionally exercise, except with the concurrence and under the advice of his ministers. Consequently the

Governor cannot, except with the consent of the latter, embody the Colonial forces with those of Her Majesty. Upon the question whether it is advisable to have two independent armies under separate commanders acting without a common plan at the same time in the same field I am not asked to give any opinion, but I imagine that Mr. Molteno's views in this respect have been misapprehended. Every person is empowered by the law of the Colony to arrest any person guilty of a serious crime, and under certain circumstances is even bound to do so. Should the person whom he so attempts to arrest resist or flee he can kill him. There is, I think, no doubt but that a body of men acting in concert may lawfully undertake the duty of arresting, and in case of resistance, kill malefactors. They may, in my opinion, act under the direction of a leader chosen by themselves, and therefore they legally act under a police officer, magistrate, or other person appointed by Government. My answer to the Governor's first question is, that, in my opinion, the appointment of a Commandant-General to direct the action of volunteers and police engaged in the Colony in the suppression of rebellion is not illegal.[57]

Unauthorised Operations

As if to confirm Frere's worst fears, the governor reported on 5 February to Lord Carnarvon details of the large-scale attack launched by colonial forces on what was known as the Tambookie [Thembu] Location, near the junction of the Black and White Kei rivers. As indicated above, this action was outside the colonial borders. In the most florid manner, he announced that great numbers of Thembu had been slaughtered and thousands of cattle taken, but not without checks to the colonial advance, frequently having to halt and await supplies and reinforcements. The result had been to extend considerably the area of disturbance northwards into Thembuland, while at the same time crippling Colonel Glyn's own movements in the Transkei. Glyn's Mfengu levies had been withdrawn without his knowledge, leaving him unable to attack and disperse the large numbers of Ngqika who had joined Sarhili in an attempt to carry the war into the colony.

He then justified his action in dismissing the Molteno ministry in his last paragraph:

The persistence of Messrs. Merriman and Molteno in starting this Tambookie campaign, their disregard of all warnings to postpone it, or to carry it on in a carefully concerted manner, so as to ensure success with the least possible bloodshed, their evasion of satisfactory replies to all requests for information, and their avowed determination to let the Governor and military authorities have nothing to say to the conduct of operations which seriously compromise the position of Her Majesty's troops on both sides of the Kei, were among the proximate causes of the present ministerial crisis.[58]

Having difficulty finding a willing replacement for Molteno, Sir Bartle Frere called upon the little-known leader of the opposition in the colonial parliament, John Gordon Sprigg, to form a new government. Gordon Sprigg was a small farmer whose property lay close to King William's Town, and he had never held any office in parliament. In classical vein, Martineau said Sprigg 'came, at Frere's summons, like Cincinnatus, literally from his farm' if not from his plough.[59] Sprigg formed his new government on 6 February and, not long afterwards, his wife was brought away from the family farm just before it was attacked by Ngqika, and its cattle driven off.

To bring this part of the narrative to a close, it is necessary to report the conclusion of the Colonial Secretary, Sir Michael Hicks Beach, regarding the tumultuous events of late January and early February, culminating in the dismissal of the Molteno government. In a letter to the governor dated 21 March 1878, he wrote:

> Without attempting at the present moment to define the precise extent of the responsibility resting upon ministers in the suppression of disturbances such as those which have occurred, I would observe that I cannot concur with Mr. Molteno if he holds that a minister has a right at any moment to appoint an officer unknown to the constitution without the sanction of Parliament, and in opposition to the judgment of the Governor, and to assign to him functions which would give him paramount authority above that of the Governor himself in all military matters, more especially after martial law had been proclaimed.
>
> It should be borne in mind that, in consequence of the peculiar conditions of the Colony and the adjacent territories, responsible government, as established at the Cape, has necessarily been made subject to a limitation not elsewhere required.[60]

There are two matters which arise here. The first is the desire 'to assign to [the commandant-general] functions which would give him paramount authority above that of the Governor himself in all military matters'. Is this really what Molteno wanted to do, or is it an exaggerated version which Frere himself chose to believe? In his biography of his father, Percy Molteno maintained that '[The commandant-general] was to be subordinate to the Governor, who in any instructions to him must act with the advice of the Cabinet and not by virtue of his office as Commander-in-Chief.'[61]

The second matter refers to what Hicks Beach called 'the peculiar conditions of the Colony', under which the Cape 'has necessarily been made subject to a limitation not elsewhere required'. This is a concept entirely foreign to this writer, and I believe is one which is not mentioned elsewhere. As will be seen, it was in any case soon superseded by other opinions.

Hicks Beach continued by emphasising the terms of Frere's office as high commissioner, under which 'you are specially required and instructed to do all such things as you lawfully can to prevent the recurrence of any irruption into Her Majesty's possessions of the tribes inhabiting the adjacent territories, and to maintain those possessions in peace and safety.' And 'all the Queen's officers and ministers, civil and military, are commanded and required to aid and assist you to this end.' But once again, there is a problem. The reference to irruption relates to the invasion of the colony by 'tribes from adjacent territories'. The Ngqika could not be so described, and far from the Thembu 'irrupting' into the colony, the reverse was the case.

It might be sufficient to mention here two statistics which have a bearing upon the feeling in the colony with regard to the governor's dismissal of his ministers. For reasons which will become plain, neither will be found in the many pages which Percy Molteno devotes to the defence of his father's actions in January and February 1878. On the other hand, while they are to be found in the work of Basil Worsfold, an acknowledged apologist for Sir Bartle Frere, they are sufficiently objective to be quoted here:

> The charge that Frere had thus violated the self-governing rights of the Colony and returned to a system of 'personal rule' was entirely invalidated by the subsequent action of the Cape Parliament and electorate. In the representative chamber the dismissal, after full debate, was approved by a majority of 37 to 22; and when the Cape Parliament, which was then in its last session, was dissolved, the electorate of the Colony endorsed this verdict in the ensuing General Election by giving the Sprigg Ministry a still larger majority.[62]

The question remains, of course, whether Frere was able to dismiss Molteno and his ministry? Not being a constitutional expert, I have relied here on the Canadian constitutionalist Alphaeus Todd, who wrote extensively on these matters. We should begin by reviewing the position of the Sovereign with regard to advice given to him by Parliament.

> Should it be needful for the Sovereign to proceed to extremity, and reject the advice of his Ministers, upon a particular occasion, it is for them to consider whether they will defer to the judgment of their Sovereign, or insist upon their

own opinion; and as a last resort they must decide whether they will yield the point of difference, or tender their resignations. For, in the words of Lord John Russell, a minister, in such a position, 'is bound either to obey the Crown, or to leave to the Crown that full liberty which the Crown must possess of no longer continuing that Minister in office'.[63]

The next matter to be considered is whether or not a Sovereign is able to dismiss his ministers.

The right of a Sovereign to dismiss his Ministers is unquestionable; but that right should be exercised solely in the interests of the state, and on grounds which can be justified to parliament. By the operation of this principle, the personal interference of the Sovereign in state affairs is restrained within reasonable limits. It is prevented from assuming an arbitrary or self-willed aspect; and is rendered constitutional and beneficent.[64]

The final question is, to what extent are the reserve powers of the Sovereign inherited by the governor of a colony?

While, under ordinary circumstances, a Constitutional Governor would naturally defer to the advice of his Ministers, so long as they continue to possess the confidence of the popular Chamber, and are able to administer public affairs in accordance with the well understood wishes of the people, as expressed through their representatives; if, at any time, he should see fit to doubt the wisdom, or the legality, of advice tendered to him; or should question the motives which have actuated his Advisers on any particular occasion, – so as to lead him to the conviction that their advice had been prompted by corrupt, partisan, or other unworthy motives, and not by a regard to the honour of the Crown, or the welfare and advancement of the community at large, the Governor is entitled to have recourse to the power reserved to him, in the Royal Instructions; and to withhold his assent from such advice. Under these circumstances, he would suitably endeavour, in the first instance, by suggestion or remonstrance, to induce his Ministers to modify or abandon a policy or proceeding which he was unable to approve. But if his remonstrances should prove unavailing, the Governor is competent to require the resignation of his Ministers, or to dismiss them from office; and to call to his councils a new Administration.[65]

This last is exactly the circumstance in which Sir Bartle Frere believed he found himself and so felt perfectly empowered to dismiss the Molteno ministry.

Chapter 8

Civil War in the Colony

It was the way of the Englishman to establish one shop, then another followed, and presently there was a town like Queenstown.

Mfanta of the Thembu

In the previous chapter, mention was made of the activities of colonial troops within and without the colony. We should now describe these proceedings, their results and their shortcomings, in some detail.

In the period from the end of December until the end of January 1878, John Merriman published a series of announcements in the government *Gazette* giving the names of scores of men whom 'the Governor has been pleased to approve' as officers of burgher forces and African levies.[1] On the contrary, Frere was most displeased that the names of most of these officers had not been submitted to him for approval. In a report to the Colonial Secretary of 20 February, the governor complained: 'As far as I can make out, not more than one or two of all the appointments gazetted . . . had been submitted to the Governor, either before or after the issue of the notification, and there are men who already hold commissions from the Governor as volunteer officers.'[2]

When one looks through the names of these officers, some stand out to those familiar with men who had commands less than a year later in the Natal Native Contingent (NNC) during the Anglo-Zulu War. Among them are Rupert La Trobe Lonsdale (commandant of Keiskammahoek district), who would be given the 3rd Regiment of the NNC; James Faunce Lonsdale (Kaffrarian Volunteers, probably present at the battle of the Springs), who would go on to command a company of the NNC at Isandlwana, and there lose his life; William John Nettleton (Port Elizabeth Volunteer Horse) would command a battalion of the NNC; Robert Develing (a lieutenant with the Alice Mfengu Levy), who became a captain in the 1/3rd NNC under

Lonsdale; and finally C.R. St Leger Shervinton (Pulleine's Rangers), who commanded a company in Nettleton's NNC battalion. It is worth taking a few moments to look at Rupert Lonsdale a little more closely, since he was to achieve some notoriety at the battle of Isandlwana on 22 January 1879.

Rupert La Trobe Lonsdale was born in Melbourne, Australia on 23 August 1849,[3] and was thus only twenty-eight years of age when the present war erupted. He was a former lieutenant in the 74th (Highland) Regiment, having been commissioned ensign in September 1868 and lieutenant in November 1871.[4] He had disposed of his commission by sale.[5] Lonsdale had been a special magistrate in the Keiskamma Hoek district when he was appointed to command an Mfengu levy.[6]

Sir Evelyn Wood met Lonsdale when he was a magistrate at Keiskammahoek in early 1878 and wrote of him:

> For the next three months Lonsdale dined with me at least twice every week, and had many other meals with me, and thus I got to know him very well. He had served in the 74th Regiment, until a marriage on insufficient means forced him out of the Army, and he chanced to go to the Cape to nurse a sick brother.[7]

Wood thought that Lonsdale was about thirty years of age at that time, and described him as 'of slight but strong build'. He noted that he led his Mfengu levy at a cracking pace which even they, 'who when paid will run 6 or 7 miles for hours in succession', found severe.[8]

Fred Carrington also befriended the newly arrived Lonsdale while the former was in Wynberg, noting in a letter of 19 December 1875 that 'the two Lonsdales [probably Rupert and his cousin James] and wife are coming to lunch or tea,' adding, 'They arrived yesterday. They are going up to Queenstown farming I hear. It is a great pity to take such a pretty little girl up into such a country, utterly unfitted for the life they lead.' A year later he wrote from Queenstown, 'At King Williamstown I met Rupert Lonsdale who, with his wife, is living at Keiskamma Hoek about thirty-three miles off where he has a magistracy worth about three hundred a year. He has a lovely life of it and says he would rejoin the service if he could.'[9]

Frank Streatfeild, yet another of the commandants of an Mfengu levy, noted in his acerbic style: 'There was an appointment at that time called "Field Commandant", and they drew pay of 25s. a day and allowances. Sir Evelyn Wood once said to me that you only had to shake any mimosa bush and a bunch of Commandants would come tumbling out of it. They commanded nothing but themselves, and that very badly.'[10]

In a memorandum dated 11 January 1878 addressed to Sir Bartle Frere, the prime minister of the Cape Colony, Mr Molteno, described an operation proposed to be undertaken by colonial troops within the colony.[11] It involved the movement of troops along the Queenstown road towards the Bolo Drift of the Kei River, where they would join Inspector Surmon of the FAMP with a small group of Europeans and a Mfengu levy commanded by Captain (later Commandant) Richard F. Rorke. The whole force was to be commanded by Commandant John Frost. Molteno explained that a third group under Commandant Friedrich X. Schermbrucker would make a demonstration to the east of the Emgwali mission station to cut off any fugitives.

The effect of this operation, it was hoped, would be to drive the Xhosa rebels down the Kei Valley and, by effecting a junction with forces at Draaibosch, prevent the Ngqika from reaching the labyrinthine security of the Amathola Mountains. Following the successful conclusion of the operation, it would then be possible to pass the Mfengu levy across the Kei to take part in clearing the Tyityaba Valley, an operation which the imperial troops were anxious to begin.

The prime minister noted that other troops under Commandant Brabant were to be reinforced to permit him to clear the Kwelegha Valley and thus allow him then to join the operations in the Kei Valley. He asked that an imperial force be sent from Draaibosch towards Ndimba's homestead, and mentioned that artillery would be helpful 'in shelling the bushy Kloofs on the Kei' to drive the Ngqika into the open.

Communications from commandants in the field were not generally released, their reports being directed to the minister for Crown lands and public works, John Merriman. They were not therefore normally available to Sir Bartle Frere. On 30 January, however, the governor received a number of reports written in the period 22 to 27 January. The covering letter was a model of brevity: 'Reports for the Information of his Excellency the Governor', accompanied by a note in pencil asking that the reports be returned 'with as little delay as possible for the purpose of being put into type'.[12]

Commandant Frost reported his early progress in a letter to Merriman dated 23 January. Without going into the daily detail given by Frost, the general movements were as follows.

Frost left on 14 January, moving along the Queenstown road in the direction of the Bolo River, joining the column under Commandant Rorke coming from the Bolo Drift. Together, they moved on the Lugilo River, where they combined with an Mfengu column under Captain J. McGregor. The latter had come from the Tsomo River at the direction of James Ayliff. On their way to the Lugilo on the 16th, near the Kabusi River, Rorke had clashed with a group of Ngqika. He reported one hundred of the enemy killed, and the capture of 2,500 cattle and more than 3,000 sheep and goats. Rorke had lost four of his Mfengu killed and seven wounded. After sweeping the country about the Lugilo, Frost had then made for Komgha, arriving there on the 18th in company with Commandant von Linsingen. He then returned over the same ground on the 19th and 20th, meeting little opposition and taking more cattle. In the meantime, Commandant Schermbrucker had sent forward a patrol to St John's mission station to catch any fugitives who might have made their way up the Kabusi. Commandant Brabant had also taken out a patrol which captured large numbers of cattle.

Frost reported,[13] and Merriman echoed, the view that the southern part of the Ngqika location had been cleared of the enemy. Spicer takes a somewhat different view, suggesting that it was only 'superficially successful'. While Frost may have thought that he had cleared the country, he had few engagements, none of them major; the Ngqika had 'simply melted away and re-grouped on the periphery'. Most of them, says Spicer, moved up to the Thomas River.[14]

Frost had reported:

> All huts en route were destroyed. The kraals were also examined and only small quantities of grain found in some of the pits, and all found was taken out and given to our horses. Almost every day, numbers of women and children are met, some of whom are making their way out of the location. Every effort made to obtain information, but without success.[15]

This scorched-earth policy was also to rebound on the government. The behaviour of the burghers was poor, to say the least. That of the Mfengu was still worse and there were rumours that Sarhili was considering retaliatory attacks on the Transkei Mfengu. Merriman tried to rein in the excesses of his commanders but received little comfort from their response. Spicer quotes a peremptory note sent by Frost to Merriman on 27 January: 'Only this morning received telegram from Wright which states that Government do not wish me to destroy huts in Quand and Bolo; this I have already done. I shall burn Sandilli's huts about there tomorrow. My instructions are to clear the country. Women must be ordered out or they will get shot. I must not be hampered.'[16]

Frost had also written, in his report to Merriman on 23 January, that almost every day many Ngqika women and children could be seen leaving their location.[17] Clearly, the depredations of the colonial troops, and the damage and loss they inflicted, were bringing the Ngqika to a parlous state. Deputy Commissary-General Strickland sent a report to General Cunynghame on 27 January in which he said that it would become necessary to feed the starving

Africans, and not only the women and children. He said that the imperial commissariat was already feeding the Gcaleka and his officers were now asking for instructions as to what was to be done for the Ngqika who were begging for food. When the governor brought this matter to the attention of the Cape government, Merriman responded that Ngqika women were acting as a commissariat for their men and the only relief the government was prepared to offer was employment. Spicer notes that the ministry had ordered two thousand tons of grain from Buenos Aires as emergency relief.[18]

On 25 January, Frost made a second sweep of the Thomas River area but, despite this action, there were sufficient Ngqika remaining to give support to a Thembu insurgency which was now also precipitated.

Gungubele Insurgency

On 22 January, John Hemming, civil commissioner for Queenstown, reported that he had mounted an expedition against Gungubele, chief of the Tshatshu Thembu, 'intended to support the special constables in making certain arrests of prisoners charged with arson, theft and assault'.[19] This was the same expedition about which Sir Bartle Frere had learned from unofficial sources, but of which he had not been officially informed, and on which he also commented on later receiving the reports.[20]

There is a certain oddity about this whole affair. For example, Hemming himself, in the same report, notes that: 'As I have no experience in such [military] matters I have given [the command to] Mr Percival Thomas . . . who has the general management of the expedition.'[21] Hemming's delegation of his military command was confirmed by a late *Gazette* entry by Merriman, dated 4 February, which announced appointments that were to date from 18 January. One of the entries read as follows: 'Tambookie Division:- John Hemming Esq., will accompany division in civil capacity. Jeremiah [*sic*] Thomas, to be Commandant with rank of Captain.'[22] Spicer makes the point that Hemming, lacking any military experience, had in fact delegated the military command to Thomas on his own authority and it seemed that Merriman had then approved that delegation retrospectively.

An undated memorandum written by Merriman, probably in response to the governor's enquiries, stated:

> 2. Gungobella and several of his people having committed various lawless acts, warrants were taken out for their arrest; and Mr Hemming . . . was directed to see them [the warrants] executed.

3. There being reason to anticipate resistance, he was accompanied by a strong force to support his orders.[23]

A number of reports of colonial operations were passed to Cunynghame, who indignantly expressed himself 'lost in astonishment at all these military operations being undertaken without my knowledge or concurrence'.[24]

In order to make any sense of this expedition, we need to look at the expedition's antecedents.[25] Gungubele was the son of Maphasa, chief of the Tshatshu clan of the Thembu people, and violently anti-white. Maphasa had fought with the Ngqika in the Eighth Frontier War, in which he had been killed. As a result of his alliance with the Xhosa, his lands, lying between the Black and White Kei rivers, were confiscated by Sir George Cathcart and named the district of Queenstown. The Thembu were supposedly removed to the east bank of the White Kei River, the new location being called the land of the 'Emigrant Thembu'. Not all of them moved, however, and many returned in later years. The Tshatshu were among those still in the colony.

In 1876, Gungubele agreed to purchase a farm for the sum of £2,200, despite advice from John Hemming that the price was grossly inflated. Spicer adds that Gungubele did not then appreciate the real magnitude of the purchase price and would not have been able to pay it, even with contributions from his people. The chief, however, ignored Hemming's advice and proceeded with the purchase, putting down a deposit of £200. In January 1877 the first instalment of £800 became due and Gungubele was unable to make the full payment. In the following October, the owner of the farm applied for a provisional order of sequestration and Gungubele was summoned to show why the order should not be made final. In the meantime, the balance of the debt, a total of £1,200, also fell due.

Hemming was particularly anxious that the sequestration of the property not proceed because, as part of the settlement, the owner would also receive a second farm which Gungubele owned in the Transkei, the title to which was held by the chief but he had yet to take possession of the property. Hemming's concern was that, if the expropriation were to proceed, it would create a precedent for possible future alienation of land from black owners. The owner, perhaps under pressure from Hemming, offered to revoke the sale, keeping the £500 already paid by Gungubele to defray his expenses. A bewildered Gungubele refused the offer, asking why the owner should keep both the farm and the money he had paid.

The chief told his people that the government would now arrest him, probably a clumsy attempt on his part to persuade them to help him. They became very agitated and declared their willingness to forcibly resist the chief's arrest. Spicer argues that Gungubele was at that moment trapped in circumstances over which he had no control. He was known to be antagonistic to British rule, was now heavily involved in legal affairs which were beyond his ken, and subject to great pressure from his councillors and people. Although prepared to defend himself, he was not overtly aggressive until confronted by the expedition sent to arrest him.

There were also other forces operating against him. When Sandile declared war, Gungubele's councillors told him that if he refused to fight he would be deposed. Furthermore, his cousin Mshweshwe was circulating rumours that Gungubele had agreed to join the Ngqika rebellion, rumours which reached the ears of John Hemming. Gungubele became aware of Mshweshwe's deceit through one of Hemming's interpreters, who also told him that he was to be arrested.

Relations between Hemming and the Tshatshu chief became more strained following advice given to Gungubele by both Sandile and Mfanta, a brother of the Thembu paramount chief Ngangelizwe, not to meet Hemming again. As the year of 1877 came to a close, frustration over the farm issue and suspicion of the intentions of the white colonists caused the crisis to deepen. There were stories that the war-cry had been heard because of rumours of Gungubele's impending arrest and, as well as making military preparations, the Tshatshu refused to pay their taxes and began raiding their neighbours' lands.

A sensible suggestion had been made that the government buy the farm under threat for Gungubele, in return for the Transkei farm. Hemming disregarded this approach and wrote to Merriman on 5 December that the chief should be 'brought to account'. Spicer continues the story:

> On 11th December, Hemming went to Bolotwa to hold his monthly [magistrate's] court and to obtain information on the state of the location. He had warned Gungubele especially to attend, but he did not appear and Hemming had to go and find him. Having had no reply from Merriman, Hemming took matters into his own hands by issuing Gungubele with an ultimatum, saying that he must apprehend those responsible for the several crimes committed recently or he himself be held responsible.[26]

Merriman's eventual reply to Hemming was that the ultimatum should include some specific charge that justified an arrest warrant, and would stand up in court, before the chief could be 'brought to account'.

Gungubele was receiving a great deal of encouragement to join the Xhosa rebellion, being told that many other people would assist him, including Sandile, Sandile's brother Anta and other notables. Mfanta even sent a message that leaders as far away as Adam Kok in Griqualand West and Morosi of the Basotho, were prepared to help. At a Tshatshu council meeting, at which it was decided to fight, Gungubele said he personally had no aggressive intentions towards the white people, despite these offers of support, but would resist any aggression towards him.

In the face of the warning signs, Gungubele did nothing to stop the marauding against his neighbours. Spicer notes that 'a body of Ngqika joined the Tshatshu in early January and were involved in an attempt to break through into Emigrant Thembuland, but were driven back . . .'[27]

In consequence of the increasing criminality, Hemming recommended that special constables be sworn in and sent to arrest the lawbreakers. In view of the likelihood that they would be met with armed resistance, Hemming further suggested that Gungubele could be pinched between his own and Frost's forces and thereby be disarmed. Merriman agreed with this assessment and that the chief was seeking to bring his neighbours into a rebellion against the government. On 14 January, he issued instructions to Hemming, stating that Gungubele should be treated as a British miscreant and that warrants be taken out bringing specific charges against him, and to attempt to serve the warrants on him. He warned Hemming not to provoke violence and authorised him to use it himself only if resistance was offered. If resistance were shown, he was to disarm the rebels and, in any case, occupy the district with his forces during the present disturbance.

Hemming collected some four hundred volunteers and marched to the Bolotwa River, where he was joined by about 250 African levies. On 24 January, with his force under the military command of Mr Thomas, Hemming moved from the Bolotwa to Gungubele's homestead on the Gwatyu, arriving shortly after sunrise. The surrounding hills were manned by armed Thembu, 'these jeering and taunting us and closing in on our rear'.[28] A few shots were fired at Hemming's force and the fighting began immediately thereafter. It lasted for two hours, during which Gungubele's homestead was overrun and the Tshatshu lost as many as 150 dead. The perfidious Mshweshwe, who had acted as a guide for Hemming, was found among the dead with thirty-two assegai wounds in his body.

Hemming sent a telegram to Merriman on 27 January with the intelligence that four hundred Ngqika were with Gungubele during the action of the 24th, the remainder being Thembu. He feared that the rebellion was spreading and that Mfanta was imitating Gungubele's activities by mustering his own men and compelling loyal Thembu to join him.[29]

A second telegram, sent to Merriman on the same date, carried news of another engagement, and further information about the Ngqika involvement:

Very severe action in broken country near junction of Kei; enemy in Krantzes, and strongly posted; Insheshine, cousin of Gungobella, cut to pieces; on our side, three other natives wounded, about 12 of the enemy killed; the enemy consisting of Tembus, Gaikas, and Hottentots; our men had to retire having expended all ammunition. Enemy did not pursue. Boers did not assist much, rather the reverse, they waited for the Kafirs to come to them, which did not take place. In action of 24th, about 300 Gaikas, who fled from Gungabella's, went over to Anta's, and took refuge in huts near the river. I must have more arms, ammunition, men, and provisions. Umfanta's men are now out with Gungobella, and I think all the Tembus will join.[30]

Merriman at last realised the serious nature of the developments that had occurred with his agreement and ordered Griffith up 'to crush all disaffection' and to arrest the leaders of the rebellion. He arrived there on 28 January, to learn that Mfanta had indeed joined the rebellion, announcing the fact by driving off fifty of Hemming's horses that same day.

Hemming reported to Griffith that he had heard that Khiva had joined Gungubele between the White and Black Kei rivers with eight hundred men. Three hundred of Anta's men had also joined, which, together with three hundred under Mfanta and Gungubele's six hundred, made a total of two thousand warriors.

There followed three days of heavy fighting until, on 4 February, the rebels were finally dispersed, but not without heavy losses on both sides. The Tshatshu were completely routed, some of them seeking refuge with Sandile's brother Anta, while others joined Mfanta, who had fled through Emigrant Thembuland to join a turbulent Thembu chief named Sitokhwe Tyhali. Gungubele himself went north to the Thomas River, seeking safety among the Ngqika refugees who had also fled there.[31]

Eastern Thembu

In the years leading up to the outbreak of the Ninth War, the Emigrant Thembu had become increasingly aware of the erosion of their independence by the British. This feeling was shared by one of the more aggressive chiefs, Sitokhwe Tyhali, the chief of the Vundhle Thembu. Walter Stanford had been appointed magistrate to Dalasile, another senior Thembu chief, in 1876,[32] and because he was the nearest magistrate to Sitokhwe, the Vundhle chief was also placed under his supervision.[33] Stanford did not see him for some months after his appointment but Sitokhwe came to his attention when the Vundhle Thembu chief had a brush with Ngangelizwe, causing the paramount chief to seek shelter in a trader's store. As a result of this incident, Ngangelizwe gave him the sobriquet Igezi, or 'madman'. Stanford relates a number of other incidents in which Sitokhwe was involved between 1876 and the start of the war.[34]

We have already seen that there was frequent, and extensive, communication between the various African peoples within, and without, the colony. Sandile actively encouraged the Thembu chiefs to join his rebellion against the British authorities. The division among the Rharhabe in favour of war, however, was also to be observed among the Thembu, so there was little likelihood that all would seek to join him, if only because of the petty jealousies among them. The fate of Sitokhwe, then, is one which, given similar circumstances, could have befallen any of the other chiefs.

The chief had had frequent disagreements with Charles Brownlee and as a punishment for Sitokhwe's frequent lawlessness, Brownlee had given half of the miscreant's land to his brother in January 1877.[35] Following Hemming's rout of the Thembu in February 1878, Sitokhwe became noticeably quieter and even reported the presence of Mfanta in his country to Ngangelizwe, while at the same time refusing to make any contribution to the levies which were then being raised by the colony. When Stanford sent out a patrol that entered Sitokhwe's district, it was fired upon by his people and the chief became a marked man. Despite Sitokhwe's earlier betrayal of Mfanta, Ngangelizwe's brother now joined him.[36]

When he refused to surrender, a force was assembled by Major H.G. Elliott that advanced from Mtentu towards the Gatberg on 21 March with three thousand volunteers and African levies. They arrived two days later, pinning Sitokhwe, Mfanta and some four or five hundred of their people against the mountain overlooking Maxongo's Hoek.

Elliott's report, dated 29 March, is extensive,[37] and is supported by accounts from his subordinates ex-Major James Boyes, John Vice and Stanford himself.[38] At 1 p.m. on the 23rd, his force moved forward in four divisions, each marching into a separate kloof towards Maxongo's Hoek, where the rebels were thought to be concealed.

Stanford's two columns on the left came under heavy fire and their levies hesitated, but when Stanford and his officers rode forward alone, the levies rallied and drove the rebels, who continued to contest almost every rock and gully, back until sunset. On the same day, a small group under Captain A. Ross went to Sitokhwe's homestead and, finding it deserted, burnt it to the ground.

The main force bivouacked overnight in Maxongo's Hoek and during the following two days they scoured the whole mountainside as far as the Barkly

Pass, only to find that Sitokhwe and Mfanta had slipped over the mountain on the first night. Elliott reported that he had lost one European and three Africans dead, with five Africans wounded. The rebels had lost, according to their womenfolk, more than sixty men. They also lost about 1,200 cattle and 2,500 sheep and goats. The majority of the force was dismissed, returning to their several stations, with only a small group remaining under Stanford to hold the district.

With this defeat, Thembu resistance in the north-east came to an end, although the grievances of the Emigrant Thembu remained unsatisfied. Gungubele was captured towards the end of March and taken to Queenstown; two weeks later Mfanta was taken and Sitokhwe was arrested on 13 April.

Persecution of Tini Maqoma

There are some similarities between the cases of Gungubele and Tini Maqoma, each of whom encountered troubles with farms they had bought. In the case of Tini, however, Spicer suggests that the difference between them was the local officials who were keen to drive him from his lands 'for the good of the district' and, by so doing, forced him into rebellion.[39]

Tini, the son of the celebrated Ngqika military strategist, Maqoma, purchased two farms in the Waterkloof area in the early 1870s, settling there with his followers.[40] Some of the latter also became tenant farmers in the same area. The passage of time saw an increase in the numbers of both people and cattle. This led to overcrowding of the population and overgrazing by the stock. The fear of an imminent war, and the drought of 1877, did nothing to alleviate these problems and, inevitably, neighbours began to lose cattle. Spicer argues that the return of the Gcaleka to their homeland from across the Mbashe River, combined with Khiva's mission to Sandile, 'focussed the spotlight of colonial fears on Sandile and the other Rharhabe chiefs'.[41] The Europeans around Fort Beaufort saw Tini, with his thousand warriors, as a distinct threat, and suspicion and fear in such a situation led to the inevitable panic. Tini was no different, being equally suspicious of the Europeans. He heard rumours that he was to be sent to Robben Island, and he would have remembered his own father dying there.

The die seemed to be cast when Mfengu were appointed as stock police in the district, a development that acted as a brake on Tini's own attempts to deal with the stock thefts. Spicer quotes W.B. Chalmers' own comment on that situation: 'There is no doubt that the employment of Fingoes against the Kafirs is most irritating to the Kafirs and that a great deal of mischief is thus created where mischief would not otherwise arise.'[42]

Tini's own actions were a function of the tension between himself and the white people of Fort Beaufort. When he gave evidence in the village in a case of theft, he took a bodyguard of two hundred warriors with him. He was reported by a local newspaper to have said, referring to the bodyguard, that while he did not look for war, he was afraid of an attack on himself and was determined to resist it if it eventuated.

The fear gripping the white farmers became apparent as, once again, they began to leave their farms: by early January 1878, the white population of some districts was reduced almost to zero while none remained in the Blinkwater. Spicer states that white volunteers patrolled the perimeter of Tini's farm. To alleviate the heightening tension Merriman suggested the appointment of a prominent officer to restore confidence but nothing materialised.

Tini's own response, with famine now threatening, was to take up arms; thefts of stock also increased. The recently appointed magistrate in Fort Beaufort was informed that Tini was concentrating his warriors in the Waterkloof, intending to seize cattle or even to attack Fort Beaufort itself. On 9 January, he recommended the disarming of Tini and his followers, although he recognised that this would lead to bloodshed. Worse, he recommended the arming of the local Mfengu. Once again, Merriman was able to defuse this situation.

By 2 February, stock theft had reached unprecedented levels and it was decided that a number of stock police, including some Mfengu, would be stationed on a farm next to Tini's. In response, Tini told Inspector Booth, who commanded the troop of police, that he (Tini) was the government in that area and that he would not give up his cattle. Booth later testified that he thought Tini was drunk at the time.

Tini then appeared at the farm where the police were stationed, accompanied by about a hundred of his warriors, and demanded that the police leave at once, otherwise he would kill them. On hearing of this threat, the magistrate, Holland, telegraphed Merriman for instructions. The minister, however, chastened by the actions of Gungubele, told him to prepare a warrant for Tini's arrest but not to serve it for a few days, to allow tempers to cool.

By this time, the Sprigg government had assumed office, and his ministers followed the same cautious line by instructing Holland not to serve the warrant. Sprigg also appointed the special commissioner whom Merriman had omitted to select, choosing W.B. Chalmers for the position. Tini apologised to Chalmers for the incident at the farm, stating that he only wished to know who had authorised the occupation of the farm, since he had not been consulted in the matter.

Inevitably, the existence of the arrest warrants became known to Tini and he countered the threat by moving to the wilderness of the Schelm (or Hermanus) Kloof, accompanied by a strong armed guard. Meanwhile, on 16 February, a police patrol following a spoor on to Tini's farm was accosted and told that the next policeman to set foot on the farm would be killed. Increasingly, Tini defied government authority by punishing the cattle thieves, who brought trouble on his people, by levying fines in cattle and firearms.

Chalmers now made a startling suggestion: he recommended that Tini be arrested, even if it led to bloodshed, and that farms in the area owned by Africans should be bought up and sold to European farmers. He also commented that it had been an error to allow the Ngqika back into the Waterkloof. He repeated this mantra often over coming weeks, and it was echoed by Holland. Sprigg agreed that lawlessness must be suppressed immediately: Tini must either surrender and be disarmed, or be compelled to do so. The prime minister appointed General Cunynghame to the command of all troops in the area and on 20 February a warrant for Tini's arrest, on a charge of sedition, was prepared.

Spicer observes that at this point: 'Chalmers realised, perhaps after the Gungubele affair, that it would be impossible to serve the warrant without sacrificing the lives of the servers.'[43] He therefore planned to surround the Waterkloof, Schelm Kloof and Blinkwater with a force large enough to put down any resistance. This was, of course, an impossible task. The perimeter of such an encirclement would have been more than eighty kilometres, in an environment far more advantageous to the rebels. This plan came to Tini's notice, simply because one of his people, a tenant farmer, was asked by the owner for his rent to be paid early, citing as his reason for so doing the fact that the tenant was to be attacked the following week! When Chalmers finally surrounded Tini's homestead on 4 March with seventeen hundred men to make the arrest, Tini had by then fled to the Waterkloof. From this fastness, he refused all Chalmers' promises of safe passage for him, his men and their cattle, were he to surrender. Spicer notes that Tini's refusal should have surprised no one, since Chalmers had informed Tini in his message that 'On account of the great trouble which the Kaffirs in Schelm Kloof and Waterkloof have given for a long time past, the Government is determined that these fastnesses shall no longer be occupied by Kaffirs.'[44]

There followed a massive campaign to bring Tini to heel, involving thousands of troops and the bombardment of the kloofs, despite the fact that he had committed no act of rebellion. It was in vain, however, because Tini slipped away to the Pirie bush, appearing in April on the Ntaba kaNdoda, where he aligned himself with Siyolo.

Spicer notes that the campaign brought to light a number of cases of excessive zeal on the part of colonial troops:

> There had been no declared rebellion, nor any formal declaration of war, nor was any warning given as in the case of the Ngqika so that those who did not wish to fight might separate themselves from those who did. Instead, Palmer's [*sic*=Chalmers'] force treated every black in the Fort Beaufort area as a rebel, and blacks on private farms were taken prisoner, their huts burnt and property confiscated as the colonial forces 'cleared' the country.[45]

Chapter 9

A War in Earnest

Gcalekaland has been well-swept, the gardens and huts destroyed and the country really cleared of its inhabitants.

Walter Currie, 1857

In an earlier chapter we left Colonel Glyn having just been appointed to the command of all troops in the Transkei, replacing Commandant Griffith, and about to begin operations against the resurgent Gcaleka.

On 27 December 1877, Glyn ordered the three columns of his Transkei Field Force to advance from the Springs, Ibeka and Idutywa.[1] He would cover almost the same ground as his predecessor, although rather more quickly. The right column was led by Major Edward Hopton while the left was commanded by Major H.G. Elliott.[2] The headquarters column under the personal command of Glyn bivouacked on the first night some six kilometres beyond the Msintsana stream at the headwaters of the Nxara River.[3] Here Colonel Glyn met Captain J.C. Robinson, RA, who had already cleared the Qora River up to this point. (Robinson had been temporarily detached from his corps and was commanding the FAMP Artillery.) That same night, Commandant Allan Maclean arrived at Glyn's camp to report that he had made a long patrol down the Kei River to its mouth, then north to the Kobonqaba River, following the river towards Kentani (Centane, Quintana), but finding no Gcaleka.

The next day, the 28th, Glyn led his column to the Lusize River. There he received despatches from his other columns, Hopton reporting that he had patrolled the Mnyameni Valley near Kentani Hill. Elliott had pushed his way from Idutywa down the west bank of the Mbashe River as far as the Bongo Mountain. He had encountered a few Gcaleka but had been able to disperse them with heavy loss to the enemy but with little to his own force.

At the Lusize River, Glyn ordered an Mfengu levy under Captain Fuller to clear the country to the mouth of the Nxara. On 29 December, having received intelligence of an assembly of Gcaleka at the junction of the Kabusi and Qora rivers, Glyn moved to high ground overlooking the Qora, from where he sent out Mfengu levies under Maclean and Veldtman (who in the meantime had been given a captain's commission, the only Mfengu chief to be so honoured). They quickly came to grips with the Gcaleka and, after a short tussle, routed them, capturing more than nine hundred cattle and some horses. After the engagement about a hundred women and children were found in the bush and these were sent under escort to Ibeka.

On 30 December, Glyn advanced through the western boundary of the Manubi Forest but found few Gcaleka, taking only fifty-eight head of cattle. Close to the Qora, he met Fuller, who had entered the forest from the south, reporting that he had 'exchanged sundry shots with the enemy who were but few in number'.[4]

Captain Nixon, RE, constructed a barrel raft and on the 31st the whole column was transported across the Qora at its mouth, taking up a position overlooking the next river to the north-east, the Jujura. There he met a party under Captain Upcher which had worked down the Icanga ridge, meticulously scouring the country without opposition and capturing five hundred cattle. While there, Glyn spotted HMS *Active* close inshore and was able to establish brief communication with Commodore Sullivan, the ship then returning to the mouth of the Mbashe at Glyn's request.

On 2 January 1878, finding the Jujura River impossible for wagons to cross, he sent the infantry and wagons, under Captain William Degacher, round via the Icanga with instructions to meet him at Malan's mission station. Glyn himself crossed the Jujura with Captain Robinson's two guns, two hundred FAMP, the 1/24th and thirteen hundred Mfengu, carrying three days' provisions. He next crossed the Shixini River, mounted the next ridge and bivouacked at the head of the Nqabarana River. The Mfengu, meanwhile, hastened to reconnoitre the Dwesa (Udwessa) Forest.

The following day, the 3rd, Glyn sent Captain Robinson and his guns to Bodi, going himself across country with a hundred mounted men as escort towards the Mbashe mouth, where he met Maclean and heard his report. Maclean said the Dwesa Forest was clear, the Gcaleka having hastily retreated at his approach, leaving five hundred cattle behind, which the commandant had snapped up.

Glyn wished to communicate with Commodore Sullivan aboard HMS *Active* and Commander Wright was sent to the Mbashe mouth with Maclean's and Fuller's Mfengu, the latter to guard the drifts. Glyn moved off to Bodi himself on 4 January. The next day, Major Boyes arrived with a number of Mfengu and Thembu levies, carrying despatches from Major Elliott, who had returned to Idutywa.

At this point, Glyn was prepared to state that he believed the Transkei was clear of Gcaleka, although, old soldier that he was, and bearing in mind Griffith's own experience, he added the caveats:

> At the same time, owing to the physical features of the country and the small force at my disposal, it is impossible in my opinion to prevent small straggling parties from being concealed in or returning into the country.
>
> At the same time, I consider that with a line of entrenched posts to be occupied for some time in carefully selected spots and patrolling constantly kept up, there need be no alarm at a repetition of the incursions of large bands of Gcalekas into the country.[5]

He announced that the first such post would be commenced that day (5 January) by Captain Nixon.

He also cautioned that his Mfengu levies had been anxious to return to their homes following the Ngqika rebellion. Glyn had sent off Inspector Maclean and his FAMP north to the junction of the Kei and Tsomo rivers to allay their fears. He had also given Captain Veldtman permission to return to the Ibeka district with his four hundred men, on condition that they make themselves available should their services be further required.[6]

On 6 January, Glyn made his way to the Shixini River, passing Malan's mission station, where he commended the site for its good water. On the 7th, he continued his march, leaving Captain Nixon and his men, together with Captain Thomas Rainforth and a company of the 1/24th, at Malan's. He marched that day for more than thirty 'hot and wearying' kilometres, making his next stop at a place he called 'Thompson's Shop', presumably a trader's store.

Glyn established his camp the next day, and sent a message to Major Elliott, advising him of his arrival. He also sent out a patrol towards the Dwesa Forest. On the 9th, he sent out Mfengu patrols both east and west which returned in the evening reporting numbers of Gcaleka with their cattle on the Bomvana side of the Mbashe River.

His next plan, having received news of Elliott, was for the latter to work down the Mbashe towards the coast, whilst Glyn did the same, working upstream from the mouth of that river. It was not to be. In the evening, he received orders from Cunynghame to return with his column to Ibeka and he departed on the 10th.[7]

While Colonel Glyn had stuck out his neck with his opinion that the Transkei had been cleared of Gcaleka, he had the wisdom to warn that there might still remain enemy groups that had been missed, or who might return once more. His fears were to be realised more quickly than he thought.

Action in the Tyityaba Valley, January 1878

On 14 January, General Cunynghame reported the events which had occurred to that date since the battles of Draaibosch on 29 and 30 December. He reported two concentrations of rebels, one being north of Komgha on the Kabusi, and a second in the Tyityaba (Chichaba) Valley near its junction with the Kei River.[8] The first were held in check by their recent mauling at the hands of Major Moore, and thus they were content to observe, but not hinder, the movement of mail and supplies along the Draaibosch–Komgha road.

On 11 January, Captain von Linsingen set out on a reconnaissance, in company with some of the German Volunteer Rifles under Captain Fischer, from Komgha towards the Kabusi River, crossing Major Moore's battleground of 29 December to get there. On his arrival at the river, he quickly set about burning homesteads, in the course of which he was confronted by Ngqika rebels in large numbers. Calling up the Volunteers, von Linsingen advanced his right wing towards the top of a large hill and, having received their first volley, 'attacked them at the point of the bayonet', driving them over the hill and down into the kloof behind. He himself was narrowly missed by three assegais hurled at him, which he calmly collected afterwards as souvenirs. Following the action, he and his men renewed their burning of Ndimba's homestead, which the action had interrupted.[9]

At that time, Cunynghame had three small detachments close to the Tyityaba Valley: one hundred of the 1/24th at Mpetu, fifty of the 88th at Pullen's farm and sixty FAMP at Smith's farm, while there were fewer than twenty men of the East London Volunteers at Fort Linsingen in the Tyityaba Valley itself, and forty more of the Volunteers at Fort Buffalo near the mouth of the Kei River. Since Fort Linsingen was located near the junction of the Tyityaba and Kei rivers, on the west bank of the Kei, we must assume that the rebels were higher up the valley. It was an area which offered considerable difficulty, the steep valley sides and the many kloofs running off on both sides of the river being heavily wooded.

The second concentration of rebels was discovered by a reconnaissance on 4 January led by Lieutenant Maurice Moore, from Pullen's farm, and Sub-Inspector Graham, FAMP, from Smith's farm near the old Fort Warden. The rebels were found 'in considerable force', with a large herd of cattle. Lieutenant Moore reported that they were attacked by the enemy with considerable vigour. They were identified later as Ngqika from a pass found on one of the bodies, but he and Graham had been able to drive them off. Moore concluded: 'Their position is extremely strong and could not be attacked, with good result, without a strong force of infantry, some mounted men and a large force of Fingoes.'[10]

It was here, then, that Colonel Glyn had planned to commence his operations before moving back across the Kei but, as we have seen, his preparations were stalled by the refusal of the colonial government to provide additional Mfengu levies.

On 6 January a frantic telegram was received from Captain Wardell at Fort Warwick near Mpetu:

> Our communications are cut off. We are surrounded on all sides by Kaffirs; are destroying everything. [Captain] Spencer [East London Volunteers] is here with his men from Fort Buffalo, all except party at Fort Linsingen. I do not see my way to relieving them at present. The enemy being so strong between us in the Chichaba, it will be as much as we can do to hold our own here; Spencer's camp was attacked last night; it adjoined our redoubt; the enemy driven off; no loss to us; expect same will occur off and on in some form, as they appear so very determined. In broad daylight, yesterday, they carried off about 100 of our Commissariat oxen. – the Chichaba is full of Kaffirs, under five chiefs. We want ammunition to complete our reserve, and also Sniders for Volunteers. I should like a Field Piece, also some rockets, our position being so very open and exposed. We have supplies for about 10 days. Ten families in laager here. Have less [?70] women and children pass night in ditch at our Fort; no other place of safety; also our horses; McLean [sic] has not returned. We are obliged to be under arms all night lately. Can you send me any sandbags? – Saturday, 2 p.m.[11]

Based at Komgha, Lieuenant-Colonel Lambert was unable to commence the relief of the beleaguered posts until 8 January. On his way to Mpetu, he met Sub-Inspector Graham at Pullen's farm, who told him that he had withdrawn his force from Smith's farm that morning, bringing away all his stores. Lambert ordered him to remain at Pullen's.

On arriving at Fort Warwick to relieve Wardell, Lambert was advised that the small party at Fort Linsingen had already been relieved by, of all people, Maphasa of the Tsonyana, who had earlier been assigned the task of watching the Kei drifts. The party which had evacuated the fort had been attacked en route to Fort Warwick but had received assistance from Spencer with some of his East London Volunteers and a detachment of the 24th.

The two threatened posts having been relieved, and still being anxious to get to grips with the rebels, Lambert consulted those on the spot on the practicality of an attack, but was dissuaded from the enterprise and evacuated Fort Warwick to return to Komgha on 8 January.[12] In a brief minute on Lambert's report, the general thought the colonel had been prudent in not attacking the rebels with the few troops under his command.[13]

Lambert was then ordered to the Tyityaba Valley for a second time, with instructions to clear the valley of rebel Ngqika, and left Komgha on 14 January with two columns, one under his command and the other commanded by Major Moore.[14] His own right column, consisting of two seven-pounder guns, 122 men of the 88th Regiment and fifty-eight men of Sansom's Horse, proceeded to Mpetu, bivouacking on the first night at Pullen's farm. While there, Captain Brabant appeared and asked permission for his men to co-operate with him the following day, suggesting that he should proceed to Mpetu early and prevent the Kafirs from crossing the Kei beyond there.

Also whilst there, he received a letter from Commandant Pattle stating that he was delayed but expected to join with his Mfengu by 4.30 the following morning. As a result, Lambert delayed his own departure until 5 a.m. but, since Pattle had not by then appeared, continued to a hill overlooking the upper Tyityaba Valley. About 7.30 a.m. he was met by Major Moore's column, which had bivouacked at a nearby farm. From here, Lambert ordered Maclean's and Streatfeild's Mfengu into the valley to begin operations. Shortly afterwards, Pattle's Mfengu also showed up, having entered the valley at Sansom's farm and driven down the left side of the valley.

Major Moore's left column consisted of Lieutenant Wilfred Heaton with sixty men of the 1/24th, Sub-Inspector White with thirty men of the FAMP, Captain Spencer with seven mounted and fifty-three foot of the East London Volunteers, and Captain von Linsingen with thirteen mounted and sixty-five foot of the Buffalo Volunteers.[15] He also had with him one FAMP artillery gun and a rocket tube. After leaving Komgha, Moore led his column towards Fort Warden. At Pullen's farm he had expected to be joined by Pattle and his Mfengu but, since Pattle was not to be found, Moore left a message to be delivered by Lieutenant Maurice Moore, ordering the commandant to send a hundred Mfengu with an officer to join his column, while Pattle and the remainder of his Mfengu were to go to the head of the Tyityaba Valley, where they would join their fellows under Maclean and Streatfeild. By 8.30 p.m., after a breakdown of the Scotch cart carrying the gun near Fort Warden, Major Moore arrived at Driver's farm which, together with Smith's farm nearby, he reported was 'in ruins'. The next morning, he contacted Lambert and they then resumed their separate operations.

Maclean reported to Lambert that there were no rebels in the upper valley and so he withdrew and proceeded to Mpetu. As the oven-like heat abated in the late afternoon, Maclean and Streatfeild volunteered to go out again. They re-entered the valley near Gray's farm and, after crossing the Tyityaba River, fell in with Pattle's Mfengu. The two forces combined to capture between two and three thousand head of cattle and three thousand sheep, which were driven into the camp that night by Maclean and Streatfeild, Pattle remaining with Moore's column. Five Ngqika had been killed, and one Mfengu.

During the evening, Brabant went by, driving what Lambert estimated to be at least four thousand cattle and five thousand sheep, en route for his camp at Annexation on the main Komgha road.

On the morning of the 16th, acting on information that there were cattle around Filmer's farm, Lambert took eighty men of his regiment, Sansom's Horse and all his Mfengu, together with one gun and some rockets, to the area. He found nothing until he mounted a ridge, from where he saw several herds of cattle. The Mfengu worked down the Mlimane stream towards Bothma's Hoek, where they seized three thousand cattle and five hundred sheep and goats. Many of the animals had to be left behind due to the searing heat of the day.

In the meantime, Lambert had pushed forward along the ridge with sixty men of the 88th, to within eight hundred metres of the enemy. In the skirmish that followed, his men had difficulty even taking a shot because the bush was so thick, and the gun could not be brought up at all due to the steepness of the terrain. Even so, Lambert reported killing between thirty-five and forty Ngqika.

Based on reports he now received from all parts of the valley, Lambert determined that 'the Kafirs were in no part of the valley to be found in any force' and decided to return with his column to Komgha, setting out on his return journey on 17 January.[16]

In the meantime, about midnight on the 14th, Pattle had joined Moore at Driver's farm.[17] At daybreak on the 15th, Moore left the farm and moved south-west towards the headwaters of the Tyityaba River. After a little more than a kilometre, hearing no gunfire and fearing for his left flank, he returned to the wagon track and followed it further east towards the Kei River until, about five kilometres from his overnight camp, he arrived at Butler's deserted homestead (not the farm, which was further east), which was also in ruins, where he stopped for breakfast.

About 9 a.m. he heard light gunfire and, taking all his mounted men except his vedettes, half of his infantry and the gun and rockets, proceeded some fifteen hundred metres to a spur running south, from where he had a good view of the Tyityaba and also across the Kei to the cliffs on the other side. He saw no movement, although about 11 a.m. he heard more gunfire and rockets fired from the further bank of the Kei. (This, it would transpire, was Colonel Glyn making further demonstrations after the battle of Nyumaga.) About 4 p.m. he went on to Butler's farm (also in ruins), seeing von Linsingen reconnoitring along one of the spurs to the south. After reaching Butler's, Moore joined von Linsingen and witnessed a sharp engagement between two or three hundred Ngqika and Pattle's Mfengu. The fight lasted from 4.45 p.m. to 6 p.m., during which as many as twenty Ngqika were killed, while the Mfengu suffered two men wounded, one of them mortally. They also deprived the rebels of some two thousand head of cattle. As a precaution against the Ngqika breaking out into the Kei Valley, Moore ordered von Linsingen back to Butler's farm while the fight was in progress; he spent the night there. On the 16th, Pattle continued his sweep towards the confluence of the Tyityaba and the Kei, in combination with Spencer's volunteers and fifty Mfengu covering his flank on the high ground. The latter force returned within three hours, driving more cattle and sheep, and also reporting that von Linsingen's blockhouse (Fort Linsingen) at the Tyityaba mouth was still standing.

With his fresh water now all but exhausted, Moore left Butler's farm at 2 p.m. and made his way back to Butler's homestead, where he bivouacked overnight.

The following morning (17 January) Moore sent von Linsingen and his men to patrol the slopes towards the river, with Spencer's Volunteers in support on the heights, the former taking a further one hundred cattle during this reconnaissance. About mid-morning, Moore received orders from Colonel Lambert to return to Komgha and began his return march at 10.30 a.m., reaching Komgha at 4.30 p.m. the same day.

In his report to General Cunynghame on the successful clearance of the Tyityaba Valley, Colonel Bellairs observed:

> The operations were most successful. They were conducted for three days in a valley district over 15 miles in length by 3 or 4 in breadth, though narrowing in parts to perhaps only one, over lofty spurs and ridges running into it, forming a series of densely wooded and impracticable ravines. The weather was intensely hot, and though both men and horses were much distressed at times, the troops did their work well and cheerfully, in a manner reflecting credit on all present.
>
> The enemy was known to have been in great force a short time previously, but strong as the position was for natives it was evacuated, the majority of the enemy dispersing in such alarm before our forces could come up with him as to allow vast herds of cattle and sheep to fall into our hands with but little resistance on his part.[18]

In a summary of this operation, Bellairs noted that Lambert and Moore, with a combined total of 420 Europeans and three guns, together with 'a strong body of Fingoes', had cleared the Tyityaba Valley, in the process killing some sixty Ngqika and, more importantly, capturing more than twelve thousand cattle and eight thousand sheep.

Battle of Nyumaga, 13 January 1878

About 11.30 p.m. on Saturday 12 January, the Tsonyana chief Maphasa warned Captain Robinson, RA, then acting resident with that chief, that a rebel force under Khiva had crossed the Kei River at the Tyityaba Drift in order to make an attack on the camp of Major Owen, then based at Nyumaga (Neumaka, Newmaga) six kilometres south-west of Kentani. This is a spot on the east bank of the Kei, close to the banks of which there is an eminence of the same name which overlooks the river. Robinson immediately sent off a message to warn Owen of the impending attack, and instructed Maphasa to watch the drifts. The chief did so, and engaged another party of rebels who tried to cross.[19]

When Major Owen received Robinson's message, he sent a message of his own to warn General Cunynghame, who in turn sent his aide-de-camp, Lieutenant Nevill Coghill, with forty FAMP, to Colonel Glyn with the same warning.[20]

Owen sent Lieutenant Thirkill to warn his men that they might expect some action in the near future. At daybreak, Owen noted that he could see the rebels mustering on a nearby hill some three kilometres from his position. He then quietly awaited the expected arrival of Colonel Glyn.

Glyn was already on the march from Ibeka and that Saturday night he was camped near Kentani Mountain when Coghill gave him the general's message. He struck camp immediately and marched with all haste towards Nyumaga.[21] Glyn arrived at Owen's camp about 3.45 p.m. on Sunday 13 January and still the rebels had not made their attack. Owen had already made his troop dispositions in anticipation of the colonel's arrival and, having heard them, Glyn ordered Owen's men to advance to the attack, leaving a hundred FAMP with Captain Robinson and his two guns to defend the camp.

According to Glyn, Owen had arranged his troops thus:

> On the right, 1 Coy 1/24th under Lieutenant Cavaye 1/24th; next to them the Naval Brigade with one Rocket Tube, under Lieutenant Cochrane, in the centre; the guns with R.A. under Lieutenant Kell, Connaught Rangers, next; Rocket Tube and Party 1/24th Regiment with Lieutenant Main R.E.

& 1 Company Connaught Rangers, under Lieutenant Thirkill on the left; in the centre were about 30 of Commandant Maclean's Fingoes, who assisted in drawing the Guns &c.[22]

Captain Veldtman was also present with his company of Mfengu and had already arranged that his men would make the first contact, then simulate a retreat to draw the rebels forward.

Of his own men, Glyn placed Inspector Chalmers' troop of FAMP at the head of a kloof on his right to guard his right rear, and Inspector Bourne's troop similarly on the left 'in direct echelon'. He placed Captain Russell Upcher with two companies 1/24th, and some Royal Marines under Lieutenant Dowding, RMLI, in support at the rear of the line.

At the crest of the hill in front of the rebels, Owen bade his men lie down. The rebels, also now advancing, hesitated at the sight of the troops and at that precise moment the action began with the firing of rockets by Lieutenant Main. Nevill Coghill gave his mother a description of this, his first action: 'Well, as I said we opened the ball with a rocket which spun over the heads of this first advancing party and buried itself in the Kloof beyond with what success I know not. The second went right in amongst them and then they resorted to their old strategies of dividing and trying to out-flank us.'[23]

The British were on a small plateau with kloofs running up into its sides, Coghill adding: 'and into these the enemy wormed on both sides of us'. Inspector Bourne was covering the most threatening kloof and opened fire. The whole line then advanced to engage the enemy.

Owen observed that the rebels were concentrating on his left, so ordered his line to change its front half left to engage them 'with a rush and a cheer'. Glyn saw that Owen's men were exposed to a very hot fire and threw in Upcher's reserve. He also sent the troop of 24th mounted infantry under Lieutenant Ralph Arthur Penrhyn Clements, who then came up on Owen's left in support. In his report, Upcher wrote that Inspector Bourne, on his left, asked for assistance and he sent one of his two companies, under Lieutenant Edgar Anstey, in reply. (Upcher reported that his men had fired seventeen hundred rounds in the engagement.)[24]

These actions tipped the scale and the rebels began to fall back. Lieutenant Charles Walter Cavaye's company, on the right with a Naval Brigade rocket battery, was also heavily engaged but outflanked their opponents and they too retreated in disorder.

Lieutenant Waldegrave Charles Fearn Kell (who belonged to the 88th, but who had by now become a de facto artillery officer of considerable skill), seeing that the left of the British line was the most threatened, moved both his guns to cover that flank, subsequently moving them to wherever they were most effective. 'On the extreme right-rear, the enemy, who attempted to turn our flank on that side, were driven back by Inspector Chalmers' Troop of F.A.M. Police.'[25]

By 6 p.m., the enemy being by then completely routed and at some distance from the camp, Colonel Glyn re-assembled his force and returned to camp, reaching it about 7.15 p.m. The enemy was thought to have lost at least fifty men, while they had also been observed removing many wounded from the field. The British force had lost none, suffering only four of the Connaught Rangers and one Mfengu wounded.

Over the next few days, Colonel Glyn continued his harassment of the rebels on the east bank of the Kei. On the 15th, he led his column out of the Nyumaga camp, intending to co-operate in the attack on the nearby Tyityaba Valley.[26] By 7.30 a.m. he had taken up a position on a ridge overlooking the Kei River, offering a good view of the lower valley on the other side of the river. He placed his guns further back on the ridge, from where they commanded a wide stretch of the river.

About 8.30 a.m., he heard heavy firing on the far side, then a number of Africans appeared driving cattle towards the nearby drift. Some of them tried to cross but were driven back by the Naval Brigade's rocket battery. Glyn sent off Commandant Maclean with his Mfengu and Inspector Chalmers' troop of FAMP after the cattle. They returned that evening with some thousand head, having killed seven rebels and having themselves lost three horses, with two Mfengu wounded.

Glyn spotted some of the Komgha column on the other side of the Kei and asked Maclean to communicate with them. Having done so, Maclean reported them to be volunteers under Captain Brabant, from East London, Glyn then complaining that he had not been informed of Brabant's participation. At the end of the day, 'finding that I could not be of further use I returned to my Camp.'[27]

On the 16th, Glyn sent Major Owen's column to a position just inland from the Kei Ebb and Flow Drift, only a few kilometres south-east of Nyumaga, there to intercept any rebels crossing the drift with their cattle. He had already despatched Upcher, with fifty men of the 24th, at 2 a.m. to set up an ambush and observe any movement of the rebels. At dawn he saw a few Xhosa but they retreated into the bush when fired upon.

Glyn, who had accompanied Owen, arrived at a small village, from where he saw a number of men driving cattle away from Brabant's column, whom Glyn spotted on the other side of the river. When they saw Owen's column, the rebels fled into the bush, leaving their cattle halfway across the river. Glyn sent Maclean and his Mfengu after both rebels and cattle, supporting them with Captain Robinson's guns. The Mfengu skirmished down to the river, killing nine rebels on the way, and captured the cattle, numbering about seven hundred, then continued across the river, where they captured another two herds. Glyn then awaited the cool of the evening before returning to a new camp which he established about eight kilometres from the Ebb and Flow Drift.

On 17 January, having received a report from a patrol sent out by Major Owen reporting a large herd of cattle being driven into a kloof on the colonial (west) bank of the Kei just above the Ebb and Flow Drift, Glyn sent off Maclean with his ever-useful Mfengu to search them out.[28]

Maclean crossed the Kei at the Ebb and Flow and entered the kloof, supported by Major Owen's guns and rocket tube. As the Mfengu entered the kloof, the rebels, with their cattle, tried to get back to the river. The mounted element of the Mfengu pursued them and, in the skirmish that followed, four Ngqika were killed and 430 cattle and 700 sheep were captured. The Ngqika made an unsuccessful attempt to re-capture their animals but were driven off by the Mfengu. A large number of women were later found in the bush, who said that they had been driven out of the Tyityaba Valley the day before.[29]

Battle of Mnyameni, 30 January 1878

On 25 January, Colonel Glyn was at at Ibeka when he received a telegram from Komgha advising him that a large party of Xhosa and their cattle had been 'driven across' into the Mnyameni bush.[30] (The Mnyameni is a small stream which curls round the western shoulder of Kentani Hill. The Tala forest lies some ten kilometres to the west of the valley.) The message included intelligence that Maphasa was also expecting an attack.

Acting on this information immediately, Glyn sent off Inspector Chalmers with a hundred FAMP to Maphasa's location but he returned without having sighted the enemy. The next day, he sent Commandant Allan Maclean with his Mfengu levy towards the Springs; Maclean reported that a large body of Xhosa were in the vicinity. Glyn then advised Komgha and the Springs of his intention to attack.

On Sunday 27 January, Glyn ordered Captain Upcher out with a column to move to the head of the Mnyameni Valley. The following day, Upcher's advanced guard was attacked by a large force of five hundred Xhosa, which he was able to drive off. He was unable to follow them into the bush, however, since the weather was very wet and his Mfengu levies had failed to arrive. When Glyn learned of this, he sent off Captain F.W. Grenfell (one of General

Cunynghame's aides-de-camp) with the mounted men of the 24th, twenty-five FAMP and three hundred Mfengu under Maclean.

Upcher described the details of his engagement in a report dated 30 January.[31] His original force consisted of about 150 men of the 1/24th, about two dozen men of the Naval Brigade, FAMP Artillery and more than ninety FAMP. He left Ibeka on the 27th and camped near Kentani Hill for the night in dense forest.

The following morning, he made a strong reconnaissance along the Mnyameni ridge, where he located the enemy on a conical hill in the direction of the Tala bush. The Xhosa fired on his FAMP advance party, who returned the fire. Upcher had orders not to attack and, having discovered the location of the enemy, attempted to withdraw the FAMP. As soon as they began to move back, however, five or six hundred Xhosa rushed to the attack. They were driven back with loss by 'two well-directed shells from Captain Robinson R.A.'[32] Upcher kept the Xhosa under scrutiny until nightfall using the FAMP under Sub-Inspector Holden. Late on the 28th, Upcher received the reinforcements under Captain Grenfell sent by Glyn.

At daybreak on the 29th, Upcher led his column out, leaving a camp guard of ninety FAMP and some of the 24th under Sub-Inspector Holden. He located the Xhosa in the same place but somewhat less in strength. Maclean and his Mfengu immediately took possession of the conical hill on which the Xhosa had been seen the previous day, where Upcher quickly established the FAMP Artillery with Captain Rainforth and his company of the 24th, together with sixty FAMP under Sub-Inspector Hatton in support, and to watch the Mnyameni bush.

Captain Robinson then put a few shells into the nearby bush and Maclean's Mfengu began the attack. In this he was supported by the Naval Brigade with rockets, a company of the 24th under the young Lieutenant Charles Atkinson, Lieutenant Clements' mounted 24th and Sub-Inspector Cochrane with another FAMP gun.

The Mfengu drove the Xhosa out of their bush retreat, straight into the Blue Jackets and Atkinson's company. The Xhosa tried to make a stand but were driven back by the men of the Naval Brigade, 'capitally led by Lieutenant Hamilton', and some Mfengu, all under the command of Captain Grenfell. The Xhosa then broke and Clements and his mounted men were sent in pursuit, following them through the Tala forest.

Upcher then rested his men for two hours, expecting that the garrison at the Springs might send their Mfengu into the bush to drive the Xhosa back towards him. When they failed to do so, he sent Maclean and his Mfengu back into the bush, supported by his whole force, where they met with considerable resistance. The Naval Brigade fired several rockets and Captain Robinson shelled part of the bush, having previously taken up a position commanding the watercourse in the valley below. They kept up this long-range fire whenever the enemy were seen. Finally, Fuller's Mfengu from the Springs joined Maclean's and the bush was cleared. The force marched back to their camp in heavy rain, Upcher estimating the Xhosa losses at about forty killed, while one sailor and three Mfengu were wounded.[33]

Captain George Deare, commanding Prince Alfred's Volunteer Guard based at the Springs, submitted his report on the engagement later than Upcher.[34] He wrote that he left the Springs during the early hours of 29 January with his unit and a company of Pulleine's Rangers under the command of Captain C.R. St Leger Shervinton. The body of Mfengu that he had expected did not arrive so he left with only six of them.

Deare advanced first along the west bank of the Butterworth (Gcuwa) River and towards the Kei. On the way, he observed Colonel Glyn's column moving along the Kentani road. Shortly after crossing the Kei River he was seen by a party of Xhosa, who then drove their cattle away from him but towards Glyn's column. Deare ordered Shervinton to attack with his rangers, providing support with his own unit. The Xhosa resisted strongly but fell back under the determined assault. There followed a period of long-range rifle fire on the enemy as they fled over a conical hill, after which Deare and Shervinton descended into the valley to capture more than three hundred cattle. The Xhosa lined the nearby hills but declined any further engagement.

Shortly afterwards, Deare saw a white flag in the Tyityaba Valley and, when he descended, he found Captain von Linsingen. He agreed to assist Deare in an attack on the conical hill, on which there remained a number of Xhosa. After taking the hill, they burnt the huts they found there and captured several women and children, with four horses. Deare was able to extract from them the fact that their opponents had been both Gcaleka and Ngqika. Captain Shervinton's report adds little to that of Deare, other than minor detail.[35]

We might here provide a few further details about the Shervinton brothers, both of whom were active in this campaign, although serving with different units. Charlie wanted his brother Tom to join him as an officer in Pulleine's Rangers and had arranged a lieutenancy for him, but Tom declined the offer because he wanted to remain in a mounted unit. By this time, Charlie had also been promoted to captain and an extremely proud Tom wrote:

Charlie is getting on splendidly. He is Captain in Pulleine's Rangers, and gets 21s. a day. He is very popular with his men, who say they will follow him wherever he chooses to lead them. When he left King William's Town they all wanted to get into his company, and actually smuggled themselves into the train, but were found out at Kei Road and were sent back to King. He is very good to me, and helps me in every way he can.[36]

While serving at the Springs, Charlie was involved in a skirmish of his own. A fellow officer described the incident:

While Shervinton was visiting a block-house a couple of miles from the 'Springs'; as evening was drawing in, it was observed from the camp through a field-glass that some two dozen natives were closing on his track. It was evident that he saw them too, for suddenly he shortened his reins and set his horse going his best. Emptying his revolver right and left as he dashed through them he left five men on the ground behind him, escaping with an assegai wound in the leg, which prevented him walking for six weeks, though able to perform his duties on horseback.[37]

A letter in a Cape newspaper described the conditions for colonial volunteers in Gcalekaland:

During three days of incessant rain, we were almost wholly without provisions, our sole food consisting of meat without even a pinch of salt, and a few mealies given us by the Fingoes. We were then ordered to start when the rations were two days overdue, and on our refusal were told that it amounted to mutiny. Eventually some broken mouldy biscuits were served out, some men being fortunate enough to get a very small quantity of bad meat. When there was meal, it was often mixed on an old mackintosh, for want of proper utensils.[38]

General Cunynghame might have felt very satisfied with his clearance of both Gcalekaland and the neighbouring Tyityaba Valley, but he could never have foreseen the combination of Xhosa forces which would strike at him next. As with the Gcaleka, many Ngqika, including Makinana, had slipped by the troops and Maphasa's people guarding the drifts, passing into the supposedly vacated Transkei.[39]

Battle of Kentani, 7 February 1878

There was now a short interval while both black and white took breath after recent events. The British held the view that operations on both sides of the Kei River had placed them in an insuperable position, which is probably true. This did not mean, however, that the Xhosa were defeated.

Spicer relates a number of incidents which throw light on what was really happening, rather than what the British thought might be taking place. He notes that Stanford, usually a good source of intelligence, reported that Sarhili had recalled all his warriors to the Transkei.[40] Colonel Glyn had also noted Gcaleka crossing the Qora on their way to the Kei. In an interview with an African correspondent at Willowvale, Spicer learned that there had been a meeting between the Gcaleka and Rharhabe chiefs at Nyumaga, just after the battle on 13 January. Sandile proposed that they fight to the last man because the English could never be trusted. Sarhili agreed, stating that he would 'never speak to the English again', but he was, despite his words, reluctant to fight to the last man, simply because the British seemed to have an inexhaustible supply of soldiers. The result was some sort of compromise in which both agreed that they would make one last effort: their target was to be the small camp at Kentani.[41]

It seems extraordinary, with Sarhili's recent experience of the attack on a fortified position at Ibeka, that he would now consider repeating what had proved to be a fruitless and costly exercise and, if nothing else, demonstrates the desperation he must have felt at his situation.

On 4 February, Maphasa reported that a major attack was imminent, with the object of obtaining ammunition. Unsure of where such an attack might take place, Glyn thought that it might fall on either Ibeka or Kentani.[42] With skilful foresight he strengthened his resources at both and, lacking sufficient artillery to cover the two places fully, strategically placed a reserve column at Tutura, a mission station about halfway between them. The column consisted of half a company of the 1/24th, twenty Royal Marines, thirty-two Pulleine's Rangers, a troop of the Frontier Light Horse and a troop of FAMP Artillery with two guns, all under the command of Captain Robinson.[43]

The force at Kentani, under the command of Captain Russell Upcher, 1/24th, consisted of twenty-five men of the Naval Brigade, two companies of the 1/24th, eighty FAMP and two troops (i.e. seventy-two men) of Carrington's Frontier Light Horse (FLH). He also had with him fourteen men of the FAMP Artillery and fourteen men of the Cape Town Volunteer Artillery, each with one gun. He was joined by two levies of Mfengu, one under Captain Veldtman and the other under Smith Poswa, totalling 560 men.[44]

The position Upcher chose to defend was overlooked at some distance to the north by Kentani Mountain, a conical eminence rising some three hundred metres over the surrounding countryside.[45] Upcher placed his headquarters in a central redoubt on a knoll to the south of the mountain, its sides descending steeply to two streams surrounding the position on three sides. Although the site is now part of a forestry plantation, the area was then quite open except for small patches of woodland in the kloofs. The two guns, one seven-pounder and one nine-pounder, were placed on opposite sides of the redoubt so as to remain mobile. Below and to the west of the redoubt, Upcher carefully concealed a number of firing pits, in each of which he secreted a few men of the 24th. He located the wagon laager a few yards to the south, guarded by some of the FAMP.

Spicer writes that Sigcawu and Khiva advised Sarhili that the best means of attack was to make an early morning approach, in order to overwhelm the camp quickly and thereby obtain the ammunition and food they needed.[46] The Ngqika under Khiva and Sandile advanced on the camp from the Kei River while Dalasile, of the Velelo clan, led the Gcaleka division up from the coast. Their two divisions totalled five thousand warriors. The original plan had been a concerted attack of Ngqika and Gcaleka together, but in the latter stages of his advance, Sandile had been shadowed by Maphasa, who now occupied a hill in his rear. The Rharhabe chief therefore sent a message to Sarhili telling him that he was unable to attack while Maphasa threatened his flank. The Gcaleka thus went into the battle without him.

About 5.30 a.m. on the wet and miserable morning of 7 February, Captain Veldtman reported the Gcaleka advance on the Kentani camp to Captain Upcher. Upcher's next actions were set out in his report:[47]

> I immediately struck tents. The men (who had been previously told off to their places) manned the shelter trenches, which I had constructed on the lines laid down for the proposed Fort.
>
> Captain Rainforth's Company were [sic] sent out in skirmishing order, and lined a small hill on our right front. Carrington's Light Horse patrolled to the North to observe the enemy; both these officers had orders to fire and retire, to bring the enemy within range of the Camp; these orders were carried out most satisfactorily.

He also sent a message to Captain Robinson at Tutura reporting the attack, which the latter received at 6.40 a.m.

The Gcaleka advanced in two divisions from the left (south) and the front (west), their total numbers being about fifteen hundred warriors according to Upcher's estimate but were probably more. At twelve hundred yards Upcher ordered into action first the nine-pounder gun of the FAMP, then shortly afterwards the seven-pounder of the Cape Town Volunteers. After another brief interval, the Naval Brigade rocket battery joined their fire to that of the guns. Despite the heavy fire directed at them, the Gcaleka steadily

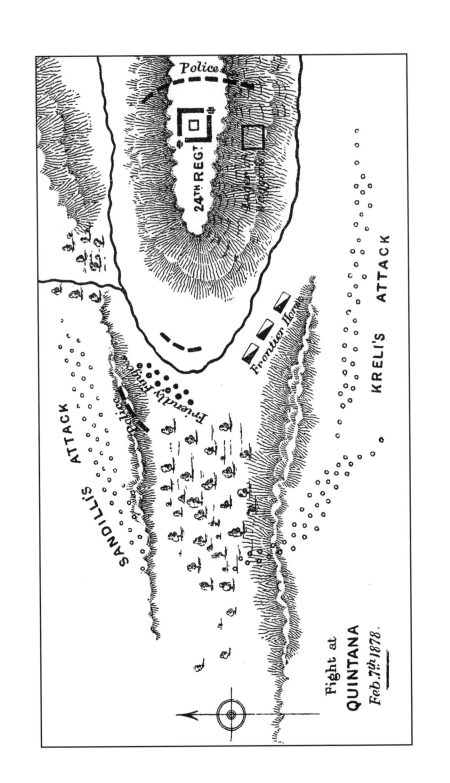

Fight at
QUINTANA
Feb. 7th 1878.

continued their advance. When they came to within nine hundred yards, the concealed men of the 24th rose up in their firing pits and poured in a series of thunderous volleys, which came as a complete surprise to the Gcaleka in front, bringing them to a halt. The division on the left flank, however, continued to move forward to within four hundred yards, being constantly reinforced from behind a hill to their rear.

The Mfengu were the closest force to the Gcaleka, Veldtman being placed on the far side of the stream to the south while Smith Poswa was located in a similar position to the west, both parties having orders to pursue 'directly the enemy was broken'. Both divisions of the Gcaleka began to give way after about twenty minutes' intensive firing and Veldtman chased the Gcaleka division on the left as far as the Qolora River, not returning to the camp until noon, killing fifty-four of the enemy in the pursuit.

Lieutenant Carrington led his FLH in a charge on the division to the front, breaking them up and driving them into the Mnyameni stream. A number of Gcaleka still hovering to the left rear (east) were driven off by the FAMP, foot and mounted, under sub-inspectors Holden and Sprenger. Carrington modestly described his own part, in a letter dated two days after the battle:

> Here I am all right after the big fight of the 7th. I was down at Upcher's camp at Quintana, and on a nasty wet morning the Kaffirs, five or six thousand, came for us. I went out with my troop to meet them and then retired. They came on with a rush with three columns. We plied them with shell, rockets and musketry, and turned them at last. I then sallied out and charged them all over the place, and then came back to camp.[48]

Sandile now approached the camp but his division was attacked by Maphasa's men in front, and by those of Xhoxho in the rear. Shaking off the irritating Tsonyana warriors, Sandile re-grouped and recommenced his advance.

With the Gcaleka apparently completely routed, and Carrington having returned from his pursuit, Upcher sent his men to breakfast. At that moment, however, word came that a second enemy force was advancing from the right flank (north-west) round the side of Kentani Hill. Upcher sent out Captain Francis Wallace Grenfell, 60th Rifles, with a party of FAMP under Sub-Inspector Hatton, Carrington's FLH and half a company of the 24th under Lieutenant Atkinson, to intercept this new threat. It was found to be the belated Ngqika under Khiva and Sandile.

Hatton soon found himself in difficulty after crossing the stream and mounting the hill, but hung on grimly until he was assisted by the troop of FLH under Captain Whalley. At one stage, the Ngqika were so close that one man received an assegai through his clothing. Together, the FAMP and Whalley's men then attacked the Ngqika, driving them back. Meanwhile, Atkinson had engaged some of the Ngqika retreating along the ridge. Grenfell ordered him to face his company about to support the Police, with which order he immediately complied.

Carrington, with a second troop of FLH under Lieutenant Davey, had engaged a number of rebels who had emerged from a kloof on the left, and were trying to outflank him. He charged straight into the Ngqika 'with great gallantry', again driving them back. In a letter to Nevill Coghill, Carrington described the scrambling fight at close quarters, and their resulting injuries:

> I rode my horse and 4 scoundrels kept potting at me and at last hit my horse in the jaw and he spun round like a top. He was only 10 yds. off so I potted him with my revolver. Another of my men had his horse shot dead under him. Another knocked out of line with a bullet in the hock. Another (a man of mine) shot thro' the thigh, another dragged off his horse by a Kafir, which Kafir he killed, but his horse has not since been seen. Sergt. Leslie was assegaied in the hand, but knocked the fellow over with the butt end of his gun and then shot him.[49]

Rainforth's company of the 24th now joined Grenfell and together the column pursued the Ngqika down the ridge, the 24th skirmishing in the centre with mounted men on each flank. Grenfell reported sixty enemy killed in the kloof.[50] He chased them to the end of the ridge then, seeing the Ngqika still flying away, left a party of Mfengu to watch them, returning with his European troops to the camp.

While Grenfell was thus engaged, Upcher had seen a group of Ngqika approaching through another wooded kloof on his right. He left Holden in charge of the camp, 'with a sufficient force', and rode out himself, leading the Naval Brigade and a company of the 24th under Lieutenant Anstey. With the aid of Smith Poswa's Mfengu, he was able to drive back the Ngqika with heavy loss, clearing the kloof after about an hour.

By 10.30 a.m. the Ngqika had retreated out of range and began to assemble 'in hundreds' on a conical hill to the right. Upcher called off the pursuit and returned with his force to the camp. To complete the coup, Upcher sent out the FAMP nine-pounder gun under Sub-Inspector Cochrane. 'He took up a good position, and worked his gun well, shelling the hill occupied by the enemy, and they fled in the direction of the Tala Bush.'

Upcher reported that the loss to the enemy had been severe, 185 bodies having been counted, but since many had fallen in the long grass, he estimated that their loss was more than two hundred. His own casualties were two Mfengu killed, with three Europeans and seven Mfengu wounded. Carrington concluded his own account of the battle in another letter to Coghill with praise for his commanding officer: 'Baby Upcher is an excellent officer.'[51] (While this may have been a well-known nickname in the officer's mess of the 1/24th, it may also have been a private joke between Upcher and Carrington, the former being born in February 1844 and the latter in August of the same year.)

Having received Upcher's note of the impending attack on Kentani in the early morning, Captain Robinson 'marched off without delay to reinforce'.[52] When he was within five kilometres of the camp it became clear that the attack had been beaten off, so Robinson calculated that his best means of rendering assistance was to take his detachment down the Tala Ridge. His advance guard reported that the enemy was gathering behind a ridge with the intention of attacking Upcher's flank. He advanced his two guns at the gallop, escorted by his troop of Carrington's FLH, and opened fire on them at 8.30 a.m. 'Two shells caused the enemy to retire, and two more sent them flying.'

Robinson then brought up his infantry and pursued the enemy for nearly two kilometres, but, believing his force was too small, chose not to enter the Tala bush. His report commended the marching ability of his infantry – 'seven miles in an hour and a half, and not a straggler'.

It is interesting to note that Maphasa's son Xhoxho assisted in the defence of the camp by engaging, and thus diverting, the rear of Sandile's division.[53] The agent in charge of the chief's location, Charles Lundell, wrote to Upcher on 9 February saying that, after visiting the site of Maphasa's fight, he had found twenty-five bodies, of which two were thought to be 'either Bomvana or Mpondo'.[54]

The momentous defeat at Kentani signalled the end of the Gcaleka campaign: they had been soundly beaten and they quickly recognised that reality. For his part, Sarhili was confirmed in his belief that there was no point in pursuing the war. The Transkei campaign was, to all intents and purposes, at an end, although small bands of Gcaleka continued to cause trouble for a short while. Sarhili returned to his homestead on the Qora River, where he was joined by Khiva. Spicer says that Makinana fled into Bomvanaland, commenting that he was referred to by Africans as a coward, being described by them as a 'good runner'.[55] Khiva would be killed, together with three of his brothers, on 15 March, by Pattle and his Mfengu.

After several times seeking terms for his surrender, and not being offered any that were satisfactory, Sarhili went into self-exile across the Mbashe River, a circumstance in which he had found himself in earlier days.

Sandile, as he had also done so often before, retreated with his supporters into the fastness of the Amathola Mountains, from where he hoped to continue his war with the British.

A Change of Leadership

There was now a change in the British military leadership, in addition to the change of government described earlier. General Cunynghame was recalled from his post, asserting that 'having by seniority attained the rank of full General, I had become too high rank to retain my command, according to the rules of the service'.[56] His aide-de-camp, Lieutenant Coghill, wrote to his mother on 23 January, giving her the news:

> You have probably seen in the papers that more regiments are being sent out here (amongst others my 2nd Batt.) also a *Major* General Thesiger. When I saw this announced I was certain that he was sent to assist the General, as indeed the General had pointed out that his successor should have assistance as the district had become too vast for the supervision of one man – judge then my surprise to find on my return from Queen's Town that it is as a *relief* and not as a *support* that he comes out – I could scarcely believe that because in the first place it is a Lieutenant-General's Command and Thesiger is only a Major General – and in the next the General has *not made a single mistake* and all his operations have been *thoroughly successful.*[57]

In truth, General Cunynghame himself confirmed the allegation that there was 'a want of cordiality between me and the Colonial Ministry'[58] and Merriman's relationship with the general was particularly poisonous. The feeling was mutual: Cunynghame described Merriman as 'a man of active temperament, unbounded ambition, strong in faith in himself, not over-courteous in manner or conciliatory in disposition, most difficult to reason with . . .'[59]

His replacement was to be Major-General the Honourable F.A. Thesiger, son of the first Baron Chelmsford. His father would pass away in October 1878, when Thesiger became the second Baron Chelmsford, but we shall refer to him throughout this work as Lieutenant-General (local rank) Thesiger.

Chapter 10

Thesiger's War

'How can I sit still when Sarhili fights? If he is overpowered . . . then I too become nothing.'

Sandile

Lieutenant-General the Honourable Frederic Augustus Thesiger was born on 31 May 1827 and was educated at Eton College. He began his military career in 1844 when he obtained a commission by purchase in the Rifle Brigade. He bought a transfer into the more acceptable Grenadier Guards in 1845 and found regular promotion thereafter. By 1868 he was a major-general, having served in the Crimea, Sardinia, Turkey and India.[1] It is fair to note that much of his service life had been spent in administration, acting as quartermaster-general and deputy adjutant-general in most of his postings. Thesiger had also served briefly as aide-de-camp to Queen Victoria in 1868. He returned from India in 1874 and spent much of the next four years on half-pay, serving in two short home postings which belied his rank, and was eventually offered appointment as deputy adjutant-general at Horse Guards, a post he 'asked permission to decline, being anxious for a command in India'. This was almost certainly due to the high cost of mess bills and entertainment in England, as opposed to India: Thesiger was not a wealthy man 'on account of limited private income'.[2] When offered the command in South Africa, he at least had no expensive mess bills to meet.

The newly appointed general arrived in South Africa on 4 March 1878 and assumed his military command (which included St Helena) on the same day, while Sir Arthur Cunynghame departed for England shortly thereafter. Thesiger was accompanied by Major John North Crealock as his assistant military secretary,[3] a man who would attract considerable opprobrium, particularly during and after the Zulu War little more than a year later.

Crealock was born in 1837 and, after an education at Rugby School, enlisted in the 95th Regiment as ensign by purchase in October 1854 and was promoted lieutenant in February 1855. He purchased his step to captain in May 1859, was promoted to brevet major in July 1872 and substantive major in March 1875. Crealock spent a long twelve years serving in India before returning home, following which he applied to accompany Thesiger as assistant military secretary.[4] The journal which he wrote during his service at the Eastern Cape has proved extremely useful to this writer, both as a diary of operations and as a vehicle for his criticism of his general and others serving under him. It also betrays Crealock as having a poor command of English and a man whose thinking was inclined to be somewhat 'woolly'.

In February and early March Thesiger's army had been boosted by the arrival at the Cape of two additional imperial battalions. The 90th Light Infantry, a single-battalion regiment led by its commanding officer, Lieutenant-Colonel H.W. Palmer, left in two vessels: the larger portion under Major Rogers, VC, on 10 January 1878 and the headquarters group under Palmer on the 12th. Palmer arrived with four companies in East London on 9 February after leaving the band and colours at Cape Town. Major Rogers' group arrived at Durban on the same day. Colonel Palmer was appointed commandant of the Fort Beaufort district and given the task of operating against Tini Maqoma and the Kroome Heights generally. The 90th left King William's Town on 18 February and arrived at Fort Beaufort on the 21st.[5]

The 2nd Battalion, 24th Regiment, unusually, joined its 1st Battalion at the same station, arriving at East London under Lieutenant-Colonel Henry James Degacher a month later, on 9 March, the last company disembarking on the 11th.[6] N/5 Battery, Royal Artillery, with 124 men and six seven-pounder guns also arrived at the same time under forty-year-old Major Arthur Harness.

In addition, a number of special service officers also arrived with Thesiger. Among them were Brevet Colonel Henry Evelyn Wood, VC, also of the 90th Regiment, and Brevet Major Redvers Henry Buller, 60th Rifles. Wood had been assistant quartermaster-general at Aldershot but resigned and left for the Cape with General Thesiger on 31 January.[7]

These two officers, working first independently and later together, were to prove outstanding soldiers in the coming months, the latter in command of Carrington's Frontier Light Horse. Captain Matthew Gosset and Lieutenant William Molyneux were to become two of Thesiger's aides-de-camp,[8] with his third, Lieutenant Hamilton, RN, being an acknowledgement of the presence at the Cape of the Naval Brigade.

General Thesiger quickly reached two conclusions, which he confided to the Secretary of State for War in his first despatch: 'I found that the impression existing here among many Officers, both Military and Civil, was that the disturbances had passed the critical stage, and that, owing to their losses in the field, and want of supplies, both Gaikas and Gcalekas will offer no further resistance.'[9] His conclusions were wrong on both counts.

Thomas River Campaign

In this same report, Thesiger described an operation, planned before his arrival, in which a column had been formed under Commandant Griffith which launched an attack on Sandile and his Ngqika in the Thomas River area in the north-east of the colony. This attack took place on 8 March and Thesiger also reported its result:

> From the reports hourly received here while this operation was going on, it appeared that Sandilli, with a large body of Kaffirs, reckoned at 800 strong, had eluded Commandant General Griffith's Forces. The various posts lying on the line Cathcart–Greytown–Stutterheim, which had been denuded of their garrisons, were therefore in considerable peril, being threatened by the Kaffirs moving Westward.[10]

Molyneux is more forthright about this incident:

> Griffith reported . . . he had captured twelve hundred head of cattle; but a portion of his force had taken the wrong road, leaving a gap in the circle surrounding the Kafirs. Sandilli at once took advantage of this, and on the morning of the 9th, the thirty men left to guard Stutterheim were astonished to see large bodies of Kafirs, within a few miles of the town, making for the Pirie bush.[11]

The Ngqika did not attack the town but certainly laid waste to outlying farms, killing some German settlers as they passed by.

When the news of the breakout reached the general, he immediately sent off all the mounted volunteers he could lay his hands on under Captain Gardner of the Albany Volunteers, with Captain Gosset as their staff officer. Crealock's journal gives little space to the result of this sally, in an entry dated 11 March: 'This force had an engagement that day in capture of 150 head of cattle and 9 killed; and the following day 150 cattle and 250 sheep.'[12] Gosset was to remain as staff officer to Commandant Fleischer's column for several days, and reported on his activities in a separate document.

Thesiger concluded his report with a bleak warning: the arrival of the two new battalions was 'not in excess of our immediate requirements' and should the situation in Natal and the Transvaal deteriorate, 'the Imperial force will certainly need reinforcing.'

The general's next report was dated 25 March and set out his plan of operations to contain, and defeat, Sandile.[13] 'A cordon of posts was formed and during the week (10th to 17th March) the Troops were busy patrolling.' His dispositions effectively encircled what is known as the Pirie (Perie) Bush, with six separate columns based at Gwengwe, Isidenge, Fort Merriman, Keiskammahoek, Bailie's Grave Post and the Pirie mission station.

Commandant Frost's position was far to the north-east, Fort Merriman being the old Fort Kabusie located near Stutterheim. Thesiger intended that Frost begin his movement early, so as to link up with Commandant Schermbrucker at Isidenge.

Following the dismissal crisis, the problem of the command of colonial troops was also a matter which General Thesiger was compelled to address, and he thought that the matter would be quickly resolved:

> Owing to the peculiar views of the late Government, and to the inexperience of the present one on first taking Office, the General in Command was at first but imperfectly informed of the exact position of the Colonial troops, and of their intended movements. This, I am happy to say, is no longer the case, and I trust that I shall shortly, with the assistance of the Colonial Government, have the entire direction of the Colonial, as I have already of the Imperial, troops; I have no reason to doubt but that I shall meet with the full support of the many excellent Officers now in the Field in Command of various Colonial Corps.[14]

He was soon to learn that this assumption was also wide of the mark.

First Pirie Bush Operation

On 16 March, the Naval Brigade returned to HMS *Active*, and Thesiger re-organised his troops into six divisions led by: Colonels Wood and Degacher, Commandants Frost, Schermbrucker, Venter and Brabant.[15]

On the same day, Thesiger issued orders for the commencement of his first operation to close in on the Ngqika in the Pirie bush, to begin on 18 March.[16] His plan was for Wood's column at Keiskammahoek to be the directing one, and it was to move in a south-easterly direction, driving the Ngqika before it towards the Pirie bush and Murray's Krantz. Commandant Frost, coming from Stutterheim, and supported by Commandant Schermbrucker, was to assist on the left flank and Commandant Brabant on the right. Meanwhile, the commanding officers at Pirie, Haynes' Mill and Isidenge were to 'use their best endeavours . . . to prevent the Kaffirs breaking out to the Southward, and to drive all that may be found opposite them in a North-Easterly direction towards Stutterheim'.

This first part of the plan was foiled by a lack of discipline on Brabant's part. Wood's own report mildly chided him: 'The Column . . . moved towards Commandant Brabant, who had ascended from Rabula and not from Bailie's Grave Post as arranged. At this time, Brabant's column moved to the lowest plateau after Cattle and, being fired on, retired with some loss.'[17] This had a knock-on effect because, as a result, Streatfeild was required to go to Brabant's assistance, later lamenting:

> This premature attack of Brabant's had been productive of no good whatever, and had entirely upset all the proposed operations of the day. I was forced to go to his assistance when sent for, and therefore both his force and mine were lost for the day, as far as the combined attack went; and also, on account of this, Wood's and the other corps remained in a state of inactivity.[18]

The forces then spent a very cold night on the mountainsides, awaiting the dawn and preparing themselves for another hard day in the bush.

Operations resumed on the 19th, with limited results. Crealock noted in his journal that the attack began with artillery fire from Haynes' Mill: 'Left camp at 5.45 a.m. for Haine's [sic] Mill, fired a few shells at 6.30 up to the heights where we believed rebels were and enjoyed the sight through our glasses of natives running. Later on, however, we found our shells in most cases had fallen among or near our own Fingoes . . .'[19]

The owner of Haynes' Mill, William Haynes, commanded his own small force of Mfengu and on this day his men were to show their true colours. Lieutenant Molyneux, one of Thesiger's aides-de-camp, took these Mfengu, with ten men of the 90th as a personal escort, to clear a part of the lower Buffalo Poort or valley. Haynes claimed that he had to guard his mill that day and sent his sixteen-year-old son to act as guide instead.[20]

When the boy had shown Molyneux the road into the bush he was sent home again, while the officer led the way forward. After struggling for about a mile through the bush, they emerged into a clearing in which was planted a mealie garden. In the meantime, Haynes' 150 Mfengu had evaporated, leaving only about forty men with Molyneux, the rest 'having made a strategic movement to the rear'. After they had offered all sorts of excuses for their comrades' retrograde action, Molyneux ordered them on: 'On bidding them to advance all together, one pointed his gun at me; I had to take it away, and rub his nose with the muzzle of my revolver.'[21]

Molyneux then went forward with two men of the 90th, ordering the Mfengu to follow him 'in a lump', with the remaining eight men of the 90th to 'drive them on from behind'. The interpreter then began to find excuses for not continuing until Molyneux was startled by a shot nearby and the whole of the Mfengu 'went down the path as if the Evil One was after them'. The origin of the shot remained a mystery but Molyneux was convinced that it came from one of his Mfengu. He had no alternative but to quit the bush as quickly and quietly as possible, and without rendering any assistance to those on the plateau.[22]

In the meantime, Wood, Brabant and Frost had cleared the plateau with the loss of one colonial officer, Captain Bradshaw, an officer with Streatfeild's Mfengu, who was allegedly shot by Dukwana, perhaps the best marksman among the Xhosa.[23]

Streatfeild was unaware of the officer's death until he returned to camp that night:

> It appears that some Kafirs had come out of the bush, and fired on the horse guard, and that a company or two of Fingoes with officers, Bradshaw among the number, had chased them into the bush and followed them up; and after a bit of a 'scrimmage' [they] were returning back to camp, when a Kafir came sneaking through the bush behind them and shot poor Bradshaw through the head. Two of the men were also shot in getting his body out of the bush. He was killed at the bottom of a deep kloof, and they had dreadful work in getting his body out of it, for the side of the kloof was very steep and rocky and in many places there was barely footing.[24]

General Thesiger spent the night at Haynes' house near the mill and Crealock waxed lyrical in his journal when describing the nocturnal conditions:

> The boards of the verandah in Mr Haine's [sic] wooden house were hard but rest was easily found by tired men, and the General and Ct Gen Griffith and Mil Sec after sharing the miller's rough but hospitable fare made up their beds (their saddles) in a sheltered corner. The thunder rolled over the forest and the giant gum trees round creaked and groaned under the blast casting weird shadows when the moon now and again threw fitful light.[25]

The operation continued on the 20th, when Wood reported his intention to clear further areas of bush. The general wanted a closer look at this action and during the day he and his party, consisting of Griffith, Crealock, Molyneux and Captain Wright, RN (commanding the Naval Brigade), made their way to Isidenge, to the east of Mount Kempt. They were also accompanied by Thesiger's interpreter (and intelligence officer), the Honourable William Drummond.[26]

On 21 March, Thesiger was met by Captain Gosset, and the general and his party were taken along a rough-hewn track to Schermbrucker's position under Mount Kempt. The party continued to Keiskammahoek via Fort Merriman, the latter distinguished as a colonial camp by the 'mass of filth' they found there. Lacking news from Wood, Thesiger was anxious to move on and so continued towards Bailie's Grave Post via the Red Hill Pass. The day's work, being in the saddle from 6 a.m. to 10.30 p.m., exhausted them and they rested for the night at Brown's House, just south of the Rabula River, where they found Streatfeild and his men.[27]

Also during this day, Wood continued to scour the bush, following a scratch plan devised by Brabant, but the results were not entirely satisfactory.[28] Meanwhile, Thesiger was confronted by a new problem: the burgher volunteers wished to return to their homes, their period of service being about to expire.[29] There was also a problem with their commissariat, and they were very short of supplies. The general lamented: '. . . it will be understood that the difficulties of command is [sic] enormously increased, and the General himself placed in an embarrassing position, when, in the middle of serious operations, a considerable portion of the force declares its intention of leaving him for their homes.'[30] This news heralded the effective end of the current operation and he returned to King William's Town to secure approval from the governor for a new levy of burgher forces.

Crealock reported 126 Ngqika killed and 682 cattle, 105 horses and 290 sheep taken between 11 and 21 March. British losses in only four days were quite significant: three officers and one private soldier, with four Mfengu also killed.[31] Captain Charles Warren, RE, commanding the Diamond Field Horse, was severely injured when a tree felled by Ngqika struck his back.[32]

Crealock jotted down three 'lessons' in his journal which he should bear in mind in future operations:

1. The General to be at the top of the mountain [Mount Kempt] and not leave any of the commanders too much discretion or liberty of action.
2. That unless roads and paths were made to connect our various parties [and] camps we should never get on and we must find out some way of getting up supplies to the troops instead of letting the troops return for supplies.
3. Introduce flag signalling.[33]

The very serious problem of communications was addressed even before
the operation was ended. There were originally only two tracks through the
area, both of them running north–south. One was the road from Burnshill,
well to the west of King William's Town, to Keiskammahoek and the other
was further east, running from Keiskammahoek over the Red Hill Pass and
down to Bailie's Grave Post. Thesiger now set his troops to work cutting new
roads through the bush, particularly in an east–west direction. Molyneux
described his own and Gosset's task as being 'in cutting a road through a
kloof to join Mount Kempt with the plateau below' at Isidenge.[34] A road
was also built for several kilometres from Bailie's Grave Post up to the Gozo
Heights.[35] Thesiger wrote: 'The effect of these [roads] must, I consider, be
looked upon as most important, as now for many years, should the rebels
again take refuge in the bush, there will be no difficulty in dealing with them
as has already been done.'[36]

On 26 March, by then having established a reasonable level of confidence in
General Thesiger, Sir Bartle Frere left King William's Town to return to Cape
Town, arriving there on 7 April. He had been away since early September the
previous year, nearly seven months, and it was vital that he get back in time for
the new session of the Cape parliament and his other administrative duties.[37]

Kroome Heights Campaign

Action was also taken in the Kroome Heights, to the north of the Fort
Beaufort–Adelaide road, where Colonel Palmer, 90th Regiment, had
been ordered to clear the Waterkloof, Schelm Kloof and Blinkwater of all
Xhosa then living there. On 3 March he began his operations: a small force
commanded by Captain Stephen John Stevens, of the 90th, consisting of a
hundred men of the 90th and two seven-pounder guns of the Royal Artillery,
was sent to occupy a position at the head of Schelm Kloof.[38]

> On the 4th March Colonel Palmer with a column composed of 300 Europeans,
> 70 Native Police and 200 Fingoes left Fort Beaufort at 9 p.m. and, making a
> night march, reached Tini Makomo's village at Blinkwater at daylight of the
> 5th, and surrounded the huts. Makomo was himself absent; but many prisoners
> were made, the rebel's cattle [taken] and their huts burnt.[39]

Heavy rain brought operations to a halt on the 6th but they resumed on
the 7th, when an attack was launched against Schelm Kloof. The Ngqika
showed little resistance and Palmer was able to penetrate into the lower
kloofs. Over the next two days the upper kloofs were scoured and all rebels

were driven out, five being reported killed and many women taken and sent away. Leaving five small posts to dominate the area, Palmer retired with the remainder of his force to his camp at Fort Fordyce on the plateau.[40]

With the expectation that he now had the area under control, Palmer issued an ultimatum to the rebels in the Kroome through W.B. Chalmers, the special commissioner. The essence of the ultimatum was that, as a result of past troubles, the Waterkloof and Schelm Kloof were now denied to Xhosa residents. The Ngqika living in the Blinkwater and Schelm Kloof, he said, had refused to leave and 'the consequences, to them, have therefore been most disastrous.'

> If the Kafirs at the back of Fort Fordyce and those in the Water Kloof, will submit, and come to me and give up all their guns, and assegais, and leave this country quickly, they will not be interfered with and I will give them passes to remove with their cattle, women and children, to [other] locations.[41]

The deadline for acceptance of these terms was noon on 15 March. The messenger returned after delivering the ultimatum without reply, and operations were commenced in the Waterkloof on 16 March.[42]

The general area of the Waterkloof has been described in an earlier chapter (see page 88). The Waterkloof valley itself has extremely steep sides clothed with heavy forest and it has but few passes into it other than its north-westerly entrance. Two of these passes are to be found on either side of the great north–south ridge on its southern side, which was then known as the 'Iron Mountain'. The kloof on the eastern side of this ridge, which represents one of the passes, was then known as 'Myers Kloof'.

One company of the 90th occupied Botha's farm, in the very centre of the Waterkloof opposite the Iron Mountain, with 220 burghers placed along the line of Myers Kloof in the south-west and two guns were placed on the north-eastern ridges under Captain Smith, RA. The passes on either side of the Iron Mountain were held by Native Police.

With these arrangements complete, Palmer led his principal force into the Waterkloof through the kloof on the western side of the Iron Mountain. His column was preceded by Native Police, flanked by Mfengu in the bush on each side. These were followed by more mounted volunteers, then by Palmer with two more companies of the 90th and two guns from the Royal Artillery. The Mfengu and Native Police guarded the entrance to the valley while the main body came through. When they arrived in the valley, Palmer found that the burghers were already engaged. He sent the Mfengu forward to support them, together with a company of the 90th. As the rebels withdrew to the east along the valley floor, they were engaged by the guns on the eastern rim of the valley 'and must have suffered heavily'.[43] The valley then being completely penetrated, Palmer turned his attention to the Iron Mountain, on the heavily timbered southern side of the Waterkloof. This was swept clean, fourteen enemy dead were counted and many cattle were taken. Among the dead was thought to be one of Tini Maqoma's councillors. Large stores of provisions and blankets were also found in caves of the various small kloofs in the valley, and were brought away.

After these operations were completed, Palmer established five more posts in the Waterkloof from which patrols were constantly made throughout the valley 'but there has been no sign of Kaffirs returning to the Water Kloof, all traces met with were of those leaving the neighbourhood.' The Kroome Mountains could finally be declared clear of Ngqika.

On 21 March, the Colonial Secretary had arranged for a thousand Mfengu to be sent from the Transkei to cover the shortage which Thesiger claimed existed. They were to arrive by 28 March and so the general arranged for his next attack to take place on that day. By then he had sorted out his columns and all were standing by to make their sweep. Thesiger noted, in his despatch of 10 April, that '[the Mfengu] did not arrive, however, until the 3rd April, and my plan of operation was consequently very seriously disturbed.'[44]

Second Pirie Bush Operation

Despite this setback, the Ngqika were found 'in considerable numbers' in the country between the 'Gozo Heights and the precipice west of Haynes' Mill [McNaghten's Kranz]' and Thesiger arranged an attack on 29 March. The assault enjoyed only partial success, the Ngqika melting away from their position, which 'if properly defended, must have entailed considerable loss on our side'.[45]

The rebels had now been confined to the Buffalo Poort, an area of such considerable extent as to compel the general to await the arrival of the Transkei Mfengu before trying to beat through it. In the meantime, Thesiger tightened his grip on the encirclement, preventing food getting in and rebels getting out. Since the Ngqika commissariat function was largely undertaken by their women, movement proved difficult to control. Even so, mealie gardens in the vicinity were destroyed and, according to Molyneux, 'portions of the bush were beaten each day.'[46]

William Ayliff led his one thousand Transkei Mfengu into Stutterheim on 4 April and from there proceeded to Isidenge. The 'grand attack' was set to commence on the 5th.[47] Thesiger's plan, in simple terms, was for the Mfengu to drive the Ngqika through the bush from Mount Kempt to Haynes' Mill, towards an arc of troops waiting to receive them. The signal for the start of the 'beat' was the firing of three guns from Mount Kempt. One cannot help but think that this scheme was considered very much akin to a day of grouse shooting in the Scottish Highlands.

The guns fired their salvo and about 6 a.m. the Mfengu began to scour the bush – from the amount of gunfire, they were seemingly engaged in the most bloody conflict. Molyneux described what actually happened:

> From almost the beginning our white comrades lining the plateaux above must have thought we were engaged in a terrific battle. Every bush-buck or blue-buck that was viewed got a tremendous volley, the men firing right or left or back, whichever way the beasts went, regardless of wounding or killing their comrades or officers; yet they carefully avoided the bases of the krantzes, the very places where the enemy might be expected to hide. They were so untrustworthy that I was not surprised to see the white officers of each corps invariably keeping together. Four white men with carbines can make a good defence; a company of Fingoes with one officer would probably run if attacked, and leave their white leader to his fate.[48]

The new campaign was in vain: the Ngqika had used the days since the end of March to slip away again.

There was more success to the north-west. Siyolo, chief of the Ndlambe Ngqika, then living on the Keiskamma River, had joined the rebels and had been defeated by Commandant von Linsingen. On this day, Siyolo was surreptitiously making his way with some twelve hundred warriors towards the Ntaba kaNdoda when he was discovered crossing the Debe Nek. He was immediately attacked by Captain Warren with his Diamond Field Horse. Siyolo was heavily defeated and fled into the nearby bush, leaving sixty dead behind him. Warren also took three hundred cattle after the engagement.[49]

On hearing of this success, Thesiger immediately diverted some of his troops to the west to continue the attack on the following morning: Wood came south down the Keiskamma River from Keiskammahoek while Streatfeild and his Mfengu descended the Rabula to cut off any retreat into the Amathola range.

First Ntaba KaNdoda Operation

On the morning of the 6th, the bush south of the Ntaba kaNdoda was shelled and around noon the Mfengu moved in. The Ndlambe melted away into the Lotutu (Tutu) bush north-west of the mountain, and the troops took possession. The Lotutu bush was then attacked in the afternoon. In the first rush, Captain Webster, leading some of his Mfengu, was shot dead. Molyneux noted: 'Poor Webster's body was carried up on an extemporised litter after dark; it was evident that he had been shot with a Snider rifle, for there was but a very small blue hole in the centre of his forehead, while the whole of the back of his head had been blown completely away.'[50]

The second sortie fared little better but the third, in the late afternoon, 'was crowned with partial success, a great portion of the wood having been occupied by the Fingoes'. The Ndlambe once again managed to steal away during the night 'and dispersed in every direction'.[51]

One group was intercepted on the 7th in a wooded kloof which was then heavily shelled by two guns, following which the kloof was cleared by two companies of the 2/24th, with the loss of one private soldier. Two Mfengu were also killed and twenty wounded. It was estimated that Xhosa losses in the first week of April were of the order of five hundred.[52]

On 15 April, General Thesiger made a tour of inspection of the Ntaba kaNdoda and Debe Nek area and found that there were still many Xhosa rebels in the vicinity, frequently raiding Mfengu homesteads during the night for supplies. As a result of this inspection he determined that further attacks were required to drive the rebels out. Unfortunately, however, he was again deprived of both colonial and African troops, both of whom chose this moment to return to their homes. These delays were clearly frustrating, Thesiger remarking in his report of 24 April: 'This lull in active operations has been most distasteful to me, feeling as I do that the only way to bring this War to an end is to constantly harass the Kaffirs, cutting off their supplies, and preventing their obtaining fresh recruits.'[53]

Second Ntaba KaNdoda Operation

The lull ended on 30 April, on which date Thesiger had determined that his new offensive against the Ntaba kaNdoda was to begin. In preparation, he moved troops to their new start points in a wide circle about the Ntaba kaNdoda. It should be mentioned here that, for the first time, a contingent of loyal Ngqika from Siwani's people was actively engaged against their brothers.

The general's plan for this assault was particularly complex and is set out below in its entirety:

On Tuesday the 30th April the Forces will advance from their respective Camps, so as to be ready to attack at daybreak.

Colonel Wood's force, as per margin, will advance in two columns, Streatfeild's and Lonsdale's Fingoes supported by 2 Companies 90th L. Infantry, will beat the bush towards the Taba Ka Indoda on the right side of the Zanyorkwe Valley. Bowker's Rovers will watch this Valley.

3 Companies 90th L.I. with 4 Guns and Diamond Field Horse will advance from Burns Hill & Makabalekile ridge on to the open ground west of the Taba Ka Indoda.

Commandant Von Linsingen's force will move up the Burnside [Hill]– Bailey's [Grave] Post road & will beat the southern slopes of the Taba Ka Indoda, in a westerly direction, & work its way eventually onto the open ground on [to] which Colonel Wood's European column will debouch.

Lt Colonel Degacher's force consisting of 5 Companies 2/24th & 4 Guns will move from Bailie's [Grave] Post to the ground near the Intaba Ka Indoda, where the Guns will be placed in position to shell the Bush.

Maclean's Fingoes will move at 2 a.m. from Bailie's [Grave] Post to the mouth of the Zanyorkwe Valley, and will beat the eastern side of the Valley bush towards the Intaba Ka Indoda.

Frontier Light Horse and 1 Company 2/24th under Major Buller, CB, 60th Rifles, will move one hour before daylight to ridge between Zanyorkwe & Congo [Gongqo] Valley.

Captain Sampson's [Sansom's] Volunteers will watch the Bush on the south side of the Intaba Ka Indoda & prevent the rebels breaking out in a South westerly direction.

Captain Comeley will watch the Bush leading from the Intaba Ka Indoda to the Perie bush & endeavour to prevent the rebels crossing from one to the other.

The Hottentots now at the drift near Bailie's [Grave] Post, will guard the last named post during the absence of the Company 2/24th Foot.[54]

By 5 a.m. on 30 April, the 1,600 European and 2,400 African troops that made up the assault forces had swung into action and the reports of the various commanders are now summarised separately, so as to offer a more comprehensive picture.

Major Hackett, 90th Regiment, commanded one of Wood's two columns, which consisted of two companies of the 90th and more than a thousand Mfengu under Streatfeild and Lonsdale. Hackett moved from the lower Rabula River to take a position in an extended line which reached from the upper Zanyorkwe River to Figland's farm, at the top of the Makabalekile spur and near the western end of the Ntaba kaNdoda escarpment. From here, his line moved north towards the Lotutu bush, while a force of volunteers was left to guard Hobbs Drift and the Rabula.

Wood himself led his second column, consisting of three companies of the 90th Regiment, thirty-five volunteers and four RA guns. He also had with him 130 Khoikhoi levies and 46 Alice Native Police. He first moved up the Makabalekile spur, to be followed shortly afterwards by Captain Warren and a part of his Diamond Field Horse, the remainder staying behind to watch the Debe Flats.[55]

As his force ascended the ridge, he noticed three to five hundred Ngqika running from the east to support another group obviously in ambush on either side of Wood's route. The trap was sprung a little too early but nevertheless the Ngqika fought with 'great spirit'.

> The column under Colonel Wood had already traversed about one-fourth of the distance when the Kaffirs formed across the bush path, and till now concealed by a turn of the path, charged the advanced guard, formed by Captain Stevens' company of the 90th Light Infantry. His men were immediately hotly engaged, and on the Captain being shot through the face, the rebels cheering charged, to be at once repulsed. Lieutenant Saltmarshe now took Captain Stevens' place, and within five minutes he was killed. The men, however, pressed on under Colour-Sergeant Smith . . .[56]

Wood called on Major Apsley Cherry to take command of the company, now without officers. The vanguard moved forward again, supported by Captain Stuart Smith's two guns firing case (or canister) shells into the bush at a range of only thirty yards. On reaching open ground, Wood paused only long enough to signal his ambulances, Scotch carts and bullock guns to come up, then moved forward again to join von Linsingen and Buller. The latter lined the bush paths leading into the Zanyorkwe and Lotutu ravines, to finally link up with the column from the lower Rabula about 4 p.m.[57]

Wood reported that he had taken about seventy head of cattle and a few horses. The many women who came out of the bush belonged to Siyolo, Edmund Sandile and Phato, and they said that Siyolo himself had defended the Makabalekile ridge. Wood also learned that Edmund Sandile and Tini Maqoma were in the Lotutu bush.[58] Wood's casualties were quite high, particularly among the Burnshill contingent: in addition to Lieutenant Saltmarshe, two privates of the 90th were also killed, with Captain Stevens and five other ranks wounded. Six of Maclean's Mfengu were also wounded.

Commandant von Linsingen organised his force into three groups. On the right he had Rautenbach (in command) and his Horse and another colonial cavalry unit, the Berlin Horse, half of whom were dismounted, together with

Maclean's and Kirsten's Mfengu. Their aim was to attack the south-east of the Ntaba kaNdoda.[59]

In the centre, under von Linsingen himself, were some foot volunteers, with several units of Mfengu. He also had three hundred of Siwani's Ngqika. Von Linsingen's left wing was commanded by Captain Warren, with his Diamond Field Horse, and Bartholomew's and Lonsdale's Mfengu. They were to move up the Makabalekile spur, then scour the southern slopes of the Ntaba kaNdoda.

Just after sunrise, the whole force was ordered forward but as they advanced they found little more than 'old traces of Kaffir encampments'. As they gained the tops of the ridges, they saw cattle and a few Ngqika to the north. Having achieved the ridge summits, the force, with the exception of Warren's Diamond Field Horse and two companies of Siwani's Ngqika, was directed to scour the western side of the Zanyorkwe Valley. Molyneux, then acting as staff officer to von Linsingen, described the effort required to reach it from his position atop the Ntaba kaNdoda: 'What a race it was! Into holes, out again, hands and faces bleeding from thorns, knees punctured, and shirt-sleeves in ribands, till after about an hour of it our left came out on the open plateau west of the Zanyorkwe Valley, and our centre force hit off the bush covering the valley's western slope.'[60]

Warren and the Ngqika were placed under the command of Colonel Wood. Of these latter, von Linsingen said:

> [They] behaved extremely well, knew no 'Single File' business and were difficult to be held in, when on the track of the enemy. They killed 7 rebels, one of these was hit by an assegai thrown from a distance of nearly 50 yards. They are very indifferently armed, having guns of a very inferior description and one half only armed with assegais.[61]

Again, von Linsingen found little evidence of rebels in the Zanyorkwe Valley, eventually joining up with Streatfeild, Lonsdale and a company of the 90th. The combined force made a three-quarter wheel to the left and assisted in scouring the remainder of the valley. He reported having killed seventeen rebels in a sharp engagement in a deep kloof leading into the Zanyorkwe Valley, in which he was supported by Warren.

General Thesiger was particularly satisfied with the system of flag signalling that had been developed from Crealock's idea:

> The system of Flag signalling was found most valuable, it enabled me to know what was happening over a large extent of broken country & to transmit the necessary orders.

Colonel Wood was able to telegraph from the position he had gained with his advance guard to the remainder of his force that had not entered the bush, 'Advance with caution', when it would have been dangerous to have sent a Messenger, & I myself was informed of what had happened, and of the names of the Officers killed and wounded &c., a very short time after the occurrence, information that could only have reached me by messenger sooner than in 3 hours . . .[62]

It is also noteworthy that Thesiger and his staff were not above the deliberate leaking of false information as to the general's immediate intentions. Molyneux explains:

Some time later, all our efforts to catch the rebels en masse proving ineffectual, and our messages going by wire through this station, suspicion fell upon the native clerks. False information was accordingly telegraphed purposely to Colonel Wood; and the Kafirs were found in the very place where the message had said that the troops were not to be employed.[63]

Early on the morning of 1 May, groups of rebel Ngqika attempted to slip through the British cordon by crossing into the Pirie bush. Some probably reached their destination but one group stumbled into the Bailie's Grave Post in the morning mist. Thesiger sent a company of the 2/24th to assist but by the time it arrived the emergency was over, one Ngqika having been killed.

At sunrise the bush between the post and the Ntaba kaNdoda, a distance of about five kilometres, was searched by Maclean's Mfengu, aided by the FLH, two companies of the 2/24th and two guns. Later in the day, von Linsingen left the Debe Nek to search the bush that the troops had not already covered. Eleven Ngqika were killed, two prisoners were taken and a hundred women and children surrendered.

On 2 May, Thesiger made a personal visit to every post round the Ntaba kaNdoda. He sent Colonel Degacher, with two companies of the 2/24th, and von Linsingen with his force, to scour the Zanyorkwe Valley again. During the afternoon, after Degacher had left to return to his camp, a group of Ngqika were found concealed under what was called 'Siyolo's Krantz'.

The position was covered by dense Bush & by large detached boulders of rock from behind which the enemy fired on anyone approaching it; one of Siwani's Kaffirs belonging to Von Linsingen's force was killed endeavouring to do so. Colonel Degacher's force returned, on receiving this intelligence, but it was found that the Guns could not be used without withdrawing the cordon of men necessary to prevent the rebels escape.[64]

Von Linsingen spent the night in the valley to prevent the rebels' escape. Despite appeals to surrender, the men refused to do so.

On 3 May, von Linsingen began his attack, Crealock noting:

About 8 a.m. Siwani's Caffres expressed a desire to attack the caves; Buller was away with Nixon at breakfast, Molyneux, Gosset and myself were looking on. Mr Clarke in charge of Siwani's men came forward and saying 'Well come on if you are so anxious' [and] led the way. A shot glanced off a rock over his head which had the effect of making all the hulking great germans [*sic*] take shelter behind a large tree . . . while Fingoes etc. crouched behind any piece of available cover. We were not awe struck by the pluck shewn by many. V. Linsingen came on the scene at this moment and taking off his coat and taking a little nip, which two things are a sign he means business, proceeded to take his men around the flank. He was anxious to withdraw those who had already gone on, as it was the wrong manner to attack, he said. This however, I refused to let him do saying as they had once gone in they had better not be withdrawn, for which they did not want much excuse. Occasional shots were now fired by the rebels and at them, but about 8.30 I observed to Gosset it was becoming rather like a rat hunt, so we returned to camp after a severe climb.[65]

By noon, von Linsingen reported that he had taken the position, twenty-one Ngqika having been killed in the operation, and two prisoners taken. On closer examination of the ground, an 'almost impracticable' path was found by which Siyolo and some of his men were thought to have stolen away during the night.

It being plain that the Ngqika had once again slipped back to the Pirie bush, Thesiger ordered his headquarters moved to King William's Town and visited the Pirie chain of posts. While doing so, he received another report that rebels were collecting in the Buffalo range above Keiskammahoek. He then arranged for Colonel Wood to attack them on the morning of 4 May. The rebels, however, had already moved down into the Gwili Gwili Valley at daybreak. Captain Robert Develing, commanding the Alice Mfengu levy serving under Rupert Lonsdale, had been watching this area for some days.

Captain Develing in command of the Alice Fingo Levy numbering only 150 men, & Captain Pohl, who had been watching for some days this part of the country, at once attacked them and after a short engagement drove them back up the hill into the Buffalo Poort Bush. 22 of the rebels were counted dead on the Field; 4 of Captain Develing's men were wounded, 1 Fingo woman and 1 man resident in the valley were killed & three wounded; Captain Develing re-took all but 10 Head of the 100 Cattle & 300 sheep which had been captured by the rebels.[66]

Thesiger concluded that the object of the Ngqika raid had been to obtain supplies, as other reports indicated that the rebels were now suffering from extreme hunger.

Third Pirie Bush Operation

The general planned to launch his next attack on the Pirie bush on 8 May, and arranged his troops as follows:

1. Colonel Wood was to move from Keiskammahoek to the Gozo Heights.
2. Colonel Degacher would move from Haynes' Mill to the plateau west of the Buffalo Poort.
3. Commandant von Linsingen would march from the Pirie mission station to join Degacher on the plateau.
4. Major Buller would move from Mount Kempt, by a path cut in April, to the same plateau.
5. Commandant Schermbrucker would move from Isidenge to Mount Kempt, and then follow Major Buller.
6. Captain Surplice, 24th, was to be guided by Haynes himself to a position below the western krantz of the Buffalo Poort, to ambush the Ngqika when driven from the plateau.[67]

The clearance of the Pirie bush began about 7 a.m. and General Thesiger again tried to command the attack from Haynes' Mill, mistakenly, according to Crealock, who felt he would have had more control had he been on Mount Kempt.

The day was not a triumph. Crealock gave two prerequisites for success: that Buller get down to the plateau unmolested, since it was reported that the Ngqika controlled the corridor; and that the tracks from the plateau down to the valley above Haynes' Mill be properly guarded to prevent the Ngqika escape.[68] Buller fulfilled his part of the arrangement but Haynes did not. In his despatch of 15 May, General Thesiger reported:

Major Buller's force descended from Mount Kempt, by Molyneux' path to the lower plateau. These forces advanced as ordered, but the Company of 2/24th under Captain Surplice and the Fingoes under Captain Haynes, instead of waylaying the path called Buller's path, went off too far to their right.

This mistake afforded an opening by which the enemy on retiring from the plateau above could escape, their retreat being covered (as actually happened) by a few determined men.[69]

Crealock offered no excuse for the indolent Haynes:

[Buller] the day previous to the attack quite satisfied himself that Mr. Haines [*sic*] knew the spot he was to hold and Capt[ain] Surplice's company of 2.24th also. Buller's own advance through the Bush was quite successful and had those paths been waylaid as ordered and counted upon, Sandilli himself would have been caught or shot and a very successful day been the result. As it was these waylaying parties went off to a place where they were useless and allowed a free passage to the Caffres to retire by.[70]

Molyneux was even more emphatic as to Haynes' incompetence:

At daybreak on the 8th the forces moved off; all went well, and they reached their assigned positions, except Captain Surplice's detachment which had Haynes of the mill as its guide. As this man Haynes knew every inch of this bush, having cut timber in it for years, he had been chosen for guide, notwithstanding that he had shirked a job some little while previously. He had been shown the exact spot for the ambush on the day before by Major Buller; yet he misled the company and rendered the whole plan abortive.[71]

It is interesting to note that Captain Surplice retired from the 2/24th in July 1878 and one might conjecture that this incident may have been a contributing factor to his decision to leave the regiment.

Wood arrived before daylight on the Gozo Heights, with four companies of the 90th. He also had two guns, with an escort of a fifth company of the 90th. He noted that both guns had suffered broken shafts 'from the guns turning upside down'. Buller arrived at break of day and Colonel Degacher a little later, the Mfengu 'being very stiff and cold from the heavy rain last night'. Schermbrucker did not arrive until 9 a.m. and von Linsingen not until noon.[72]

Wood's operation began when he sent two companies of the 90th and the Mfengu to beat across the plateau but no enemy was to be found. Some five hundred of them were reported to have passed down the Buller–Haynes' Mill path before Maclean's Mfengu had closed the gap.

Wood needed to know in which direction the Ngqika had gone and Buller went off down the same path and then turned north. The Ngqika were

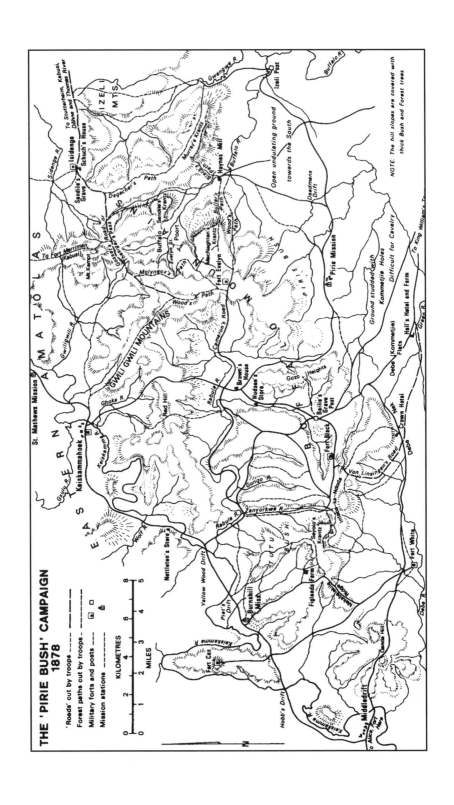

THE 'PIRIE BUSH' CAMPAIGN
1878

'Roads' cut by troops ————
Forest paths cut by troops - - -
Military forts and posts ▣ ▢
Mission stations ———— ⛪

MILES
0   1   2   3   4   5
KILOMETRES
0   4   8

NOTE. The hill slopes are covered with thick Bush and Forest trees discovered holding the same rocks as they had on 29 March. What followed is recorded in a report by Major Buller:

> Colonel Wood now sent up Colonel Degacher with two Companies of the 24th, but owing to some misconception, they formed on the right where there were no Kaffirs. I then brought up the Frontier Light Horse and while forming them for attack, I regret to state that Captain McNaughten [*sic*] was killed and Captain Whalley severely wounded.[73]

Buller's account is emphatically contradicted in the regimental account written by officers of the 2/24th:

> Soon afterwards, very heavy firing was heard in the direction Major Buller had taken, and information was brought that the Frontier Light Horse had been suddenly fired upon and had lost two officers and several men killed and wounded. The hospital stretchers of the 24th were asked for and sent up, and two companies in support; but only H Company went forward as C was withheld for the protection of the guns which had come up with Colonel Wood's column . . .
>
> This report [by Major Buller] was entirely erroneous. For, as we have seen, information was brought of the loss sustained by the Frontier Light Horse, and stretchers were asked for, before even the order to support was given; Lieut.- Colonel Degacher was talking to Colonel Wood at the time; and further, as [H] company was marching up [the] hill to support, it met the wounded officer (Captain Whalley) and men being brought down in the 24th stretchers.[74]

These two versions are but one example of the confusion which could be caused when fighting over such difficult terrain.

Wood sent off Maclean's and Lonsdale's Mfengu to turn the rebels' flanks. Before Maclean could take up his position, having further to travel, Lonsdale pressed down on the Ngqika flank while Buller led his men, with some Stutterheim Police and a few men of the 24th, down the path and cleared it with a cheer. The rebels, with the exception of five men, retired. The latter, armed with double-barrelled shotguns, made a stand, killing Private Davies, FLH, and one Mfengu, and wounding another, before all five were killed. During this time, Wood's artillery shelled the bush, aiming at smoke from fires indicating the positions of other rebels. He reported killing only eight Ngqika, although there were reports of some falling over a nearby precipice and a recently buried body was also found.

In spite of the stringent precautions taken by Thesiger to keep the operation a secret, Buller was of the opinion that 'the enemy knew of our intended attack, for there were no signs of a hurried departure', an opinion shared by his general.[75]

The next day, Thesiger scoured the western portion of the Buffalo Valley in a vain attempt to regain the initiative lost the previous day. The only result was a wounded Captain A.G. Godwin-Austen of 'B' company, 2/24th. Fatefully, Lieutenant Gonville Bromhead assumed command of the company.

Thesiger's plans had thus far been largely reactive, and he seems to have sent units all over the countryside at the first report of an Ngqika presence, a pattern of behaviour that he would repeat at Isandlwana with fatal consequences. Now he determined 'that from [10 May] two distinct forces should daily harass the enemy occupying the Intaba Ka Indoda and Peri [*sic*] bushes.'[76] On that day, Commandant von Linsingen was despatched to the Ntaba kaNdoda area with three companies of Colonel Degacher's 2/24th under Major Wilsone Black, one company of volunteer infantry, seventy-nine mounted infantry, and Allan Maclean's 550 Mfengu. Von Linsingen also took with him Siwani's loyal Ngqika.

The general also ordered the construction of two earth forts as the centre of these operations: Colonel Wood built his eponymous Fort Evelyn on the Gozo Heights 'for a garrison for two companies and two guns';[77] Fort Black, named after Major Wilsone Black of the 24th, was built to the east of the Ntaba kaNdoda, for a garrison of one company and two guns, to command the Zanyorkwe Valley.[78]

On 11 May, 'parties of rebels unaware of the return of our forces' were shelled in the Zanyorkwe Valley by a battery under Major Harness while Maclean's Mfengu combed through the valley once again. A day later, none were to be found in their usual haunts but some were located in the late morning to the east of the Makabalekile Ridge. Von Linsingen immediately attacked them, inflicting a loss of thirty-three killed.[79]

Colonel Wood reported that Commandant Lonsdale had also left the Gozo Heights at 3 a.m. on the 12th, and, after descending to Haynes' Mill, entered the eastern valley of the Buffalo Poort. With Captain Harber on the right and Captain Duncombe on the left (two more future NNC officers), they ascended what was known as Sandile's Krantz and engaged about five hundred Ngqika whom they found there. Lonsdale reported forty-four rebels killed and eighteen women prisoners. His own force suffered the loss of one man, with five wounded. The prisoners taken by Lonsdale reported that they were greatly disheartened and 'straitened for food'. Thesiger was also greatly encouraged to receive news from Charles Brownlee that Sandile had made enquiries as to the terms he might be offered.[80]

On 14 May, a general order was published, announcing that the Diamond Field Horse, under Captain Warren, RE, had been called home.[81] On 16 May, a force of police and burghers, having heard that a body of rebels had made its way across the Keiskamma, probably intending to enter the Fish River bush, followed them up and defeated them near Breakfast Vlei, with a loss to the enemy rebels of twenty-four killed.

During the next week, reports filtered in that both the Ntaba kaNdoda and Pirie districts were being evacuated by the Ngqika, the constant harassment and resulting privation breaking their spirit. A report of 22 May stated that the rebels 'have dispersed themselves over the face of the country in numerous small marauding parties . . . Owing to this new phase which the war has assumed, travelling has become dangerous for small parties and greater precautions have become necessary for ensuring the safety of convoys.'[82]

On 20 May, a report was received that Tini Maqoma had dissociated himself from Sandile and had returned to the Waterkloof.[83] The following day, General Thesiger felt sufficiently confident in the situation in the colony to begin a seventeen-day tour of inspection of the Transkei, accompanied by his staff.[84] As he left, an attack was launched on the Waterkloof by colonial troops, dispersing the rebels who had taken residence there. Tini Maqoma was reported captured in the attack.[85]

Death of Sandile

On 29 May, a patrol consisting of two companies of Lonsdale's Mfengu engaged a hundred Ngqika in the bush to the north of Isidenge Hill, driving them towards Fort Merriman and St Andrews. (There was some initial confusion as to the date of this engagement, it first being reported as taking place on 30 May.) Dukwana, formerly an elder at the Mgwali mission station and a bodyguard to Sandile, was amongst the slain. The chief was reported to have been an excellent marksman and did much of the execution during the engagement. Seventeen rebels were killed and two Mfengu were also lost, with four wounded – shot, it was said, by Dukwana.[86]

Thesiger wrote a despatch on 2 June from Ibeka, part way through his tour of inspection.[87] In it he summarised the situation for his masters at the War Office in London. He began by reporting that 'nothing of importance' had occurred during the previous two weeks and that colonial and imperial forces continued to harass the rebels. He confirmed the view that they were 'dispersing over the country'. He also confirmed that Tini Maqoma had indeed been captured near Fort Beaufort and that his brother Tapi had also been taken. Meanwhile, Siyolo was thought to have taken refuge in the Fish River bush, while Sandile had left the Pirie bush and was seeking safe haven with his brother Anta.

He noted that the prominent chief Dukwana, a close colleague of Sandile, had been killed in the fighting of 29 May when Lonsdale's Mfengu had attacked the party of Ngqika. His positive identification was the result of finding a letter on the body from Rev. John Cumming, a missionary at Emgwali mission station, to Dukwana.

Thesiger concluded by suggesting that the evidence in the colony, together with his inspection of the Transkei, led him to think that the war was slowly drawing to an end: 'Reviewing the situation of affairs in the colony & its frontiers, I am of opinion that matters are tending, altho' slowly, to a conclusion of the disturbances.'[88]

On 5 June, the diary of operations contained further news:

> It is asserted by the natives, and believed by the Under Secretary for Native Affairs, that Sandilli was killed in the action of 30 May [sic] at the same time as Dukwana; but that his body was removed by his relatives.
>
> [It] is also asserted that Siyolo has been killed in the Fish River bush.
>
> The Water and Schelm Kloofs have again been cleared of rebels, and a brother of the chief Oba killed.[89]

The rebel chiefs, it seems, were falling like nine-pins.

Thesiger's despatch of 12 June was even more positive, and it also contained further details of casualties among the Ngqika chiefs. He claimed that the rebels had now been 'driven completely from the fastnesses of the Buffalo Range' and the energy of the various commanders had resulted, as he had predicted, in either the death or capture of the rebel leaders. Thesiger also mentioned in an aside that an error had been made in the date of the engagement in which Sandile and Dukwana had been killed, and should have been recorded as 29 May. A search had been made for Sandile's body and it had been recovered from a bush location on 7 June.[90]

A post-mortem was carried out on the body on 8 June by Dr Herbert Everitt, a medical officer and captain in the Tarkstadt Volunteers. It read, in part:

> From external appearances I am of opinion that death had taken place about four days [previously]. The left side of the face, left orbit, and right arm, and one

or two smaller patches had been eaten away by animals. I found a bullet wound having entrance posteriously in the right hypochondriac region, a little above the right loin, and its aperture of exit anteriously three inches to the right of the ensiform cartilage, through the seventh and eighth ribs, the bullet fracturing the ribs extensively in its course both back and front. There was injury to the right lobe of [the] liver, and fragments of ribs were driven into [the] abdominal cavity. From the inflammation and extravasation about the wound I should judge the injury to have been received some days before death; and from the extensive laceration of soft parts, comminution of bone and size of apertures, [I] am of opinion that the wound was caused by a Snider bullet.[91]

Milton asserts that Sandile had abandoned his dependence on alcohol during the last few months of his life.[92]

Sandile was buried by Commandant Schermbrucker, commanding the Stutterheim contingent, at Schuch's farm, about three kilometres east of Mount Kempt, on 9 June:

In accordance with instructions I had the dead body of Sandilli decently and properly, but without any military consideration, buried at Isidenge this morning at 11 o'clock. The interment was witnessed by all the European forces in the camp, by a number of Imperial troops from Mount Kemp who passed through here on patrol under command of Major Dunbar at the time of the burial, and by about 500 Fingos of Commandants Streatfield [sic] and Maclean's levies.[93]

There is a myth that the chief's head was removed before burial, and that it was taken back to England by Fred Carrington and kept on his mantelpiece. This is demonstrably untrue, since Carrington had left the Eastern Cape for the Transvaal much earlier than Sandile's death.[94] Furthermore, the remains were excavated in 2005 and found to be intact, including the skull. Incidentally, they were also confirmed as being those of Sandile.[95]

The general's despatch of 12 June continued that Siyolo had been killed in the Fish River bush and that other leaders had either been killed or captured. Sandile's sons Edmund and Mathanzima had sent a message from their sanctuary at Thomas River asking to surrender now that their father was dead. The only other leaders still at large were Ndimba and Makinana. In a later paragraph, Thesiger reported that Ndimba had surrendered and that Sandile's half-brother Anta had died two days earlier, the latter having been ailing for some time and not having joined the rebellion.

End of the War

Following the death of Sandile, and the death or capture of so many other Ngqika leaders, the rebels' morale collapsed. They were already assailed by hunger and cold, death and disease. By mid-June the rebellion had run its course. On 2 July, General Thesiger reported the capture of both Edmund Sandile and Mathanzima,[96] and a general amnesty had been declared by Sir Bartle Frere the previous day. The war was finally over and the once-great Xhosa people had been reduced to their lowest ebb. Total losses during the war were reported on 21 June as being:[97]

	Xhosa	*British*
Killed	3,680	12 officers
		48 men
		133 Africans
Wounded		10 officers
		47 men
		161 Africans
Captured	171 men	
	1,522 women and children	
	45,336 cattle	
	579 horses	

Thus the Ninth Frontier War in the Eastern Cape came to a close, but its effects would continue to resound through the decades to follow. General Thesiger had already made arrangements for some of his troops to move to Natal, and the 24th and 90th regiments were soon to follow. It was July 1878 and already Sir Bartle Frere was considering the possibility of conflict with the Zulu king, Cetshwayo kaMpande.

Epilogue

The Kaffirs should be made to know and feel that the white man was master of the land.

J. Gordon Sprigg, February 1878

The death of Sandile brought an end to the ninth and last frontier war, and with its end came the complete military and civil subjugation of the Xhosa people. This was consolidated by the government in two ways: further confiscation of Xhosa land and the disarmament of all indigenous Africans.

Shortly after his installation in February 1878, the new prime minister, J. Gordon Sprigg, announced that black Africans would have to atone for their guilt in starting the war.[1] He announced plans to re-settle the Ngqika as British subjects in small villages in locations on a non-tribal basis. The old practice of chiefly control of land would be replaced by the introduction of individual tenure for each family head. Finally, the power of the traditional chiefs was to be further eroded by giving magistrates more power, and by payments to government-appointed headmen.[2]

These matters were overshadowed by the dismissal debates which dominated the next parliamentary sitting in May 1878. Nevertheless, amendments were made to the Native Locations Act of 1876, amendments which included the redefinition of an African location as any collection of more than five huts per square mile occupied by non-employees of the land-owner. Such locations were temporarily permitted to remain, but were soon abolished by proclamation. Spicer notes that this measure was quickly introduced and in the East London area, 'black squatters and tenant farmers were ruthlessly evicted without any alternative land being provided.' Such evictions, of course, increased the population density of existing locations and the consequent movement of Xhosa people into white employment.[3]

Re-Settlement of the Xhosa

The government announced that the Ngqika were to be removed from the colony and established in a location in the Transkei. This was a measure long considered in earlier days but now it was to be implemented. The first people to be removed were, remarkably, not the rebel clans but those who had chosen not to support Sandile and the war party: the people of Feni, Kona and the recently deceased Anta were to be moved across the Kei River, the announcement being deliberately delayed until the last day of sitting of the 1878 parliament.

It was also announced that there was to be no white settlement in the Transkei, at least for the time being. This last caused such an uproar among the frontier colonists that Sprigg was forced to back down and, during the parliamentary recess of 1878, two land boards were created: one for the allotment of white farms in the Ngqika territory and the other to divide Gcalekaland into European farms and black locations.

Spicer suggests that there was some difficulty for the government finding adequate reasons to justify the movement of the Ngqika into the Transkei, and that two were put forward. The first, and least convincing, was that it removed the Africans from the influence of alcohol, because no canteens were to be permitted in the new locations. The second, put forward by Sprigg himself, was that 'The advantages of the new system of village settlement, closer magisterial supervision and the imminent introduction of individual tenure, outweighed any emotional attachment to their old land that the Ngqika might have had.'4

When told of their impending removal on 6 August 1878, the loyal Ngqika were astonished at the arbitrary manner in which this decision had been taken, without reference to the chiefs concerned. Charles Brownlee met Anta's people on 2 September:

> I explained to them that in their interests as well as those of the Colony the Government after mature consideration had decided on moving the Gaikas from their present location and settling them across the Kei, that at the peace of 1850 they were told as a tribe and through their Chiefs that they would be permitted to live as British subjects West of the Kei so long as they conducted themselves in a peaceful and orderly manner, that they had not fulfilled those conditions, they had robbed the Colonial farmers to an enormous extent, and their principal Chief [Sandile] with many of his adherents had gone into rebellion against the Government, and the Gaikas had thus as a tribe forfeited the right, to occupy this land, but as many of them had remained loyal to Government they would not be worsted by the action of those who had gone into rebellion, they would be liberally provided for in land across the Kei, every man would obtain title to his land, and having title neither Government nor Chief could remove them from the land which would be

their own, and an inheritance for their children, that they would be placed under the care and supervision of magistrates and would be located on their land as British subjects . . .[5]

Anta's brother Kaltom replied that they had remained loyal to the British through the Cattle Killing and the late war, had suffered from drought and the loss of cattle to the rebel Ngqika, and he begged the government to re-consider its decision to move them. Brownlee was implacable, emphasising the permanent land tenancy that was to be made available to them; the Africans soon recognised their helplessness and accepted the decision with as much grace as the circumstances permitted.

The other clans reacted in much the same manner and within days the migration had begun. On 5 September, Brownlee sent a sorrowful note to Cape Town:

You doubtless remember Old Tyala, the chief councillor among the Gaikas, who did all in his power to keep the Gaikas out of the rebellion, and who urged on Sandilli the arrest of Makinnon and Kiva. I have just received the following from Wright: – The death of Tyala is reported this morning, no cause stated except that he had a short time before expressed a wish to die owing to the misfortunes that had come on the tribe. He had been ailing some time. According to his light, he was a noble character and appears to have died of a broken heart, satisfactory intelligence received regarding the movement of the Gaikas; now that they find the thing decided upon they are much more reconciled to the movement.[6]

The Transkei was divided from north to south into two districts, the western one to be named Kentani and the other in the east called Willowvale. The Ngqika were to be settled in Kentani. Matthew Blyth was appointed chief magistrate of the new area, to be called Transkei, which also included Mfenguland, Ibeka and Idutywa.[7]

The migration began on 6 September 1878 and reports soon showed that the movement proceeded without difficulty. On the 13th, the secretary for native affairs was able to send a telegram from Nqamakwe: 'Matters in this part satisfactory. Gaikas on the move through Kei to the late Galeka location, under the charge of European Officers; food has been purchased for them on the way.'[8] On 14 September, the Colonial Secretary reported that 'the main body of Sandilli's people will cross the Kei today.'[9] By the 17th, they had reached their prescribed locations and begun to settle in. There had been no trouble throughout, little stock loss and no deaths. Spicer notes that, in all, 7,664 people moved across the Kei, taking with them more than 6,500 cattle.[10]

When the re-settlement was complete, according to Theal: 'The whole of the old Gaika location west of the Kei thus became vacant. It was divided into farms, which were sold on quitrent tenure by public auction to Europeans, so that the colony gained that tract of land in reality by the rebellion.'[11]

A son of the missionary William Shaw, Mr F.B. Shaw, was appointed magistrate to the Ngqika and took up residence in the Kentani location on 1 October 1878.[12]

The new location of Willowvale was to be the circumscribed new home of the Gcaleka. Their original lands had first been reduced to accommodate the Mfengu. Now they had been reduced by half again to accommodate the Ngqika.

Following the battle of Kentani on 7 February, Colonel Eustace, still the chief magistrate of the Gcaleka, had taken up residence at Ibeka and settled Bhotomane's and Maphasa's people close by.

The new magistrate for the Gcaleka, Frank Streatfeild, was appointed in January 1879 and set up his residence in what became the village of Willowvale. The remainder of the Gcaleka were moved into the Willowvale location.[13] There was one exception: Sarhili.

Disarmament

The second plank of Sprigg's native policy was the disarmament of Africans. This applied not only to the Ngqika and Gcaleka, who were disarmed when they were re-settled in their new locations, but was extended to include all black Africans within the British sway, meaning the Mfengu, Thembu and others beyond the borders of the colonial government.

It was heralded by the introduction of an Act for the Preservation of Peace in the Colony, better known, perhaps, as the Peace Preservation Act of 1878. Under the terms of the Act, the governor could proclaim that within certain districts it was unlawful to own arms and all those in possession, other than authorised persons (mainly officials and members of the armed forces) and those with a licence, were to hand in their arms, for which compensation would be paid. The compensation also became an issue because it was set at face value rather than the original cost of the weapon.

Limitations on space preclude the examination of this matter in great detail; suffice to say that the policy was stoutly resisted by the non-Xhosa and so outraged the Basotho that they went to war over the issue in 1880.[14]

The Fate of Sarhili

After his defeat at Kentani, Sarhili had gone into hiding in a remote area of the Transkei. He made several enquiries as to the terms to be imposed on his surrender but they came to nothing. Despite the declaration that the war was over and an amnesty declared for all rebels except their leaders, the hunt for Sarhili went on.

A special patrol under the command of Lieutenant Teignmouth Melvill, including a mounted section of the 1/24th, was sent out specifically to hunt him down. It failed to capture him. According to a report of 18 July, 'Kreli and his followers were found in the forest and followed until sundown; three prisoners were taken but Kreli escaped and from this date until the 23rd August, no traces of him could be found, although constant patrols were made, night and day, into Bomvanaland as well as Gcalekaland.'[15]

Sarhili crossed the Mbashe River, passing through Bomvanaland into the country of the Mpondo. There he took refuge with the chief Gwadiso, despite the fact that Moni, the paramount chief, had already accepted British rule in the previous January. The Pondo chief Nqwiliso reported his presence and Sarhili narrowly avoided capture.

He remained in Pondoland for about a year, after which he re-crossed the Mthatha River and took up residence on the Bomvana side of the Mbashe. In 1881, he was offered a free and unconditional pardon, with residence near his old homestead of Holela, but he refused. He continued to ask to be allowed to return to his country and the government had concerns about his potential influence. In 1883, he was pardoned and allowed to settle in the Mbashe Valley. He was subsequently offered permanent habitation in three locations, including Qolora, provided that he accept British rule and its laws and regulations. The old chief was now backed into a corner and finally acquiesced. He died in 1892.[16]

Sandile's sons, Gonya (Edmund) and Mathanzima were found sheltering in the Thembu Sitokhwe's homestead on 30 June 1878.[17] Gonya was subsequently found guilty of sedition and was condemned to death, which was later commuted to life imprisonment. His brother Mathanzima was sentenced to twenty years' penal servitude. They were released in 1888 through the intercession of Charles Brownlee.[18]

Although Gcalekaland had now been conquered, and there were several attempts to secure its annexation to the Cape Colony in the next few years, the Home government steadily refused the necessary letters patent. They were finally granted and, in August 1885, an Act for the annexation was passed into law.[19]

Further Colonial Expansion

In a memorandum dated 4 June 1878, Sir Bartle Frere was preparing for further acquisition of territory to the north of the Cape Colony, in the area known as 'Kaffraria'. This was not the same as the earlier 'British Kaffraria' but described all the country north of the Kei River and south of the Drakensburg Mountains, as far as the southern border of Natal. This embraced the territories of the Gcaleka, Bomvana, Thembu (Tambookies), including the Emigrant Thembu, Mpondo and Griqualand East.

Frere suggested that there were four steps towards acceptance of Africans as British subjects, and each of these various territories was already positioned at one of the stages in their relationship with the Crown:

1. Conquest or request. People who had been conquered, or had chosen to come under the protection of the Crown, but which still retained their own customs. Such people included the Gcaleka, Mpondo and Bomvana. In such cases, an administrator was appointed as Resident or Chief Magistrate without the intervention of the chief.

2. Application to the Crown to authorise the colony to annex the territory. When approval was given, then a resolution to that effect was passed by both houses of the parliament. The Thembu were at this stage in the process.

3. Letters patent were issued by the Queen and an Act was passed by the colonial legislature to annex the territory. Such an Act had already been passed with regard to Fingoland, the Idutywa Reserve and Griqualand East but had not yet received royal assent.

4. Assent being received, an order in council was issued and the annexation was complete. Basotholand had arrived at this point.[20]

As early as August 1878, the right bank of the St Johns River, from a point some twenty kilometres inland to the sea, had been annexed.[21] By the year 1885, the territories of all of the people mentioned above had been annexed to the Cape Colony. It would not be too many more years before the map of South Africa between the Mbashe River and Natal was also coloured pink, and on 31 May 1910 the Union of South Africa as we know it today was formed by the annexations which had gone before and the inclusion of the two Boer republics.[22]

Later Developments

In the years following union, the indigenous Africans became what Pixley Izaka Seme called 'hewers of wood and drawers of water' and the South

African Native National Congress (SANNC), forerunner of the African National Congress (ANC), was formed in 1912.[23] There followed a series of legislative measures in the early twentieth century which gradually further restricted the rights of indigenes.

The introduction of the policy of 'apartheid' (or separation) by the newly elected National Party government in 1948 began almost immediately, in which white people were to be treated entirely differently from those designated 'black' or 'coloured'. A decade later, those designated 'black' were deprived of their citizenship and removed to 'homelands', large tracts of South Africa that were set aside for African habitation. Those in which the Xhosa were circumscribed were called Ciskei and Transkei.

It was only in April 1994, when the African National Congress won the national election, and thus became the majority party in the parliament, that apartheid, with all its cruel legislative apparatus, was struck down and racial equality was finally re-introduced. It was an ironic twist of history that many of the leaders of the ANC were Xhosa.

Notes

Introduction

1 BPP C.2100, Enclosure in No. 43, p. 52: Thesiger to Secretary of State for War, 12 March 1878, para. 3.
2 Geoffrey Blainey, *Tyranny of Distance: How Distance Shaped Australia's History*, Melbourne: Macmillan, 1975.
3 C. de B. Webb, 'Lines of Power: The High Commissioner, the Telegraph and the War of 1879', *Natalia*, Vol. 8, December, 1993.
4 BPP 216, No. 8, p. 19: Grey to Sir E.B. Lytton, 20 July 1859.
5 Eric A. Walker (ed.), *The Cambridge History of the British Empire, Vol. VIII: South Africa, Rhodesia and the High Commission Territories*, London: Cambridge University Press, 1963, pp. 24–5.
6 Walker, pp. 28–9.
7 Walker, pp. 40ff.
8 A.T. Bryant, *Olden Times in Zululand and Natal*, London: Longmans, Green, 1929, pp. 3–4.
9 The prefix 'ama' used here simply provides the definite (or indefinite) article; the reader will quickly perceive the tautology. Such prefixes will be omitted in future references.
10 Bryant, *Olden Times*, chapter 1, *passim*.
11 Jeff Guy, *The Destruction of the Zulu Kingdom: The Civil War in Zululand, 1879–1884*, Pietermaritzburg: University of Natal Press, 1994, pp. 22ff.
12 Guy, p. 22.
13 Noël Mostert, *Frontiers: The Epic of South Africa's Creation and the Tragedy of the Xhosa People*, London: Jonathan Cape, 1992, p. 902.
14 Walker, p. 45.
15 J.B. Peires, *The House of Phalo: A History of the Xhosa People in the Days of Their Independence*, Berkeley: University of California Press, 1981, pp. 29, 46.

Chapter 1

1 Donald Moodie (ed.), *The Record, or a Series of Official Papers Relative to the Condition and Treatment of the Native Tribes of South Africa*, Cape Town: A.A. Balkema, 1960, p. 9.
2 Quoted in Mostert, p. 110.
3 Mostert, p. 110.
4 Moodie, Part 1, p. 280 (approval); tourist pamphlet *Castle of Good Hope*. (building and completion).

5 Moodie, Part 1, p. 280: Instructions to van Riebeeck to permit discharge of employees for the purpose of establishing their own farms.

6 Moodie, Part 1, p. 205: 6 April 1660.

7 Mostert, p. 139.

8 Walker, p. 130. See also Moodie, Part 1, p. 372.

9 Mostert, pp. 160–1.

10 John Milton, *Edges of War: A History of Frontier Wars 1702–1878*, Kenwyn: Juta & Co., 1983, p. 10.

11 George McCall Theal, *History of South Africa under the Administration of the Dutch East India Company 1652–1795*, Vol. I, London: Swan Sonnenschein, 1897, p. 426.

12 Mostert, p. 162.

13 Milton, p. 24.

14 Milton, pp. 24–5.

15 Mostert, p. 218.

16 See Theal, *History of South Africa under the Administration of the Dutch East India Company*, chapter XI, for a close examination of the San conflict.

17 Mostert, p. 219.

18 Mostert, pp. 220ff.

19 Milton, p. 25.

20 See the genealogical tables for the various people described.

21 Milton, p. 19.

22 Milton, pp. 19–20.

23 Peires, *The House of Phalo*, pp. 46–7.

24 Peires, *The House of Phalo*, chapter 4, *passim*.

25 Milton, p. 28.

26 Mostert, pp. 227ff.

27 Mostert, pp. 229ff; Milton, p. 29.

28 Milton, p. 30.

29 Moodie, Part 3, p. 110.

30 Milton, p. 31.

31 Mostert, p. 241.

32 Mostert, pp. 237–8.

33 Milton, pp. 34–5.

34 See for example, J.S. Marais, *Maynier and the First Boer Republic*, Cape Town: Maskew Miller, 1944.

35 Mostert, p. 249.

36 Mostert, p. 250.

37 Milton, pp. 36–7.

38 Mostert, pp. 268ff.

39 Mostert, p. 270.

40 George McCall Theal, *Records of the Cape Colony, Copied for the Cape Government from the Manuscript Documents in the Public Record Office, London, Vol. I: Feb. 1793 to Dec. 1796*, printed for the Government of the Cape Colony, 1797, p. 175.

41 Milton, p. 40.
42 Mostert, pp. 266, 272.
43 Mostert, p. 274.
44 Mostert, pp. 274–5.
45 Mostert, p. 290.
46 Milton, pp. 44ff.
47 John Barrow, *An Account of Travels into the Interior of Southern Africa*, Vol. II, London: Cadell & Davies, 1806, p. 130.
48 Mostert, pp. 291–2.
49 Mostert, pp. 292–3.
50 John Shipp, *Memoirs of the Extraordinary Military Career of John Shipp, Late a Lieutenant in His Majesty's 87th Regiment*, London: Fisher Unwin, 1890, p. 66.
51 Mostert, p. 295.
52 Milton, p. 47.
53 Marais, pp. 113–14.
54 Mostert, pp. 319–20.
55 Walker, pp. 191–2.
56 Mostert, pp. 323ff.
57 Milton, pp. 49–50.
58 Mostert, p. 326.
59 Mostert, p. 327.
60 Mostert, pp. 32–8.
61 Mostert, p. 329.
62 Mostert, p. 331.
63 Mostert, pp. 332-3.
64 Mostert, pp. 334–5.
65 Mostert, p. 340. See also Theal, *Records of the Cape Colony*, Vol. V, pp. 222ff: Instructions to General Baird.
66 Quoted in Sir George E. Cory, *The Rise of South Africa: A History of the Origin of South African Colonial Development towards the East from the Earliest Times to 1857*, Cape Town: C. Struik, 1910, Vol. I, p. 145.
67 Milton, p. 56.
68 Mostert, p. 342.

Chapter 2

1 Milton, pp. 56–7.
2 Milton, p. 57.
3 Milton, pp. 58–9.
4 C.W. Hutton (ed.) *The Autobiography of the Late Sir Andries Stockenström, Bart*, Vol. I, Cape Town: J.C. Juta, 1887, pp. 30–1.
5 Mostert, pp. 364ff.
6 Mostert, p. 372.
7 Moodie, Part 5, p. 17: Collins to Caledon, 6 August 1809.
8 Moodie, Part 5, pp. 18–19: Collins to Caledon, 6 August 1809.

9 Many of the troops who took part in the invasion of the Cape had subsequently been sent off to invade the River Plate area in South America.

10 Mostert, pp. 373–4.

11 Mostert, p. 375.

12 Mostert, p. 378. The unit was also called the 'Cape Corps'.

13 Mostert, p. 379.

14 Milton, p. 61.

15 Cory, pp. 241–2.

16 Theal, *Records of the Cape Colony*, Vol. XIII, 1901, p. 236: Colonel Graham's report, 2 January 1812.

17 The names of the twelve dead can be found in WCA, CO 2580/4: Report from Graaff-Reinet to the governor, 19 February 1812.

18 Hutton, Vol. I, pp. 59ff.

19 Mostert, p. 385.

20 Mostert, pp. 385–6.

21 Old and infirm, Chungwa had been taken to a secret hiding place by his bodyguards. He was found there by a group of Boers, who immediately shot him dead in his bed. See Milton, p. 62; Hutton, Vol. I, p. 61.

22 Mostert, p. 386.

23 Mostert, p. 388.

24 Mostert, p. 389.

25 Mostert, p. 391.

26 Milton, p. 65.

27 Peires, *The House of Phalo*, pp. 69ff.

28 Mostert, p. 449.

29 Mostert, pp. 450–1.

30 Milton, p. 67.

31 Mostert, p. 451.

32 Milton, p. 68.

33 Milton, pp. 68–9; Mostert, pp. 466–7. See also F. Herbst and D. Kopke, 'Site of the Battle of Amalinde', *Military History Journal*, Vol. 13, No. 5, June 2006.

34 Mostert, pp. 467–8.

35 Thomas Pringle, *Narrative of a Residence in South Africa*, Cape Town: Struik, 1966, p. 286.

36 Mostert, pp. 468–9.

37 Mostert, pp. 471–2.

38 Mostert, pp. 473–4.

39 Milton, p. 69.

40 Milton, pp. 69–70.

41 Milton, p. 70.

42 Mostert, pp. 474–5.

43 A shell containing a cylindrical canister full of metal balls or shot. When the shell is fired, the canister disintegrates and the shot is dispersed in a conical array, having a devastating effect upon the target. Also known as 'case shot'.

44 Mostert, pp. 475ff; Milton, pp. 71ff.

45 Mostert, p. 482.

46 Mostert, pp. 484–5.

47 Mostert, p. 487.

48 Mostert, p. 488.

49 Mostert, pp. 488–9.

50 Hutton, Vol. I, p. 155.

51 Mostert, p. 489.

52 Mostert, pp. 489–90.

53 Mostert, pp. 490–1.

54 Theal, *Records of the Cape Colony*, Vol. XI, 1902, pp. 337–41: Somerset to Earl Bathurst, 15 October 1819. See also BPP 538: Report from the Select Committee on Aborigines (British Settlements), Part I, August 1836, pp. 47–8.

55 Quoted in Milton, p. 80.

56 BPP 538: Report from the Select Committee on Aborigines, British Settlements. (August 1836), p. 679.

57 Mostert, p. 508.

58 Timothy Stapleton, *Maqoma: Xhosa Resistance to Colonial Advance 1798–1873*, Johannesburg: Jonathan Ball, 1994, pp. 82–3; Mostert, p. 509.

59 Stapleton, p. 9.

60 Mostert, p. 510.

61 Mostert, p. 514.

62 Milton, pp. 80–1.

63 Mostert, pp. 479–80.

64 Milton, p. 82.

65 Mostert, pp. 541ff.

66 Mostert, p. 544.

67 Milton, p. 83.

68 Dan Wylie, *Myth of Iron: Shaka in History*, Scottsville: University of KwaZulu-Natal, 2006, *passim*.

69 Mostert, p. 606.

70 Mostert, p. 616.

71 Milton, p. 92.

72 Mostert, p. 578.

73 Mostert, p. 617.

74 Mostert, pp. 608–9.

75 Mostert, p. 614.

76 Mostert, p. 612.

77 Hutton, Vol. I, pp. 298–9.

78 Mostert, pp. 618–19.

79 Stapleton, p. 63.

80 Mostert, pp. 621–2.

81 Mostert, pp. 631–2.

82 Mostert, p. 632.

83 Mostert, p. 633.

84 Hutton, Vol. I, pp. 319ff.

85 Mostert, p. 634.

86 BPP 538, p. 9: Evidence of Captain Robert Scott Aitchison, 31 July 1835.

87 Mostert, p. 635.

88 BPP 538, p. 9: Evidence of Captain Robert Scott Aitchison to Select Committee, 31 July 1835.

89 BPP 252, p. 119: Somerset to Military Secretary, 11 December 1834.

90 Mostert, pp. 651–2.

91 BPP 538, p. 567: Response of Chief Tshatsu to the question 'Was not Hintza considered as the head of the Caffre chiefs?'.

92 Mostert, p. 666.

93 Milton, pp. 103–11.

94 Related in Mostert, pp. 671–2.

95 Mostert, pp. 669–70.

96 BPP 503, p. 48: Maqoma to D'Urban, 1 January 1835.

97 BPP 503, p. 49: Statement of the Frontier Caffres to D'Urban.

Chapter 3

1 Mostert, p. 658.

2 A.L. Harington, *Sir Harry Smith: Bungling Hero*, Cape Town: Tafelberg Publishers, 1980, chapter 1, *passim*.

3 Harington, p. 14.

4 Harington, pp. 16–17.

5 Dorothy E. Rivett-Carnac, *Hawk's Eye*, Cape Town: Howard Timmins, 1966, p. 68.

6 Milton, pp. 111–12.

7 Milton, p. 113.

8 John Jarvis Bisset, *Sport and War: Or Recollections of Fighting and Hunting in South Africa from the Years 1834 to 1867*, London: John Murray, 1875, pp. 8–11.

9 Mostert, p. 685.

10 Milton, p. 114.

11 BPP 279, Enclosure 1 in No. 3: General Order, 16 March 1835.

12 BPP 279, Enclosure 6 in No. 3: Notice, 13 April 1835.

13 Mostert, p. 712.

14 BPP 279, Enclosure 7 in No. 3: Notice, 3 May 1835.

15 Mostert, pp. 715–16; see also BPP 279, Enclosure 7 in No. 3: Notice, 3 May 1835.

16 Mostert, pp. 717–18.

17 R.E. Gordon, *Shepstone: The Role of the Family in the History of South Africa, 1820–1900*, Cape Town: A.A. Balkema, 1968, p. 87. Shepstone said D'Urban threatened that, for every Mfengu murdered, he would 'put to death two kaffirs'.

18 Milton, p. 120.

19 Gordon, pp. 87–8. There were many more than six thousand. According to a return of 15 May 1835, there were 16,800 men, women and children, together with 22,000 head of cattle. See BPP 279, p. 27: Sub-enclosure in Enclosure 8 in No. 3.

20 Mostert, pp. 721–2.

21 BPP 279, Enclosure 12 in No. 3: Notice, 15 May 1835.

22 What follows is based upon a report by Harry Smith in BPP 279, Enclosure 18 in No. 23, pp. 48ff: Smith to D'Urban, 18 May 1835.

23 BPP 279, Enclosure 18 in No. 23, p. 49: Colonel Smith's report on the death of Hintsa.

24 BPP 279, Enclosure 18 in No. 23, p. 49: Colonel Smith's report on the death of Hintsa.

25 Mostert, pp. 725–6.

26 Milton, p. 125.

27 BPP 279, Enclosure 19 in No. 3: Notice, incorporating the treaty with Sarhili, 24 May 1835.

28 BPP 279, Enclosure 19 in No. 3: Notice, incorporating the treaty with Sarhili, 24 May 1835; Mostert, p. 731.

29 Mostert, p. 743.

30 Mostert, pp. 745–6.

31 Mostert, pp. 750–1.

32 BPP 279, No. 3: D'Urban to Aberdeen, 19 June 1835.

33 Mostert, p. 742.

34 Mostert, p. 775.

35 BPP 279, pp. 59ff: Glenelg to D'Urban, 26 December 1835.

36 Mostert, p. 756.

37 BPP 279, p. 67: Glenelg to D'Urban, 26 December 1835.

38 BPP 279, pp. 71: Glenelg to D'Urban, 26 December 1835.

39 Mostert, pp. 789.

40 Hutton, Vol. II, p. 45.

41 Mostert, p. 790.

42 Mostert, pp. 792–3.

43 Mostert, p. 796.

44 Mostert, pp. 793–4.

45 Mostert, pp. 796–7.

46 Hutton, Vol. II, p. 203.

47 Mostert, p. 805.

48 Mostert, p. 804.

49 Gordon, p. 94.

50 Mostert, p. 823.

51 Milton, p. 148.

52 Mostert, p. 826.

53 J.M. Meintjes, *Sandile: The Fall of the Xhosa Nation*, Cape Town: T.V. Bulpin, 1971, p. 115.

54 Mostert, p. 825.

55 BPP 635, p. 201–2: Evidence of Sir George Napier to Select Committee, 23 June 1851.

56 Mostert, p. 845.

57 Mostert, p. 842.

58 Mostert, pp. 842–3.

59 Sandile slapped a storekeeper who had locked his store on seeing Sandile approach, then entered the store and took a number of items without payment. See Meintjes, p. 136.

60 Meintjes, pp. 140ff.

61 Milton, p. 157.

62 Milton, pp. 160–1.

63 Mostert, p. 880.

64 Milton, p. 161.

65 Milton, p. 163.

66 Milton, pp. 162–3.

67 Milton, pp. 163–4.

68 Bisset, p. 87.

69 Bisset, pp. 88ff.

70 Meintjes, p. 151.

71 Mostert, p. 903.

72 Mostert, p. 904.

73 BPP 786, Enclosure B in No. 18: Governor's reply to Maqomo's message.

74 BPP 786, Enclosure C in No. 18: Maitland's meeting with Xhosa chiefs, 30 September 1846.

75 Milton, p. 168.

76 BPP 786, No. 19, p. 195: Maitland to Earl Grey, 26 November 1846.

77 Milton, p. 169.

78 Mostert, p. 914.

79 BPP 912, No. 10, p. 27: Pottinger to Grey, 20 February 1847.

80 Mostert, pp. 915–16.

81 Mostert, p. 917.

82 Mostert, p. 918.

83 Mostert, p. 922.

84 Bisset, pp. 124ff.

85 Milton, p. 171.

86 Mostert, pp. 927–8.

87 Milton, p. 171.

Chapter 4

1 G.C. Moore-Smith (ed.), *The Autobiography of Lieutenant-General Sir Harry Smith*, Vol. II, London: John Murray, 1902, p. 228.

2 Milton, p. 173.

3 BPP 969, No. 7, p. 24: Smith to Grey, 28 December 1847.

4 BPP 969, Enclosure 1 in No. 18, pp. 49ff: Proceedings of 7 January 1848.

5 Mostert, pp. 940–1.

6 BPP 217, *passim*.

7 Milton, p. 178.

8 Milton, p. 179.

9 BPP 1334, Sub-enclosure 1 in Enclosure in No 4, p. 17: Maclean to MacKinnon, 26 August 1850.

10 BPP 1334, No. 7, p. 28: Smith to Grey, 21 October 1850; and No. 9, p. 38: Smith to Grey, 31 October 1850. The proclamation deposing Sandile was published in Enclosure 5 to this despatch, dated 30 October 1850.

11 BPP 1334, Sub-enclosure 1 in Enclosure 1 in No 9, pp. 41–2: Brownlee to MacKinnon, 30 October 1850.

12 BPP 1334, Enclosure 1 in No. 14, p. 59: Mackinnon to Smith, 2 December 1850.

13 BPP 1334, Enclosure 5 in No 9, p. 44: Proclamation deposing Sandile as chief of the Rharhabe.

14 BPP 1334, Enclosure 2 in No 15, pp. 66f: Memorandum of movements, 14 December 1850.

15 BPP 1334, No. 15, p. 63: Smith to Grey, 20 December 1850. See also Milton, p. 181.

16 BPP 1334, Enclosure 1, No. 16, p. 73: Mackinnon to Smith, 24 December 1850. For the attack at the Boma Pass see also Bisset, chapter XVII and T.J. Lucas, *Camp Life and Sport in South Africa: Experiences of Kaffir Warfare with the Cape Mounted Rifles*, London: Chapman & Hall, 1878, chapter XIII.

17 Lucas, pp. 169–70.

18 Bisset, p. 133.

19 Lucas, pp. 175–6.

20 Bisset, pp. 149–50.

21 BPP 1334, Enclosure 2, No. 16, p. 73: MacKinnon to Smith, 25 December 1850.

22 Cory Library, MS779: Blanckenberg, P.B., 'The Treachery at Auckland'.

23 Milton, p. 190.

24 BPP 1380, No. 3, p. 4: Smith to Grey, 4 February 1851.

25 Sarah Ralph, diary, *Martello Magazine*, Fort Beaufort Museum, Nos 3–6 inclusive.

26 BPP 1380, Enclosure in No. 3, p. 7: Report of parley with rebel leaders at Fort Armstrong, 22 January 1851.

27 Milton, pp. 195ff.

28 *Grahamstown Journal*, 25 February 1851.

29 Milton, p. 202.

30 BPP 1428, Enclosure 6 in No. 26, p. 161: Return of killed, wounded and missing in action.

31 Milton, p. 206.

32 For details of this campaign see BPP 1428, No. 34 and enclosures, p. 202ff: Smith to Grey, 19 November 1851.

33 BPP 1428, Enclosure 6 in No. 38, p. 226: Instructions to Somerset, 28 November 1851.

34 BPP 1635, No. 6 and enclosures, pp. 23ff: Smith to Grey, 16 February 1852.

35 BPP 1428, No. 21, pp. 253ff: Grey to Smith, 14 January 1852.

36 BPP 1635, No. 10, pp. 62ff: Smith to Grey, 17 March 1852.

37 Milton, p. 216.

38 Harington, pp. 223ff.

39 Mostert, p. 1150.

40 At the end of the war, Cathcart wrote a long despatch to Earl Grey in which he set out the state of the frontier as he found it, then a detailed report of his subsequent actions. See BPP 1635, No. 51, pp. 218ff: Cathcart to Grey, 11 February 1853.

41 Milton, pp. 217–18.

42 Milton, pp. 218–19.

43 Mostert, pp. 1153–4.

44 Mostert, p. 1158.

45 Milton, p. 219.

46 BPP 1635, Enclosure 1 in No. 53, p. 231: Proclamation of peace with Sarhili, 14 February 1853.

47 Sir George Cathcart, *Correspondence of Lieutenant-General the Hon. Sir George Cathcart KCB Relative to Military Operations in Kaffraria . . .*, London: John Murray, 1856, pp. 204ff.

48 Milton, pp. 221f.

49 Milton, p. 223.

50 Mostert, pp. 1165–6.

51 Peires, *The House of Phalo*, pp. 65–6.

52 The details of the movement to 'responsible government' may be traced in BPP 181: (181-I and 181-II) Correspondence regarding the Establishment of Responsible Government at the Cape of Good Hope, and the Withdrawal of Troops from that Colony, April and June 1870.

53 The disease is now recognised as contagious bovine pleuropneumonia (CBPP) and is caused by mycoplasma mycoides SC. It was brought to South Africa via infected bulls imported from Holland in 1853. The disease is spread by direct droplet infection, especially at watering places and in cattle enclosures. See *Contagious Bovine Pleuropneumonia (Lungsickness)*, National Department of Agriculture, Directorate Animal Health, Pretoria, 1996.

54 J.B. Peires, *The Dead Will Arise: Nongqawuse and the Great Cattle-Killing Movement of 1856–7*, Jeppestown: Jonathan Ball, 2003, pp. 93–4.

55 Charles Pacalt Brownlee, *Reminiscences of Kaffir Life and History*, Lovedale: Lovedale Mission Press, 1896, pp. 138–9: letter to Colonel John Maclean, chief commissioner, 28 June 1856.

56 Peires, *The Dead Will Arise*, pp. 99–100. Charles Brownlee thought that she was a ventriloquist: Brownlee, p. 135.

57 Peires, *The Dead Will Arise, passim.*

58 Peires, *The Dead Will Arise*, p. 347.

59 Mostert, pp. 1226–7.

60 Brownlee, *Reminiscences*, p. 165.

61 Milton, pp. 237–8.

62 Mostert, pp. 1229–30.

63 Mostert, pp. 1230ff.

64 Milton, pp. 243–4.

65 Milton, p. 245.

66 Milton, pp. 249–50.

67 Mostert, pp. 1240–1.

68 Mostert, pp. 1241–2.

69 Milton, p. 251.

70 See BPP 3436: Correspondence relative to the annexation of British Kaffraria to the Cape of Good Hope, February 1865, *passim*.

71 Mostert, pp. 1245.

72 BPP 181, No. 1, pp. 1–2: Carnarvon to Wodehouse, 26 January 1867.

73 BPP 181, No. 2, pp. 3ff: Wodehouse to Carnarvon, 16 July 1867.

74 BPP 181, No. 2, p. 5: Wodehouse to Carnarvon, 16 July 1867.

75 BPP 181, No. 3, pp. 13–14: Buckingham and Chandos to Wodehouse, 9 December 1867.

76 BPP 181, No. 5, pp. 15–17: Earl Granville to Wodehouse, 9 December 1869.

77 Quoted in Milton, p. 166.

78 Phyllis Lewson (ed.), *Selections from the Correspondence of J.X. Merriman*, Cape Town: Van Riebeeck Society, 1960, pp. ixff.

79 Basil Worsfold, *Sir Bartle Frere: A Footnote to the History of the British Empire*, London: Thornton Butterworth, 1923, p. 12.

80 Worsfold, chapters 2 and 3.

81 Cornelius W. de Kiewiet, *The Imperial Factor in South Africa: A Study in Politics and Economics*, London: Frank Cass, 1965, p. 129.

82 Worsfold, p. 55.

83 Quoted in John Martineau, *Life and Correspondence of Sir Bartle Frere*, Vol. II, London: John Murray, 1895, p. 164.

84 BPP 457: Copies of the Letters Patent appointing Sir Harry Smith governor of the Cape of Good Hope.

85 Worsfold, p. 48.

86 Martineau, Vol. II, p. 179.

87 Gen. Sir A. T. Cunynghame, *My Command in South Africa 1874–78*, London: Macmillan, 1879, pp. 1–2.

88 Major G. Tylden, *The Armed Forces of South Africa 1659–1954*, Johannesburg: Frank Connock Publications, 1954, pp. 57–60.

89 Cunynghame, p. 306.

Chapter 5

1 BPP C.1961, p. 68–9: Memorandum of Brownlee, 28 August 1877.

2 BPP C.1961, Enclosure in No. 83, p. 160–1: Eustace to Brownlee, 18 August 1877.

3 Mr West White Fynn, *East London Daily Dispatch*, 11 May 1911.

4 Dr A.W. Burton, Cory Library, MS14, 254/13: The Nchayechibi War.

5 Burton, MS14, 254/13: What happened after the brawl on the Qcuwa river?

6 Burton, MS14, 254/13: What happened after the brawl on the Qcuwa river?

7 Burton, MS14, 254/13: What happened after the brawl on the Qcuwa river?

8 Quoted in M.W. Spicer, 'The War of Ngcayecibi 1877–8', unpublished MA Thesis, Rhodes University, Grahamstown, 1978, p. 74.

9 BPP C.1961, Enclosure in No. 83, p. 160–1: Eustace to Brownlee, pp. 166–7.

10 BPP C.1961, Enclosure 1 in No. 30, p. 82: Eustace to Frere, 1 September 1877.

11 Burton, MS14, 254/13: What happened after the brawl on the Qcuwa river?

12 Burton, MS14, 254/13: What happened after the brawl on the Qcuwa river?

13 BPP C.1961, Enclosure 1 in No. 30, p. 82: Eustace to Frere, 1 September 1877.

14 BPP C.1961, Enclosure 2 in No. 30, p. 82ff: Melvill to Glyn, 2 September 1877. Much of what follows is also drawn from this report.

15 BPP C.1961, No. 30, pp. 80–1: Frere to Carnarvon. 5 September 1877.

16 Spicer, p. 86.

17 BPP C.1961, Enclosure 3 in No. 30, p. 85: Chalmers to Commandant James Bowker, 2 September 1877.

18 Martineau, Vol. II, p. 195.

19 BPP C.1961, No. 39, p. 92ff: Frere to Carnarvon, 25 September 1877.

20 BPP C.1961, Enclosure 1 in No. 39, p. 96–7: Frere to Sarhili, 20 September 1877.

21 Spicer, p. 95–6.

22 Langalibalele was chief of the amaHlubi people who lived in Natal. When he was required to hand in firearms he held illegally, he refused to comply and fled across the Drakensberg Mountains into Lesotho. He was eventually apprehended and sent to Robben Island after a farcical trial. His people were badly treated by the Natal government as a result. See R.O. Pearse, et al. (eds), *Langalibalele and the Natal Carbineers: The Story of the Langalibalele Rebellion, 1873*, Ladysmith: Ladysmith Historical Society, 1973, 1976; ; and BPP C.1141: Langalibalele and the amaHlubi Tribe, being remarks upon the official record of the trials of the Chief, his sons and *induna* and other members of the amaHlubi tribe. (January 1875.)

23 Charles Duncan Griffith in W.J. de Kock and D.W. Kruger (eds), *Dictionary of South African Biography*, Vol. II, Cape Town: Human Sciences Research Council, 1977, pp. 276–7.

24 BPP C.1961, Enclosure 2 in No. 49, p. 123: Frere to Cunynghame, 1 October 1877.

25 BPP C.1961, Enclosure in No. 43, p. 106.

26 BPP C.1961, Enclosure in No. 43, p. 107.

27 BPP C.1961, Enclosure in No. 43, pp. 105.

28 BPP C.1961, Enclosure in No. 43, p. 107.

29 BPP C.1961, No. 39, p. 95: Frere to Carnarvon, 25 September 1877.

30 Spicer, p. 98.

31 Spicer, p. 98.

32 BPP C.1961, Enclosure 3 in No. 39, pp. 99ff: Merriman to J. Rose Innes, 24 September 1877.

33 Spicer, p. 101.

34 Chalmers' report, and General Cunynghame's comments upon it, are in BPP C.1961, Enclosure 2 in No. 102, pp. 199–200.

35 BPP C.1961, Enclosure 2 in No. 102, pp. 199–200.

36 The mail ship *Windsor Castle* was wrecked on 16 October 1876 en route to the Cape (*Illustrated London News*, 2 December 1876).

37 BPP C.1961, Enclosure in No. 61, p. 145.

38 Ex-CMR, *With the Cape Mounted Rifles: Four Years' Service*, London: Richard Bentley & Son, 1881, p. 77.

39 Spicer, p. 106.

40 Cunynghame, p. 321.

41 This material was drawn from the early chapters of Kathleen Shervinton, *The Shervintons, Soldiers of Fortune*, London: T. Unwin, 1899.

42 Ex-CMR, p. 84.

43 What follows is described in Griffith's report in BPP 1961, Enclosure in No. 61, pp. 145–6.

44 Cunynghame, p. 321.

45 BPP C.1961, Enclosure in No. 61, p. 146.

46 BPP C.1961, Enclosure in No. 61, p. 146.

47 Spicer, p. 108, n. 23.

48 BPP C.1961, No. 52, p. 128: Cunynghame to Under-Secretary of State for War, 10 October 1877.

49 BPP C.1961, No. 42, p. 102: Frere to Carnarvon, 28 September 1877.

50 BPP C.1961, Enclosure 2 in No. 42, pp. 103–4: Cunynghame to Frere, 24 September 1877.

51 BPP C.1961, Enclosure 3 in No. 42, p. 104: Cunynghame to Frere, 26 September 1877.

52 BPP C.1961, No. 42, pp. 102–3: Frere to Carnarvon, 28 September 1877.

53 BPP C.1961, Enclosure 4 in No. 42, p. 104: Frere to Cunynghame, 28 September 1877.

54 BPP C.1961, Enclosure in No. 51, pp. 127–8.

55 BPP C.1961, Enclosure C in No. 84, p. 173: Stockenström opinion, 19 October 1877.

56 BPP C.1961, No. 44, p. 109, para. 19: Frere to Carnarvon, 3 October 1877.

57 Lewson, *Selections from the Correspondence of J.X. Merriman*, pp. 27–8.

58 Lewson, *Selections from the Correspondence of J.X. Merriman*, p. 28, n. 3.

59 BPP C.1961, Enclosure 1 in No. 49, p. 123: Frere to Cunynghame, 1 October 1877.

60 BPP C.1961, Enclosure 1 in No. 49, p. 120: Cunynghame to Frere, 28 September 1877, para. 2.

Chapter 6

1 BPP C.1961, Enclosure in No. 61, pp. 143–4: Griffith to military secretary, 10 October 1877.

2 BPP C.1961, Enclosure in No. 61, pp. 143–4: Griffith to military secretary, 10 October 1877.

3 Spicer, pp. 120–1.

4 The action at the 'Springs' is described in BPP C.1961, Enclosure in No. 61, p. 144: Griffith to military secretary, 10 October 1877.

5 D.B. Hook, *With Sword and Statute: On the Cape of Good Hope Frontier*, Cape Town: J.C. Juta, 1905, pp. 238ff.

6 Ex-CMR, p. 109.

7 BPP C.1961, Enclosure D in No. 84, pp. 174: Merriman's telegram reply, 15 October 1877.
8 This was probably also the site of the future battle of Kentani.
9 What follows is based upon the following reports: BPP C.1961, Enclosure A in No. 85, pp. 174–5: Hook's report, 23 October 1877, pp. 175–6.
10 BPP C.1961, Enclosure A in No. 85, pp. 174–5: Griffth's report, 23 October 1877.
11 BPP C.1961, Enclosure A in No. 85, pp. 175–6: Elliot's report, 18 October 1877.
12 BPP C.1961, Enclosure 3 in No. 102, pp. 202–3: Griffith's report, 5 November 1877.
13 BPP C.1961, Enclosure 3 in No. 102, pp. 202–3: Griffith's report, 5 November 1877.
14 BPP C.1961, Enclosure 2 in No. 107, pp. 219–20: Griffith's report, 20 November 1877.
15 J.W. Macquarrie, *The Reminiscences of Sir Walter Stanford*, Cape Town: Van Riebeeck Society, 1958, p. 86.
16 BPP C.2000, Enclosure in No. 10, pp. 14ff: Griffith to deputy adjutant-general, 29 November 1877.
17 BPP C.1961, Enclosure 3 in No. 102, p. 201: Proclamation, signed by Merriman, 21 November 1877.
18 Spicer, p. 136.
19 Spicer, p. 128.
20 Spicer, p. 125.
21 Spicer, p. 127.
22 BPP C.2000, Enclosure 1 in No. 38, pp. 53–4: Brownlee, memorandum on Mackinnon, 14 December 1877.
23 BPP C.2000, Enclosure 1 in No. 38, p. 53: Brownlee memorandum, 14 December 1877.
24 Spicer, p. 128.
25 Spicer, p. 129.
26 Spicer, p. 126ff.
27 Spicer, p. 131.
28 BPP C.1961, No. 102, pp. 197–8: Frere to Carnarvon, 21 November 1877.
29 Spicer, p. 133.
30 BPP C.2000, Enclosure 2 in No. 38, pp. 54ff: Chalmers to Merriman, 11 December 1877.
31 BPP C.2000, Enclosure 2 in No. 38, p. 56: Chalmers to Merriman, 11 December 1877.
32 BPP C.1961, No. 92, pp. 180: Frere to Carnarvon, 20 November 1877.
33 BPP C.1961, Enclosure 3 in No. 102, p. 201: Proclamation, 21 November 1877.
34 Spicer, p. 136.
35 BPP C.2000, No. 13, p. 29: Frere to Carnarvon, 5 December 1877.
36 BPP C.2000, Sub-enclosure 3 in Enclosure in No. 19, p. 37: Telegram, Wardell to Cunynghame, 2 December 1877.
37 The detail of what follows can be found in BPP C.2000, Enclosure 1 in No. 22, pp. 43–4: Bourne's report, 3 December 1877.

38   BPP C.2000, Sub-enclosure 6 in Enclosure in No. 19, p. 38: Griffith to Merriman, 3 December 1877.

39   Spicer, p. 138, n. 138.

40   BPP C.2000, Sub-enclosure 7 in Enclosure in No. 19, p. 38: Griffith to Cunynghame, 5 December 1877.

41   BPP C.2000, Enclosure in No. 19, p. 36: Cunynghame to Secretary of State for War, 5 December 1877.

42   BPP C.2000, Enclosure in No. 18, p. 34: Commodore Sullivan to Admiralty, December 1977.

43   BPP C.2000, Enclosure in No. 24, p. 45: Commodore Sullivan to Simon's Bay, 16 December 1877.

44   'Kroomen' were experienced fishermen from the Kroo tribe in what is now Liberia in West Africa, often used as seamen by the Royal Navy at the time.

45   Fleet-Surgeon Henry F. Norbury, *The Naval Brigade in South Africa During the Years 1877–78–79*, London: Sampson Low, Marston, Searle and Rivington, 1880, p. 88.

46   Norbury, p. 89.

47   Norbury, p. 95.

48   Norbury, p. 96.

49   Norbury, pp. 102–3.

50   Merriman to Molteno, 3 December 1877, quoted in Spicer, p. 139.

51   Merriman to Molteno, 15 December 1877, quoted in Spicer, p. 139.

52   BPP C.2000, No. 22, pp. 42–3: Frere to Carnarvon, 12 December 1877.

53   George McCall Theal, *History of South Africa from 1873 to 1884: Twelve Eventful Years*, Vol. I, London: George Allen & Unwin Ltd, 1919, p. 80.

54   Colonel G. Hamilton-Browne, *A Lost Legionary in South Africa*, London: T. Werner Laurie, 1912, chapter IV, *passim*.

55   The name is often spelled 'Shervington' in other secondary accounts, but see Shervinton, *passim*.

56   Philip Gon, *Send Carrington! The Story of an Imperial Frontiersman*, Graighall: A.D. Donker, 1984, chapter 1, *passim*.

57   Spicer, pp. 140–1.

58   Spicer, pp. 144–5.

59   Spicer, pp. 145–6.

60   Cunynghame, pp. 341–2.

61   BPP C.2000, Enclosure in No. 86, p. 125: Brownlee to Wright, 23 December 1877.

62   Spicer, p. 146.

63   BPP C.2000, Enclosure in No. 86, pp. 126–7: Lt Craigie to D.A.G., 25 December 1877.

64   BPP C.2000, Enclosure in No. 86, p. 127: Brownlee, record of Siwani meeting, no date.

65   Spicer notes that Tainton had 'responsibility for blacks in the King William's Town district'; see Spicer, p. 153, n. 40.

66 BPP C.2000, No. 80, p. 116: Frere to Carnarvon, 2 January 1878. See also BPP C.2000, Enclosure in No. 86, pp. 136–7: Civil Commissioner, Panmure, to Merriman, 1 January 1878. These accounts name the murdered brothers as 'Painton'.

67 BPP C.2000, No. 10, p. 11: Frere to Carnarvon, 4 December 1877. These accounts name the murdered brothers as 'Painton'.

68 Quoted in P.A. Molteno, *The Life and Times of Sir John Charles Molteno*, London: Smith, Elder & Co., 1900, p. 338, n. 1.

69 Captain Henry Hallam Parr, *A Sketch of the Kafir and Zulu Wars: Guadana to Isandhlwana*, Kegan Paul, London, 1880, pp. 75–6. Hallam Parr has the wrong date here.

70 Spicer, p. 155.

71 Spicer, p. 143.

72 BPP C.2000, Enclosure in No. 86, p. 129: Unsigned telegram from Komgha, 29 December 1877, 1 p.m.

73 BPP C.2000, Enclosure in No. 86, p. 129: Unsigned telegram from Komgha, 29 December 1877, 5.08 p.m.

74 BPP C.2000, Enclosure in No. 90, pp. 144–5: Report of Major H.G. Moore on first action at Draaibosch, 31 December, 1877. See also National Army Museum, Chelmsford Papers, 6807-386-1/7: Brevet Moore to Lieutenant-Colonel Lambert, 31 December 1877.

75 TNA, WO 32/7385: Victoria Cross: Award to Major (now Brevet Lieutenant-Colonel) H. Moore, 88th Regt, for action against Kaffirs, South Africa.

76 BPP C.2000, Enclosure in No. 90, pp. 145–6: Report of Major H.G. Moore on second action at Draaibosch, 31 December, 1877.

77 BPP C.2000, Enclosure in No. 90, pp. 144–5: Return of killed and wounded.

78 BPP C.2000, Enclosure in No. 90, p. 143: Bellairs' comment on Moore's report, 6 January 1878.

79 Brownlee, pp. 317–18.

80 BPP C.2000, Enclosure in No. 86, p. 128: Brownlee memorandum, 29 December 1877.

81 Spicer, pp. 156–7.

Chapter 7

1 Spicer states that Molteno arrived on the 8th (Spicer, p. 161) presumably relying on Molteno's biographer (Molteno, p. 300). Theal gives 9 December as the date of his arrival (Theal, *History of South Africa from 1873 to 1884*, Vol. I, p. 100).

2 Molteno, p. 300.

3 Molteno, p. 301.

4 BPP C.2079, No. 9, pp. 12–13: Frere to Carnarvon, 16 January 1878.

5 BPP C.2079, Enclosure 1 in No. 9, pp. 113-15: Bellairs to Cunynghame, 16 January 1878.

6 BPP C.2079, Enclosure 1 in No. 86, p. 183: Bellairs memorandum, undated.

7 BPP C.2079, No. 9, pp. 12–13: Frere to Carnarvon, 16 January 1878.

8 BPP C.2079, Enclosure 1 in No. 86, p. 182: Minute for Ministers, 11 January 1878.

9 Lewson, *Selections from the Correspondence of J.X. Merriman*, p. 35.

10 Lewson, *Selections from the Correspondence of J.X. Merriman*, pp. 35–6.

11 Lewson, *Selections from the Correspondence of J.X. Merriman*, pp. 37–8. The emphasis is in the original.

12 BPP C.2079, Enclosure 1 in No. 86, p. 184: Minute for Ministers, 12 January 1878.

13 BPP C.2079, Enclosure 1 in No. 86, p. 184: Frere to Molteno, 12 January 1878.

14 BPP C.2079, Enclosure 1 in No. 86, pp. 184–5: Notes of meeting of Frere and Molteno, 11 January 1879.

15 BPP C.2079, Enclosure 1 in No. 86, p. 185: Molteno to Frere, 12 January 1878.

16 BPP C.2079, Enclosure 1 in No. 86, p. 186: Frere to Molteno, 14 January 1878.

17 BPP C.2079, Enclosure 1 in No. 86, pp. 186–7: Frere to Molteno, 14 January 1878.

18 BPP C.2079, Enclosure 1 in No. 86, p. 191: Minute to Frere, 18 January 1878.

19 Molteno, p. 301.

20 BPP C.2079, Enclosure 1 in No. 86, p. 191: Frere to ministers, 21 January 1878.

21 BPP C.2079, Enclosure 1 in No. 86, pp. 188–9: Molteno to Frere, 19 January 1878.

22 BPP C.2079, Enclosure 1 in No. 86, pp. 188–9: Memorandum, 19 January 1878.

23 BPP C.2079, Enclosure 1 in No. 86, pp. 189–90: Frere to Molteno, 22 January 1878.

24 BPP C.2079, Enclosure 1 in No. 86, p. 190: Molteno to Frere, 22 January 1878.

25 BPP C.2079, No. 10, pp. 191–5: Frere's memorandum, 26 January 1878.

26 BPP C.2079, Enclosure 1 in No. 86, pp. 191ff: Frere to Molteno, 26 January 1878.

27 Quoted in Phyllis Lewson, 'The First Crisis in Responsible Government in the Cape Colony', MA thesis, University of Witwatersrand, 1940, published in *Archives Year Book for South African History*, No. 5, Part II, 1942, pp. 247–8.

28 BPP C.2079, Enclosure in No. 32, p. 44: Strickland to surveyor-general of ordnance, 21 January 1878.

29 BPP C.2079, Enclosure in No. 32, p. 45: Warneford to commissary-general, undated.

30 BPP C.2079, Sub-enclosure C in Enclosure in No. 32, pp. 45–6:

31 BPP C.2079, No. 10, p. 19: Telegram, Frere to Carnarvon, 29 January 1878.

32 BPP C.2079, No. 47, p. 77: Frere to Carnarvon, 30 January 1878.

33 BPP C.2079, Enclosure 1 in No. 86, pp. 196ff, 31 January 1878.

34 BPP C.2079, Enclosure 1 in No. 86, p. 199: Minutes of Executive Council meeting, 1 February 1878.

35 BPP C.2079, Enclosure 1 in No. 86, p. 200ff: Minutes of Executive Council meeting, 2 February 1878.

36 BPP C.2079, Enclosure 1 in No. 86, pp. 202–3: Minute in reply by Mr Molteno, 2 February 1878.

37 BPP C.2079, Enclosure 1 in No. 86, p. 201: Minutes of Executive Council meeting, 2 February 1878.

38 BPP C.2079, Enclosure 1 in No. 86, p. 201: Minutes of Executive Council meeting, 2 February 1878.

39 Martineau, Vol. II, p. 210.

40 Martineau, Vol. II, p. 210, footnote.

41 Lewson, *Selections from the Correspondence of J.X. Merriman*, p. 37.

42 BPP C.2079, Enclosure 1 in No. 86, p. 210: Brownlee to Frere, 6 February 1878.

43 BPP C.2079, Enclosure 1 in No. 86, p. 206: Frere to Stockenström, 6 February 1878.

44 BPP C.2079, Enclosure 1 in No. 86, p. 207: Stockenström to Frere, 6 February 1878.

45 BPP C.2079, Enclosure 1 in No. 86, p. 207: Frere to Stockenström, 7 February 1878.

46 BPP C.2079, Enclosure 1 in No. 86, p. 207: Stockenström to Frere, 8 February 1878.

47 BPP C.2079, Enclosure 1 in No. 86, p. 207: Frere to Stockenström, 8 February 1878.

48 BPP C.2079, Enclosure 1 in No. 86, p. 207: Stockenström to Frere, 9 February 1878.

49 BPP C.2079, Enclosure 1 in No. 86, p. 208: Stockenström to Frere, 9 February 1878.

50 BPP C.2079, Enclosure 1 in No. 86, p. 208: Frere to Stockenström, 9 February 1878.

51 BPP C.2079, Enclosure 1 in No. 86, pp. 208–9: Stockenström to Frere, 14 February 1878.

52 BPP C.2079, Enclosure 1 in No. 86, p. 209: Frere to Stockenström, 26 February 1878.

53 BPP C.2079, Enclosure 1 in No. 86, p. 209: White to Frere, 6 February 1878.

54 BPP C.2079, Enclosure 1 in No. 86, p. 209: White to Frere, 7 February 1878.

55 BPP C.2079, Enclosure 1 in No. 86, p. 210: Frere to White, 8 February 1878.

56 BPP C.2079, Enclosure 1 in No. 86, p. 210: Frere to White, 15 February 1878.

57 BPP C.2079, Enclosure 1 in No. 86, p. 217: Stockenström's legal opinion, undated.

58 BPP C.2079, No. 53, pp. 86–7: Frere to Carnarvon, 5 February 1878.

59 Martineau, Vol. II, p. 211.

60 BPP C.2079, No. 75, pp. 124–5: Sir Michael Hicks Beach to Frere, 21 March 1878. Hicks Beach had taken over the position of Secretary of State for the Colonies in February 1878.

61 Molteno, p. 321.

62 Worsfold, p. 61.

63 Alphaeus Todd, *On the Position of a Constitutional Governor Under Responsible Government (1878)*, Ottawa, 1878, p. 6.

64 Todd, *On the Position of a Constitutional Governor Under Responsible Government*, p. 7.

65 Todd, p. 23.

Chapter 8

1 See, for example, BPP C.2079, Enclosures in No. 84, pp. 169ff: Appointments.

2 BPP C.2079, No. 84, p. 161: Frere to Carnarvon, 20 February 1878.

3 TNA, WO 42/70(I): his certificate of baptism shows a birth date of 28 August, with a note that it 'should be 23'. Lonsdale's unusual forename has been a source of error to compilers and writers for many years. J.P. Mackinnon and S.H. Shadbolt, *The South African Campaign of 1879*, London: Sampson, Low, Marston, Searle and Rivington, 1880, p. 388, gives his initials as 'R. de La T.'; Donald Morris, *Washing of the Spears: The Rise and Fall of the Zulu Nation*, London: Jonathan Cape, 1965, p. 264, calls him 'Rupert de la Tour', an error duplicated by John Laband in *Lord Chelmsford's Zululand Campaign 1878–1879*, Stroud: Army Records Society/Alan Sutton Publishing, 1994, p. 278.

4 H.G. Hart, *New Annual Army List for 1872*, London: John Murray, 1872: 74th Regiment.

5 H.G. Hart, *New Annual Army List for 1874*, London: John Murray, 1874. See also Charles L. Norris-Newman, *In Zululand with the British Throughout the War of 1879*, London: W.H. Allen, 1880, p. 21.

6 BPP C.2220, No. 10, pp. 19–20: Frere to Hicks Beach, 23 July 1878.

7 Evelyn Wood, *From Midshipman to Field Marshal*, London: Methuen, 1906, Vol. I, p. 301.

8 Wood, Vol. I, p. 302.

9 Carrington Letters, Museum of the Royal Welsh, Brecon.

10 Frank N. Streatfeild, *Reminiscences of an Old 'Un*, London: Eveleigh Nash, 1911, pp. 148–9.

11 BPP C.2079, Enclosure in No. 86, p. 182: Minute from Molteno to Frere, 11 January 1878.

12 BPP C.2079, Enclosure 2 in No. 46, p. 69: Molteno to Frere, 27 January 1878.

13 BPP C.2079, Enclosure 4 in No. 46, pp. 70–1: Frost to Merriman, 23 January 1878.

14 Spicer, p. 164.

15 BPP C.2079, Enclosure 4 in No. 46, p. 71: Frost to Merriman, 23 January 1878.

16 Quoted in Spicer, p. 165.

17 BPP C.2079, Enclosure 4 in No. 46, p. 71: Frost to Merriman, 23 January 1878.

18 Spicer, pp. 165–6.

19 BPP C.2079, Enclosure 3 in No. 46, pp. 69–70: Hemming to chief commissioner, 22 January 1878.

20 BPP C.2079, Enclosure No. 6 in No. 46, p 72: Frere's minute for ministers, 28 January 1878.

21 BPP C.2079, Enclosure 3 in No. 46, pp. 69–70: Hemming to Merriman, 22 January 1878.

22 BPP C.2079, Enclosure in No. 84, p. 171: Appointments, 4 February 1878.

23 BPP C.2079, Enclosure in No. 84, p. 165: Undated Merriman memorandum.

24 BPP C.2079, Enclosure 8 in No. 46, p. 72: Cunynghame, 28 January 1878.

25 Unless otherwise indicated, the following is based upon Spicer, pp. 186ff.

26 Spicer, p. 192.

27 Spicer, p. 194.

28 BPP C.2079, Sub-enclosure 5 in No. 46, p. 71: Hemming to Merriman, 24 January 1878.

29 BPP C.2079, Enclosure 15 in No. 46, p. 76: Hemming to Merriman, 27 January 1878.

30 BPP C.2079, Enclosure 16 in No. 46, p. 76: Hemming to Merriman, 27 January 1878.

31 Spicer, pp. 196ff.

32 Macquarrie, p. 53.

33 Macquarrie, p. 56.

34 Macquarrie, pp. 57–8.

35 Spicer, p. 199.

36 Spicer, pp. 200ff.
37 BPP C.2220, Enclosure 1 in No. 11, pp. 20–1: Elliott to secretary of native affairs, 29 March 1878.
38 BPP C.2220, Annexures 1–3 in Enclosure 1 in No. 11, pp. 22ff.
39 Unless otherwise stated, what follows is drawn from Spicer, pp. 203ff.
40 Theal, *History of South Africa from 1873 to 1884*, Vol. I, p. 27.
41 Spicer, p. 204.
42 Quoted in Spicer, pp. 204–5.
43 Spicer, p. 209.
44 Spicer, p. 210.
45 Spicer, p. 211.

Chapter 9

 1 BPP C.2079, Enclosure in No. 236, A, pp. 34–5.
 2 BPP C.2000, Enclosure in No. 86, p. 131: Cunynghame to Frere, 27 December 1877.
 3 TNA, WO 32/7679: A. Glyn to Cunynghame, 5 January 1878.
 4 TNA, WO 32/7679: A. Glyn to Cunynghame, 5 January 1878.
 5 TNA, WO 32/7679: A. Glyn to Cunynghame, 5 January 1878. Elsewhere, this information is given in two separate despatches.
 6 BPP C.2079, Enclosure in No. 23, pp. 34–5: Report A, Glyn to Cunynghame, 5 January 1878.
 7 BPP C.2079, Enclosure in No. 23, pp. 34–5: Report B, Glyn to Cunynghame, 12 January 1878.
 8 TNA, WO 32/7680: Cunynghame to Frere, 14 January 1878.
 9 TNA, WO 32/7680: Von Linsingen to Lambert, 11 January 1878.
10 TNA, WO 32/7680: Moore to Lambert, 5 January 1878.
11 TNA, WO 32/7680: Wardell to D.A.G., 6 January 1878. See also BPP C.2079, Sub-enclosure B in Enclosure 1 in No. 9, p. 17.
12 TNA, WO 32/7680: Lambert to Cunynghame, 10 January 1878.
13 BPP C.2079, Sub-enclosure B2 in Enclosure 1 in No. 9, p. 18: Cunynghame minute, undated.
14 BPP C.2079, Enclosures in No. 32, pp. 47–8: Lambert to D.A.G., 18 January 1878.
15 BPP C.2079, Sub-enclosures in No. 39, pp. 48–9: Moore to Lambert, 18 January 1878.
16 BPP C.2079, Sub-enclosures in No. 39, pp. 47–8: Lambert to Bellairs, 18 January 1878.
17 What follows is also found in Moore's report in BPP C.2079, Sub-enclosures in No. 39, pp. 48–9.
18 BPP C.2079, Enclosures in No. 32, p. 46: Bellairs to Cunynghame, 22 January 1878.
19 TNA, WO 32/7680: A, Robinson to Glyn, 15 January 1878.
20 TNA, WO 32/7680: B, Owen to Glyn, 14 January 1878.
21 TNA, WO 32/7680: C, Glyn to D.A.G., 17 January 1878.

22 TNA, WO 32/7680: Glyn to D.A.G., 17 January 1878.

23 NAM 7112-38-1-42, Coghill letters: Coghill to his mother, 15 January 1878.

24 TNA, WO 32/7680: Upcher to Glyn, 17 January 1878.

25 TNA, WO 32/7680: Glyn to D.A.G., 17 January 1878.

26 TNA, WO 32/7680: Glyn to Cunynghame, 17 January 1878.

27 TNA, WO 32/7680: Glyn to Cunynghame, 17 January 1878.

28 TNA, WO 32/7680: C, Glyn to D.A.G., 18 January 1878.

29 TNA, WO 32/7680: C, Glyn to D.A.G., 17 January 1878.

30 BPP C.2079, Enclosures in No. 65, p. 113: Glyn to D.A.G., 31 January 1878. See also TNA, WO 32/7686, *passim*.

31 BPP C.2079, Enclosures in No. 32, pp. 113–14: Upcher to Glyn, 30 January 1878.

32 NAM 6807-386-1-7: Upcher to Glyn, 30 January 1878.

33 NAM 6807-386-1-7: Upcher to Glyn, 30 January 1878.

34 BPP C.2079, Enclosure 1 in No. 81, p. 146: Deare to Glyn, 30 January 1878.

35 BPP C.2079, Enclosure 1 in No. 81, p. 147: Shervinton to Glyn, 31 January 1878.

36 Shervinton, p. 14.

37 Shervinton, p. 16.

38 Shervinton, p. 11.

39 Spicer, p. 163.

40 Spicer, p. 167.

41 Spicer, pp. 166–7.

42 BPP C.2079, Enclosure 1 in No. 81, pp. 148–9: Glyn to D.A.G., 12 February 1878.

43 TNA, WO 32/7691: Glyn to DAG, 12 February 1878.

44 BPP C.2079, B, Enclosure 1 in No. 81, pp. 150: Upcher to Glyn, 8 February 1878. See also TNA, WO 32/7681, *passim*.

45 What follows, unless otherwise stated, is based on Upcher's report of the battle in TNA, WO 32/7681: Upcher to Glyn, 5 February 1878.

46 Spicer, p. 168.

47 TNA, WO 32/7681: Upcher to Glyn, 5 February 1878. Unless otherwise stated, what follows is based on this report.

48 Museum of the Royal Welsh, Brecon, Carrington Letters: Ibeka, Transkei: 9 February 1878.

49 Patrick Coghill (compiler), *Whom the Gods Love*, Halesowen: privately published, 1968, p. 85.

50 BPP C.2079, C. Enclosure 1 in No. 81, pp. 151–2: Grenfell to Upcher, 7 February 1878.

51 Coghill, p. 86.

52 BPP C.2079, D. Enclosure 1 in No. 81, p. 152: Robinson to Upcher, 9 February 1878.

53 Spicer, p. 169.

54 BPP C.2079, E, Enclosure 1 in No. 81, p. 152: Lundell to Upcher, 9 February 1878.

55 Spicer, p. 170.

56 Cunynghame, p. 374.

57 NAM 7112-38-1-45, Coghill letters: Coghill to his mother, 23 February 1878. Emphasis in the original.

58 Quoted in Spicer, p. 174.
59 Cunynghame, pp. 310–11.

Chapter 10

1   Lord Chelmsford's obituary, *The Times*, 10 April 1905.
2   NAM 6807/386-18-34: Copy of letter from Chelmsford to military secretary Horse Guards seeking employment, 1 January 1881.
3   Chris Hummel (ed.), *The Frontier Journal of Major John Crealock 1878*, Cape Town: Van Riebeeck Society, 1989, p. 19.
4   Hummel, pp. 1–2.
5   Alex M. Delavoye, *Records of the 90th Regiment, The Kaffir War 1877-78*, London: Richardson, 1880, pp. 222–3.
6   Museum of the Royal Welsh, Brecon, Accession No. B451-81: *Records of the 24th: The Kaffir War 1877/1878, 2nd Battalion*.
7   Wood, Vol. I, p. 296.
8   Major-General W.C.F. Molyneux, *Campaigning in South Africa and Egypt*, Macmillan: London, 1896, p. 17.
9   TNA, WO 32/7688: Thesiger to Secretary of State for War, 12 March 1878.
10 TNA, WO 32/7688: Thesiger to Secretary of State for War, 12 March 1878.
11 Molyneux, p. 41.
12 Hummel, p. 24.
13 TNA, WO 32/7688: Thesiger to Secretary of State for War, 25 March 1878.
14 TNA, WO 32/7688: Thesiger to Secretary of State for War, 12 March 1878.
15 Theal, *History of South Africa from 1873 to 1884*, Vol. I, p. 121.
16 TNA, WO 32/7688: Operations … in the Perie [*sic*] Bush, 16 March 1878.
17 TNA, WO 32/7688: Wood to D.A.G., 22 March 1878.
18 Frank N. Streatfeild, *Kaffirland: A Ten Months' Campaign*, London, Sampson, Marston, Searle and Rivington, 1879, p. 116.
19 Hummel, p. 40.
20 Molyneux, pp. 56–7.
21 Molyneux, p. 57.
22 Molyneux, p. 57–8.
23 Molyneux, p. 58.
24 Streatfeild, *Kaffirland*, pp. 121–2.
25 Hummel, p. 42.
26 Hummel, p. 43.
27 Hummel, pp. 44-7.
28 TNA, WO 32/7688: Wood to D.A.G., 22 March 1878.
29 Molyneux, p. 60.
30 TNA, WO 32/7688: Thesiger to Secretary of State for War, 25 March 1878.
31 TNA, WO 32/7688: Crealock, summary of killed and wounded &c. between 11 & 21st March 1878.
32 Hummel, p. 35, n. 44.
33 Hummel, p. 47.

34 Molyneux, p. 62.
35 Molyneux, p. 61.
36 TNA, WO 32/7688: Thesiger to Secretary of State for War, 10 April 1878.
37 Theal, *History of South Africa from 1873 to 1884*, Vol. I, pp. 107–8.
38 TNA, WO 32/7690: Thesiger to Secretary of State for War, 24 April 1878.
39 TNA, WO 32/7690: Summary of operations carried on under Col. Palmer 90th LI in clearing the Kerumo [Kroome] Range, Beaufort District.
40 TNA, WO 32/7690: Summary of operations carried on under Col. Palmer 90th LI in clearing the Kerumo [Kroome] Range, Beaufort District.
41 TNA, WO 32/7690: Copy of ultimatum, 14 March 1878.
42 TNA, WO 32/7690: Summary of operations carried on under Col. Palmer 90th LI in clearing the Kerumo [Kroome] Range, Beaufort District.
43 TNA, WO 32/7690: Thesiger, summary of operations carried on under Col. Palmer 90th LI Regt in clearing the Kerumo [Kroome] Range, Beaufort District.
44 TNA, WO 32/7688: Thesiger to Secretary of State for War, 10 April 1878.
45 TNA, WO 32/7688: Thesiger to Secretary of State for War, 10 April 1878.
46 Molyneux, p. 62.
47 Molyneux, p. 63. TNA, WO 32/7688: Thesiger to Secretary of State for War, 10 April 1878.
48 Molyneux, p. 64.
49 TNA, WO 32/7688: Thesiger to Secretary of State for War, 10 April 1878.
50 Molyneux, p. 69.
51 TNA, WO 32/7689: Diary of QMG Department, 6 April 1878.
52 TNA, WO 32/7689: Diary of QMG Department, 7 April 1878.
53 TNA, WO 32/7690: Thesiger to Secretary of State for War, 24 April 1878.
54 TNA, WO 32/7692: Thesiger to Secretary of State for War, 5 May 1878.
55 TNA, WO 32/7692: Wood to D.A.G., 13 April.
56 Delavoye, p. 228.
57 Wood, p. 317.
58 TNA, WO 32/7692: Wood to D.A.G., 13 April 1878.
59 TNA, WO 32/7692: Von Linsingen to D.A.G., 1 May 1878.
60 Molyneux, p. 81.
61 TNA, WO 32/7692: Von Linsingen to D.A.G., 1 May 1878.
62 TNA, WO 32/7692: Chelmsford to Secretary of State for War, 5 May 1878. See also TNA, WO 32/7692: Wood to D.A.G., 13 May 1878 'The Lieutenant General himself must have noticed the greater benefit of signalling which is eminently adapted for this country intersected by deep ravines.'
63 Molyneux, p. 75.
64 TNA, WO 32/7692: Chelmsford to Secretary of State for War, 5 May 1878.
65 Hummel, p. 81.
66 TNA, WO 32/7692: Chelmsford to Secretary of State for War, 5 May 1878.
67 TNA, WO 32/7692: Chelmsford to Secretary of State for War, 15 May 1878.
68 Hummel, p. 84.
69 TNA, WO 32/7692: Thesiger to Secretary of State for War, 15 May 1878.

70 Hummel, p. 84.

71 Molyneux, p. 87.

72 TNA, WO 32/7692: Wood to D.A.G., 8 May 1878.

73 TNA, WO 32/7692: Wood to D.A.G., 8 May 1878. His name was spelled McNaghten but modern maps show the krantz named after him as 'McNaughtens'.

74 Regimental Museum, Royal Welsh, Brecon, Records of the 2nd Battalion 24th Regiment, The Kaffir War, Accession No. B451-81.

75 TNA, WO 32/7692: Thesiger to Secretary of State, 15 May 1878.

76 BPP C.2144, Enclosure in No. 55, pp. 78ff: Thesiger to Secretary of State for War, 15 May 1878.

77 TNA, WO 32/7692: Thesiger to Secretary of State for War, 15 May 1878; see also Molyneux, p. 88, Hummel, p. 90.

78 TNA, WO 32/7692: Thesiger to Secretary of State for War, 15 May 1878. See also Molyneux, p. 88, who also does not give the fort a name, although Hummel, p. 90 does. I have searched for the remains of this fort and what was found was too large and did not sufficiently command the Zanyorkwe Valley. I suspect that its remains were lost when the Heroes Acre project was built.

79 TNA, WO 32/7692: Thesiger to Secretary of State for War, 15 May 1878.

80 TNA, WO 32/7692: Thesiger to Secretary of State for War, 15 May 1878.

81 BPP C.2144, Enclosure in No. 58, p. 85: General order dated 14 May 1878.

82 TNA, WO 32/7693: Diary of QM General's Department, 22 May 1878.

83 BPP C.2144, Enclosure in No. 57, p. 85, Telegram from Thesiger to Frere, no date. See also TNA, WO 32/7693: Diary of QM General's Department, 20 May 1878.

84 TNA, WO 32/7694: Review of general situation and tour of inspection by General Thesiger, passim.

85 TNA, WO 32/7693: Diary of the QM General's Dept, 23 May 1878.

86 TNA, WO 32/7695: Diary of the QM General's Dept, 30 May 1878.

87 BPP C.2144, Enclosure 1 in No. 94, pp. 177–8: Thesiger to Secretary of State for War, 2 June 1878.

88 BPP C.2144, Enclosure 1 in No. 94, pp. 177–8: Thesiger to Secretary of State for War, 2 June 1878.

89 TNA, WO 32/7695, Enclosure 2 in No. 91: Diary of QM General's Operations, 29 May to 5 June 1878.

90 BPP C.2144, Enclosure in No. 100, pp. 194ff: Thesiger to Secretary of State for War, 12 June 1878. Also see TNA, WO 32/7696, Thesiger to Secretary of State for War, 12 June 1878.

91 BPP C.2144, Enclosure 4 in No. 99, p. 193: Medical officer, 8 June 1878.

92 Milton, p. 272.

93 BPP C.2144, Enclosure 3 in No. 99, p. 193: Schermbrucker to Bellairs, 9 June 1878.

94 Gon, Send Carrington!, pp. 122–3.

95 Daily Dispatch, 2 June 2005: 'Sandile's Head Unearthed'.

96 BPP C.2144, Enclosure 2 in No. 126, p. 253: Thesiger to Secretary of State for War, 2 July 1878.

97 BPP C.2144, Enclosure 3 in No. 110 pp. 239–40: D.A.G. to military secretary, 21 June 1878.

Epilogue

1 Spicer, p. 215.
2 Spicer, p. 217.
3 Spicer, pp. 219ff.
4 Quoted in Spicer, p. 222.
5 BPP C.2220, Enclosure 1 in No. 79, pp. 240–1: Brownlee to secretary for native affairs, 5 September 1878.
6 BPP C.2220, Enclosure 2 in No. 79, p. 242: Brownlee to Littleton, 5 September 1878.
7 Theal, *History of South Africa from 1873 to 1884*, Vol. I, p. 137.
8 BPP C.2220, Enclosure 2 in No. 79, p. 243: secretary for native affairs to Frere, 13 September 1878.
9 BPP C.2220, Enclosure 2 in No. 79, p. 243: Colonial Secretary to Frere, 14 September 1878.
10 Spicer, p. 223.
11 Theal, *History of South Africa from 1873 to 1884*, Vol. I, p. 138.
12 Theal, *History of South Africa from 1873 to 1884*, Vol. I, p. 138.
13 Theal, *History of South Africa from 1873 to 1884*, Vol. I, p. 139.
14 The matter is dealt with at some length by Spicer, pp. 218–20.
15 Regimental Museum of the Royal Welsh, Brecon, Accession No. BCRMR 1959.46, entry for 18 July 1878.
16 Spicer, pp. 229–30.
17 Spicer, p. 201.
18 Milton, p. 281.
19 Walker, p. 530.
20 BPP C.2144, Enclosure 2 in No. 89, p. 166: Minute for Ministers, 4 June 1878.
21 BPP C.2220, Enclosure in No. 60, p. 159: Telegram, Thesiger to Frere, 31 August 1878.
22 Walker, pp. 633–60.
23 Douglas Oakes (ed.) *Illustrated History of South Africa: The Real Story*, New York: Readers Digest, 1988, pp. 288–9.

Bibliography

I. Manuscripts

A. The National Archives, London

WO 32/7385 Victoria Cross: Award to Major (now Brevet Lieutenant Colonel) H. Moore, 88th Regt, for action against Kaffirs, South Africa.

WO 32/7679 Reports by General Sir A. Cunynghame, General Officer Commanding, on operations in Galekaland. Reports of local commanders.

WO 32/7680 Reports on operations in Chichaba [Tyityaba] Valley and Transkei. Relations with civil government over separation of Command.

WO 32/7681 Report by General Cunynghame on Battle of Quintana.

WO 32/7682 Recommendations for awards and promotion for officers by General Cunynghame.

WO 32/7688 Reports by General Thesiger on assuming command and on operations. General situation and state of forces, with maps.

WO 32/7689: Kaffir War: Diary of operations from outbreak of war 26 September 1877 to 17 April 1878 by Quarter Master General's department.

WO 32/7690 Report by General Thesiger on general situation. Summary of operations, Kerumo [Kroome] Range, Beaufort District, with maps.

WO 32/7691: Kaffir War: Diary of operations, 15 April – 1 May.

WO 32/7692: Kaffir War: Reports by General Thesiger on general situation. Report of operations by local commanders, with maps.

WO 32/7693 Diaries of operations, 1 May–29 May.

WO 32/7694: Kaffir War: Review of general situation and tour of inspection by General Thesiger. Report on patrol into Bomvanaland.

WO 32/7695 Diary of operations by Quarter Master General's Department, 29 May to 19 June.

WO 32/7696 Report by General Thesiger on end of hostilities on Eastern Frontier of Cape Colony and death and capture of rebel chiefs. Acknowledgement of services of troops. Situation in Transvaal and Griqualand West.

WO 42/70(I): Rupert Lonsdale's service record.

B. National Army Museum, London

1. Chelmsford Papers 6807/386
File 18.

2. Coghill Papers 7112-38
File 1.

C. Regimental Museum Royal Welsh, Brecon
Carrington Letters.
Records of the 1st Battalion, 24th Regiment: The Kaffir War 1877–1878, Accession No. BCRMR 1959.46
Records of the 2nd Battalion, 24th Regiment, The Kaffir War 1877–1878, Accession No. B451-81.

D. Cory Library, Rhodes University, Grahamstown, South Africa
MS14-254-13: Dr A.W. Burton, 'The Ninth Kaffir War'.
MS779: Blanckenberg, P.B., 'The Treachery at Auckland'.

E. Western Cape Archives, Cape Town
CO2580/4: Report of death of Anders Stockenstrom.

II. Official Publications

British Parliamentary Papers
Papers shown in parentheses ( ) are Sessional Papers, those in square brackets [ ] are Command Papers.

(216) Copies of Correspondence . . . which has taken place between the Colonial Office and Governor Sir George Grey respecting his Recall from the Cape of Good Hope and his subsequent re-appointment, . . . April 1860.

(217) Transportation – Convicts: Transportation (Cape of Good Hope), April 1849

(252) Papers relative to the Condition and Treatment of the Native Inhabitants of Southern Africa within the Borders of the Colony of the Cape of Good Hope, June 1835.

(279) Cape of Good Hope: Caffre War and Death of Hintza, May 1836.

(538) Report from the Select Committee on Aborigines (British Settlements), Part I, August 1836.

(503) Copies or Extracts of any Further Despatches which have been received from, or addressed to, the Governor of the Cape of Good Hope relative to the late Caffre War . . ., July 1837.

(786) Correspondence with the Governor of the Cape of Good Hope relative to the state of the Kaffir Tribes on the Eastern Frontier of the Colony, February 1847.

(912) Correspondence with the Governor of the Cape of Good Hope relative to the state of the Kaffir Tribes on the Eastern Frontier of the Colony, February 1848. (In continuation of Papers presented in February 1847.)

[969] Correspondence with the Governor of the Cape of Good Hope relative to the state of the Kaffir Tribes on the Eastern Frontier of the Colony, July 1848.

[1334] Correspondence with the Governor of the Cape of Good Hope relative to the state of the Kaffir Tribes and the Recent Outbreak on the Eastern Frontier of the Colony, March 1851.

[1380] Correspondence with the Governor of the Cape of Good Hope relative to the state of the Kaffir Tribes and the Recent Outbreak on the Eastern Frontier of the Colony, May 1851.

(457) Copies of the Letters Patent appointing Sir Harry Smith Governor of the Cape of Good Hope, 1851.

(635) Report from the Select Committee on the Kaffir Tribes, together with the proceedings of the Committee, Minutes of Evidence, Appendix and Index, August 1851.

[1428] Correspondence with the Governor of the Cape of Good Hope relative to the state of the Kaffir Tribes and the Recent Outbreak on the Eastern Frontier of the Colony, February 1852.

[1635] Correspondence with the Governor of the Cape of Good Hope relative to the state of the Kafir tribes, and to the recent outbreak on the eastern frontier of the colony, May 1853.

[3436] Correspondence relative to the Annexation of British Kaffraria to the Cape of Good Hope, February 1865.

(181) (181-I and 181-II) Correspondence regarding the Establishment of Responsible Government at the Cape of Good Hope, and the Withdrawal of Troops from that Colony, April and June 1870.

BPP C.1141: Langalibalele and the amaHlubi Tribe, being remarks upon the official record of the trials of the Chief, his sons and *induna* and other members of the amaHlubi tribe. (January 1875.)

[C.1961] Further Correspondence respecting the Affairs of South Africa, February, 1878. (Continues C. 1883.)

[C.2000] Further Correspondence respecting the Affairs of South Africa, April, 1878. (Continues C. 1961.)

[C.2079] Further Correspondence respecting the Affairs of South Africa, July, 1878. (Continues C. 2000.)

[C.2100] Further Correspondence respecting the Affairs of South Africa, 1878, in continuation of C. 2079, July 1878.

[C.2144] Further Correspondence respecting the Affairs of South Africa, in continuation of C. 2100, August 1878.

[C.2220] Further Correspondence respecting the Affairs of South Africa, December, 1878. (Continues C. 2079.)

III. Newspapers

East London Daily Dispatch, 1911.
London Gazette, various.
Graham's Town Journal, 1851, 1870, 1880.
The Times, 1905.

IV. Books and Compilations

Barrow, John, *An Account of Travels into the Interior of Southern Africa*, Vol. II, London: Cadell & Davies, 1806.

Bisset, John Jarvis, *Sport and War: Or Recollections of Fighting and Hunting in South Africa from the Years 1834 to 1867*, London: John Murray, 1875.

Blainey, Geoffrey, *The Tyranny of Distance: How Distance Shaped Australia's History*, Melbourne: Macmillan, 1975.

Brownlee, Charles Pacalt, *Reminiscences of Kaffir Life and History*, Lovedale: Lovedale Mission Press, 1896.

Bryant, A.T., *Olden Times in Zululand and Natal*, London: Longmans, Green, 1929.

—— *The Zulu People as They Were Before the White Man Came*, Pietermaritzberg: Shuter and Shooter, 1949.

Cathcart, Sir George, *Correspondence of Lieutenant-General the Hon. Sir George Cathcart KCB Relative to Military Operations in Kaffraria . . .*, New York: Negro Universities Press, 1969; originally published London: John Murray, 1856.

Coghill, Patrick (compiler), *Whom the Gods Love*, Halesowen: privately published, 1968.

Cory, Sir George E., *The Rise of South Africa: A History of the Origin of South African Colonial Development towards the East from the Earliest Times to 1857*, six volumes, London: Longmans, Green, 1910–1940.

Cunynghame, General Sir A.T., *My Command in South Africa 1874–78*, London: Macmillan, 1879.

De Kock, W.J. and Kruger, D.W. (eds), *Dictionary of South African Biography*, Vol. II, Cape Town: Human Sciences Research Council, 1977.

Delavoye, Alex M., *Records of the 90th Regiment, The Kaffir War 1877–78*, London: Richardson, 1880.

Ex-CMR, *With the Cape Mounted Rifles: Four Years' Service*, London: Richard Bentley & Son, 1881.

Gon, Philip, *The Road to Isandlwana: The Years of an Imperial Battalion*, Johannesburg: A.D. Donker, 1979.

—— *Send Carrington! The Story of an Imperial Frontiersman*, Craighall: A.D. Donker, 1984.

Gordon, R.E., *Shepstone: The Role of the Family in the History of South Africa, 1820–1900*, Cape Town: A.A. Balkema, 1968.

Guy, Jeff, *The Destruction of the Zulu Kingdom: The Civil War in Zululand, 1879–1884*, Pietermaritzburg: University of Natal Press, 1994.

Hamilton-Browne, Colonel G., *A Lost Legionary in South Africa*, London: T. Werner Laurie, 1912.

Harington, A.L., *Sir Harry Smith: Bungling Hero*, Cape Town: Tafelberg Publishers, 1980.

Hart, H.G., *New Annual Army List for 1872*, London: John Murray, 1872.

—— *New Annual Army List for 1874*, London: John Murray, 1874.

—— *New Army List for April, 1878*, London: John Murray, 1878.

Hook, D.B., *With Sword and Statute: On the Cape of Good Hope Frontier*, Cape Town: J.C. Juta, 1905.

Hummel, Chris (ed.), *The Frontier Journal of Major John Crealock 1878*, Cape Town: Van Riebeeck Society, 1989.

Hutton, C.W. (ed.), *The Autobiography of the Late Sir Andries Stockenström, Bart*, two volumes, Cape Town: J.C. Juta, 1887.

de Kiewiet, Cornelius W., *The Imperial Factor in South Africa: A Study in Politics and Economics*, London: Frank Cass, 1965.

Laband, John (ed.), *Lord Chelmsford's Zululand Campaign, 1878–1879*, Stroud: Army Records Society/Alan Sutton Publishing, 1994.

Lewson, Phyllis (ed.), *Selections from the Correspondence of J.X. Merriman*, Cape Town: Van Riebeeck Society, 1960.

Lucas, T.J., *Camp Life and Sport in South Africa: Experiences of Kaffir Warfare with the Cape Mounted Rifles*, London: Chapman & Hall, 1878.

Mackinnon, J.P. and Shadbolt, S.H., *The South African Campaign of 1879*, London: Sampson, Low, Marston, Searle and Rivington, 1880.

Macquarrie, J.W., *The Reminiscences of Sir Walter Stanford*, Vol. I, Cape Town: Van Riebeeck Society, 1958.

Marais, J.S., *Maynier and the First Boer Republic*, Cape Town: Maskew Miller, 1944.

Martineau, John, *Life and Correspondence of Sir Bartle Frere*, Vol. II, London: John Murray, 1895.

Meintjes, Johannes, *Sandile: The Fall of the Xhosa Nation*, Cape Town: T.V. Bulpin, 1971.

Milton, John, *The Edges of War: A History of Frontier Wars 1702–1878*, Kenwyn: Juta, 1983.

Morris, Donald R., *The Washing of the Spears: The Rise and Fall of the Zulu Nation*, London: Jonathan Cape, 1965.

Molteno, P.A., *The Life and Times of Sir John Charles Molteno*, London: Smith, Elder, 1900.

Molyneux, Major-General W.C.F, *Campaigning in South Africa and Egypt*, London: Macmillan, 1896.

Moodie, Donald (ed.), *The Record, or a Series of Official Papers Relative to the Condition and Treatment of the Native Tribes of South Africa*, Cape Town: A.A. Balkema, 1960.

Moore-Smith, G.C. (ed.), *The Autobiography of Lieutenant-General Sir Harry Smith*, two volumes, London: John Murray, 1902.

Mostert, Noël, *Frontiers: The Epic of South Africa's Creation and the Tragedy of the Xhosa People*, London: Jonathan Cape, 1992.

Norbury, Fleet-Surgeon Henry F., *The Naval Brigade in South Africa During the Years 1877–78–79*, London: Sampson Low, Marston, Searle and Rivington, 1880.

Norris-Newman, Charles L., *In Zululand with the British Throughout the War of 1879*, London: W.H. Allen, 1880.

Oakes, Douglas (ed.), *Illustrated History of South Africa: The Real Story*, New York: Readers Digest, 1988.

Parr, Captain Henry Hallam, *A Sketch of the Kafir and Zulu Wars: Guadana to Isandhlwana*, London: Kegan Paul, 1880.

Pearse, R.O. et al. (eds), *Langalibalele and the Natal Carbineers: The Story of the Langalibalele Rebellion, 1873*, Ladysmith: Ladysmith Historical Society, 1973, 1976.

Peires, J.B., *The House of Phalo: A History of the Xhosa People in the Days of Their Independence*, Johannesburg: Ravan Press, 1981.

—— *The Dead Will Arise: Nongqawuse and the Great Cattle-Killing Movement of 1856–7*, Jeppestown: Jonathan Ball, 2003.

Pringle, Thomas, *Narrative of a Residence in South Africa*, Cape Town: Struik, 1966.

Rivett-Carnac, Dorothy E., *Hawk's Eye*, Cape Town: Howard Timmins, 1966.

Shervinton, Kathleen, *The Shervintons, Soldiers of Fortune*, London: T. Unwin, 1899; reprinted by Kessinger Publishing, 2011.

Shipp, John, *Memoirs of the Extraordinary Military Career of John Shipp, Late a Lieutenant in Her Majesty's 87th Regiment*, London: Fisher Unwin, 1890.

Smithers, A.J., *The Kaffir Wars 1779–1877*, London: Leo Cooper, 1973.

Stapleton, Timothy, *Maqoma: Xhosa Resistance to Colonial Advance 1798–1873*, Johannesburg: Jonathan Ball, 1994.

Streatfeild, Frank N., *Kaffirland: A Ten Months' Campaign*, London: Sampson, Marston, Searle and Rivington, 1879.

—— *Reminiscences of an Old 'Un*, London: Eveleigh Nash, 1911.

Theal, George McCall, *History of South Africa under the Administration of the Dutch East India Company 1652–1795*, two volumes, London: Swan Sonnenschein, 1897.

—— *History of South Africa from 1873 to 1884: Twelve Eventful Years*, Vol. I, London: George Allen & Unwin Ltd, 1919.

—— *Records of the Cape Colony, Copied for the Cape Government from the Manuscript Documents in the Public Record Office, London*, thirty-six volumes, Cape Town: Government of the Cape Colony, 1897–1906.

Todd, Alphaeus, *On the Position of a Constitutional Governor Under Responsible Government (1878)*, Ottawa, 1878.

Tylden, Major G., *The Armed Forces of South Africa 1659–1954*, Johannesburg: Frank Connock Publications, 1954.

Walker, Eric A. (ed.), *The Cambridge History of the British Empire, Vol. VIII: South Africa, Rhodesia and the High Commission Territories*, London: Cambridge University Press, 1963.

Wood, Evelyn, *From Midshipman to Field Marshal*, London: Methuen, 1906.

Worsfold, Basil, *Sir Bartle Frere: A Footnote to the History of the British Empire*, London: Thornton, Butterworth, 1923.

Wylie, Dan, *Myth of Iron: Shaka in History*, Scottsville: University of KwaZulu-Natal, 2006.

V. Pamphlets, Theses, Articles and Other Papers

Contagious Bovine Pleuropneumonia (Lungsickness), National Department of Agriculture, Directorate Animal Health, Pretoria, 1996.

Herbst, F. and Kopke, D., 'Site of the Battle of Amalinde', *Military History Journal*, Vol. 13, No. 5, June 2006.

Lewson, Phyllis, 'The First Crisis in Responsible Government in the Cape Colony', MA thesis, University of Witwatersrand, 1940, published in *Archives Year Book for South African History*, No. 5, Part II, 1942.

Ralph, Sarah, diary, *Martello Magazine*, Fort Beaufort Museum, Nos 3–6 inclusive.

Spicer, Michael W., 'The War of Ngcayecibi 1877–8', unpublished MA thesis, Rhodes University, Grahamstown, 1978.

Webb, C. de B., 'Lines of Power: The High Commissioner, the Telegraph and the War of 1879', *Natalia*, Vol. 8, December 1993.

Index